# Business
# Accounting

Jill Hussey and Roger Hussey

palgrave
macmillan

First published 1999 by
MACMILLAN PRESS LTD
Houndmills, Basingstoke, Hampshire RG21 6XS
and London
Companies and representatives
throughout the world

ISBN 0–333–73081–X

A catalogue record for this book is available
from the British Library.

This book is printed on paper suitable for recycling and made from fully managed and sustained forest sources.

Typeset in Great Britain by
Aarontype Limited
Easton, Bristol

Printed and bound in Great Britain by
Antony Rowe Ltd, Chippenham and Eastbourne

# Contents

# PART III   MANAGEMENT ACCOUNTING

# Preface

Accounting information lies at the heart of any business. If we are to fully appreciate the activities of companies and other business organisations, it is essential to understand their financial operations. It is therefore not surprising that accounting forms an integral part of the syllabus of many courses in universities and other institutions of higher and further education.

In recent years there has been a dramatic growth of interest in the two main subdivisions of accounting: financial accounting and management accounting. This book covers both subjects in a clear, direct style. It is suitable as a course text, supplemented by lectures, on a variety of business and management courses and other programmes of study.

*Business Accounting* covers the key elements of financial and management accounting and is ideal for a one-year course. The book is divided into 23 chapters which are presented in a logical teaching sequence. The text includes activities which are designed to promote understanding of the principles and the solutions add to the student's knowledge as well as providing an introduction to the next learning point. At the end of each chapter there are a variety of exercises, which are intended for self-assessment by the student, with answers at the back of the book.

JILL HUSSEY
ROGER HUSSEY

# Part I

# Introduction to Accounting

# 1 The Nature of Accounting

## 1.1 Introduction

*Accounting* is a key activity in any organisation, regardless of size or the nature of its activities. An accounting system can provide information on the financial performance of a business for its owners, directors and managers for management purposes, and for the Inland Revenue and the Customs and Excise for tax purposes. In addition, the information may be used by competitors, customers and suppliers to assess the strength of the business, as well as employees, trade unions, pressure groups and others who are interested in the activities of the organisation. Day-to-day accounting information is needed in order to run the business and an accounting system allows a record of all the business's economic transactions to be kept. In addition, it helps management to make decisions which have financial implications and aids the planning of future activities.

Because of its crucial importance in an organisation, and its complexity, accounting can be divided into two main streams: *financial accounting* and *management accounting*. In this chapter we consider what accounting is about in general and what these two subdivisions are most concerned with. We also discuss some of the *assumptions* accountants use when carrying out their work.

## 1.2 Definition of Accounting

In its broadest form, *accounting* is concerned with identifying, measuring, recording and communicating the economic transactions of organisations. We shall now consider each of these activities separately:

- *Identifying* economic transactions in most cases is fairly straightforward. Examples include selling goods to customers, paying wages, purchasing new stock and buying machinery or equipment.
- *Measuring* economic transactions is done using money as the form of measurement. For example, instead of saying that the business has sold

20 kg of grain, we say that the business has sold 20 kg of grain at 30p per kg. Therefore the total sale is £6.

- *Recording* the economic transactions is essential. They are either recorded in handwritten books of accounts or on suitable computer software such as a spreadsheet program or specialist accounting package.
- *Communicating* the economic transactions is done by producing financial statements. These are records, set out in a particular format, which summarise one particular financial aspect of the business. The three main forms of financial statement are the *cash flow statement, profit and loss account* and *balance sheet*. We shall be looking at each of these financial statements in more detail in Part II.

The following activity allows you to carry out the basic accounting procedures of identifying, measuring and recording in monetary terms the building of some office shelves.

---

## Activity

A business buys 5 litres of paint, 20 metres of timber and employs a carpenter for 2 days to build shelves in an office. If paint costs £4 per litre, timber costs £2.50 per metre and the carpenter charges £50 per day, what is the total cost of the shelves?

---

The cost can be calculated in a number of stages. You need to multiply the cost of paint per litre by the amount used. You also need to multiply the cost of timber per metre by the amount used. Finally, you need to calculate the cost of employing the carpenter by multiplying his daily rate by the number of days. The order in which you work out the figures does not matter, as long as you arrive at three figures which when added together make up the total cost of the job:

|  | £ |
|---|---|
| Cost of paint (£4 × 5 litres) | 20 |
| Cost of timber (£2.50 × 20 metres) | 50 |
| Cost of labour (£50 × 2 days) | 100 |
| Total cost of the shelves | 170 |

In more complex examples it is not so easy to identify and measure the economic events in monetary terms. We shall be looking at some of the problems in subsequent chapters.

Although we have looked at the main definition of accounting, as we saw above the subject can be divided into *financial accounting* and *management accounting*. These two forms of accounting can be further broken down into such activities as *bookkeeping, auditing* and *costing*. However, in this chapter we start by looking at financial accounting and management accounting.

## 1.3 **Financial Accounting**

*Financial accounting* aims to present a *true and fair view* of economic transactions through financial statements. Essentially, this implies that the financial statements are a faithful reflection of the economic activities of the organisation. The financial statements are drawn up within a *regulatory framework* which is very important for large companies. This means that the organisation must prepare the financial statements according to legislation and other regulations. In addition, the financial statements use a number of *accounting assumptions* which have been established as general principles. We shall be looking at these assumptions later in this section. Generally, an organisation's financial statements are considered to give a true and fair view if they comply with the regulatory framework and normal accounting assumptions. However, in a very small number of cases, the organisation may have to ignore specific regulations in order to ensure that the financial statements give a true and fair view and that the users of the accounts are not misled.

Financial accounting can be divided into a number of specific activities, such as the following:

- *bookkeeping*, which is concerned with recording business transactions;
- *auditing*, which is the thorough examination of the financial records of an organisation to confirm that the financial statements give a true and fair view (an audit is legally required for limited companies);
- *corporate recovery*, which is an increasingly important area of accounting and covers the provision of insolvency services and advice to companies in financial difficulties;
- *taxation advice*, which is governed by legislation and involves individuals and businesses.

## Activity

Are the following statements true or false?

A financial accountant can give advice on the following matters:

**a** how to arrange financial affairs so that the least amount of tax is incurred;
**b** the best way to borrow money for a specific project;
**c** the likely profit to be made on a huge rock concert;
**d** carrying out financial transactions in foreign currencies;
**e** deciding on the best way to provide for a pension;
**f** calculating VAT payments;
**g** trading in stocks and shares.

You may have been puzzled by some of these statements, but you would be right if you said that they are all the concern of the financial accountant. However, as in other professions, there are specialists who may concentrate on specific areas. For financial accountants this is particularly true of matters relating to financial investment and taxation. In small businesses there may be only one financial accountant who carries out all the above activities, but a large organisation is more likely to employ specialists, who are not necessarily qualified accountants, to deal with different aspects of accounting.

Financial accounting is a complex activity and accountants use certain *accounting assumptions* when identifying, measuring, recording and communicating economic transactions. It is important that all accountants use the same assumptions, otherwise the same economic transactions would be viewed in different ways by different accountants. The assumptions accountants use are also known as *accounting concepts, conventions, principles, rules, axioms* or *postulates*, but all these terms refer to the same thing.

Some of the main assumptions which underpin accounting cannot be properly understood until we have looked at financial statements in detail in Part II. However, at this stage we can introduce the following important assumptions which are used in everyday accounting:

- The *going concern concept* requires the accountant to compile the financial statements on the basis that the business is a going concern. This means that it is assumed that the business will continue to operate and that as far as is known there is no intention to close it.
- The *consistency concept* requires the accountant to deal in the same way with items of a similar nature. It also requires him or her to be consistent from one accounting period to the next. This allows financial information to be compared easily.
- The *prudence concept* requires the accountant to take a cautious view of an organisation's economic transactions. No profits or revenues must be anticipated, unless it is almost certain that they will be achieved. On the other hand, all costs and losses must be accounted for whether the amount is known or is only an estimate.
- The *money measurement concept* requires the accountant to prepare the financial statements by measuring items in terms of monetary values. You came across this assumption in the first activity in this chapter. For example, rather than record the number of haircuts in a year in the financial statements, the accountant for a hairdressing business must record the value of the haircuts, which will be used as the figure for sales. Thus, 1,680 haircuts at £10 per head becomes a sales figure of £16,800.
- The *stable unit of measurement concept* assumes that the currency holds its value over time, although this is not the case in reality. You know from experience that prices can fluctuate and in all probability you will have to pay more or less to replace items you bought in the past. For example, 4 years ago a business may have been able to buy a ream of printed stationery for £45, but today it would cost £50. On the other hand, it may have paid £180 for a desk four years ago, but today a similar desk may cost only £150. The accountant records the actual prices paid, although

they may vary over time. This presents some serious problems, which we shall examine in later chapters.

- The *business entity concept* requires the accountant to describe the business in the financial statements as a separate entity. This means that the business is considered to exist separately from its owner(s). Thus, for accounting purposes, Snippers Barber Shop, for example, is regarded as being quite separate from its owner, George Garibaldi.

In recent years the regulation of accounting has changed dramatically and over time our opinions of the importance and meaning of the accounting assumptions have changed, and will continue to do so. Nevertheless, they provide an *accounting framework* in which financial accountants can carry out their work. The following activity demonstrates their importance.

---

## Activity

A business bought a machine for the production department at the beginning of the year for £1,500. It is estimated that the machine will generate profits for the next 10 years. 6 months later the chief accountant finds out that if the machine had to be sold it would be worth only £1,000. Using the going concern concept, which of these two figures should be shown in the accounts?

---

You may have found this question quite difficult to answer. The clue lies in understanding what we mean by a going concern. As we have already seen, a 'going concern' is a business that will continue to operate for the foreseeable future. This means that there is no intention to close the business or significantly reduce any of its activities. In other words, the business does not have to sell its machine and therefore the machine would be shown in the accounts at £1,500, as it is anticipated that it will continue to generate profits.

Next we consider what situation a business might be in if it were not a going concern. You are probably aware of the consequences of a business closing or going into liquidation. The activities of the business cease, the workforce is made redundant and any assets the business owns, such as buildings, vehicles, office equipment, etc. are liquidated. This means that they are sold and the money used to pay any outstanding debts. If the business is a going concern the correct figure for the machine is the price which was paid for it: £1,500. If the business is not a going concern, the figure would be the machine's estimated second-hand value of £1,000. However, if there was no going concern concept, either of these figures might be used and this would be very confusing to the users of accounting information.

At this stage you may find the individual accounting assumptions fairly difficult to understand. However, as they are fundamental to the preparation of financial statements, it is important to know of their existence and we will show how they are applied in later chapters.

## 1.4 **Management Accounting**

*Management accounting* uses a range of techniques and methods, both financial and statistical, to provide information to management. We shall be looking at these in some detail in Part III of this book. A management accountant is concerned with identifying why the information is required so that the most appropriate technique can be used to supply information to managers. The managers of the business need this information to enable them to plan the progress of the business, control the activities and understand the financial implications of any decisions they may take. Unlike financial accounting, management accounting is not governed by legislation or other regulations.

Cost accounting is part of management accounting. It is concerned with establishing *budgets* and *standard costs*. It is also concerned with establishing *actual costs*. The different costing methods used can be classified into two main groups, depending on the nature of production. *Specific-order costing* is used to assess the individual costs of performing each discrete *job, contract* or *batch. Continuous-operation costing* is used in industries where the product or service is homogeneous and results from a continuous operation.

To illustrate the difference between financial accounting and management accounting we can look at the example of the office shelves again:

- A financial accountant would be interested in the total cost of £170 so that it can be recorded as the economic transaction.
- A management accountant would be more concerned with informing managers how much the individual elements, such as the paint, the timber and the labour, cost. A management accountant would also want to calculate how much the shelves actually cost and compare it with a plan or budget of what it was estimated they would cost. In setting the plan, the management accountant would also want to look at a number of different ways and costs involved in building the shelves so that the managers can decide the most appropriate way.

## **Activity**

Classify the following activities into financial accounting and management accounting activities:

**a** Auditing the books of an organisation.
**b** Managing an organisation's tax affairs.
**c** Analysing the financial implications of management decisions.
**d** Preparing the financial statements at the year end.
**e** Ensuring compliance with legal and other regulations.
**f** Providing financial information for managers.
**g** Keeping the financial records of an organisation.

By now you are probably more confident about deciding which activities involve financial accounting and which can be classified as management accounting. With the exception of **c** and **f**, all the above activities are concerned with financial accounting.

The *purpose* of management accounting is to provide managers with financial and statistical information to help them carry out their responsibilities. The responsibilities of managers in any organisation can be classified as planning, controlling and decision-making. Therefore the financial information they require should help them to control the resources for which they are responsible, plan how those resources can be most effectively used and decide what course of action they should take when a number of options are open.

## Activity

Imagine you are a manager and decide whether you would require the following information for planning, controlling or decision-making:

**a** The amount claimed for taxi fares by staff last month.
**b** The prices charged by a new supplier for materials.
**c** The cost of running the office photocopier.
**d** The cost of employing subcontracted staff, compared with using your own employees.
**e** The cost of making a component, compared with buying it from an outside supplier.

Items **d** and **e** should be easy to define because in both circumstances you are choosing between alternatives and are therefore making decisions. With items **a** and **c** you are mainly concerned with controlling costs, although you might want the information to make plans for future expenditure. Item **b** could be concerned with planning future costs or you may be about to decide whether to change to another supplier. This decision may have arisen because you are trying to control costs. Although the boundaries between planning, controlling and decision-making are blurred, financial and statistical information has a very important role to play and it is the management accountant who provides this information.

Management accounting is concerned with providing accounting information that is of *value* to managers. Therefore, it offers a number of general advantages, such as helping the organisation to be more profitable or, in a non-profit organisation, ensuring that it is providing value for money.

## Activity

What other advantages do you consider a management accounting system offers to organisations? Draw up a list of the advantages under the headings of planning, controlling and decision-making.

Your list may include some of the following examples:

**Planning**
- the price of products or services;
- the number of employees that will be needed and what they should be paid;
- planning the quantity of each product or service which must be sold to achieve a desired level of profit;

**Controlling**
- unnecessary expense and waste;
- the amount of investment made in plant and machinery;
- the cost of running different departments.

**Deciding**
- whether to make or buy a particular component;
- whether it is financially worthwhile investing in new technology;
- which products or services to offer if there is a shortage of skilled labour.

## 1.5  Relationship between Financial and Management Accounting

Although accounting can be divided into *financial* and *management* accounting, you should not be misled into thinking that there is no relationship between these two activities, since both draw from the same data sources and both generate financial information. However, there are some important differences which relate to the accuracy, level of detail and timing of the information produced.

Financial accounting mainly operates on the basis of an annual reporting cycle. It is strictly regulated and because the information must be as accurate as possible, it is often some months after the financial year end before the financial accounts are issued. The accounts are drawn up for the entire business and therefore contain aggregated information which is presented in the way required by legislation. By contrast, management accounting is not regulated and the aim is to present the information to managers when they want it and in the form they want it. In most management accounting systems reports for each activity in each part of the organisation are produced on a monthly or more frequent basis. Consequently they are very detailed. Because the reports must be produced very frequently, some figures may be only estimates.

In a business where the financial and management accounting systems are well designed and are operating efficiently, if the periodic management accounts for the different parts of the organisation were aggregated the resulting totals would be very similar to the figures in the financial accounts. However, there would be some differences. For example, the financial accounts would contain details of interest payments, dividends paid to shareholders and tax payments. There may also be minor differences due to some figures in the management accounts being estimated. If there were any significant differences, they would be investigated by the firm's accountant.

Some small businesses do not operate a separate management accounting system because of the additional costs involved or because their operations are so simple they do not require such frequent detailed information. Instead, they may rely on the financial accounts, which can also be produced quarterly or half-yearly, and other sources of information such as their order books and bank statements.

## 1.6 The Accounting Profession

As well as doing accountancy work, a qualified accountant must have passed a number of rigorous examinations set by one of the following recognised professional bodies:

- The Institute of Chartered Accountants in England and Wales (ICAEW)
- The Institute of Chartered Accountants in Ireland (ICAI)
- The Institute of Chartered Accountants in Scotland (ICAS)
- The Association of Chartered Certified Accountants (ACCA)
- The Chartered Institute of Management Accountants (CIMA)
- The Chartered Institute of Public Finance and Accountancy (CIPFA)

Each institution sets its own examinations. If you have an appropriate degree, you may receive exemptions from some elements of the professional examinations. Once qualified, an accountant can become a member of the *accounting profession* by joining one of the above recognised accountancy bodies. Members of the different professional bodies work in professional practice, such as a firm of accountants, or in industry, commerce or financial and public administration.

## Activity

Membership of which professional body/bodies would be best for the following work?

**a** An accountant in a professional practice.
**b** A management accountant in industry.
**c** A treasurer in a local authority.
**d** An accountant in an area health authority.

A qualified accountant is not necessarily restricted to only one area of work. However, an accountant in a professional practice is likely to be a member of the Institute of Chartered Accountants in England and Wales (or Ireland or Scotland) or a member of the Association of Chartered Certified Accountants.

Membership of the Chartered Institute of Management Accountants would be most appropriate for a management accountant in industry. Membership of either the Chartered Institute of Public Finance and Accountancy or the Association of Chartered Certified Accountants would be appropriate for a treasurer in a local authority or an accountant in the National Health Service.

As well as the main recognised professional bodies, there are a number of other associations and societies. For most of them you need to take examinations to become a member. There are two bodies which offer second-tier qualifications. These are intended for individuals who do not wish to become fully qualified accountants or do not have the educational qualifications to register directly with one of the main professional bodies as a student. One of the most established of these is the *Association of Accountancy Technicians (AAT)*, which was set up in 1980. More recently, the Association of Chartered Certified Accountants, has begun offering individuals the opportunity to obtain recognition for their work in accounting technical or support roles. This qualification is linked to the BTEC NVQs in accounting.

## 1.7  Conclusions

In this chapter we have looked at the two main divisions of accounting and examined the roles of financial and management accountants in organisations. We have introduced some of the main assumptions which underpin accounting and begun to investigate the effect they have on the financial statements of a business. We have examined the purpose of management accounting and how it helps managers do their jobs. We have also looked at the ways in which accountants can qualify and become members of the recognised professional bodies.

Having completed this chapter, you should now be able to:

- describe what is meant by the term 'accounting';
- differentiate between financial accounting and management accounting;
- explain the roles of financial and management accountants;
- describe six of the main accounting assumptions;
- describe the purpose and value of management accounting;
- identify the main professional bodies.

## Exercises

Complete the following sentences:

1 Accounting is concerned with ......................................................................
2 Financial accounting is concerned with ......................................................
3 Management accounting is concerned with .................................................
4 A qualified accountant must be a member of .............................................
5 The prudence concept requires ...................................................................

Are the following statements true or false?

**6** Businesses should always produce financial statements on a going concern basis.

**7** Companies are required by law to publish management accounts.

**8** The 'consistency concept' means that accountants normally cannot change the way in which items of a similar nature are treated from one accounting period to another.

**9** The 'money measurement concept' means that the figures shown in the financial statements are always given in pounds sterling.

**10** The main value of management accounting is the help it gives to managers.

You may wish to read more widely than this book to answer the following questions fully, but you can check the main points by referring to the appropriate sections in this chapter.

**11** Describe the key features of the definition of accounting. (Section 1.2)

**12** What are the main differences between the activities of a financial accountant and those of a management accountant? (Sections 1.3 and 1.4)

**13** What are the benefits of management accounting? (Section 1.4)

**14** If you wanted to qualify as an accountant and work in a professional practice, which of the professional accounting bodies would you eliminate from your choice? (Section 1.5)

Multiple choice questions (more than one answer may apply):

**15** Which of the following are normally the responsibility of a financial accountant:

**a** calculating liability for tax

**b** calculating the cost of a project

**c** identifying the financial implications of investing in alternative types of equipment

**d** keeping proper accounting records of transactions.

**16** A management accountant is normally most concerned with:

**a** ensuring that an organisation pays the correct amount of tax

**b** providing information that will be of use to managers ·

**c** auditing the books of an organisation

**d** keeping financial records of transactions.

**17** The financial statements of a business are usually prepared on the assumption that:

**a** it will close the next day

**b** it will continue in the foreseeable future ·

**c** it is not known whether it will continue

**d** it will continue for only one month.

**18** In applying the prudence concept, the accountant ensures that:

**a** all possible profits and revenues are included

**b** all possible costs and losses are included ·

**c** all possible revenues and costs are included

**d** all possible profits and losses are included.

**19** A major advantage of using money as a unit of measure is that:

**a** it is not stable because of inflation

**b** it allows a value to be put on employees' loyalty

c items are shown in the financial statements at their second-hand values
d it allows different activities to be summarised in the accounts.

**20** By law, a management accountant must be:

a a member of a professional accountancy body
b a holder of a degree in accountancy
c authorised by the Department of Trade and Industry
d none of these.

Practice questions:

**21** Explain the different roles of financial and management accountants.
**22** Explain the importance of the assumptions used by accountants, and describe any **four**.
**23** Describe the main disadvantages of using money as a unit of measurement to record business transactions.
**24** Consider a business where you have had work experience or any other organisation with which you are familiar, What aspects of the business do you think are important which are not shown in the financial statements?
**25** Describe a situation in which two of the main accounting concepts might be in conflict. Explain what you consider the correct accounting treatment should be.

(Answers on p. 312)

# 2 The Users and Uses of Financial Information

## 2.1 Introduction

*Financial information* is only important because it is useful to those who use it. Who uses the information depends to a large extent on the type and size of the business. For example, financial information relating to a small news agency business is only likely to be used by the owners and the tax authorities. However, the financial information relating to a large, multinational company has a much wider range of users. A user's level of interest depends on the purpose for which the financial information will be used. For example, a manager working in a division of a large company is likely to require detailed information in order to run the department; someone contemplating lending £1m to the company is likely to need information for assessing what the chances are of getting the loan repaid at a later date.

In this chapter we explain the structure of the main *types* of business organisation. This enables us to consider any regulations businesses have to comply with concerning the provision of financial information, as well as suggesting who might be interested in such information. We then identify the principal *sources* of financial information that are available before going on to consider the potential *users* and *uses* to which it may be put.

## 2.2 Types of Business Organisation

*Business organisations* range from the very small, such as a corner shop, to large multinational companies. Not only do they differ in size, but in their legal structure and in the type of person who may be interested in financial information about them. Before we look at the users and uses of financial information, we need to consider the main types of business organisation which generate such information. In doing this we will concentrate on organisations that have been set up with a view to making a profit, rather than not-for-profit organisations, such as charities and social clubs.

15

Business organisations can be divided into *unincorporated bodies* and *corporate bodies*. An unincorporated body is an individual or a group of individuals, such as a *sole trader* or a *partnership*, who pursue a common business purpose. A corporate body or corporation also comprises individuals who pursue a common business purpose, but by the process of legal incorporation the business becomes a legal person or entity, such as a *limited company*.

A *sole trader* is a self-employed individual who is the sole owner of his or her business and is in business with a view to making a profit. Examples range from a window cleaner to a business consultant; from a photographer to a biographer; from a fisherman to a farmer; from a baker to a wedding dress-maker. They are found in both manufacturing and service industries. A sole trader may run the business alone or employ full-time or part-time staff. There are no specific formalities required to form a one-person business, but one crucial characteristic is that a sole trader has *unlimited liability*. This means that he or she is personally liable for any debts the business may incur. This extends beyond any original investment and could mean the loss of personal property. A sole trader is relatively free from financial regulation in setting up and running the business, but often experiences difficulty in obtaining finance.

A *partnership* is a form of business in which two or more people join together in business with a view to making a profit. Examples range as widely as those cited for sole traders. Many professional firms such as accountants, doctors, dentists, vets and solicitors are partnerships. The partners may run the business alone or employ full-time or part-time staff. The agreement to form a partnership is a contract. It may be verbal or written, or contained in special document known as a deed. In the absence of a *partnership agreement*, the *Partnership Act 1890* sets out the relationship between the partners.

## Activity

What sort of financial matters do you think partners ought to agree before they start the business?

The most obvious one is how they are going to divide the profit, but there are others. For example, how much money they will each invest in the business and will some or all of them will be entitled to a salary? If the partners are in dispute, and there is no written or verbal agreement, the terms of the Partnership Act 1890 apply. The most important terms in respect of the financial relationship of the partners are as follows:

- Partners share profits, losses and capital (the amount the partners have invested in the business) equally.
- No partner is entitled to a salary.

- No interest is payable on the capital invested by each of the partners.
- If a partner makes a loan to the partnership, interest is payable at 5%.

The maximum number of partners in a firm is restricted to 20. Professional firms, such as solicitors and accountants, are not subject to this limitation. Like a sole trader, partners have unlimited liability. Each partner can make the other(s) liable for his or her acts.

## Activity

To help you identify the similarities and differences between the two types of business organisation, decide whether the following characteristics apply to a sole trader, a partnership, or both:

**a** There is only one owner.
**b** There is a maximum number of owners.
**c** There are no formalities involved when starting the business.
**d** There should be a contract of agreement.
**e** The owner(s) have unlimited liability.
**f** The business is an unincorporated body.

The first important difference to note is that whereas a sole trader is the only owner of the business, **a**, a partnership is under multiple ownership. However, you might say that because there is a maximum of one owner in a sole trader business and normally a maximum of 20 owners in a partnership, **b**, this is something both types of business have in common. Another important difference is that whereas there are no formalities involved in setting up business as a sole trader, **c**, the relationship between partners in a partnership must be formalised. You might argue that partners do no need a contract of agreement, because if there is none, the Partnership Act 1890 sets out their relations, **d**. However, what this means is that a standard agreement is applied, which may not be appropriate in all circumstances. Perhaps the most important characteristic is that both sole traders and partnerships are liable for any debts incurred, **e**. In addition, both sole traders and partnerships are unincorporated bodies, **f**.

A *limited company* is the modern name for a joint-stock company and is the most important and highly regulated form of business organisation. A limited company is a corporate body which is legally separate from its owners, the shareholders. The owners have *limited liability*. This means that the shareholders' financial liability is limited to the amount they have invested, even if the company fails owing significant amounts to its creditors. Limited companies are more closely regulated than partnerships and sole traders and financial information on their activities is readily available. They can be divided into *public limited companies* and *private limited companies*. The main differences between a public limited company and a private limited company are:

- a public company must state in its memorandum of association that it is a public company;
- a public limited company's name must end with the words 'public limited company' or the abbreviation 'plc' or 'ccc', the Welsh equivalent; a private limited company's name must end with the word 'limited' or the abbreviation 'Ltd';
- a public limited company may advertise its shares and invite the public to buy them and its shares can then be freely bought and sold; a private limited company's shares are only available privately.

The shares of a UK public limited company are listed on the *London Stock Exchange (LSE)*. There are a number of places where shares in such companies can be bought and sold. A firm of brokers is usually the best place if you are wealthy and seeking investment advice. Most banks and other financial institutions also offer the service and try to keep the process as informal and fast as possible. In addition, share shops are becoming more common in major stores. When new shares are issued newspapers carry advertisements in the form of a prospectus containing an application coupon. Whichever method you use to buy shares, it is best to obtain professional advice unless you are very knowledgeable, since every investment carries some risk as well as the chance of making a gain.

Because limited companies are so important to the economy, information about them, particularly public limited companies, is readily available and we will concentrate on public limited companies for the remainder of this chapter.

---

## Activity

What do you think are the main advantages of a limited company over a partnership?

---

One of the main advantages is that shareholders who invest in a limited company have their liability limited to the amount they have agreed to invest, even if the company goes into liquidation. With a partnership, the individual partners are liable for the debts of the business, even if they personally did not incur them. In addition, there is no restriction on the number of shareholders in a limited company, whereas the maximum number of partners in a partnership is 20. This imposes a constraint on size in partnerships which has economic implications. Limited companies usually find it easier to raise finance than partnerships. Public limited companies raise finance by issuing shares on the Stock Exchange, but even private limited companies find it relatively easy to raise loans because the financial regulations imposed on them give lenders some confidence in the financial information they provide. Limited companies have an unlimited life whereas partnerships have a finite life. When a shareholder dies, his or her shares can be transferred to someone else and the company continues, but when a partner dies, the partnership ceases.

## 2.3 Sources of Financial Information

Before looking at the potential *sources of company and industry information*, we need to discuss what we mean by *financial information*. If you were asked to give an example, you might suggest the country's balance of payments figure, a company's profits, or your salary or grant. These are all examples of financial information, but we need a formal definition of the term before we look at further examples. For our purposes, financial information can be considered to be information about something expressed in terms of money.

---

## Activity

Draw up a list of financial information you come in contact with during a typical day. If you have a job, draw up two lists; in the first, list financial information you come across at work and in the second financial information from outside your workplace.

---

If you have read the newspapers, watched television or listened to the radio today, you will probably have received some financial news. This may have been on the state of the economy, the value of contracts won by well known companies or the pay of famous people. If you have done any shopping today, you will have compared prices and been given receipts which itemise and total your purchases.

You may be surprised by the length of your list(s), even if you have only included the main examples. It will also be clear that some financial information affects you and what you are doing directly, whereas other financial information does not. For example, at home you may have a telephone bill showing a huge amount due for the quarter. As a result you may have decided to control the number of calls you make in future. At work you may have received a quotation for materials from a supplier. You may be intending to use the quotation to help you decide which supplier to order from. These are examples of financial information which have direct impact on your activities. Other examples may have less direct impact. You may have read or heard that a major company has just announced record profits. If you have no contact with that company, you may simply conclude that it indicates a prosperous national economy which may bring you some indirect benefits. If you are a shareholder or an employee of the company concerned, you will probably have a much greater interest.

The main and most comprehensive source of financial information on a limited company is its *annual report and accounts*. A limited liability company is obliged under the *Companies Act 1985* to publish an annual report and accounts, which is a public document. Other types of organisation are also legally obliged to produce financial information on their annual activities. For example, central and local government, health authorities, charities, building societies and nationalised industries all produce some form of annual financial report. Because of the importance of the annual report and accounts of limited companies as a source of financial information, we shall be examining this document in more detail in Chapter 11.

## Activity

Does any organisation with which you are involved or have an interest in, produce an annual financial report of some kind? If it is publicly available, you should obtain a copy. If the report is not publicly available, find out why.

You may have had some difficulty with this activity. If you tried to obtain an annual financial report for a division or department in a large organisation you may have found that one is not available for that particular section, only for the organisation as a whole. If you attempted to get information for a sole trader or a partnership, you will almost certainly have found that the financial statements are confidential and you cannot obtain a copy.

In recent years computer databases, such as *Datastream*, *Extel* and *Financial Analysis Made Easy (FAME)*, have also become major sources of financial information for those with sophisticated requirements. As a general guide, the following are useful sources of printed information:

- *Investors' Chronicle* is a weekly publication containing in-depth reviews on companies and industries.
- *Kompass* is a two-part publication. Volume 1 is a classified catalogue of products and services giving the names of manufacturers, wholesalers and distributors. Volume 2 contains information on over 30,000 companies.
- *The Stock Exchange Year Book* contains information on the operation of the Stock Exchange and on companies' directors, accounts and dividends.
- *Who Owns Whom* is an annual directory in two parts. Volume 1 lists parent companies and gives their subsidiaries; Volume 2 lists the subsidiaries by name and gives the parent companies.
- An increasingly important source of information is the *Internet*. There are a number of sites on the World Wide Web you can access to obtain information on both UK and international companies.

## Activity

Prepare a brief guide on the main sources of company information available to you and how to use them. The guide should enable you to find information not only on financial matters, but also on the following topics:

- products and services;
- brand and trade names;
- relationships between companies;
- facts and figures on particular industries;
- facts and figures on particular companies;
- comment and opinion on companies and industries.

## 2.4 Potential Users of Financial Information

We are confronted with *financial information* at home and at work. We may be so used to reading and hearing it that we do not think about what messages we are being given, and why. If you have managed to obtain a copy of the annual report and accounts for your organisation or any other in which you are interested, you will find that it is a lengthy document containing a large amount of complex and detailed information. It is easy to appreciate that the *owners* of the organisation have an interest in a financial view of the organisation and the *directors* and *managers* find such information useful in a number of ways. But who else might find the information useful, and why?

## Activity

List the various groups of people who might find the annual report and accounts of an organisation useful and give examples of how they might use it.

The contents of your list will depend to a large extent on the type of organisation you had in mind, but the potential users of financial information are:

- shareholders and prospective shareholders;
- lenders;
- trade unions and employees generally;
- managers;
- analysts and advisers;
- business contacts, including suppliers, customers and competitors;
- the government;
- the public.

## Activity

Use the copy you have obtained of the annual financial report and identify the information of greatest interest to the above groups.

## 2.5 Uses of Financial Information

Using our list of potential users of financial information in section 2.4, we can suggest why each group may find it useful:

- *Shareholders*, who are those people who invest in the company, require information for share trading decisions and for generally evaluating the performance of the organisation. As they are the owners of the company, they are also interested in how the directors are managing it on their behalf and the amount of dividend they will receive.
- *Lenders*, who lend money to the company, have similar interests to those of the shareholders, but are most interested in knowing whether the interest will be paid and the loan repaid.
- *Trade unions and employees generally* are interested in the security of employment and the possibility of wage increases.
- *Directors and managers* are interested in the overall performance of the organisation. Managers are likely to be interested in information about their own part of the organisation and will find management accounting information particularly useful.
- *Analysts and advisers*, such as stockbrokers, require the same information as the users they represent (investors, for example), but in greater detail.
- *Business contacts*, such as suppliers, creditors and customers, are interested in such matters as the ability of the organisation to pay its bills, the current and future supply of goods and services offered, price and product information, and the organisation's future prospects.
- *The government*, as well as requiring information for the same reasons as the other groups, needs information to estimate the effects of existing and proposed taxation and other financial and economic measures. It also needs information to estimate economic trends, such as the likely balance of payment figure. The Inland Revenue and the Customs and Excise also require financial information for tax-collecting purposes.
- *The public* may wish to have information about the role of the organisation as an employer, its contributions to political and charitable groups, the impact of its activities on the balance of trade, the community and the environment.

To understand how financial information can be helpful, we need to identify the uses to which it can be put. One way of doing this is to define the responsibilities of any job or activity.

## Activity

Sally Lunn is the manager of a small tea shop. Here is a list of her responsibilities:

- ordering and controlling stock;
- supervising two full-time and two part-time staff;
- ensuring the security of premises;
- keeping cash records and daily banking;
- general display and maintenance of the shop;
- serving customers;
- resolving customers' complaints.

Construct a list of your own responsibilities in any work you have experienced. This may be a holiday job or a voluntary job such as work in a sports or social club, or helping to organise a student activity.

No matter what job you are describing, it is likely that your responsibilities can be classified under one of the following major activities:

- *Controlling* – A large number of responsibilities are concerned with ensuring that the organisation makes progress towards its set objectives. For control to be effectively maintained, financial information is required on such matters as the various costs of products and processes, monitoring labour efficiency and identifying the sources and purpose of all expenditure. Similarly for social activities, such as organising a student ball, information is needed to ensure that a loss is not made.
- *Planning* – Without plans and policies a business has no sense of direction or purpose. Financial information allows plans and policies to be formulated and helps people in the organisation understand the targets and standards which it intends to achieve. For example, a manager needs to know what profit it is hoped the business will make. Even on a personal level you need information in order to plan holidays, whether you need to take a holiday or weekend job, etc.
- *Decision-making* – In establishing plans, it is necessary to decide which of the various courses of action should be taken. We need to know the financial implications of our actions in order to select the most appropriate plan. On a personal level we may need to make a decision between buying a car or using public transport; in business a manager may need to make a decision between using machinery or labour on an activity.

You should now be able to look at any financial information you currently receive and decide whether it helps you in the activity of controlling, planning or decision-making. This may be information you receive at work or through any social organisation you are involved with. Alternatively it may be personal financial information you receive such as bank statements, bills, a student loan, etc.

## Activity

Classify the information you receive according to whether it helps you in controlling, planning or decision-making. You may find that some types of information help with more than one activity.

Once you have completed your list, compare it with the one you drew up for the previous activity. The information should match! For example, if you decided that most of your responsibilities are concerned with controlling, then most of the information you receive will be ticked under that heading on the table. If this is not the case, you have identified financial information which you require, but do not currently receive; or you do receive it, but cannot use it because you do not understand it. In later chapters we shall be looking at different types of financial information and identifying the types most relevant to your responsibilities.

## 2.6 Conclusions

In this chapter we have looked at the different types of business organisation – sole traders, partnerships and limited companies – and compared them. We have examined the sources of financial information and identified potential users. In addition, we have looked at how the uses to which it might be put by managers can be classified as the headings of planning, controlling and decision-making.

Having completed this chapter, you should now be able to:

- describe the main types of business organisation;
- list the potential users of financial information and the uses to which it may be put;
- describe the importance of financial information to management;
- assess the usefulness of financial information to you.

## Exercises

Complete the following sentences:

1 A sole trader and a partnership have unlimited liability, which means that ...........................................................................................................................
2 The main source of financial information on a limited liability company is
...........................................................................................................................
3 Financial information can assist managers in their responsibilities of
...........................................................................................................................
4 Shareholders require information about a company for ...............................
5 Lenders require financial information on a company to ...............................

Are the following statements true or false?

**6** A sole trader is personally responsible for all debts incurred by the business.

**7** If partners do not make an agreement on the share of profit the rules of the Partnership Act 1890 apply.

**8** Only public limited companies have to publish an annual report and accounts.

**9** If two or more persons own a business they must include the word 'partnership' in its name.

**10** Only limited companies quoted on the Stock Exchange have to produce an annual report and accounts.

You may wish to read more widely than this book to answer the following questions fully, but you can check the main points by referring to the appropriate sections in this chapter.

**11** Distinguish between a incorporated and an unincorporated organisation. (Section 2.2)

**12** Identify and describe three sources of financial information on limited companies. (Section 2.3)

**13** Identify four potential users of financial information and describe how they might use it. (Sections 2.4 and 2.5)

**14** Explain how financial information assists managers in their controlling and planning activities. (Section 2.5)

Multiple choice questions (more than one answer may apply):

**15** The best source of financial information about a company is:

   **a** the *Financial Times*
   **b** the *Stock Exchange Official Year Book*
   **c** the annual report and accounts
   **d** the *Investors' Chronicle*.

**16** To form a partnership you must:

   **a** have at least two partners
   **b** have at least four partners
   **c** register the business name with the Department of Trade and Industry
   **d** make your financial results public.

**17** The Companies Act 1985 applies to:

   **a** all partnerships
   **b** all limited companies
   **c** all public limited companies
   **d** all private limited companies.

**18** A limited company offers the advantage of:

   **a** being very easy to establish
   **b** complete financial secrecy
   **c** no legal formalities to meet
   **d** limited financial risk to its owners.

**19** If a partnership wishes to buy new premises, the most appropriate way to raise money would be to:

   **a** issue shares to the public
   **b** obtain a mortgage

**c** obtain a bank overdraft

**d** use a factoring organisation.

**20** What are the disadvantages of a public limited company?

**a** restriction on the number of owners

**b** highly regulated

**c** some difficulty in raising finance

**d** can be vulnerable to being taken over.

Practice questions:

**21** Explain the difference between a partnership and a private limited company.

**22** Describe the main sources you would use to obtain financial information about a public limited company.

**23** Describe the advantages and disadvantages of setting up in business as a sole trader.

**24** Describe the information needs of three different types of users of financial information and discuss how well these needs are met by the annual report and accounts.

**25** Describe the main features of a partnership and explain their importance to anyone considering starting such a business.

(Answers on p. 313)

# Part II

# Financial
# Accounting

# 3 The Importance of Cash

## 3.1 Introduction

The two main reasons why businesses fail are because either they do not have enough *cash* or cannot obtain sufficient *credit*. The closure of the business may be due to a number of factors, but in the end it closes because the electricity has been cut off, suppliers refuse to provide goods or services and employees cannot be paid. Thus, cash is crucial if a business is to survive. Because of the importance of cash, the managers of the business and other interested parties need to know the past cash position and the likely future cash position. They need to know whether they are going to run out of cash and need to arrange credit or have sufficient funds not to worry. The key financial statements allowing them to do this are the *cash flow statement*, which looks at the past, and the *cash flow forecast*, which attempts to predict the future. There is no legal requirement to prepare these statements, but all well managed organisations do so, as they are an essential source of information for running the business.

In this chapter we describe how to construct and use cash flow forecasts and statements. This allows us to explain the critical difference between cash and profit and paves the way for a detailed examination of profit in subsequent chapters.

## 3.2 Profit and Cash

The term *cash* refers to all money, whether in the form of coins, notes, cheques or any other way of making payment which does not involve the use of *credit*. The cash receipts and payments of an organisation are recorded in a *cash book* which is normally part of a bookkeeping system known as *double-entry bookkeeping*. We discuss this in detail in Chapter 4. Cash is of great importance to both individuals and organisations. Without sufficient cash an individual or organisation may become bankrupt. However, not all transactions are for immediate cash; many are credit transactions.

29

An accounting *profit* or *loss* can be made whether the transactions are for cash or on credit and is the difference between the sales and the costs incurred in putting the goods in a saleable condition during the financial period, regardless of whether cash is paid or received.

## Activity

Imagine that you have bought a second-hand fax machine for £60 which you decide to sell straight away by advertising it in the newspaper. The advertisement costs £10 and you sell the fax machine for £120. All this takes place in August and you have no other business transactions. What is your profit for the month of August?

a £120
b £60
c £70
d £50
e £110.

You should have found the answer by *deducting all the costs you incurred in August* when selling the fax machine from the *value of the sale*. This can be shown in a simple statement as follows:

| Profit and loss account for the month of August | | |
|---|---|---|
| | £ | £ |
| **Sales** | | 120 |
| *Less* **Cost of sales** | | |
| Cost of fax machine | 60 | |
| Advertising | 10 | 70 |
| **Profit** | | 50 |

As the statement shows, the answer is a profit of £50, **d**. However, the financial statement does not tell us anything about cash. For example, it does not tell us if cash has been received for the sale of the fax machine or whether the costs have actually been paid or merely incurred. To emphasise the difference between profit and cash we will make the example slightly more complex.

## Activity

The information remains as above, but you allow the buyer to collect the fax machine now, in August, but pay in September. What is your profit or loss in August in these circumstances?

**a** A loss of £120
**b** A profit of £60
**c** A loss of £70
**d** A profit of £50
**e** A loss of £130.

You may have been misled into thinking that you have now made a loss of £120 (the amount owing to you), or £70 (the costs you have incurred). Neither figure is correct. The answer is still a profit of £50. It is very important to remember that a profit and loss account is not a record of cash paid into and out of the business. We look at the profit and loss account in more detail in Chapter 6.

## 3.3 Constructing a Cash Flow Forecast

When we calculate profit we are concerned with the intentions of the parties and the transactions they have entered into, regardless of whether any cash has changed hands. If we want to know about the cash aspects of transactions we need to construct a statement which will tell us about cash.

## Activity

Still using the same example, imagine that you have agreed to sell the fax machine on credit, but a few days later you receive a solicitor's letter informing you that if you do not pay your overdue electricity bill immediately, the supply will be cut. Which of the following actions do you think is the best one to take and which is the worst? Give your reasons.

**a** Allow the electricity to be cut off and have it reconnected later when you have been paid for the fax machine.
**b** Use your savings to pay the bill.
**c** Borrow money to pay the bill
**d** Ask the person who bought the fax machine to pay you immediately.

All the alternatives have advantages and disadvantages, and you may be able to think of other courses of action. If the electricity is cut off, it may prevent you from carrying out your business activities. Although using your savings remedies the situation, you will lose any interest your savings might be earning. Borrowing money would also prevent the electricity being cut off, but you would incur interest charges and have to repay the loan. You may think that the best solution would be to ask the buyer of the fax machine to pay you immediately, but he or she may not be able to do so.

From this example you can appreciate that not only do we require a record of what has happened to cash in the past, but also a statement that will show us what is likely to happen to cash in the future. Such a statement is known as a *cash flow forecast*. Because of the importance of cash, most organisations prepare a cash flow forecast. It usually covers a 12-month period and is divided into months. The cash flow forecast predicts as accurately as possible the *amount* of cash that is expected to come in and go out of the organisation, and the expected *timing* of the cash transaction.

For example, Sarah Wick sets up a business trading in candles in January 1998. She calls the business Candlewick Enterprises. She plans to purchase candles for £1.50 each and sell them for £2.00 each from a market stall and through mail order. Her supplier will allow her 1 month's credit. The sales from the market stall will represent 25% of total sales and her customers will pay cash. The remaining 75% of sales from mail orders will give customers 2 months' credit. The following table shows the number of candles Sarah expects the business to purchase at £1.50 each during the first 6 months' trading, and the amount of cash she expects to pay each month, taking into account that her supplier allows 1 month's credit.

|  | Jan | Feb | Mar | Apr | May | Jun | Total |
|---|---|---|---|---|---|---|---|
| Number of candles | 400 | 400 | 500 | 560 | 600 | 600 | 3,060 |
| Purchase price (£) | 0 | 600 | 600 | 750 | 840 | 900 | 3,690 |

Having looked at the expected purchases, we can now look at the sales Sarah hopes Candlewick Enterprises will achieve. The following table shows the number of candles Sarah expects the business to sell at £2 each during the first 6 months of trading and the anticipated amount of cash received each month, taking into account that 25% of customers will pay cash and the remaining 75% have 2 months' credit.

|  | Jan | Feb | Mar | Apr | May | Jun | Total |
|---|---|---|---|---|---|---|---|
| Number of candles | 400 | 400 | 500 | 560 | 600 | 600 | 3,060 |
| Cash sales (£) | 200 | 200 | 250 | 280 | 300 | 300 | 1,530 |
| Credit sales (£) | 0 | 0 | 600 | 600 | 750 | 840 | 2,790 |

The movements of cash are given specific names and it is important to use them to avoid confusing them with other terms which you will learn later in connection with the profit and loss account.

- *Positive cash flow* is the cash coming in. In the above example it is from sales, but it can be from other sources, such as a loan.
- *Negative cash flow* is the cash going out. In the above example it is for purchases, but it refers to any payment, such as wages, rent, electricity, insurance, etc.
- *Net cash flow* is the difference between the positive and negative cash flows.
- A *cash surplus* arises if more cash comes in than goes out.
- A *cash deficit* arises if more cash goes out than comes in. As it is a negative figure, it is usually shown in brackets.

## Activity

The following table is drawn up from the forecast cash flow figures for Candlewick Enterprise's purchases and sales which we calculated above. Calculate the subtotals for cash inflows and outflows and use them to work out the anticipated cash surplus or cash deficit for each month and the cumulative cash position for each month:

| | Jan £ | Feb £ | Mar £ | Apr £ | May £ | Jun £ | Total £ |
|---|---|---|---|---|---|---|---|
| **Cash in** | | | | | | | |
| Cash sales | 200 | 200 | 250 | 280 | 300 | 300 | 1,530 |
| Credit sales | 0 | 0 | 600 | 600 | 750 | 840 | 2,790 |
| Subtotal | | | | | | | |
| **Cash out** | | | | | | | |
| Purchases | 0 | 600 | 600 | 750 | 840 | 900 | 3,690 |
| Subtotal | | | | | | | |
| **Cash surplus/(deficit)** | | | | | | | |
| **Cumulative cash position** | | | | | | | |

Your completed table should look like this:

| | Jan £ | Feb £ | Mar £ | Apr £ | May £ | Jun £ | Total £ |
|---|---|---|---|---|---|---|---|
| **Cash in** | | | | | | | |
| Cash sales | 200 | 200 | 250 | 280 | 300 | 300 | 1,530 |
| Credit sales | 0 | 0 | 600 | 600 | 750 | 840 | 2,790 |
| Subtotal | 200 | 200 | 850 | 880 | 1,050 | 1,140 | 4,320 |
| **Cash out** | | | | | | | |
| Purchases | 0 | 600 | 600 | 750 | 840 | 900 | 3,690 |
| Subtotal | 0 | 600 | 600 | 750 | 840 | 900 | 3,690 |
| **Cash surplus/(deficit)** | 200 | (400 ) | 250 | 130 | 210 | 240 | |
| **Cumulative cash position** | 200 | (200 ) | 50 | 180 | 390 | 630 | 630 |

You may find the following points helpful:

- The *total column* shows the *cash receipts* and *cash payments* for the entire 6 months. If we deduct the payments for the 6 months (£4,295) from the receipts £4,320) there is a cash surplus of £25.
- The *figures in brackets* represent deficits. In the months of February, March, April and May there is a cumulative cash deficit.
- The *cumulative cash position* in the *total column* should always agree with the figure for the previous month. This represents a cross-check on the accuracy of the calculations.
- Accountants use the word 'purchases' to mean the purchase of goods which will be sold. Other costs incurred are given specific names.

However, the purchase of candles is not the only cost the business will incur. The other costs are:

- *Advertising*: £25 per month payable 1 month in arrears.
- *Telephone*: £45 per quarter payable at the end of each quarter.
- *Market stall*: £15 per month payable at the end of the month.
- *Postage and packaging*: £60 payable each month commencing in February.

We now have all the information needed to construct the following complete cash flow forecast for Candlewick Enterprises.

**Candlewick Enterprises**
**Cash flow forecast January–June 1998**

|  | Jan £ | Feb £ | Mar £ | Apr £ | May £ | Jun £ | Total £ |
|---|---|---|---|---|---|---|---|
| **Cash in** | | | | | | | |
| Cash sales | 200 | 200 | 250 | 280 | 300 | 300 | 1,530 |
| Credit sales | 0 | 0 | 600 | 600 | 750 | 840 | 2,790 |
| Subtotal | 200 | 200 | 850 | 880 | 1,050 | 1,140 | 4,320 |
| **Cash out** | | | | | | | |
| Purchases | 0 | 600 | 600 | 750 | 840 | 900 | 3,690 |
| Advertising | 0 | 25 | 25 | 25 | 25 | 25 | 125 |
| Telephone | 0 | 0 | 45 | 0 | 0 | 45 | 90 |
| Market stall | 15 | 15 | 15 | 15 | 15 | 15 | 90 |
| Postage and packaging | 0 | 60 | 60 | 60 | 60 | 60 | 300 |
| Subtotal | 15 | 700 | 745 | 850 | 940 | 1,045 | 4,295 |
| **Cash surplus/(deficit)** | 185 | (500) | 105 | 30 | 110 | 95 | |
| **Cumulative cash position** | 185 | (315) | (210) | (180) | (70) | 25 | 25 |

Most accountants adopt the layout we have illustrated when constructing cash flow forecasts. The main points to remember are as follows:

- The heading should state the *name* of the person or organisation and the *period* to which the forecast refers.
- The columns should be labelled with the *months* to which they relate.
- The *cash in*, in this case the cash and credit sales, is given in the first rows and subtotalled.
- The *cash out*, itemised separately, is given in the next rows and subtotalled.
- The subtotal of cash out is deducted from the subtotal of cash in to give the *cash surplus* or *deficit* for the month.
- The final row calculates the *cumulative cash position*.
- The final column is the *total of all cash movements* for that particular item.

If you have seen cash flow forecasts before, perhaps a pro forma given by a bank in a business pack, you may have noticed some differences in layout. Do not let this confuse you, because the principles are exactly the same. In the above example, the final column gives the total for the period for each item. It is calculated by adding all the rows (except the subtotals) horizontally. Once you have inserted the item totals you can calculate the subtotals by adding the appropriate groups of item totals vertically.

One important conclusion we can draw from Candlewick Enterprise's cash flow forecast is that the business will have problems. Although there will be a cash surplus at the end of January, by the end of February this will turn into a negative cumulative cash position of £315. There won't be a positive cumulative cash position again until the end of June. Based on these predictions, Sarah would go out of business before the end of February and clearly she must make some decisions before she starts her business.

## 3.4 Planning Capital Requirement

At the moment Sarah has not planned to invest any cash into the business herself. The cash flow forecast has shown that there will be a cash deficit which must be overcome. The first step in this situation is to find out whether the owner is able and willing to invest cash in the business. The amount of money invested by the owner is known as *capital*.

---

## Activity

Sarah is willing to invest cash in her business and she wants to find out how much she will need to make sure Candlewick Enterprises stays solvent during the first 6 months. How much capital do you think the business requires to ensure that there is no cash deficit in any month?

**a** £185
**b** £500
**c** £315
**d** £25
**e** £775.

---

The correct answer is £315. Sarah would have to invest this in February to ensure that the business does not show a cash deficit in any month. The following cash flow forecast shows the position if this amount were invested in the business.

**Candlewick Enterprises**
**Revised cash flow forecast January–June 1998**

|  | Jan £ | Feb £ | Mar £ | Apr £ | May £ | Jun £ | Total £ |
|---|---|---|---|---|---|---|---|
| **Cash in** | | | | | | | |
| Capital | 0 | 315 | 0 | 0 | 0 | 0 | 315 |
| Cash sales | 200 | 200 | 250 | 280 | 300 | 300 | 1,530 |
| Credit sales | 0 | 0 | 600 | 600 | 750 | 840 | 2,790 |
| Subtotal | 200 | 515 | 850 | 880 | 1,050 | 1,140 | 4,635 |
| **Cash out** | | | | | | | |
| Purchases | 0 | 600 | 600 | 750 | 840 | 900 | 3,690 |
| Advertising | 0 | 25 | 25 | 25 | 25 | 25 | 125 |
| Telephone | 0 | 0 | 45 | 0 | 0 | 45 | 90 |
| Market stall | 15 | 15 | 15 | 15 | 15 | 15 | 90 |
| Postage and packaging | 0 | 60 | 60 | 60 | 60 | 60 | 300 |
| Subtotal | 15 | 700 | 745 | 850 | 940 | 1,045 | 4,295 |
| **Cash surplus/(deficit)** | 185 | (500) | 105 | 30 | 110 | 95 | |
| **Cumulative cash position** | 185 | 0 | 105 | 135 | 245 | 340 | 340 |

## 3.5 Planning, Control and Decision-making

So far we have been concerned mainly with cash *planning*. This obviously involves making *decisions* about various activities. For example, unless Sarah invests £315 in the business in February, the business will go bankrupt after only two months. If she has no savings to use as capital, she must make some other plans and decisions. Her main choices are to:

- obtain a bank overdraft;
- allow only 1 month's credit to the mail order customers;
- see if her supplier will allow 2 months' credit;
- control more closely the cash expected to go out on telephone and postage and packaging;
- look for a cheaper market stall.

A cash flow forecast gives financial information which can be used to help make decisions about whether to revise planned activities. Thus, the plans become more realistic and the business is more likely to be successful. But no matter how realistic the plans are, events seldom turn out exactly as predicted. Therefore, it is important to establish *control* of the cash movements on a regular basis by comparing the actual movements of cash each month against the original plans. If things are not turning out as planned, corrective action can then be taken. Without this comparison of the actual results with the plan, there will be no control.

The following *cash flow statement* shows the actual cash flows for Candlewick Enterprises for the first 3 months' trading. The heading reflects the fact that it is no longer a forecast, but statement of the actual cash flows.

**Candlewick Enterprises**
**Actual cash flow statement January–March 1998**

| | Jan £ | Feb £ | Mar £ | Apr £ | May £ | Jun £ | Total £ |
|---|---|---|---|---|---|---|---|
| **Cash in** | | | | | | | |
| Cash sales | 160 | 180 | 200 | | | | 540 |
| Credit sales | 0 | 0 | 480 | | | | 480 |
| Subtotal | 160 | 180 | 680 | | | | 1,020 |
| **Cash out** | | | | | | | |
| Purchases | 0 | 600 | 600 | | | | 1,200 |
| Advertising | 25 | 25 | 25 | | | | 75 |
| Telephone | | | 45 | | | | 45 |
| Market stall | 20 | 20 | 20 | | | | 60 |
| Postage and packaging | 0 | 60 | 60 | | | | 120 |
| Subtotal | 45 | 705 | 750 | | | | 1,500 |
| **Cash surplus/(deficit)** | 115 | (525) | (70) | | | | |
| **Cumulative cash position** | 115 | (410) | (480) | | | | (480) |

As you can see, not everything has turned out as planned: the total number of candles sold is lower than anticipated, the market stall rent is higher, and it looks as if Sarah is paying the advertising costs in the month in which they are incurred. Even if she had introduced the £315 capital as planned, there would still be a cash deficit. However, she has arranged an overdraft with the bank.

## Activity

Sarah must revise her plans for the remaining 3 months. Suggest what action she might take.

You may think that Sarah would be in a better position if she compared her actual cash flow with her plan on a monthly basis, instead of waiting for 3 months. Certainly, control is improved with frequency and most businesses carry out this sort of exercise every month. Given the position Sarah is now in, you should have suggested that she:

● introduces more capital than planned;
● revises her planned sales for the remaining 3 months to a more realistic figure based on the first 3 months' actual figures;
● revises the number of candles she will purchase in view of her substantial stock;

- takes the month's credit on advertising;
- sees if a cheaper market stall can be rented or consider discontinuing the market stall.

If Sarah revises her cash flow forecast, she may decide that it is no longer worthwhile continuing the business. We have not yet allowed for the interest she must pay on her overdraft and the fact that she will have to pay back the money she has borrowed from the bank. Cash flows sometimes show unpleasant information, but they are essential to the effective running of any business.

## 3.6   Using Cash Flow

In the previous sections we have seen that a cash flow forecast is useful in a number of ways. In particular it helps both individuals and organisations to:

- ensure that they have sufficient cash coming in to meet any future payments;
- ensure that they have sufficient cash to carry out planned activities;
- plan for any bank overdraft or loan which may become necessary;
- make decisions about investing any cash surplus;
- control cash flows by comparing actual events against the plans.

Although it is difficult to make general rules about interpreting a cash flow forecast because it depends on the particular business, the following list includes questions you should think about.

- Is all the cash due to the business being collected as soon as possible? Although it may be necessary to give credit to customers, it should not be so extensive as to result in cash problems.
- Are all the payments made by the due date, but not too early? To pay before you have to is poor cash management, but you do not want to receive a court order for non-payment.
- Can credit agreements be arranged with suppliers so that payment is delayed?
- If any large payments have to be made – for example, for purchasing a vehicle or equipment – is it possible to agree instalments with the supplier?
- Is there sufficient cash or access to finance to ensure that the business does not go bankrupt?
- If there is a cash surplus, has a decision been made to invest it wisely so that interest is received?

In using a cash flow statement you will make alterations to your predictions and drawing up statements by hand is very tedious. However, using a computer spreadsheet program makes things considerably easier and allows greater detail to be recorded and increased sophistication in the analysis. Nevertheless, it is important to remember that a cash flow forecast is only as good as your predictions.

## Activity

Using your own bank statement, construct a cash flow forecast for yourself for the next 6 months. You may wish to use a spreadsheet program to do this. Now decide how many of the above questions are relevant to your own cash flow and attempt to answer them.

## 3.7 Conclusions

In this chapter we have considered the difference between profit and cash, and the importance of cash as a resource. We have examined two financial statements: the cash flow forecast which is used to predict the likely future cash position and the cash flow statement which shows the actual past cash position. In addition, we have looked at the principles of planning and controlling cash, and the impact that future cash flows have on decision-making. We have also seen how business activities may have to be modified and decisions taken to ensure that the business is financially viable.

Having completed this chapter, you should now be able to:

- explain the difference between profit and cash;
- construct and interpret a cash flow forecast;
- describe the critical importance of cash as a major resource;
- describe the principles for monitoring and controlling cash;
- identify the uses of a cash flow forecast.

## Exercises

Complete the following sentences:

1 The term 'cash' refers to .......................................................................................
2 Profit is ............................................................................................................
3 Positive cash flow is ...........................................................................................
4 Negative cash flow is ..........................................................................................
5 Net cash flow is .................................................................................................

Are the following statements true or false?

6 A cash deficit arises if more cash comes in than goes out.
7 A cash flow forecast can be used to decide whether the profit the business plans to earn is sufficient.
8 A cash flow forecast can be used to determine whether the business requires a loan.

**9** The cumulative cash flow figure is important only if it is negative.
**10** Cash flows are best drawn up on a quarterly basis.

You may wish to read more widely than this book to answer the following questions fully, but you can check the main points by referring to the appropriate sections in this chapter.

**11** Describe the difference between profit and cash. (Section 3.2)
**12** What procedures would you use when preparing a cash flow forecast? (Section 3.3)
**13** What are the main reasons why individuals and organisations should plan and control their cash flows? (Sections 3.3–3.6)
**14** Why do banks request cash flow forecasts from businesses seeking a loan? (Section 3.6)

Multiple choice questions (more than one answer may apply)

**15** Negative cash flow is:

    **a** cash flowing into an organisation
    **b** cash flowing out of an organisation
    **c** sales made to customers
    **d** a cash deficit.

**16** If a business anticipates a cash deficit, it can take corrective action by:

    **a** making all payments as soon as possible
    **b** extending the credit it gives to customers
    **c** delaying any payments it has to make
    **d** purchasing more goods for stock.

**17** If sales are made on credit, the transaction should be entered in the cash flow forecast:

    **a** when it is anticipated the customer will pay
    **b** when it is anticipated that the customer will take the goods away
    **c** when it is anticipated the customers will place the order
    **d** 2 months after the goods are delivered.

**18** A cash surplus is:

    **a** the amount of money invested by the owner(s)
    **b** the profit the business expects to make
    **c** when more cash goes out than comes in
    **d** when more cash comes in than goes out.

**19** If 35% of sales are made on 2 months' credit and the total sales figure for January is £4,500:

    **a** £1,575 cash should be received in January
    **b** £2,925 cash should be received in February
    **c** £1,575 cash should be received in March
    **d** £2,925 cash should be received in March.

**20** If 1,200 items at £4.50 each are purchased in January with a 33% deposit to be paid in that month and the balance to be paid within 2 months, the balancing figure will be:

    **a** £3,600 in March
    **b** £3,600 in April
    **c** £4,800 in March
    **d** £4,800 in April.

Practice questions:

**21** Calculate the missing figures in the following cash flow statement:

|  | January £ | February £ |
|---|---|---|
| **Cash in** | | |
| Cash sales | 200 | ? |
| Credit sales | 500 | 600 |
| Subtotal | 700 | ? |
| **Cash out** | | |
| Purchases | ? | 650 |
| Other expenses | 200 | 220 |
| Subtotal | ? | ? |
| **Cash surplus/(deficit)** | (100) | (70) |
| **Cumulative cash position** | (100) | ? |

**22** Discuss the main features involved in interpreting a cash flow forecast.

**23** Philip Trigg has negotiated with two manufacturers of electric circuit boards to carry out assembly work for them as a subcontractor. He anticipates assembling the following numbers of assembly boards for each manufacturer during 1998:

| Month | Firm A | Firm B |
|---|---|---|
| January | 120 | 200 |
| February | 130 | 200 |
| March | 130 | 240 |
| April | 150 | 240 |
| May | 140 | 240 |
| June | 140 | 220 |
| July | 160 | 220 |
| August | 160 | 270 |
| September | 170 | 270 |
| October | 140 | 270 |
| November | 140 | 230 |
| December | 120 | 210 |

Firm *A* has agreed to pay £6.60 for each board assembled and Firm *B* £6.50. Firm *A* will pay 2 months after the work has been done, but Firm *B* will pay 1 month after the work has been done. Philip anticipates the following expenses:

| | |
|---|---|
| Rent of workshop | £6,000 per annum, payable at the beginning of each quarter |
| Lighting and heating | £120 per month, payable 1 month in arrears |
| Telephone | £50 per quarter, payable at the end of each quarter |
| Packaging | 10% of sales, payable in the month following the month in which the sales occur |
| Miscellaneous expenses | £25 each month |
| Tools and equipment | £2,500 in January, £1,000 in February and £500 in March |

Draw up a cash flow forecast for Philip Trigg for the 6-month period January to June and calculate the amount of capital he needs to invest in the business to prevent a cash deficit in any month.

**24** Using the information given in Question 23, imagine that Philip has negotiated a bank loan of £5,000 at 12% per annum which he receives in January. He has to pay the interest on at the end of each quarter. In addition, he wishes to draw £500 per month from the business for his personal use. Construct a cash flow forecast for Philip Trigg for the 6-month period January to June. Explain what action Philip might take to resolve any cash deficit that occurs during the period.

**25** Think of a business that you would like to start. Draw up a list of all the expenses the business would incur and indicate the source of the information you would need to calculate the figures for the forecast cash outflows of the business.

(Answers on p. 314)

# 4 The Accounting System

## 4.1 Introduction

In Part I we discussed the importance of financial information, together with the main users and uses. In order to generate financial information, a business needs to establish an *accounting system*. The nature of the system depends on the type of business and the size of the organisation, but there are common features since procedures must be established to allow all financial transactions to be recorded. These procedures involve raising *source documents*, such as invoices, purchase orders and credit notes, so that those responsible in the business are made aware that a transaction has taken place and the details of the transaction can be recorded.

In most organisations transactions are recorded in an accounting system known as *double-entry bookkeeping*. This ensures that an arithmetical check on the accuracy of the records is made and that financial statements can be prepared from the records to summarise all the transactions that have taken place during any particular period of time. Large organisations carry out thousands of transactions every day and need highly sophisticated computerised accounting systems. Smaller businesses use either computerised or manual accounting systems. In this chapter we describe a simple manual system in order to explain double-entry bookkeeping, although the principles are the same whether the system is computerised or not.

## 4.2 Source Documents

In the previous chapter we noted that not all transactions between businesses are for immediate cash; many are credit transactions. An organisation needs a system for recording these transactions and must create a number of different documents in the process. Such documents are known as *source documents* and are the foundation on which the financial records of the business are built.

In large organisations goods are purchased on credit and a number of external and internal documents are necessary to record the activities. First, the purchaser issues a *purchase order* and sends it to the supplier. This document specifies the quantity, type and price of the goods ordered. When the purchaser receives the goods, they are examined to ensure that they match the items on the purchase order and a *goods received note (GRN)* is raised. Copies of the goods received note are sent to the accounts department, the purchase department and the stores department. When the stores department receives the goods the details are recorded on a *stores record card* so that the stores manager has a record of the goods available. Items are released by the stores department only on receipt of a properly authorised *stores requisition*, the fourth document in this chain. When the items are issued, the stores record card is adjusted to show the decrease in stock.

On receipt of the purchase order the supplier sends the goods to the purchaser with an accompanying *delivery note*. The purchaser signs the delivery note and returns it to the supplier as proof of receipt. Next, the supplier issues an *invoice* showing the amount the purchaser will have to pay. If the purchaser is dissatisfied with any of the goods and returns them, the supplier issues a *credit note* showing the value of the goods returned which the purchaser will no longer have to pay. If the supplier receives many orders from the same purchaser, rather than requiring payment of each invoice, the supplier may issue a monthly statement showing a summary of all the invoices and credit notes during the period and the balance due.

In addition to recording transactions for goods, businesses must also record labour costs. In manufacturing industries *clock cards* may be used to record the time spent at work by employees and *job cards* to record the amount of time spent on each job. The job cards are then reconciled with the clock cards. The wages office prepares the *payroll* by calculating the wages from the clock cards for the workers paid on a time basis and from the job cards if there is an incentive scheme. In service industries *time sheets* may be used to record how much time has been spent on each job so that clients can be charged for the time spent on their work.

## Activity

Design a flow diagram to illustrate the external and internal movement of source documents which are raised when goods are bought on credit.

In constructing your diagram you will have experienced some of the difficulties in establishing and maintaining systems in an organisation. It is necessary to ensure that each stage of the transaction is monitored, that the appropriate personnel are kept informed and that the records are correctly referenced and dated. The system needs to be designed so that if there is an error or a query, the appropriate source document can be traced and the problem resolved. Designing an accounting system in a large organisation is a task for specialists and the recording of the transactions will be computerised. However, whether the system is computerised or manual, it is normally based on the principles of double-entry bookkeeping.

## 4.3 Double-entry Bookkeeping

*Double-entry bookkeeping* is the most efficient and effective method for recording financial transactions in a way which allows the easy preparation of financial statements. In a double-entry bookkeeping system, every transaction is recorded twice. This reflects the dual nature of business transactions and provides an arithmetical check. In order to understand the principles of double-entry bookkeeping, you need to remember that the business is a separate entity from its owner(s) when it carries out its activities. Therefore, it can enter into transactions with the owner(s).

All businesses need resources, and these are known as *assets*. Examples include, cash, stock, office furniture and equipment, vehicles, plant and machinery and premises. But before the business can acquire any assets it must have funds. In a new business the most likely source of funding is the owner. The amount invested by the owner is known as the *capital*. Capital is a *liability* of the business because the business owes the money to the owner. If no one else has funded the business, the assets of the business are equal to the capital and this can be shown in the form of an equation:

$$Assets = Capital$$

However, the business may also have received funding from the bank or other lender in the form of a loan, in which case the equation becomes:

$$Assets = Capital + Other\ liabilities$$

This is known as the *accounting equation* and it is important to remember that the equation must always balance. In Chapter 7 you will see that the accounting equation is the basis of an important financial statement known as the *balance sheet*.

## Activity

A business finances the purchase of some new computer equipment by borrowing £10,000 from the bank. How does this affect the accounting equation?

In this case the business will increase its assets by £10,000 (the new equipment), but at the same time it will increase its liabilities by £10,000 (the bank loan). Thus, the accounting equation becomes:

$$(\text{Assets} + £10,000) = \text{Capital} + (\text{Other liabilities} + £10,000)$$

In a manual double-entry bookkeeping system, all transactions are recorded in an *account*, and each account is kept on a separate page. Although the pages may be loose-leaf or bound, they are kept in a book. The books of accounts are known as *ledgers*. The following illustration of one page in the ledger shows the account where the transactions concerning computer equipment are recorded:

**Computer equipment account**

| Date | (Debit) | £ | Date | (Credit) | £ |
|------|---------|---|------|----------|---|
|      |         |   |      |          |   |
|      |         |   |      |          |   |
|      |         |   |      |          |   |
|      |         |   |      |          |   |
|      |         |   |      |          |   |

The page is divided into six columns. The left-hand side is referred to as the *debit* side and the right-hand side is called the *credit* side. The date that the transaction takes place is inserted in either the first or the fourth column, the nature of the transaction in the second or the fifth column, and the amount involved in the third or the sixth column. You need to remember if you are going to debit an account, you should enter the item on the left-hand side. A *debit entry* means one that is on the left-hand side of the account. If you are going to credit an account, you should enter the item on the right-hand side of the account. A *credit entry* means one that is on the right-hand side of the account.

## 4.4 Recording Assets and Liabilities

In order to keep the accounting equation balanced, every transaction conducted by the business is entered once on the debit side of one account and once on the credit side of another account. The rules for recording transactions which involve *assets* and *liabilities* are as follows:

- *Debit* the asset account to show an *increase* in an asset.
- *Credit* the asset account to show a *decrease* in an asset.
- *Credit* the account to show an *increase* in a capital or liability account.
- *Debit* the account to show a *decrease* in a capital or liability account.

To illustrate these rules we will take a business which commenced on 1 January 1998. The owner of the business is Nick Mulch and he has invested £5,000 in his business, Mulch Garden Design. His girlfriend, Louise, has given the business a loan of £2,000. All the money is kept in the bank. Therefore, there are two transactions to record: the capital invested by Nick and the loan given by Louise. Each transaction will require a debit entry to be made to one account and a corresponding credit entry of the same amount made to another account.

Three accounts need to be opened: *a capital account* for the money invested by the owner, Nick; a *loan account* for the loan from Louise; and a *bank account* to show the money held at the bank:

### Capital account

| 1998 | | £ | 1998 | | £ |
|------|--|---|------|--|---|
| | | | 1 January | Bank | 5,000 |
| | | | | | |

### Loan account

| 1998 | | £ | 1998 | | £ |
|------|--|---|------|--|---|
| | | | 1 January | Bank | 2,000 |
| | | | | | |

### Bank account

| 1998 | | £ | 1998 | | £ |
|------|--|---|------|--|---|
| 1 January | Capital | 5,000 | | | |
| 1 January | Loan | 2,000 | | | |
| | | | | | |

If you study these accounts, you can see that the rules for recording transactions have been stringently applied. The transaction of the owner introducing £5,000 capital has been shown as a credit in the capital account and because the assets of the business have increased by this same amount, the bank account has been debited with £5,000. Thus, there is a corresponding debit entry for the credit entry.

With regard to the loan, when Louise gave the £2,000 loan to the business, its liabilities increased by that amount, so the loan account has been credited. Having made a credit entry in that account, a debit entry must be made in another account. In this case it is the bank account, since the loan means an increase in the assets of the business. As you can see, for each transaction you need to record the date, the name of the account where the corresponding entry is made and the amount. This allows you to trace it at a later date if you have any problems with the records.

We will now extend our example by showing the transactions entered into by the business on 2 January 1998. Mulch Garden Design pays £3,000 from the bank account for premises; £1,000 for machinery and £500 for equipment. The bank account is already open, so we can continue to use it. However, we need to open three new asset accounts to record these latest transactions:

### Bank account

| 1998 | | £ | 1998 | | £ |
|------|------|-------|-----------|-----------|-------|
| 1 January | Capital | 5,000 | 2 January | Premises | 3,000 |
| 1 January | Loan | 2,000 | 2 January | Machinery | 1,000 |
| | | | 2 January | Equipment | 500 |

### Premises account

| 1998 | | £ | 1998 | | £ |
|------|------|-------|------|--|--|
| 2 January | Bank | 3,000 | | | |

### Machinery account

| 1998 | | £ | 1998 | | £ |
|------|------|-------|------|--|--|
| 2 January | Bank | 1,000 | | | |
| | | | | | |

### Equipment account

| 1998 | | £ | 1998 | £ | |
|------|------|-----|------|---|--|
| 2 January | Bank | 500 | | | |

These records reflect the transactions that have taken place. For example, the bank account is an asset account. When the business received the capital of £5,000 from Nick and the loan from Louise, these amounts were debited to the bank account to show the increase in assets represented by the amount of money held at the bank. When the business paid for items such as the machinery, the bank account was credited. If you take the total of all the debit entries in the bank account and *deduct* the total of all the credit entries, the resulting figure is £2,500, which is the amount of money the business now has left at the bank.

## Activity

The business repays £1,500 to Louise on 3 January and on the same day returns £250 worth of equipment to the supplier because it is faulty and receives a refund which is paid into the bank. Make the necessary entries in the accounts.

The updated accounts should look like this:

### Bank account

| 1998 | | £ | 1998 | | £ |
|------|--|---|------|--|---|
| 1 January | Capital | 5,000 | 2 January | Premises | 3,000 |
| 1 January | Loan | 2,000 | 2 January | Machinery | 1,000 |
| 3 January | Equipment | 250 | 2 January | Equipment | 500 |
| | | | 3 January | Loan | 1,500 |

### Loan account

| 1998 | | £ | 1998 | | £ |
|------|--|---|------|--|---|
| 3 January | Bank | 1,500 | 1 January | Bank | 2,000 |
| | | | | | |

### Equipment account

| 1998 | | £ | 1998 | | £ |
|------|--|---|------|--|---|
| 2 January | Bank | 500 | 3 January | Bank | 250 |
| | | | | | |

## 4.5 Recording Revenues and Expenses

As well as needing accounts for its assets and liabilities, a business must have accounts for its *revenues* and *expenses*. Revenue is the monetary value of the sale of goods or services to customers. Expenses are the monetary value of assets used to obtain those revenues; in other words, the day-to-day costs of running the business. The rules for recording transactions which involve revenues and expenses are as follows:

- To show an increase in an expense account, *debit* the account.
- To show a decrease in an expense account, *credit* the account.
- To show an increase in a revenue account, *credit* the account.
- To show a decrease in a revenue account, *debit* the account.

As you will see, every transaction involves making a credit entry to one account and a debit entry to another account. First we will explain what is meant by an increase in an expense account and an increase in a revenue account. Suppose Mulch Garden Design spends £200 on printing advertisements in the form of promotional leaflets, and £20 on posting them to potential customers. Prior to this date the business has not incurred any expenses, so the monetary value was nil. Now it has incurred some and we need to show the increase in the appropriate expense accounts:

### Bank account

| 1998 | | £ | 1998 | | £ |
|---|---|---|---|---|---|
| 1 January | Capital | 5,000 | 2 January | Premises | 3,000 |
| 1 January | Loan | 2,000 | 2 January | Machinery | 1,000 |
| 3 January | Equipment | 250 | 2 January | Equipment | 500 |
| | | | 3 January | Loan | 1,500 |
| | | | 4 January | Advertising | 200 |
| | | | 4 January | Postage | 20 |
| | | | | | |

### Advertising account

| 1998 | | £ | 1998 | | £ |
|---|---|---|---|---|---|
| 4 January | Bank | 200 | | | |
| | | | | | |

**Postage account**

| 1998 | | £ | 1998 | | £ |
|------|------|------|------|------|------|
| 4 January | Bank | 20 | | | |
| | | | | | |

As the business has paid for the advertising leaflets and postage, its cash assets at the bank must have decreased by the amount of these expenses. Therefore, these two transactions resulted in debit entries to the expense accounts and both were credited to the bank account.

## Activity

On 5 January Mulch Garden Design pays £50 for the cleaning of the premises. On 6 January the business lets part of its display gardens for a wedding reception and receives £350 in rent. Make the necessary entries in the appropriate accounts.

You should not have had too much difficulty with this. The cleaning expenses were a pair of straightforward entries. The receipt of rent may have caused you to think because we have not illustrated any similar transactions. However, as long as you remembered the rule that you show an increase in revenues by *crediting* the revenue account (in this case, rent received), the corresponding entry had to be to debit the bank account to show an increase in cash assets of £350:

**Bank account**

| 1998 | | £ | 1998 | | £ |
|------|------|------|------|------|------|
| 1 January | Capital | 5,000 | 2 January | Premises | 3,000 |
| 1 January | Loan | 2,000 | 2 January | Machinery | 1,000 |
| 3 January | Equipment | 250 | 2 January | Equipment | 500 |
| 6 January | Rent received | 350 | 3 January | Loan | 1,500 |
| | | | 4 January | Advertising | 200 |
| | | | 4 January | Postage | 20 |
| | | | 5 January | Cleaning | 50 |
| | | | | | |

**Cleaning account**

| 1998 | | £ | 1998 | | £ |
|---|---|---|---|---|---|
| 5 January | Bank | 50 | | | |
| | | | | | |

**Rent received account**

| 1998 | | £ | 1998 | | £ |
|---|---|---|---|---|---|
| | | | 6 January | Bank | 350 |
| | | | | | |

## 4.6 Recording Purchases, Sales and Stock

Of course, it is not much use a business advertising its goods unless it has purchased some it can sell. Buying goods is an expense and therefore it is necessary to open a *purchases account* to record such transactions. As the purchase account is an expense account, when the business buys goods the transaction is recorded as a debit. However, when the business sells the goods they are *not* shown as a credit in the purchases account for two reasons. First, they will not be sold at the same price as they were purchased for because the business wants to make a profit. Because we want to show the profit on a financial statement known as the *profit and loss account* (see Chapter 6), we do not want to lose it in the detail of the purchases account. The second reason is that at the end of a financial period it is likely that there will be some unsold goods left which are known as *stock*. Stock requires special treatment which we shall be describing at the end of this section.

Instead of crediting sales to the purchases account, a *sales account*, which is a revenue account, is opened. If the goods are sold to customers for cash, the sale is shown as a credit in the sales account and the corresponding entry is a debit in the bank account. The latter entry reflects the increase in cash assets held at the bank. We need to look at a new example to shown how this is done.

Kate Burton starts off a designer clothes shop called Kool Kate on 1 July by investing £10,000 in the business. On that day she purchases equipment costing £4,000, stock costing £4,000 and pays £500 for advertising. On 2 July she sells stock for £2,800 and buys a small, second-hand car for £1,000. On 3 July she sells stock for £3,500 and purchases further stock for £2,000. The entries in the accounts look like this:

## Capital account

| 1998 | | £ | 1998 | | £ |
|------|------|------|---------|------|--------|
| | | | 1 July | Bank | 10,000 |
| | | | | | |

## Bank account

| 1998 | | £ | 1998 | | £ |
|--------|---------|--------|--------|-------------|-------|
| 1 July | Capital | 10,000 | 1 July | Equipment | 4,000 |
| 2 July | Sales | 2,800 | 1 July | Purchases | 4,000 |
| 3 July | Sales | 3,500 | 1 July | Advertising | 500 |
| | | | 2 July | Car | 1,000 |
| | | | 3 July | Purchases | 2,000 |
| | | | | | |

## Equipment account

| 1998 | | £ | 1998 | | £ |
|--------|------|-------|------|------|------|
| 1 July | Bank | 4,000 | | | |
| | | | | | |

## Advertising account

| 1998 | | £ | 1998 | | £ |
|--------|------|-----|------|------|------|
| 1 July | Bank | 500 | | | |
| | | | | | |

## Purchases account

| 1998 | | £ | 1998 | | £ |
|--------|------|-------|------|------|------|
| 1 July | Bank | 4,000 | | | |
| 3 July | Bank | 2,000 | | | |
| | | | | | |

**Sales account**

| 1998 | | £ | 1998 | | £ |
|---|---|---|---|---|---|
| | | | 2 July | Bank | 2,800 |
| | | | 3 July | Bank | 3,500 |
| | | | | | |

**Motor vehicle account**

| 1998 | | £ | 1998 | | £ |
|---|---|---|---|---|---|
| 2 July | Bank | 1,000 | | | |
| | | | | | |

In this example we have referred to the goods that the business is buying and selling as *stock*. However, we will not use a *stock account* until the end of the financial period, as we explain in a moment. Instead, the purchases and sales of goods have been recorded in separate accounts, named *purchases account* and *sales account*, respectively. Accountants use the term 'purchases' by itself to mean purchases of goods for resale. Do not confuse this with purchases of other assets, such as equipment or machinery.

There is one final aspect of purchases and sales of goods which we must consider. Perhaps the business has purchased goods and had to return them to the supplier because they are faulty, or for other reasons. Alternatively, perhaps a customer returns goods to the business. The first transaction requires a *returns outward account* (or *purchases returns account*) to be opened. The second transaction requires a *returns inward* (or *sales returns account*) to be opened.

The following example illustrates the returns outward account. On 1 July Kool Kate purchases goods from the usual supplier, but later £200 worth are found to be faulty. They are returned to the supplier on 12 July and a refund of £200 is received the same day. These transactions are recorded as follows:

**Bank account**

| 1998 | | £ | 1998 | | £ |
|---|---|---|---|---|---|
| 1 July | Capital | 10,000 | 1 July | Equipment | 4,000 |
| 2 July | Sales | 2,800 | 1 July | Purchases | 4,000 |
| 3 July | Sales | 3,500 | 1 July | Advertising | 500 |

| 12 July | Returns outward | 200 | 2 July | Car | 1,000 |
| | | | 3 July | Purchases | 2,000 |
| | | | | | |

**Returns outward account**

| 1998 | | £ | 1998 | | £ |
|---|---|---|---|---|---|
| | | | 12 July | Bank | 200 |
| | | | | | |

As you can see, the bank account has been debited to show the increase in cash assets due to the cash refund by the supplier, but rather than crediting the purchases account to record the goods which were returned, a returns outward account has been opened and this provides an accurate record of what has happened. This information will be used when the profit and loss account is drawn up later.

## Activity

The same principles are applied if one of the customers returns goods. Show how the transactions are recorded in the accounts if one of Kool Kate's customers returns £500 worth of goods to the business on 14 July and the business gives the customer a refund the same day.

The transaction should be recorded as follows:

**Bank account**

| 1998 | | £ | 1998 | | £ |
|---|---|---|---|---|---|
| 1 July | Capital | 10,000 | 1 July | Equipment | 4,000 |
| 2 July | Sales | 2,800 | 1 July | Purchases | 4,000 |
| 3 July | Sales | 3,500 | 1 July | Advertising | 500 |
| 12 July | Returns outward | 200 | 2 July | Car | 1,000 |
| | | | 3 July | Purchases | 2,000 |
| | | | 14 July | Returns inward | 500 |
| | | | | | |

**Returns inward account**

| 1998 | | £ | 1998 | | £ |
|---|---|---|---|---|---|
| 14 July | Bank | 500 | | | |
| | | | | | |

## 4.7 Credit Transactions

So far in the examples we have used, all the receipts and payments have been for cash. However, many business transactions are made on *credit* and the receipt or payment of cash does not take place until a later date. This requires accounts to be opened for *creditors* (those individuals and entities to whom the business owes money and *debtors* (those individuals and entities who owe the business money). Thus, a debtor is an *asset* to the business and a creditor is a *liability* of the business. The rules of double-entry bookkeeping for making entries into asset and liability accounts therefore apply to debtors and creditors.

First we consider an example where a customer of the business has not paid cash, but has obtained goods on credit. Suppose the clothes sold by Kool Kate for £2,800 on 2 July were bought on credit by Philippa Merton. The entry in the sales account will still be a credit, but instead of debiting the bank account as an increase in cash assets, we need to debit Philippa Merton's account. This is because, by obtaining the goods on credit, Philippa is a debtor because she has not yet paid for the goods:

**Sales account**

| 1998 | | £ | 1998 | | £ |
|---|---|---|---|---|---|
| | | | 2 July | Philippa Merton | 2,800 |
| | | | | | |

**Philippa Merton**

| 1998 | | £ | 1998 | | £ |
|---|---|---|---|---|---|
| 2 July | Sales | 2,800 | | | |
| | | | | | |

As you can see, because Philippa Merton is an asset account (that is, a person who owes the business cash), we have followed the rules for asset accounts. Before 2 July she owed the business nothing, but after the sales transaction on that date, she owed Kool Kate £2,800. This increase in debtor assets is shown by debiting the Philippa Merton account. The debtor's account has been opened in Philippa Merton's name so that a record can be kept of who owes Kool Kate money.

## Activity

On 20 July Philippa Merton pays £750 of the money she owes to Kool Kate. Show how this transaction will be recorded in the accounts.

The accounts will be amended as follows:

### Bank account

| 1998 | | £ | 1998 | | £ |
|---|---|---|---|---|---|
| 1 July | Capital | 10,000 | 1 July | Equipment | 4,000 |
| 3 July | Sales | 3,500 | 1 July | Purchases | 4,000 |
| 12 July | Returns outward | 200 | 1 July | Advertising | 500 |
| 20 July | Philippa Merton | 750 | 2 July | Car | 1,000 |
| | | | 3 July | Purchases | 2,000 |
| | | | 14 July | Returns inward | 500 |
| | | | | | |

### Philippa Merton

| 1998 | | £ | 1998 | | £ |
|---|---|---|---|---|---|
| 2 July | Sales | 2,800 | 20 July | Bank | 750 |
| | | | | | |

As you can see, cash assets have increased by £750 and debtor assets have decreased by the same amount. Note that in the bank account we have deleted the entry on 2 July for sales of £2,800 because we have now decided that Philippa Merton did not pay cash but took the goods on credit. The debit entry is therefore to the Philippa Merton account and the sales account remains untouched.

Next we consider a case where the business has not paid cash but has obtained goods or services on credit. In such a case the business has acquired a liability and you will need to use the double-entry rules for increasing and decreasing liability accounts. On 26 July Kool Kate purchases goods on credit from Pank Patel for £1,500. On 28 July Kool Kate pays the debt in full. The transactions are recorded as follows:

### Purchases account

| 1998 | | £ | 1998 | | £ |
|---|---|---|---|---|---|
| 1 July | Bank | 4,000 | | | |
| 3 July | Bank | 2,000 | | | |
| 26 July | Pank Patel | 1,500 | | | |
| | | | | | |

### Pank Patel

| 1998 | | £ | 1998 | | £ |
|---|---|---|---|---|---|
| 28 July | Bank | 1,500 | 26 July | Purchases | 1,500 |
| | | | | | |

### Bank account

| 1998 | | £ | 1998 | | £ |
|---|---|---|---|---|---|
| 1 July | Capital | 10,000 | 1 July | Equipment | 4,000 |
| 3 July | Sales | 3,500 | 1 July | Purchases | 4,000 |
| 12 July | Returns outward | 200 | 1 July | Advertising | 500 |
| 20 July | Philippa Merton | 750 | 2 July | Car | 1,000 |
| | | | 3 July | Purchases | 2,000 |
| | | | 14 July | Returns inward | 500 |
| | | | 28 July | Pank Patel | 1,500 |
| | | | | | |

Having worked through the examples in the preceding sections, you may have noticed how easy it is to make a mistake and enter a transaction as a credit or a debit in both two accounts, rather than as a credit on one account and a debit on the other. Although you may have found the process somewhat tedious, it is essential that you understand these important principles before moving on to the subsequent chapters in this book. If your employment involves accounting, you will need to acquire basic book-keeping skills.

## 4.8 Conclusions

Double-entry bookkeeping is a crucial procedure for recording accounting transactions. The system ensures that the records are mathematically accurate and permits the profit and loss account and balance sheet to be prepared. It captures the dual nature of transactions by making a debit and a corresponding credit entry for every financial transaction. A debit entry is recorded on the left-hand side of the account and a credit entry on the right-hand side. There are separate rules for recording assets and liabilities, revenues and expenses.

Having completed this chapter, you should now be able to:

- describe a range of source documents;
- explain the principles of double-entry bookkeeping;
- record entries for assets and liabilities;
- record entries for expenses and sales.

## Exercises

Complete the following sentences:

**1** A goods received note is raised by ............................................................................:
**2** Clock cards are used to ................................................................................................
**3** Double-entry bookkeeping is ......................................................................................
**4** Capital is .....................................................................................................................
**5** The accounting equation is .........................................................................................

Are the following statements true or false?

**6** A job card records the total time an employee spends at work.
**7** A debit to an asset account shows an increase.
**8** A debit to a liability account shows an increase.
**9** The purchase of goods is debited to a stock account.
**10** A debtor is someone to whom you owe money.

You may wish to read more widely than this book to answer the following questions fully, but you can check the main points by referring to the appropriate sections in this chapter.

**11** Describe the source documents used for recording labour costs (Section 4.2)
**12** What is the importance of the accounting equation? (Section 4.3)
**13** What is the function of a purchases return account? (Section 4.6)
**14** What are the principles of double-entry bookkeeping? (Sections 4.3–4.7)

Multiple choice questions (more than one answer may apply):

**15** Using the accounting equation, if assets are £25,000 and liabilities are £16,000, capital is:

**a** £41,000
**b** £9,000
**c** £50,000
**d** £16,000.

**16** The accounting entries to record a loan taken out by a business are:

  **a** debit the bank account and debit the loan account
  **b** credit the loan account and debit the bank account
  **c** credit the loan account and credit the bank account
  **d** credit the bank account and debit the loan account.

**17** If a business purchases goods for cash for later resale, the accounting entries are:

  **a** debit the stock account and credit the bank account
  **b** credit the stock account and debit the bank account
  **c** debit the purchases account and credit the stock account
  **d** debit the purchases account and credit the bank account.

**18** If a customer who has received goods on credit subsequently pays the business, the accounting entries are:

  **a** debit the creditor's account and credit the bank account
  **b** debit the debtor's account and credit the creditor's account
  **c** credit the debtor's account and debit the bank account
  **d** credit the creditor's account and debit the bank account.

**19** If a business returns goods it has received on credit to its supplier, the accounting entries are:

  **a** debit the sales account and credit the returns outward account
  **b** credit the purchases account and debit the returns outward account
  **c** debit the purchases account and credit the returns outward account
  **d** credit the returns outward account and debit the creditor's account.

**20** The accounting entries to record a customer who pays for goods which had been sold on credit are:

  **a** credit the sales account and debit the creditor's account
  **b** debit the bank account and credit the creditor's account
  **c** debit the bank account and credit the debtor's account
  **d** debit the debtor's account and credit the bank account.

Practice questions:

**21** On 1 March 1998 Jack Castle starts a business, Castle Tours, with £5,000 capital and a £5,000 loan from the bank. He keeps £300 of the loan as cash pays the balance of the loan and the capital into the business's bank account. Show the bookkeeping entries.
**22** Clive Ashley owns Ashley Kennels. On 1 August 1998 the business purchases £1,500 of dried dog food on credit from Bowin Ltd. On 2 August £50 of the food is returned to the supplier as it was beyond its sell-by date. Show the bookkeeping entries.
**23** Mary's Cake Shop has £2,500 in the bank. On 1 March 1998 goods to the value of £3,000 were purchased on credit from Goodwin Wholesale Ltd. On 12 June Mary's Cake Shop pays £1,000 to Goodwin Wholesale Ltd. Show the bookkeeping records.

**24** Rex Bendall starts an agricultural fencing business, Wellworth Fencing, with £50,000 capital which he has inherited. On 1 June 1998 he opens a bank account for the business and pays in the capital into it, buys a lorry for £16,000, pays for insurance costing £1,400 and pays 3 months' rent on premises in advance of £4,500. On 2 June he purchases equipment for £5,400 and fencing materials from Timber Supplies for £850. In addition he pays for advertising in the local press which costs £420. On 4 June he buys a further £120 of fencing materials from Timber Supplies on credit. Draw up the books of accounts.

**25** Pamela Lawley has a gift shop called Lavender & Lace. On 4 July the cash account of the business looked like this:

**Cash account**

| 1998 | | £ | 1998 | | £ |
|---|---|---|---|---|---|
| 1 July | Opening balance | 500 | 1 July | Postage | 25 |
| 2 July | Cash sales | 138 | 1 July | Window cleaning | 10 |
| 3 July | Cash sales | 192 | 1 July | Stationery | 15 |
| | | | 1 July | Parking | 2 |
| | | | 1 July | Stationery | 36 |
| | | | 1 July | Petrol | 18 |
| | | | 2 July | Parking | 2 |
| | | | 2 July | Postage | 31 |
| | | | 2 July | Purchases | 104 |
| | | | 3 July | Parking | 2 |
| | | | 3 July | Petrol | 18 |
| | | | 3 July | Purchases | 89 |
| | | | | | |

Draw up the accounts to show the corresponding entries.

(Answers on pp. 315–20)

# 5 The Trial Balance

## 5.1 Introduction

The *trial balance* is a list of the balances of all the individual accounts in the accounting system. All the debit balances are entered in one column and all the credit balances in the other. The sum of these two columns should be the same. As the name implies, a trial balance is a test to see whether the double-entry bookkeeping system has been maintained accurately and the debit and credit totals balance. If they do not balance, checks must be made to identify and rectify any errors and the trial balance drawn up again. It may take a number of trials before the totals of the debit and credit columns balance. In this chapter we explain how to calculate whether individual accounts have a *debit* or a *credit* balance, how to construct a trial balance from the figures and how to identify errors if the columns do not balance.

## 5.2 Balancing the Accounts

Before you can construct a trial balance, you need to know how to determine the debit or credit balance on each of the individual accounts. The rules for *balancing the accounts* are very straightforward. We will continue to use the example of Kool Kate from Chapter 4 to illustrate them. At the end of a financial period, which may be the end of the month, the end of the quarter, the end of the year, or any other period decided by the business, all the individual bookkeeping accounts are balanced using the following rules.

1 If the account contains entries on each side which are equal to one another, they can be double underlined to close the account for that financial period. This means that there is no outstanding balance on this account at the end of the period. The Pank Patel account is an example of this:

### Pank Patel

| 1998 | | £ | 1998 | | £ |
|------|------|------|------|------|------|
| 28 July | Bank | 1,500 | 26 July | Purchases | 1,500 |
| | | | | | |

**2** If the account contains only one entry, insert the balancing figure on the opposite side and carry this down to the same side as the original entry to start the next period. The term *carried down* is often abbreviated to c/d; *brought down* is abbreviated to b/d. Kool Kate's motor vehicle account provides an example of this. You can see that we have complied with the rules of double-entry bookkeeping: for every debit entry there is a corresponding credit entry and vice versa. We have credited the closing balance of £1,000 and debited an opening balance of the same amount:

### Motor vehicle account

| 1998 | | £ | 1998 | | £ |
|------|------|------|------|------|------|
| 2 July | Bank | 1,000 | 31 July | Balance c/d | 1,000 |
| 1 August | Balance b/d | 1,000 | | | |
| | | | | | |

**3** If the account contains a number of entries, add up both sides. If both sides are the same, insert the totals and double underline them. This means that there is no outstanding balance on this account. An extension of Kool Kate's debtor account for Philippa Merton provides an example of this:

### Philippa Merton

| 1998 | | £ | 1998 | | £ |
|------|------|------|------|------|------|
| 2 July | Sales | 2,800 | 20 July | Bank | 750 |
| 5 July | Sales | 200 | 28 July | Bank | 2,550 |
| 8 July | Sales | 100 | | | |
| 12 July | Sales | 200 | | | |
| | | 3,300 | | | 3,300 |
| | | | | | |

If both sides do not agree, first insert the balancing figure on the side with the lower amount and then insert the totals, which should now be equal, and double underline them. Complete the entry by carrying down the balancing figure on the opposite side as the opening balance for the new financial period. Kool Kate's bank account provides an example of this:

**Bank account**

| 1998 | | £ | 1998 | | £ |
|---|---|---|---|---|---|
| 1 July | Capital | 10,000 | 1 July | Equipment | 4,000 |
| 3 July | Sales | 3,500 | 1 July | Purchases | 4,000 |
| 12 July | Returns outward | 200 | 1 July | Advertising | 500 |
| 20 July | Philippa Merton | 750 | 2 July | Car | 1,000 |
| 28 July | Philippa Merton | 2,550 | 3 July | Purchases | 2,000 |
| | | | 14 July | Returns inward | 500 |
| | | | 28 July | Pank Patel | 1,500 |
| | | | 31 July | Balance c/d | 3,500 |
| | | 17,000 | | | 17,000 |
| 1 August | Balance b/d | 3,500 | | | |
| | | | | | |

## Activity

Calculate the closing balances of the remaining accounts for Kool Kate from Chapter 4. These are the capital account, the sales account, the purchases account, the equipment account, the returns inward account, the returns outward account and the advertising account.

You should not have had too much difficulty with this activity if you followed the rules. You can check your closing balances in the next section, where they are used to construct the trial balance.

## 5.3  Constructing a Trial Balance

When all the accounts have been balanced off, some of them will have been closed completely and will show no balance brought down to commence the next financial period, whereas others will show either a *debit* or a *credit* balance. The debit balances normally represent the assets and expenses of the business and the credit balances normally represent the capital, revenue and liabilities of the business. The list of balances is drawn up in a financial statement at a particular point in time known as a *trial balance*.

If you have made a debit entry for every credit entry and vice versa, the total of the debit balances should be equal to the total of the credit balances. If errors are present, it may require a number of trials to get the two columns to balance. When you have achieved this, the arithmetical accuracy of the double-entry bookkeeping system is proven and the trial balance can be used to draw up the *final accounts*. The final accounts are two important financial statements known as the *profit and loss account* and the *balance sheet*, which we be examining in Chapters 6 and 7.

Continuing to use the example of Kool Kate, we can now calculate the closing balances for the accounts and construct a trial balance:

### Kool Kate
### Trial balance as at 31 July 1998

|  | Debit £ | Credit £ |
|---|---|---|
| Capital at beginning of year |  | 10,000 |
| Sales |  | 6,800 |
| Purchases | 7,500 |  |
| Cash at bank | 3,500 |  |
| Equipment | 4,000 |  |
| Motor vehicles | 1,000 |  |
| Returns inward | 500 |  |
| Returns outward |  | 200 |
| Advertising | 500 |  |
|  | 17,000 | 17,000 |

*Note*: At 31 July the business had stock of £4,000.

Looking at the two columns, you will see that the debit column is a list of all the expenses (for example, purchases), which will appear on the *profit and loss account*, and assets (for example, premises) which will appear on the *balance sheet*. The credit column is a list of the capital and the liabilities which will appear on the *balance sheet* and the sales or revenues which will appear on the *profit and loss account*.

You will see that at the end of the trial balance there is a note which states that the business has stock of £4,000 at 31 July. As discussed earlier in this chapter, when goods are purchased, a debit is made to the purchases account and when goods are sold, a credit is made to the sales account. However, it is likely that at the end of a financial period the business will still have stock remaining which it will hope to sell in the next financial period and make a profit. To account for this properly, the business must carry out a stock-take at the end of the financial period. Some businesses close to allow a manual counting of stock and its valuation to take place; others operate an automated stock control system which allows up-to-date stock figures to be read off at any time. In this example the stock is valued at £4,000 at the end of the period.

## Activity

A business purchased 100 items at £2 each with a view to selling them at £2.40 each. At the end of the year 20 items remained unsold. However, due to a decline in the market the business can now sell them for only £1.50 each. Calculate the value of the closing stock at the year end.

You may have calculated the closing stock as 20 items at £2 each (£40) but the value of the closing stock is 20 items at £1.50 each (£30). This is because there is an important accounting rule which states that closing stock must be valued at cost or net realisable value, whichever is the *lower* figure. *Net realisable value* is the price the business expects to get for the stock *less* any costs incurred in selling it.

## 5.4 Other Transactions

You will remember that Kate started her business on 1 July 1998 and we drew up the trial balance after the end of the first month's trading on 31 July 1998. This provides a simple example, but we can now extend this to draw up a trial balance for the first 6 months' trading. This allows us to introduce a number of new types of transaction. Instead of drawing up separate accounts using double-entry bookkeeping as we did in Chapter 4, we are going to focus on the nature of the transaction. However, the principles of double-entry bookkeeping still apply.

- *Carriage* – The business may have to pay delivery charges for raw materials or goods. This is sometimes referred to as *carriage inward*. It is an expense of the business and therefore appears in the debit column of the trial balance. It is regarded as part of the cost of purchasing the raw materials or goods. Sometime the business has to bear the cost of delivery of its goods to customers, and this is known as *carriage outward*. This is also an expense and appears in the debit column of the trial balance.
- *Discounts* – When a business purchases goods it may be able to negotiate a trade discount and pay slightly less than the normal price. In such a case only the net price (the price *after discount*) is entered into the accounts. Another form of discount sometimes available is a cash discount which is offered to encourage customers to pay promptly. When a business offers a cash discount to customers it is referred to in the supplier's accounts as *discounts allowed*. It is treated as an expense of the business and appears in

the debit column of the trial balance. When a business receives cash discounts from its suppliers it is referred to in the customer's accounts as *discounts received* and appears in the credit column of the trial balance.

- *Petty cash* – As well as maintaining a bank account, a business may keep a very small amount of cash on the premises, known as *petty cash*. This is used to pay miscellaneous expenses, such as window cleaning, travelling expenses or the milk bill. A cash account must always appear in the debit column of the trial balance because it is an asset. The bank account can also appear in the debit column when the business has a credit balance at the bank, which is an asset. However, if the business has a debit balance (overdraft) at the bank it appears in the credit column of the balance sheet because it is a liability.

- *Miscellaneous income* – In addition to revenue from the sales of their main trading activities, many businesses have *miscellaneous income*. Examples include rent from part of their premises, or commission from acting as an agent for another business. As this represents revenue, it appears in the credit column of the trial balance. It is important that any miscellaneous income is recorded separately and not included in the normal sales.

- *Stock account* – In Chapter 4 we mentioned that the *stock account* is somewhat special and that separate accounts are maintained for purchases and sales. At the end of a financial period (the maximum being a year) a physical count of stock is carried out, and this is often referred to as *stock-taking*. If there is an adequate system for recording the number of items in stock, only a sample of the stock needs to be counted to confirm that the records are accurate. Once the total number of items in stock is known, the value can be calculated by multiplying the number of items by the original cost per item. However, some items may be worth less than what was paid for them because of such factors as a change in fashion or technological advances which make them out of date. The general rule used by accountants is to value stock either at cost or the net selling price, whichever is *lower*. The net selling price is the figure you would expect to receive if the stock were sold, *less* any selling costs. When constructing a trial balance, it is usual to show the figure for closing stock as a footnote because it will be needed when the final accounts are drawn up.

- *Drawings* – Drawings are the cash drawn by a sole trader in anticipation of the profit he or she hopes to receive at the until the end of the financial year. A sole trader owns the business and therefore all the profit belongs to him or her and it is normal to make regular withdrawals of cash. A drawings account is opened and each time the sole trader pays himself or herself, a credit entry is made to the bank account and a debit entry is made to the drawings account. Therefore, the drawings account appears in the debit column of the trial balance. The cash withdrawn by the sole trader is always referred to as drawings. If you see the terms *salaries* or *wages* in the accounts or trial balance, these payments refer to amounts paid by the sole trader to employees.

## Activity

Draw up a trial balance for Kool Kate as at 31 December 1998. A stock-take on that date shows 180 items which cost £20 each and could be sold for £45, and 200 items which cost £16 each and could be sold for £14. The account balances after the first 6 months of trading are as follows:

|  | £ |
|---|---|
| Capital at beginning of year | 10,000 |
| Sales | 52,400 |
| Wages | 2,400 |
| Purchases | 38,700 |
| Cash | 300 |
| Cash at bank | 2,800 |
| Equipment | 4,000 |
| Motor vehicles | 1,000 |
| Returns inward | 900 |
| Returns outward | 800 |
| Advertising | 3,400 |
| Carriage inward | 960 |
| Discounts allowed | 1,200 |
| Discounts received | 680 |
| Drawings | 12,000 |
| Telephone | 600 |
| Shop overheads | 1,220 |

Your completed trial balance should look like this:

**Kool Kate**
**Trial balance as at 31 December 1998**

|  | Debit £ | Credit £ |
|---|---|---|
| Capital at beginning of year |  | 10,000 |
| Sales |  | 6,800 |
| Wages | 2,400 |  |
| Purchases | 38,700 |  |
| Cash | 300 |  |
| Cash at bank |  | 2,800 |
| Equipment | 4,000 |  |
| Motor vehicles | 1,000 |  |
| Returns inward | 900 |  |
| Returns outward |  | 800 |
| Advertising | 3,400 |  |
| Carriage inward | 960 |  |
| Discounts allowed | 1,200 |  |
| Discounts received |  | 680 |
| Drawings | 12,000 |  |
| Telephone | 600 |  |
| Shop overheads | 1,220 |  |
|  | 66,680 | 66,680 |

*Note*: Stock at 31 December is £6,400.

## 5.5  Limitations of a Trial Balance

A *trial balance* is a list of the balances of all the individual accounts which shows all the debit balances in one column and all the credit balances in another. If the principles of double-entry bookkeeping have been adhered to, with a debit for every credit, the sum of the debit column in the trial balance will be the same as the sum of the credit column. If they do not balance, checks must be made to identify any discrepancies.

## Activity

A trial balance detects arithmetical errors. What other mistakes can be made in recording transactions in the individual accounts which are not revealed by the trial balance?

Errors which are not revealed by a trial balance are where the accounting transaction:

- has not been recorded in the books of accounts at all;
- has been recorded in the wrong accounts – for example, in the premises account instead of the equipment account;
- has been recorded in the wrong class of account – for example, in an asset account instead of a liability account;
- has been correctly recorded, but the wrong amount was entered;
- has been recorded in the correct accounts, but on the wrong side of both accounts.

Finally, a common error is to transpose numbers; for example, writing £320 instead of £230. To find out whether this is the reason for your trial balance not balancing, calculate the difference between the total of the debit and credit columns on the trial balance. If this figure is divisible by 9, you have probably transposed a number somewhere and you should check for this error.

## 5.6  Conclusions

At the end of a financial period, which may be for any convenient length of time, the accounts are balanced. A trial balance is then prepared which lists the credit and debit balances from the individual accounts and if the totals of the two columns are equal, we can assume that the records are mathematically accurate. However, other errors are not revealed by the trial balance. Once the two columns agree, it is possible to draw up what are known as the final accounts from the trial balance. These are the profit and loss account and the balance sheet, and we shall be looking at these two important financial statements in Chapters 6 and 7, respectively.

Having completed this chapter, you should now be able to:

- balance off accounts;
- construct a trial balance;
- discuss the treatment of stock;
- explain the limitations of a trial balance.

## Exercises

Complete the following sentences:

**1** The purpose of a trial balance is ............................................................................
**2** The credit column of a trial balance is a list of all ............................................
**3** To find out if you have transposed figures in the accounts you ......................
**4** In double-entry bookkeeping, for every debit entry ........................................
**5** The final accounts prepared from a trial balance are ......................................

Are the following statements true or false?

**6** A trial balance detects only arithmetical errors.
**7** The debit column of a trial balance is a list of all expenses and assets.
**8** Sales should always be in the debit column of a trial balance.
**9** Returns inward should always be in the debit column of a trial balance.
**10** If there is no closing balance on an account it will not appear in the trial balance.

You may wish to read more widely than this book to answer the following questions fully, but you can check the main points by referring to the appropriate sections in this chapter.

**11** What are the rules for closing off accounts. (Section 5.2)
**12** How is a trial balance constructed? (Section 5.3)
**13** How does a business determine the value of stock at the year end? (Section 5.4)
**14** What are the limitations of the trial balance? (Section 5.5)

Multiple choice questions (more than one answer may apply):

**15** The debit column of the trial balance shows:

    **a** all the expenses and sales accounts
    **b** all the sales and liability accounts
    **c** all the expenses and asset accounts
    **d** all the liability and expenses accounts.

**16** When goods are returned to the supplier as faulty:

    **a** a debit entry is made to the sales account
    **b** a credit entry is made to the returns outward account
    **c** a debit entry is made to the returns outward account
    **d** a credit entry is made to the returns outward account and a debit entry is made to the sales account.

**17** At the end of a financial period, a credit on the bank account suggests that:

    **a** assets have increased over the period
    **b** assets have decreased over the period
    **c** there is money in the bank
    **d** there is an overdraft at the bank.

**18** At the end of a financial period, a credit balance outstanding on a stock account suggests that:

**a** assets have increased over the period
**b** there has been no change in assets during the period
**c** assets have decreased over the period
**d** a bookkeeping error has been made.

**19** Which one of the following errors should show in a trial balance:

**a** if a debit had been made to an asset account instead of an expense account
**b** if a debit had been made to both an asset account and an expense account
**c** if both a debit and a credit entry have been omitted
**d** if a debit and a credit entry have been recorded but in the wrong accounts.

**20** At the end of a financial period a trial balance:

**a** must always balance first time
**b** will never balance if entries have been made to the wrong accounts
**c** will balance once any arithmetical errors have been corrected
**d** will balance if the figures are transposed.

Practice questions:

**21** Show the closing balance on the following bank account at 20 October:

**Bank account**

| 1998 | | £ | 1998 | | £ |
|---|---|---|---|---|---|
| 1 October | Opening balance | 6,400 | 2 October | Purchases | 750 |
| 12 October | Sales | 1,800 | 3 October | Advertising | 1,120 |
| 15 October | Paul Plummer | 950 | 16 October | Purchases | 2,300 |
| 18 October | Paul Plummer | 950 | 18 October | Janet Mayo | 780 |
| 20 October | Sales | 1,450 | 20 October | Purchases | 3,400 |
| | | | | | |
| | | | | | |
| | | | | | |
| | | | | | |

**22** Construct a trial balance from the following list of balances taken from the accounts of Jean's Farm Eggs, calculating the figure for capital:

| | £ |
|---|---|
| Purchases | 17,500 |
| Bank | 13,500 |
| Sales | 16,800 |
| Equipment | 24,000 |
| Vehicles | 21,000 |
| Offices expenses | 2,000 |
| Capital | ? |

**23** The following account is that of a debtor to the business, Turner Tyres:

**Turner Tyres**

| 1998 | | £ | 1998 | | £ |
|------|-------|-------|------|---|---|
| 2 May | Sales | 850 | | | |
| 12 May | Sales | 1,650 | | | |
| 18 May | Sales | 260 | | | |
| 21 May | Sales | 400 | | | |
| 25 May | Sales | 640 | | | |

On 31 May Turner Tyres pays 50 per cent of the amount due. Show this entry in the accounts as well as the closing balance on the Turner Tyres account.

**24** Construct a trial balance for Harlech Health Food from the following list of balances, calculating the figure for purchases:

| | £ |
|---|---|
| Capital | 18,000 |
| Wages | 1,600 |
| Bank | 1,500 |
| Equipment | 2,000 |
| Rent | 1,400 |
| Sales | 26,200 |
| Returns inward | 900 |
| Returns outward | 460 |
| Discounts allowed | 720 |
| Discounts received | 620 |
| Miscellaneous expenses | 390 |
| Purchases | ? |

**25** During 1998 Country Furniture had sales which were three times the amount of its purchases and trading expenses which were 25 per cent of the figure for purchases. The business has £4,000 in the bank at 31 December 1998, the year end, and this is half the amount it has incurred in trading expenses. Premises were purchased for £75,000 and one-third of this was funded by a bank loan. Draw up a trial balance for Country Furniture as at 31 December 1998 and show the figure for capital. Stock at the beginning of the year was the equivalent of 2 months' sales.

(Answers on pp.320–2)

# 6 The Profit and Loss Account of a Sole Trader

## 6.1 Introduction

The *financial performance* or *profitability* of a business is one aspect that is of key interest to its owners and other stakeholders. To find out what profit a business has made, a *profit and loss account* must be drawn up. A profit and loss account is a financial statement that shows the financial performance of the business over a period of time. It does not show the movements of cash; as you know from Chapter 3, a cash flow statement does that.

To construct a profit and loss account we need to determine the financial period we are interested in. This may be a year, but it could be for a shorter period, such as 3 months or even 1 month. All the sales for the financial period need to be taken into account, irrespective of whether they were for cash or on credit: in other words, irrespective of whether they have been paid for or not. Then the costs incurred in achieving the sales during the financial period are matched against the sales. In this chapter we describe how a simple profit and loss account for a *sole trader* is constructed. We also explain how the difference between profit and cash can be analysed for a financial period.

## 6.2 The Accruals Concept

We looked at six of the main *accounting assumptions* in Chapter 1. Accounting assumptions are used in maintaining accounting records and preparing financial statements and provide an essential *accounting framework* for all types of organisations. We are now going to introduce another concept which is critical for constructing a profit and loss account.

The *accruals* or *matching concept* requires that all revenue and costs are recognised as they are earned and incurred, not when cash is received or paid, and they are matched in the period to which they relate. It lies at the heart of all financial statements.

## Activity

Name four of the other accounting concepts which are used in the preparation of financial statements.

---

If you did not have to refer to Chapter 1 to answer this question you are doing very well! If you had difficulty remembering them, you should revise them now. The six concepts we introduced were as follows:

- the going concern concept;
- the consistency concept;
- the prudence concept;
- the money measurement concept;
- the stable unit of measurement concept; and
- the business entity concept.

If you read other books on accounting you may find some other concepts mentioned. It is important to remember that the concepts we identified in Chapter 1 are applied to the financial statements of sole traders, partnerships and limited companies. We will be looking at the financial statements of partnerships and limited companies in Chapters 9 and 11.

## 6.3 Constructing a Profit and Loss Account

In Chapter 3 we constructed a cash flow forecast for Candlewick Enterprises. You will remember that in the forecast for January to June, Sarah Wick planned to end up with a cash surplus of £340, after investing £315 of her own money in the business. If she achieves this, would you consider that her *financial performance* was satisfactory?

---

## Activity

Draw up a list of questions you would like to ask Sarah after her first 6 months in business to find out if she thinks it is a financial success.

---

You may have thought of the following questions:

- Did she consider that £340 was a satisfactory cash balance to plan for at the end of the first six months?
- Did she actually achieve it?
- How much profit did she hope to achieve for the first 6 months?
- How much profit did she actually make?
- Were her planned and achieved cash surplus and profit adequate, considering the money, time and effort she put into the business?

- Were her achievements typical for her line of business?
- Would she have been better off using her money, time and effort in some other enterprise?
- Has she built up a business which in itself is worth something, either in respect of the assets it has acquired (cash, stock, etc.) or in potential?

This is a formidable list of questions and you may think that answering some of them will be very difficult. Although the cash flow forecast provides some answers, there are other factors which must be taken into consideration when we look at financial performance. We can prepare a financial statement, known as a *profit and loss account*, to help us find some of the answers to these questions and measure financial performance. The word *account* literally means 'a history of'. The profit and loss account is therefore a history of the business's financial performance over a period of time.

In Chapter 3 we looked at a simple profit and loss account concerning a second-hand fax machine, which is reproduced below.

---

**Profit and loss account for the month of August**

|  |  | £ | £ |
|---|---|---:|---:|
| | **Sales** | | 120 |
| *Less* | **Cost of sales** | | |
| | Cost of fax machine | 60 | |
| | Advertising | 10 | 70 |
| | **Profit** | | 50 |

---

You may remember the principle that *profit is not cash*. In other words, the figures for sales and costs do not take into account whether the purchaser of the computer has paid for it or whether the business has yet paid for the advertising. In a profit and loss account we are concerned with matching *sales* with the *cost of those sales*. This *matching* or *accruals concept* is yet another assumption used by accountants and it is extremely important to apply it when constructing a profit and loss account. Using the accruals concept, expenses and revenues must both refer to the same accounting period and will be taken into the profit and loss account as they arise and not when cash is paid or received. By using the accruals concept we can arrive at a figure of profit for the financial period that describes the financial performance of the business, regardless of cash movements in and out of the organisation.

Managers in trading organisations are not only interested in the single figure of profit, but in more detailed information. Therefore, it is usual to show the profit the company makes on trading (buying and selling goods) separately. This is referred to as the *trading* or *gross profit* because not all the expenses of the business have been met. All the other expenses of the business are deducted from the gross profit to arrive at a figure of *net profit*. All this information is shown on one account which is known as the *trading and profit and loss account*. This is a key financial statement and it provides information on the financial performance of an organisation over a specified period of time. Sometimes the statement is headed 'profit and loss account' (without the word 'trading') or may be called a 'profit statement' depending on the type of organisation and the exact information it contains. Whichever title is used, the heading should always include the period to which it relates.

First we will look at the two sections of the trading and profit and loss account separately and then combine them in the full account. We will continue to use the example of Sarah Wick's business, Candlewick Enterprises, and find out whether it has made an actual profit for the first 3 months. This means that in drawing up the trading and profit and loss account we can forget the division of the figures between the individual months, since we are interested in the transactions which took place only in that quarter. To arrive at the figures for the three months we need to look more closely at the actual sales and purchases for each of the 3 months. You will find it helpful to refer to the actual cash flow statement in Section 3.5 of Chapter 3:

|  | Purchases | | Cash sales | | Credit sales | |
|---|---|---|---|---|---|---|
|  | Number | £ | Number | £ | Number | £ |
| January | 400 | 600 | 80 | 160 | 240 | 480 |
| February | 400 | 600 | 90 | 180 | 270 | 540 |
| March | 500 | 750 | 100 | 200 | 300 | 600 |

We have entered the figures in the months in which the transactions took place, not when the cash was paid or received. If you look at the actual cash flow statement in Chapter 3, you will see that the 400 candles purchased in January were not paid for until February. Similarly, the £480 due for the 240 candles sold in January on credit was not received until March. The other point to note is that although the business purchased the same number of candles as planned, the actual sales were much lower each month.

## Activity

How much stock (unsold candles) did Candlewick Enterprises have at the end of March and what was its total cost?

There are a number of ways you could have calculated the answer. It does not matter at this stage how you calculated the figure, as long as you understand the principles involved. You may find the following layout useful, which is one accountants use for more complex examples:

|  | | Number of candles | Number of candles |
|---|---|---|---|
| **Purchases during the 3 months** | | | 1,300 |
| *Less* **Actual sales during the 3 months** | | | |
| | Cash sales | 270 | |
| | Credit sales | 810 | 1,080 |
| **Closing stock at 31 March** | | | 220 |

Therefore, the closing stock of 220 candles, which cost £1.50 each, is valued at £330.

Using the above figures, we can now draw up a *trading account* for Candlewick Enterprises which is the trading portion of the profit and loss account and shows the *gross profit*:

**Candlewick Enterprises**
**Trading account for the 3 months ending 31 March 1998**

|  | | £ | £ |
|---|---|---|---|
| **Sales** | | | |
| | Cash sales | 540 | |
| | Credit sales | 1,620 | 2,160 |
| *Less* | **Cost of sales** | | |
| | Purchases | 1,950 | |
| *Less* | Closing stock | 330 | 1,620 |
| | **Gross profit** | | 540 |

This trading account shows a gross profit of £540 for the 3 months. We can cross-check this by doing a small calculation. We know that the business buys each candle for £1.50 and sells it for £2.00, thus making a gross profit of 50p on each candle. As 1,080 candles have been sold in the three months, the total gross profit must be $1,080 \times 50p = £540$. Obviously, in a more complex business, you could not carry out these simple calculations. 'Gross' simply means before something else is deducted. In this case the something is the other expenses that the business has incurred during the same 3 months. Under the heading of *cost of sales* we are calculating the cost of the candles which have been sold. Sometimes this is called the *cost of goods sold*.

We can now complete the remainder of the trading and profit and loss account by deducting all the other expenses.

**Candlewick Enterprises**
**Trading and profit and loss account for the 3 months**
**ending 31 March 1998**

|  |  | £ | £ |
|---|---|---:|---:|
| **Sales** |  |  | 2,160 |
| *Less* | **Cost of sales** |  |  |
|  | Purchases | 1,950 |  |
| *Less* | Closing stock | 330 | 1,620 |
|  | **Gross profit** |  | 540 |
| *Less* | **Expenses** |  |  |
|  | Advertising | 75 |  |
|  | Telephone | 45 |  |
|  | Market stall | 60 |  |
|  | Postage and packing | 180 | 360 |
|  | **Net profit** |  | 180 |

Although the business had only paid postage and packing for 2 months, we have entered the figure for 3 months as those expenses had been incurred for each month. It could be that at the time of making up the trading and profit and loss account, Sarah did not know the exact the figure for postage and packing for March or she may not have received the telephone bill for the first quarter. However, if it is known that the business has incurred but not paid an expense in a financial period, then an amount known as an *accrual* must be shown. If the figure is not known with certainty, an estimate must be made. Accruals arise because of the *accruals* or *matching concept* and ensure that we include all the relevant expenses for a financial period, even if they are only estimates.

## 6.4 The Profit and Loss Account and Cash Flow Statement Compared

In Chapter 3 we saw that Candlewick Enterprise's actual cash flow for the 3 months showed a negative closing cash balance at the end of March of £480, assuming that Sarah had not invested any money in the business.

## Activity

How did Candlewick Enterprises make a net profit of £180 and yet be overdrawn by £480? There is an apparent discrepancy of £660. List the items that you think caused this difference by comparing the items in the profit and loss account and the actual cash flow statement shown in Section 3.5 of Chapter 3.

The items causing the apparent discrepancy are as follows:

- Sarah has allowed 2 months' credit to her credit customers. Credit sales for the 3 months were £480 plus £540 plus £600 (total £1,620), but the business has only been paid for the first of these 3 months (£480) and is still owed £1,140 at the end of March.
- On the other hand, Sarah has negotiated 1 month's credit from her suppliers. At the end of March the business owes the suppliers for the purchases for the month of March which amounted to £750 (January's purchases were paid in February, and February's in March).
- Sarah took no credit for the expenses relating to advertising, telephone, market stall or miscellaneous expenses, so there is no discrepancy between profit and cash flow here. However, the business did not pay the £60 per month for postage and packing until the month following the month in which the expense was incurred.
- At 31 March the business has 220 candles in stock. These cost £1.50 each and this is how they have been valued in the profit and loss account; whether they have been paid for or not is a separate issue. Therefore, the total value of stock is £330.

In order to make the position clear, we will summarise these items under the headings of 'good news' and 'bad news'. The good news is where Candlewick Enterprises has assets and the bad news is where the business has incurred liabilities.

|  | £ | £ |
|---|---|---|
| **Good news (assets)** | | |
| Cash the business is owed by customers | 1,140 | |
| The business has unsold stock which cost | 330 | 1,470 |
| **Bad news (liabilities)** | | |
| Cash the business owes its suppliers | 750 | |
| Cash the business owes for postage and packing | 60 | 810 |
| **Difference** | | 660 |

As you can see, the difference between the assets and the liabilities is £660. This explains the apparent discrepancy between the net profit of £180 and the actual overdraft at 31 March of £480.

There are a number of important lessons to be learned from the principle that profit is not the same as cash and these can be used to run a business more efficiently:

- Giving credit to customers may have the advantage of increasing sales and thus potential profit, but results in a delay before the sales value is realised in the cash flow. In extreme cases this means that an organisation can make a good profit, but at the same time fail because of lack of cash.

- Building up stock to an unnecessarily high level can have an adverse effect on cash flow. Buyers who take advantage of bargains, such as special discounts, often forget this, perhaps because they consider that cash flow is the concern of the accountant and not of the organisation as a whole.
- Taking credit from suppliers is one way of improving cash flow; after all, it is a form of free finance. However, if an organisation takes more than its agreed credit, it runs the risk of gaining a bad reputation. This may lead to difficulty in obtaining credit in future, and even to the discontinuation of supplies.

## 6.5 **Depreciation**

There is one more expense, known as *depreciation*, which must be considered. Candlewick Enterprises owns a small van which Sarah bought second-hand for £1,300 just before she started trading in January. It is used to carry stock to the market stall and make deliveries to credit customers. The garage has told Sarah that it has about 4 years' useful life left, after which time she will probably be able to sell it for scrap and get about £100. The business has the benefit of the use of the van so it must be shown in the trading and profit and loss account.

---

## **Activity**

Which of the following figures do you consider it would be fair to charge to the 3 months' profit and loss account for the use of the van?

a   £1,300
b   £1,200
c   £300
d   £150
e   £75.

---

The clue to the correct figure is the word 'fair'. You might argue that the total cost of the van to the business will be £1,200 (that is the purchase price of £1,300 less the £100 scrap value). However that cost is for 4 years' use and it would not be fair to charge the full amount against 3 months' trading. There are several ways in which Sarah could calculate a figure, but there is a fairly simple method, which is widely used, known as the *straight line method of depreciation*. This means that the cost is apportioned evenly over the useful life of the asset. The first step is to deduct the estimated scrap value from the cost:

$$£1,300 - £100 = £1,200$$

Next, divide the result by the expected life of the asset:

$$\frac{£1,200}{4 \text{ years}} = £300 \text{ per annum}$$

If you want the depreciation for part of a year, take the appropriate proportion of the depreciation rate:

$$£300 \times \tfrac{1}{4}(3 \text{ out of } 12 \text{ months}) = £75$$

So we need to deduct a further £75 as an expense from Sarah's gross profit as follows:

|  |  | £ | £ |
|---|---|---|---|
| | **Gross profit** | | 540 |
| *Less* | **Expenses** | | |
| | Advertising | 75 | |
| | Telephone | 45 | |
| | Market stall | 60 | |
| | Postage and packing | 180 | |
| | Depreciation | 75 | 435 |
| | **Net profit** | | 105 |

There have been numerous attempts to describe depreciation in a comprehensible way. Here are some of them:

- Depreciation is the spreading of the benefit of using the van over the 4 years of its useful life.
- Sarah's business uses up the asset over the 4 years and therefore the annual depreciation charge is an expense of the business.
- The annual depreciation charge of £300 is an attempt to spread the expenditure incurred in buying the van over the whole of its useful life.
- Depreciation is a charge for the use of the van.

The best way to consider depreciation is as the cost spread or apportioned on an arbitrary basis over the financial periods in which the business will benefit from the use of the van (in this case, 4 years). Depreciation is not a cash flow. The cash flow occurred in December when the business bought and paid for the van. That was why there was a nil cash balance at the beginning of January. If you want to reconcile Candlewick Enterprise's new, reduced profit with the cash flow, you will need to include the £75 depreciation in the reconciliation.

## 6.6  Doubtful Debts

Sarah may not realise that some of the customers she has allowed to buy on credit may not pay because they have moved away, gone bankrupt or died. At the moment she has entered the credit sales for the 3 months in the profit and loss account. If she wants to be *prudent*, which is one of the concepts used by accountants, she should make some allowance for the fact that not all credit customers will pay. If she does not do this, her profit may be overstated. To reduce the profit figure to a more prudent amount, Sarah should make a *provision for doubtful debts*. This is an estimate of how much of the amount owing to the business will not be paid. As it is an estimate, it will not be exact, but Sarah and her accountant can use their experience to decide what provision to make. The provision for doubtful debts appears with the other expenses in the trading and profit and loss account.

## Activity

If a provision for doubtful debts of $2\frac{1}{2}$% is made at the end of the quarter, what amount should be entered in the profit and loss account of Candlewick Enterprises?

**a**   £54.00
**b**   £40.50
**c**   £28.50.

The first amount is $2\frac{1}{2}$% of the total sales figure of £2,160. As this includes cash sales, this answer is wrong because these have been paid for. The figure of £40.50 is $2\frac{1}{2}$% of the total credit sales of £1,620. However, of this amount the business received a payment of £480 in March. The amount due is the balance of £1,140 and it is against this figure that we make our provision of $2\frac{1}{2}$%. Therefore, the correct answer is £28.50. As this is only an estimate, Sarah will probably round it up to £29 when entering it in the profit and loss account. However, we will not adjust the profit and loss account for the first 3 months, but we will be looking at the provision for doubtful debts again in Chapter 7, when we examine the 6 months' figures.

## 6.7  The Continuing Business

So far we have drawn up the profit and loss account only for the first 3 months' trading. Profit and loss accounts can be drawn up for any financial period of time, although the maximum period would be 1 year. However, there are some slight complications where the trading and profit and loss account is drawn up in a *continuing business*. This should cause you no great problems, but you must remember what happened at the end of the previous financial period and make suitable adjustments for any stock held.

## Activity

In the quarter April to June Candlewick Enterprises buys another 1,500 candles on credit at £1.50 each and sells 1,400 of them, 25% for cash and 75% on credit at £2 each. Calculate the gross profit for the 3 months April to June.

You may have found this activity fairly easy, perhaps not even needing to draw up a trading account. However, it is important to do so to ensure that all the relevant information is shown. The new trading account should look like this:

**Candlewick Enterprises**
**Trading account for the three months ending 30th June 1998**

|  |  | £ | £ |
|---|---|---|---|
| **Sales** | | | |
| | Cash sales | 700 | |
| | Credit sales | 2,100 | 2,800 |
| *Less* | **Cost of sales** | | |
| | Opening stock | 330 | |
| *Add* | Purchases | 2,250 | |
| | Total available for sale | 2,580 | |
| *Less* | Closing stock | 480 | 2,100 |
| | **Gross profit** | | 700 |

The main difference in a continuing business is that there is an *opening stock*. The opening stock figure is the same as the closing stock figure on the previous trading and profit and loss account. The calculations for the actual number of candles would be:

| | | |
|---|---|---|
| | Number of candles at 31 March (i.e. on 1 April) | 220 |
| *Add* | Purchases April to June | 1,500 |
| | Number of candles available for sale | 1,720 |
| *Less* | Actual number of candles sold | 1,400 |
| | Closing stock at 30 June | 320 |
| | Total cost of closing stock (320 × £1.50) | £480 |

This method may seem quite laborious, but it is essential that you remember it, as you will need to know it for more complex examples and when we look at the balance sheet in Chapter 7.

## 6.8 Conclusions

In this chapter we have described how to construct a simple trading and profit and loss account and compared and reconciled it with the cash flow statement. We have investigated the relationship between purchases, stock and cost of sales, and we have given a basic explanation of the principle of depreciation. We have also examined the difference between profit and cash and looked at the relationship between profit and cash flow in the life of a business.

Having completed this chapter, you should now be able to:

- apply the accruals accounting concept;
- describe what is meant by financial performance;
- construct a simple profit and loss account;
- describe the principles for measuring financial performance;
- compare a profit and loss account with a cash flow statement;
- explain the differences between profit and cash at different stages in an organisation's life.

## Exercises

Complete the following sentences:

**1** Gross profit is ................................................................................................................
**2** Net profit is ..................................................................................................................
**3** An accrual is ................................................................................................................
**4** Depreciation is .............................................................................................................
**5** A provision for doubtful debts is intended to show ....................................................

Are the following statements true or false?

**6** Straight line depreciation is calculated by dividing the scrap value of an asset by the expected useful life.
**7** The cost of sales figure is calculated by adding the figure for opening stock to purchases and then deducting the figure for closing stock.
**8** The cost of sales is equal to gross profit.
**9** Depreciation is shown as an addition to gross profit.
**10** An increase in the provision for doubtful debts is shown as an expense in the profit and loss account.

You may wish to read more widely than this book to answer the following questions fully, but you can check your answers by referring to the appropriate sections in this chapter.

**11** Explain the purpose of the cost of sales adjustment in the profit and loss account. Include a worked example in your explanation. (Section 6.3)
**12** Describe the differences between a profit and loss account and a cash flow statement. (Section 6.4)
**13** Define depreciation and explain one method of accounting for it. (Section 6.5)
**14** What is a provision for doubtful debts and how is it accounted for in the profit and loss and balance sheet? (Section 6.6)

Multiple choice questions (more than one answer may apply):

**15** The trading account of a business shows:

  **a** the cash left after sales less cost of sales
  **b** the gross profit of a business
  **c** the net profit of a business
  **d** none of these.

**16** The correct calculation of cost of goods sold requires inclusion of:

  **a** all expenses, suitably matched for the period
  **b** all expenses, suitably matched for the period, but excluding depreciation
  **c** all expenses, suitably matched for the period, but excluding depreciation plus the cost of goods purchased
  **d** closing stock of goods.

**17** The realisation convention in the trading account means that profit is only realised when:

  **a** cash is received and paid
  **b** goods are paid for
  **c** goods are sold
  **d** expenses are correctly matched.

**18** During the year a business makes credit sales of £127,000 and receives payments from its customers of £89,000. At the year end a provision of 5% is made for doubtful debts. The correct figure is:

  **a** £6,350
  **b** £1,900
  **c** £4,450
  **d** £13,100.

**19** A company buys a delivery van for £36,000 which it is considered will last for 5 years and have a scrap value of £8,000. What is the annual depreciation charge to the profit and loss account?

  **a** £36,000
  **b** £8,000
  **c** £8,800
  **d** £5,600.

**20** During the year a business purchases 300 items at £6 each and sells 260 items for £10 each and has 10 items stolen. The value of the closing stock is:

  **a** £240
  **b** £300
  **c** £180
  **d** £60.

Practice questions:

**21** Insert the missing figures in the following examples.

|  | a £ | b £ | c £ | d £ | e £ |
|---|---|---|---|---|---|
| Opening stock | 100 | ? | 1,020 | ? | 14,960 |
| Purchases | ? | 680 | ? | 1,924 | ? |
|  | 500 | 730 | ? | 2,156 | ? |
| Closing stock | 50 | ? | 1,550 | 150 | 18,815 |
| Cost of sales | 450 | 520 | 9,680 | ? | 159,715 |

**22** Insert the missing figures in the following examples.

|  | a<br>£ | b<br>£ | c<br>£ | d<br>£ | e<br>£ |
|---|---|---|---|---|---|
| Sales | 10,000 | ? | 17,000 | 18,150 | ? |
| Cost of sales | 6,000 | 450 | ? | ? | 24,590 |
| Gross profit | ? | 150 | 3,500 | 17,470 | 3,160 |
| Total expenses | 3,500 | ? | ? | ? | ? |
| Net profit | ? | 50 | 250 | 2,100 | 740 |

**23** Insert the missing figures in the following examples.

|  | a | b | c | d | e |
|---|---|---|---|---|---|
| Cost of asset | £10,000 | ? | £16,400 | £1,500 | £24,750 |
| Scrap value | £2,000 | £500 | £1,400 | ? | £1,850 |
| Useful life | 4 years | 3 years | 30 years | 5 years | ? |
| Annual depreciation charge | ? | £3,000 | ? | £260 | £2,290 |

**24** A business purchases machinery in July 1993 for £120,000 with an expected life of 8 years and a residual value of £24,000. The business uses the straight line method of depreciation. In the year of purchase the business charges depreciation only for the period it has owned the asset. The business's year end is 31 December. Describe the correct treatment for the purchase of this machinery in the profit and loss account and the cash flow statement.

**25** Describe what is meant by the term 'cost of goods sold' and the importance of the calculation in arriving at a figure of gross profit. Your answer should be illustrated with a worked example.

(Answers on pp.322–3)

# 7 The Balance Sheet of a Sole Trader

## 7.1 Introduction

In addition to the profit and loss account, which shows the financial performance of a business over a period of time, the owners and other stakeholders are interested in its *financial position* at a particular moment in time; in other words, a snapshot of what the business owns and what it owes at a particular date. The *balance sheet* is a financial statement which shows the financial position of the business on a particular date at the end of a financial period. This may be at the end of the financial year, or at the end of a shorter period, such as 3 months or even 1 month. It shows what *assets* or resources the business has, such as premises, vehicles, stock and cash. It also shows what *liabilities* or debts the business has, such as a bank loan or overdraft, amounts owed to other businesses, and the amount of *capital* the owner(s) have invested in the business.

Two different formats can be used to present the balance sheet. We will start by describing the *horizontal format*, which is relatively easy to understand, before going on to the *vertical format*, which is the layout most commonly adopted by businesses. At the end of the chapter we explain the relationship between the three financial statements: the cash flow statement, the profit and loss account and the balance sheet.

## 7.2 Purpose of the Balance Sheet

In Chapter 6 we looked at the profit and loss account, which measures financial performance over a period of time. In the case of Candlewick Enterprises, this period was the first 3 months' trading, ending 31 March 1998. In this chapter we are going to look at a financial statement known as the *balance sheet*, which measures the *financial position* of an organisation at one particular moment in time.

We will continue to use the example of Candlewick Enterprises and we shall start by going back to 28 December 1997, before the business started trading in January 1998. On that day, Sarah Wick opened a business bank account with her personal savings of £1,300. She decided not to put any more of her own money into the business unless absolutely necessary. On 30 December she paid for the van she knew she would need for the business, making out a cheque for £1,300 drawn on the business account. The important thing to note is that Sarah Wick and Candlewick Enterprises are completely separate entities. This is one of the *accounting assumptions* we discussed in Chapter 1. You may have noticed in Chapter 6 that we were looking at the profit and loss account of Candlewick Enterprises. This separation of Sarah from her business is particularly important when we look at balance sheets. The balance sheet shows us the financial position of the *business* and not that of its owner.

We are now going to draw up the first balance sheet of Candlewick Enterprises as at midnight on 28 December, after Sarah paid £1,300 into her business bank account. A balance sheet is a financial snapshot of the business at that date. It shows all the business' *assets*, such as land, premises, stock, cars, cash, etc. The business can obtain these resources only by borrowing funds. You will remember from Chapter 3 that in a new business the most likely source of funding is the owner. The amount invested by the owner is known as the *capital*. Capital is a *liability* of the business because the business owes the money to the owner. Additional funds may be supplied by people or institutions. These other sources of funds are known as *liabilities* and are also shown on the balance sheet. The balance sheet illustrates what is known as the *accounting equation*, which means that at any one point in time, all the assets owned by the business have the same total value as all the liabilities of the business. The accounting equation can be expressed as an equation:

$$\text{Assets} = \text{Capital} + \text{Other liabilities}$$

In the case of the balance sheet for Candlewick Enterprises, the only asset owned by the business is the cash in the business bank account. The only liability of the business is the £1,300 capital that Sarah has invested in the business. On 28 December the balance sheet for Candlewick Enterprises looks like this:

**Candlewick Enterprises**
**Balance sheet as at 28 December 1997**

| | £ | | £ |
|---|---|---|---|
| **Assets** | | | |
| Cash at bank | 1,300 | **Capital** | 1,300 |

As you can see, the date at which the balance sheet is drawn up is given at the top of the statement. The assets are shown on the left-hand side of the balance sheet and liabilities on the right-hand side. This form of presentation is known as the *horizontal format*. Although most modern balance sheets, particularly those published by major companies, present the balance sheet vertically, with assets on top and liabilities below, we will use the horizontal presentation for the moment because it emphasises the accounting equation.

In theory a balance sheet can be prepared at any moment in time. So we will move forward to 31 December (the day after Sarah bought and paid for the van) and prepare a balance sheet as at that date. As you can see, the asset of cash has been completely replaced by the van, because all the cash has been spent on buying the van:

**Candlewick Enterprises**
**Balance sheet as at 31 December 1997**

|  | £ |  | £ |
|---|---|---|---|
| **Assets** |  |  |  |
| Van | 1,300 | **Capital** | 1,300 |

Now we will move on to 3 January. Sarah has started trading by buying 60 candles at £1.50 each on credit. You will remember from Chapter 6 that her supplier allows her 1 month's credit. Now the balance sheet looks like this:

**Candlewick Enterprises**
**Balance sheet as at 3 January 1998**

|  |  | £ |  |  | £ |
|---|---|---|---|---|---|
|  | **Assets** |  |  | **Capital** | 1,300 |
|  | Van | 1,300 | *Add* | **Current liabilities** |  |
| *Add* | Stock of candles | 90 |  | Trade creditors | 90 |
|  |  | 1,390 |  |  | 1,390 |

As you can see, the balance sheet still balances, but with increased figures. This is significant. The business has £1,390 worth of assets and these have been financed partly by Sarah and partly by her supplier (the *trade creditor*). Trade creditors are a useful source of finance and usually they do not charge interest on the amount owing until it becomes due, unlike the bank on overdrafts or loans.

It is traditional to classify assets as *fixed* or *current*, and list them separately. Fixed assets include buildings, plant and machinery, furniture and vehicles, etc. which have been bought to keep in the business. Examples of current assets, which are part of the manufacturing and trading cycle, include stock, debtors and cash. Liabilities are separated into *capital, long-term liabilities* and *current liabilities. Current liabilities* include creditors and any bank overdraft. Nowadays current liabilities are known as *creditors: amounts due within one year*, which is a more specific term. *Debtors*, which were cited above as being an example of a current asset, are those who owe the business money. *Creditors*, which are an example of a current liability, are those to whom the business owes money. We can now redraft the last balance sheet to conform with these conventions:

---

**Candlewick Enterprises**
**Balance sheet as at 3 January 1998**

|  |  | £ |  |  | £ |
|---|---|---|---|---|---|
|  | **Fixed assets** |  |  | **Capital** | 1,300 |
|  | Van | 1,300 | *Add* | **Creditors: amounts due within one year** |  |
| *Add* | **Current assets** |  |  | Trade creditors | 90 |
|  | Stock | 90 |  |  |  |
|  |  | 1,390 |  |  | 1,390 |

---

Now we will move on to 6 January. The business has sold the following stock:

- Cash sales 10 at £2 each = £20
- Credit sales 20 at £2 each = £40

---

## Activity

Using the following pro forma, draw up the new balance sheet as at 6 January. Any profit the business has made should be shown beneath the figure for capital. It appears on the liability side because it is owed by the business to the owner. At this stage in trading you can ignore the fact that, strictly speaking, a proportion of business operating expenses should be *deducted* from the profit.

**Candlewick Enterprises**
**Balance sheet as at 6 January 1998**

|  | £ |  | £ | £ |
|---|---|---|---|---|
| **Fixed assets** |  | **Capital** |  |  |
| Van |  | *Add* Profit |  |  |
| **Current assets** |  | **Creditors: amounts due within one year** |  |  |
| Stock |  | Trade creditors |  |  |
| Debtors |  |  |  |  |
| Cash |  |  |  |  |

---

First you need to calculate the gross trading profit:

|  |  | £ |
|---|---|---|
|  | **Sales** | 60 |
| *Less* | **Cost of sales** |  |
|  | 30 candles at £1.50 | 45 |
|  | **Gross profit** | 15 |

The remaining stock is 30 candles (60 *less* 30 sold) at £1.50 = £45. The debtors are the credit sales customers who now owe for 20 candles at £2 = £40. The cash at bank (previously nil) is now increased by the cash sales. So the new balance sheet looks like this:

**Candlewick Enterprises**
**Balance sheet as at 6 January 1998**

|  | £ |  | £ | £ |
|---|---|---|---|---|
| **Fixed assets** |  | **Capital** | 1,300 |  |
| Van | 1,300 | *Add* Profit | 15 | 1,315 |
| **Current assets** |  | **Creditors: amounts due within one year** |  |  |
| Stock | 45 | Trade creditors |  | 90 |
| Debtors | 40 |  |  |  |
| Cash | 20 |  |  |  |
|  | 1,405 |  |  | 1,405 |

## 7.3 Constructing a Horizontal Balance Sheet

We could continue to construct a series of balance sheets covering Sarah's business on a day-to-day basis throughout January, February and March, but this would be somewhat tedious. So we will move on to 31 March and construct the balance sheet as at that date. Before we do so, it is useful to review the transactions affecting the balance sheet which have taken place in the first 3 months' trading:

- Sarah invested £1,300 capital in the business and used it to purchase a van.
- The depreciation on the van over the 3-month period is £75.
- At 31 March the closing stock of candles was £330 (220 candles at £1.50).
- Customers bought £1,620 worth of candles, but had only paid £480 which was for goods bought in January. They still owe for candles bought in February and March because the business allows them 2 months' credit.
- Cash sales of £540 were made in the quarter.
- £750 is owed to trade creditors for 500 candles purchased in March which will be paid for in April. An amount of £1,200 has already been paid for candles. There is £60 owing for postage and packaging, although £120 has already been paid.
- The business made a net profit of £105 in the first quarter. This is shown in the profit and loss account in Chapter 6, and is the figure after charging depreciation on the van.
- Cash payments were made for advertising (£75), telephone (£45) and market stall rent (£60) during the quarter.

Before we can construct a balance sheet for Candlewick Enterprises, we need to know what cash or overdraft the business has at the end of March.

In Chapter 3 we drew up a statement of the actual cash flows into and out of the business, but some adjustments have now been made which need to be incorporated. As we are interested only in the cash position at the end of the quarter we do not need to show the monthly cash flows, so a *cash statement* will be sufficient to help us find the missing figure. The heading reflects the fact that the statement only shows the cash position and not the actual cash flows:

---

**Cash statement as at 31 March 1998**

| Cash in | £ | Cash out | £ |
|---|---|---|---|
| Capital | 1,300 | Van | 1,300 |
| Credit sales | 480 | Purchases | 1,200 |
| Cash sales | 540 | Advertising | 75 |
| Subtotal | 2,320 | Telephone | 45 |
| Balancing figure (overdraft) | 480 | Market stall | 60 |
| | | Postage and packaging | 120 |
| | 2,800 | | 2,800 |

---

## Activity

Using the above information, complete the following balance sheet:

**Candlewick Enterprises**
**Balance sheet as at 31 March 1998**

| | £ | £ | | £ | £ |
|---|---|---|---|---|---|
| **Fixed assets** | | | **Capital** | 1,300 | |
| Van | 1,300 | | *Add* Profit | ___ | |
| *Less* Depreciation | 75 | | **Creditors: amounts due within one year** | | |
| **Current assets** | | | Trade creditors | | |
| Stock | | | Overdraft | ___ | |
| Debtors | ___ | ___ | | | ___ |
| | | ═══ | | | ═══ |

Your completed balance sheet should look like this:

---

**Candlewick Enterprises**
**Balance sheet as at 31 March 1998**

| | £ | £ | | £ | £ |
|---|---|---|---|---|---|
| **Fixed assets** | | | Capital | 1,300 | |
| Van | 1,300 | | *Add* Profit | 105 | 1,405 |
| *Less* Depreciation | 75 | 1,225 | **Creditors: amounts due within one year** | | |
| **Current assets** | | | Trade creditors | 810 | |
| Stock | 330 | | Overdraft | 480 | 1,290 |
| Debtors | 1,140 | 1,470 | | | |
| | | 2,695 | | | 2,695 |

---

## 7.4  Constructing a Vertical Balance Sheet

Although it is perfectly legal to present the balance sheet in the horizontal format as we have done, in practice most organisations use the *vertical format*. Many students find the horizontal format easier to understand because it demonstrates the accounting equation:

$$\text{Assets} = \text{Capital} + \text{Other liabilities}$$

However, this is also true of the vertical format because the above equation can also be expressed as:

$$\text{Assets} - \text{Other liabilities} = \text{Capital}$$

The diagram below shows a simple model of the horizontal format. It is made up of four separate blocks of information, and the sum of the blocks on the left-hand side is equal to the sum of the blocks on the right-hand side. We have used percentages to represent the values of each block. The equation it represents is as follows:

$$\text{Fixed assets } (60\%) + \text{Current assets } (40\%)$$

$$= \text{Capital } (70\%) + \text{Other liabilities } (30\%)$$

Thus, in the model fixed assets (representing 60% of total assets) plus current assets (representing 40% of total assets) is equal to capital (representing 70% of total liabilities) plus other liabilities (representing 30% of total liabilities):

**Balance sheet: Horizontal format model**

| | | | |
|---|---|---|---|
| Fixed assets | 60% | Capital | 70% |
| Current assets | 40% | Other liabilities | 30% |

The four blocks of information can be rearranged and the next model shows the vertical format. As you know from the equation, if a block of information is moved to the other side it must become a *deduction* if the two sides are to continue to balance. The model represents the same equation, but now it has been rearranged to read:

Fixed assets (60%) + [Current assets (40%) – Other liabilities (30%)]

$\quad$ = Capital (70%)

Thus, in the second model fixed assets (representing 60% of total assets) plus current assets (representing 40% of total assets) less other liabilities (representing 30% of total liabilities) is equal to capital (representing 70% of total liabilities):

---

**Balance sheet: Vertical format model**

| | |
|---|---|
| Fixed assets | 60% |
| *Add* Current assets | 40% |
| *Less* Other liabilities | 30% |
| Capital | 70% |

---

Current assets *less* other liabilities gives the figure for *net current assets* which in this example represent 10% of total assets. Net current assets are also known as *working capital*. With this information, we can now draw up the balance sheet for Candlewick Enterprises using the vertical format:

---

**Candlewick Enterprises**
**Balance sheet as at 31 March 1998**

| | | £ | £ | £ |
|---|---|---|---|---|
| **Fixed assets** | | | | |
| | Van | 1,300 | | |
| *Less* | Depreciation | 75 | | 1,225 |
| | **Current assets** | | | |
| | Stock | 330 | | |
| | Debtors | 1,140 | 1,470 | |

| *Less* **Creditors: amounts due within one year** | | | |
|---|---|---|---|
| Trade creditors | 810 | | |
| Overdraft | 480 | 1,290 | |
| **Working capital/Net current assets** | | | 180 |
| | | | 1,405 |
| Capital | | 1,300 | |
| *Add* Profit | | 105 | 1,405 |

## 7.5 Relationship Between the Three Financial Statements

We have now looked at three financial statements for Candlewick Enterprises: the cash flow statement in Chapter 3, the profit and loss account in Chapter 6 and the balance sheet in Chapter 7. You may have noticed that when we constructed the balance sheet, some of the figures from the other two statements were needed. The obvious items are the *overdraft* from the cash flow statement and the *net profit* from the profit and loss account. The *closing stock* from the profit and loss account also appeared in the balance sheet, and the difference between the figure for purchases in the profit and loss account of £1,950 and the cash actually paid of £1,200 is shown as trade creditors £750 in the balance sheet. You are now beginning to see the relationship between the three financial statements!

So far, we have only looked at the financial statements for Candlewick Enterprises for the first 3 months of trading. We will now look at the second quarter. The following table shows when the actual transactions for cash sales, credit sales and purchases of stock took place, not when cash was received or paid, during the 6-month period January to June:

| | Jan | Feb | Mar | Apr | May | Jun | Total |
|---|---|---|---|---|---|---|---|
| | £ | £ | £ | £ | £ | £ | £ |
| Cash sales | 160 | 180 | 200 | 200 | 240 | 240 | 1,220 |
| Credit sales | 480 | 540 | 600 | 600 | 720 | 720 | 3,660 |
| Purchases | 600 | 600 | 750 | 600 | 600 | 600 | 3,750 |

You will remember that credit customers pay 2 months after the sale and purchases are paid for in the month following the transaction. The value of stock at 30 June is £90. During the second quarter, the following expenses were incurred:

- Advertising – £25 per month payable 1 month in arrears.
- Telephone – £45 per quarter payable at the end of each quarter.
- Market stall – £25 per month payable at the end of the month.
- Postage and packaging – £60 per month payable 1 month in arrears.

Depreciation on the van remains at £75 per month. Sarah did not make any provision for doubtful debts as at 31 March, but has decided to allow 5% of debtors for doubtful debts as at 30 June. She draws out £50 per month for her own use and has arranged overdraft facilities with the bank.

## Activity

Construct a cash flow statement for Candlewick Enterprises for the 3-month period April to June. It is important to incorporate any relevant figures from the previous quarter and you will therefore need to refer to the actual cash flow statement for Candlewick Enterprises for the period January to March in Section 3.5 in Chapter 3 (p. 000).

You may find the following notes helpful:

- From the actual cash flow statement for the first quarter we know that at the end of March there was a cumulative cash deficit of £480. This should be shown as cumulative cash brought forward (b/f) at the beginning of April.
- The cash received for credit sales in April and May was for credit sales which took place in February and March.
- Purchases are paid for 1 month in arrears. Therefore, those made in March are paid for in April.
- Postage and packaging is paid for 1 month in arrears. Therefore, postage and packaging for March are paid for in April.
- Sarah's monthly drawings must be shown.

Your completed cash flow statement should look like this:

### Candlewick Enterprises
### Actual cash flow statement April–June 1998

|  | April £ | May £ | June £ | Total £ |
|---|---|---|---|---|
| **Cash in** |  |  |  |  |
| Cash sales | 200 | 240 | 240 | 680 |
| Credit sales | 540 | 600 | 600 | 1,740 |
| Subtotal | 740 | 840 | 840 | 2,420 |
| **Cash out** |  |  |  |  |
| Purchases | 750 | 600 | 600 | 1,950 |
| Advertising | 25 | 25 | 25 | 75 |
| Telephone | – | – | 45 | 45 |
| Market stall | 25 | 25 | 25 | 75 |
| Postage and packaging | 60 | 60 | 60 | 180 |
| Drawings | 50 | 50 | 50 | 150 |
| Subtotal | 910 | 760 | 805 | 2,475 |
| **Cash surplus/(deficit)** | (170) | 80 | 35 | (55) |
| **Cumulative cash b/f** | (480) | (650) | (570) | (480) |
| **Cumulative cash c/f** | (650) | (570) | (535) | (535) |

## Activity

Draw up a profit and loss account for Candlewick Enterprises for the 3-month period April to June. It is important to incorporate any relevant figures from the previous quarter. Therefore, you will need to refer to the profit and loss account for Candlewick Enterprises for the period January to March in Section 6.3 in Chapter 6.

You may find the following notes helpful:

- Sarah's drawings are not shown on the profit and loss account, but will be shown on the balance sheet as a withdrawal from the profit figure.
- From the profit and loss account for the first quarter we know that at the end of March the figure for closing stock was £330. This becomes the figure for opening stock at the beginning of April. On 30 June Candlewick Enterprises had a closing stock of £90.
- Sarah Wick decided to make a provision for doubtful debts of 5% of debtors at the end of the quarter. We need to know the figure for debtors at the end of June so that we can calculate the provision for doubtful debts:

|  |  | £ |
|---|---|---:|
| | Debtors at 31 March (from balance sheet) | 1,140 |
| *Add* | Total cash and credit sales April to June | 2,720 |
| | | 3,860 |
| *Less* | Cash received (from cash flow statement) | 2,420 |
| | Debtors at 30 June | 1,440 |
| | Provision for doubtful debts (5% × £1,440) | 72 |

Your completed profit and loss account should look like this:

### Candlewick Enterprises
### Trading and profit and loss account for the
### 3 months ending 30 June 1998

|  |  | £ | £ |
|---|---|---:|---:|
| | **Sales** | | 2,720 |
| *Less* | **Cost of sales** | | |
| | Opening stock | 330 | |
| *Add* | Purchases | 1,800 | |
| | | 2,130 | |
| *Less* | Closing stock | 90 | 2,040 |
| | **Gross profit** | | 680 |
| *Less* | **Expenses** | | |
| | Advertising | 75 | |
| | Telephone | 45 | |
| | Market stall | 75 | |
| | Postage and packing | 180 | |
| | Depreciation | 75 | |
| | Provision for doubtful debts | 72 | 522 |
| | **Net profit** | | 158 |

## Activity

Construct a horizontal and a vertical balance sheet for Candlewick Enterprises as at 30 June. You will need to refer to the cash flow statement and the profit and loss account you have just drawn up for the second quarter and the balance sheet as at 31 March which you drew up earlier in this chapter in Section 7.4.

You may find the following notes helpful:

- *Profit* is added to capital and then drawings are deducted.
- The *provision for doubtful debts* is shown as a deduction from debtors.
- The *cumulative depreciation* on the van is shown as a deduction from the original cost of the van.

Your completed balance sheets should look like this:

### Candlewick Enterprises
### Horizontal balance sheet as at 30 June 1998

| | £ | £ | £ | | | £ | £ |
|---|---|---|---|---|---|---|---|
| **Fixed assets** | | | | Opening capital at 1 April | 1,405 | | |
| Van | | 1,300 | | *Add* Profit | 158 | | |
| *Less* Cumulative depreciation | | 150 | 1,150 | | 1,563 | | |
| **Current assets** | | | | *Less* Drawings | 150 | 1,413 | |
| Stock | | | 90 | **Creditors: amounts due** | | | |
| | | | | **within one year** | | | |
| Debtors | 1,440 | | | Trade creditors | | 600 | |
| *Less* Provision for doubtful | 72 | 1,368 | 1,458 | Postage and packaging | | 60 | |
| debts | | | | | | | |
| | | | | Overdraft | | 535 | 1,195 |
| | | | 2,608 | | | | 2,608 |

### Candlewick Enterprises
### Vertical balance sheet as at 30 June 1998

| | | £ | £ | £ | £ |
|---|---|---|---|---|---|
| | **Fixed assets** | | | | |
| | Van | | | 1,300 | |
| *Less* | Cumulative depreciation | | | 150 | 1,150 |
| | **Current assets** | | | | |
| | Stock | | 90 | | |
| | Debtors | 1,440 | | | |
| *Less* | Provision for doubtful debts | 72 | 1,368 | 1,458 | |
| *Less* | **Creditors: amounts due within one year** | | | | |
| | Trade creditors | | 600 | | |
| | Postage and packaging | | 60 | | |
| | Overdraft | | 535 | 1,195 | 263 |
| | | | | | 1,413 |
| | **Opening capital at 1 April** | | | 1,405 | |
| *Add* | Profit | | | 158 | |
| | | | | 1,563 | |
| *Less* | Drawings | | | 150 | 1,413 |

## 7.6 Conclusions

In this chapter we have looked at a financial statement known as the balance sheet which shows the financial position of a business, not its owner, at one particular point in time. We have examined the significance of the accounting equation and its relationship with the horizontal and vertical presentations of the balance sheet. We have created a statement in both formats which shows what the business has in the way of assets and how these have been financed. We have constructed balance sheets for both a new business and for a continuing business. We have also investigated the relationship between the cash flow statement, the profit and loss account and the balance sheet and drawn them up in a single exercise.

Having completed this chapter, you should now be able to:

- describe what is meant by the term 'financial position';
- differentiate between assets and liabilities;
- apply the accounting equation;
- construct a simple balance sheet for a new or a continuing business using the horizontal or the vertical format;
- explain the relationship between the cash flow statement, the profit and loss account and the balance sheet.

## Exercises

Complete the following sentences:

1 The accounting equation demonstrates that at any one point in time ...............
2 In the UK, the most common presentation of the balance sheet is ....................
3 Debtors represent ..........................................................................................
4 Creditors represent ........................................................................................
5 Drawings are ..................................................................................................

Are the following statements true or false?

6 Fixed assets are bought to keep in the business.
7 Current liabilities are normally paid within 1 year of the balance sheet date.
8 Drawings are shown under current assets.
9 Depreciation is shown in the cash flow statement.
10 The provision for doubtful debts is added to debtors in the balance sheet.

You may wish to read more widely than this book to answer the following questions fully, but you can check the main points by referring to the appropriate sections in this chapter.

11 Are the following balance sheet items an example of a fixed asset, current asset or a liability: (Section 7.2)

    Creditors
    Debtors
    Freehold buildings
    Factory machinery
    Cash.

**12** Explain the importance of the accounting equation. (Section 7.2)

**13** Identify and explain the main headings on a vertical balance sheet. (Section 7.4)

**14** Describe the term 'drawings' and how it is shown in the cash flow statement, the profit and loss account and the balance sheet. (Section 7.5)

Multiple choice questions (more than one answer may apply):

**15** The items which a business owns or has use of in the long term are known as:

**a** current assets
**b** capital
**c** current liabilities
**d** fixed assets.

**16** If a firm purchases a vehicle on credit which it intends to use in the business, it will be classified as a:

**a** current liability
**b** current asset
**c** fixed asset
**d** long-term liability.

**17** A business buys equipment for £5,000 on credit. This transaction will:

**a** increase assets and decrease liabilities
**b** increase assets and increase liabilities
**c** decrease assets and decrease liabilities
**d** decrease assets and increase liabilities.

**18** If the figure of capital is missing in a exam question, it can be found by:

**a** adding fixed assets and current assets
**b** deducting liabilities from total assets
**c** adding liabilities to total assets
**d** deducting liabilities from current assets.

**19** A business has assets of £15,000 and liabilities of £8,000. Therefore the capital is:

**a** £23,000
**b** £7,000
**c** £8,000
**d** £15,000.

**20** A business decides to depreciate its assets by £2,000 per annum. This figure will appear in:

**a** all three financial statements
**b** the cash flow statement and the balance sheet only
**c** the profit and loss account and the balance sheet only
**d** the cash flow statement and the profit and loss account only.

Practice questions:

**21** Insert the missing figures in the following examples.

|             | a<br>£ | b<br>£ | c<br>£ | d<br>£ | e<br>£ |
|-------------|--------|--------|--------|--------|--------|
| Capital     | ?      | 14,000 | 6,050  | 3,200  | ?      |
| Liabilities | 3,600  | ?      | 7,120  | ?      | 25,160 |
| Assets      | 12,000 | 15,400 | ?      | 18,000 | 37,160 |

**22** Using the following information for Nick Lucas, draw up balance sheets in both vertical and horizontal formats as at 31st December 1998:

| | £ |
|---|---|
| Machinery | 94,000 |
| Stock | 32,000 |
| Cash at bank | 6,000 |
| Freehold land and buildings | 100,000 |
| Fixtures and fittings | 42,000 |
| Debtors | 12,000 |
| Creditors | 30,000 |

**23** The following transactions have taken place in a business. Enter the name of the balance sheet item(s) affected under the appropriate column and indicate whether there has been an increase or decrease. The first has been done for you:

| | Asset | Liability | Capital |
|---|---|---|---|
| Stock purchased on credit | +Stock | +Creditors | |
| Cash paid for stock | | | |
| Loan repaid | | | |
| Cash received from debtor | | | |
| Cash withdrawn by owner | | | |

**24** Explain the relationship between the cash flow statement, the profit and loss account and the balance sheet. Illustrate your answer with worked examples.

**25** Why is a balance sheet claimed to be a statement of the financial position of a business? What limitations do you think it has?

(Answers on pp. 323–5)

# 8 The Final Accounts of a Sole Trader

## 8.1 Introduction

In this chapter we bring together some the knowledge you have gained from earlier chapters in this book. In Chapters 5–7 we have described how a trial balance can be drawn up from the accounting records of a business and explained the purpose and content of the profit and loss account and balance sheet. We are now at the stage where we can draw up the *final accounts of a sole trader* from the trial balance. The final accounts are the *profit and loss account* and the *balance sheet*. This is a crucial stage in the accounting process. It transforms the trial balance, which is an arithmetical check of the business's accounting records, into two financial statements which are used to communicate the accounting information to various users.

We start by looking at the adjustments which must be made to the trial balance before the final accounts can be drawn up. The first financial statement to be drawn up is always the profit and loss account. This is followed by the balance sheet which, if all the procedures have been followed correctly, should balance.

## 8.2 Adjustments to the Trial Balance

When a business reaches the end of its chosen financial period, whether it is a month, a quarter or a year, there is considerable interest in knowing the final results. Tremendous pressure is put on the accountants to prepare the profit and loss account and balance sheet as soon as possible. However, this cannot be done until all the accounts are balanced and the trial balance drawn up. Even in a small business this can be a lengthy process, so the accountant must start the work as soon as possible.

The first stage is to close all the individual accounts at the end of the financial period. However, it is quite likely that some transactions will not have been recorded. For example, some invoices may not have been received although the goods and services have been used by the business. These might include electricity and telephone bills, which are rarely received in time to be entered into the books when the trial balance is prepared. In other cases the business may know the amount, but the invoice has not yet been received from the supplier. It would be misleading for the accountant to report a figure of profit if all the costs incurred during the financial period had not been included. Therefore, certain *adjustments to the trial balance* must be made.

An *accrual* is an estimate in the accounts of a business of a liability that is not supported by an invoice or a request for payment at the time when the accounts are prepared. In this chapter we will show accruals as notes at the end of the trial balance and this is the way you would normally encounter them in exam questions. The amount of the accrual is listed as one of the expenses in the profit and loss account; it also appears as a liability in the balance sheet, as it has not yet been paid for. For example, if the electricity bill has already been received and recorded in the accounts for £5,000, but it is estimated that a further £750 is owed for the financial period, then the amount shown in the profit and loss account will be £5,750, and in the balance sheet £750 is added to the current liabilities.

Now we will look at the opposite situation. A *prepayment* is a payment made by the business for goods or services before they are received. For example, telephone line rental or insurance may have been paid in advance. Supposing an invoice was received and recorded for a year's insurance premium of £8,000 for the period to 30 June 1999 but the business's financial year ends on 31 December 1998. It would be misleading to include the full amount, as the business has only had the benefit of half the year's cover. Therefore, only half of the cost (£4,000) is charged to the profit and loss account and the remainder appears as a current asset in the balance sheet. It is a current asset because the amount was recorded in the books in the current year, but the business will enjoy the benefits of a further 6 months' cover in the following financial year. In this chapter we will show any prepayments as a note at the end of the trial balance.

## Activity

A business is preparing its accounts for the year ending 31 December 1998. Its records show that the following telephone bills have been recorded:

£880 to 31 March 1998
£860 to 30 June 1998
£890 to 30 September 1998.

What adjustment should be made to the trial balance, and what amounts appear in the profit and loss account and balance sheet?

This is where we need to make an estimate for the final quarter, as the actual amount is not known. One way to estimate it is to take the average for the previous three quarters. This gives a figure of £876.66, which would probably be rounded up to £880. At the end of the trial balance we would note that there is an accrual for telephones of £880. The full charge for telephones in the profit and loss account will be the four quarters totalling £3,510. In the balance sheet an additional current liability will be recorded of £880, representing the estimated amount.

## 8.3 The Trial Balance with Adjustments

We can now construct a *trial balance with adjustments* for accruals and prepayments. This will be used as the basis for drawing up the profit and loss account and balance sheets in the following sections.

Granville Dukes owns an art gallery called Oil & Water and employs a part-time sales assistant. In addition to buying and selling prints and maps, Granville also sells a few original paintings on behalf of a friend. The business receives a commission for doing this. The business originally rented a premises in the centre of the town, but purchased its own property at the end of the first year of trading when a considerable sum was spent on fixtures and fittings. To fund this development, Granville negotiated an interest-free loan from an aunt on the understanding that it would be paid back at the end of 5 years and she would receive copies of the final accounts. The business has been in existence for 2 years and the following trial balance is for the second year (*see page 105*).

You will remember from Chapter 5 that all the items in the debit column of the trial balance represent *assets*, which are shown in the balance sheet, or *expenses*, which appear in the profit and loss account. The credit column represents *sales and income*, which are shown in the profit and loss account, or *capital, liabilities and provisions*, which appear in the balance sheet.

When preparing final accounts from a trial balance and any adjustments shown in the notes, it is helpful to tick each figure every time you use it. By the time you have completed the profit and loss account and balance sheet, all the figures in the trial balance will be ticked once and all the adjustments in the notes will be ticked twice. If your balance sheet does not balance, look through the example again and make certain all the figures have the right number of ticks.

## 8.4 The Profit and Loss Account

We are going to prepare a *profit and loss account* which is similar in structure and content to the one described in Chapter 6. There will be two main parts to it. In the first part we will show the sales and then deduct the costs to the business of the goods which have been actually sold. This will give a subtotal of gross profit. A common mistake is to forget to deduct closing stock when

## Oil & Water
### Trial balance as at 31 December 1998

|  | Debit £ | Credit £ |
|---|---|---|
| Sales |  | 116,740 |
| Purchases | 62,680 |  |
| Wages | 14,550 |  |
| Community services | 12,000 |  |
| Insurance | 2,580 |  |
| Electricity | 800 |  |
| Advertising | 2,200 |  |
| Telephone | 800 |  |
| Miscellaneous expenses | 560 |  |
| Commissions received |  | 3,200 |
| Stock at 1 January | 35,600 |  |
| Premises | 120,000 |  |
| Fixtures and fittings | 20,000 |  |
| Debtors | 6,100 |  |
| Creditors |  | 12,450 |
| Cash in hand | 500 |  |
| Bank overdraft |  | 980 |
| Long-term loan |  | 40,000 |
| Capital |  | 120,000 |
| Drawings during year | 15,000 |  |
|  | 293,370 | 293,370 |

*Notes*:
The stock at the end of the year is valued at £31,400.
Insurance paid in advance is £280.
The estimate for telephone bill not received is £250.
The estimate for electricity used but not yet billed is £150.
Community services charge prepaid at 31 December is £1,800.
Commissions due but not yet invoiced amount to £360.
Depreciation on the premises is set at 5%; fixtures and fittings at 20%.

calculating the cost of sales, or becoming confused as to which stock figures should be added or deducted from purchases. The rule is:

Cost of sales = Opening stock + Purchases − Closing stock.

We will add the commission income to the gross profit. This is so that we can easily see the gross profit resulting from the main activity of buying and selling maps and prints. This figure will be very important when we come to analyse accounts in a later chapter. From the gross profit we will deduct all the other operating expenses of the business to arrive at the figure of net profit.

The first step is to take account of notes at the end of the trial balance and calculate the adjusted figures to be entered in the profit and loss account.

Insurance £2,580 – £280 prepaid = £2,300
Community services £12,000 – £1,800 prepaid = £10,200
Electricity £800 + £150 accrued = £950
Telephone £800 + £250 accrued = £1,050
Commissions received £3,200 + £360 owing = £3,560
Depreciation on premises at 5% per annum = £6,000
Depreciation on fixtures and fittings at 20% per annum = £4,000

Now we are ready to construct the profit and loss account:

### Oil & Water
### Trading and profit and loss account for the year ending
### 31 December 1998

|  |  | £ | £ |
|---|---|---:|---:|
| | **Sales** | | 116,740 |
| *Less* | **Cost of sales** | | |
| | Opening stock | 35,600 | |
| *Add* | Purchases | 62,680 | |
| | | 98,280 | |
| *Less* | Closing stock | 31,400 | 66,880 |
| | **Gross profit** | | 49,860 |
| *Add* | Commission | | 3,560 |
| | | | 53,420 |
| *Less* | **Expenses** | | |
| | Wages | 14,550 | |
| | Insurance | 2,300 | |
| | Community services | 10,200 | |
| | Electricity | 950 | |
| | Advertising | 2,200 | |
| | Telephone | 1,050 | |
| | Miscellaneous expenses | 560 | |
| | Depreciation – Premises | 6,000 | |
| | Depreciation – Fixtures and fittings | 4,000 | 41,810 |
| | **Net profit** | | 11,610 |

## Activity

Supposing that during the course of the year £5,000 of stock was stolen from Oil & Water, so that the figure is overstated on the profit and loss account. What would be the impact if the true figure were substituted?

The greatest impact would be on the *gross profit* and the *net profit*. These would both decrease by £5,000. If a business has stock stolen or it has deteriorated so that the value is less, it should be noticed during stock-taking. The reduced figure of stock is shown in the profit and loss account, so that the loss in stock is borne by the business. Because of the impact of closing stock values on profit, this is one area where fraud can be perpetrated by enhancing stock values and thus increasing profit.

## 8.5 The Balance Sheet

The *balance sheet* should cause no problems, because all the figures in your trial balance which have not already been ticked once must go into the balance sheet, and all the notes must be ticked twice:

### Oil & Water
### Balance sheet as at 31 December 1998

|  | £ Cost | £ Depre-ciation | £ Net book value |
|---|---|---|---|
| **Fixed assets** |  |  |  |
| Premises | 120,000 | 6,000 | 114,000 |
| Fixtures and fittings | 20,000 | 4,000 | 16,000 |
|  |  |  | 130,000 |
| **Current assets** |  |  |  |
| Stock |  | 31,400 |  |
| Debtors |  | 6,460 |  |
| Prepayments |  | 2,080 |  |
| Cash |  | 500 |  |
|  |  | 40,440 |  |
| *Less* **Creditors: amounts due within one year** |  |  |  |
| Creditors | 12,450 |  |  |
| Accruals | 400 |  |  |
| Bank overdraft | 980 | 13,830 |  |
| **Net current assets** |  |  | 26,610 |
| Total assets *less* current liabilities |  |  | 156,610 |
| *Less* **Creditors: amounts due after more than one year** |  |  | 40,000 |
| **Total net assets** |  |  | 116,610 |
| Capital at beginning of year |  | 120,000 |  |
| *Add* Profit for year |  | 11,610 |  |
|  |  | 131,610 |  |
| *Less* Drawings |  | 15,000 | 116,610 |

We have used a slightly different format than in earlier chapters, but this should have caused you few problems. The points to note are:

**1** The cost of the *fixed assets* has been shown less the depreciation to give the *net book value*. This is sometimes referred to the *carrying amount*. The depreciation is a cumulative figure. In future years, when the annual depreciation is charged to the profit and loss account, the figure of cumulative depreciation in the balance sheet will increase by the same amount. Thus, the net book value will decrease each year.

2 We have shown the *prepayments* and *accruals* separately. These are normally small amounts and would be added to debtors and creditors respectively.

3 The *loan* from Granville's aunt represents long-term finance, and is therefore shown as creditors: amounts due after more than one year.

## Activity

If you were Granville's aunt, would you be content with this year's figures?

If you look at the results you can see that although the business made a profit of £11,610, Granville drew out £15,000 for his own use. If he intends to make the same level of drawings each year, the business must increase its profits. In addition, the balance sheet shows that there is an overdraft, so there is no money to pay back any of the loan at the moment. On the other hand, the business does own its own premises which could be sold at the end of the 5 years to repay the loan. However, this would most probably force the business to close. Perhaps the results for the next year will be better and by then there will be no cause for concern. However, if you have lent a large amount of money to a business, you will want to keep an eye on it. The profit and loss account and balance sheet allow you to do this. We have demonstrated that even at a superficial level it is possible to draw some conclusions about the business from these financial statements. In Chapter 12 we will explain how you can use ratio analysis to make a more complete interpretation.

## 8.6 Conclusions

A trial balance is constructed at the end of the financial period to check the accuracy of the credit and debit balances in the accounting records. If the correct procedures have been followed, the totals of the debit and credit columns should balance. The figures summarised in the trial balance from the accounting records are used to draw up final accounts. These are the profit and loss account and the balance sheet.

However, before this can be done, it is usually necessary to make a number of adjustments to the trial balance to represent transactions which have not yet gone through the books. It is important to ensure that these items are reflected twice in the final accounts. This can be done by ticking each item on the trial balance and each adjustment when it is used in the final accounts. If every figure is correctly treated, each item in the trial balance will be ticked once and each adjustment will be ticked twice.

Having completed this chapter, you should now be able to:

- make adjustments to a trial balance for accruals;
- make adjustments to a trial balance for prepayments;
- prepare a profit and loss account from a trial balance;
- prepare a balance sheet from a trial balance.

## Exercises

Complete the following sentences:

**1** An accrual is ................................................................................................................
**2** A prepayment is ...........................................................................................................
**3** Net current assets are calculated by ...............................................................................
**4** Drawings are ...............................................................................................................
**5** Net book value is .........................................................................................................

Are the following statements true or false?

**6** Accruals are shown under current assets on the balance sheet.
**7** Drawings are shown on the profit and loss account.
**8** The annual depreciation is deducted from the cost of an asset to give the net book value.
**9** Purchases are added to opening stock in the profit and loss account.
**10** Purchases are added to closing stock in the profit and loss account.

You may wish to read more widely than this book to answer the following questions fully, but you can check the main points by referring to the appropriate sections in this chapter.

**11** Explain what is meant by accruals and prepayments, and how they affect the trial balance. (Section 8.2)
**12** Describe the items which are included in the cost of sale calculation in the profit and loss account. (Section 8.4)
**13** Explain how you would show profit and drawings on the balance sheet. (Section 8.5)
**14** Describe how you would treat depreciation in the profit and loss account and balance sheet. (Sections 8.3–8.5)

Multiple choice questions (more than one answer may apply):

**15** Insurance expenses recorded in the books are £2,800 and there is a prepayment of £500. Therefore:

    **a** £3,300 will be shown in the profit and loss account
    **b** £2,300 will be shown in the profit and loss account
    **c** a prepayment of £3,300 will be shown in the balance sheet
    **d** a prepayment of £500 will be shown in the balance sheet.

**16** If a fixed asset cost £30,000, has a scrap value of £6,000 and a life of 4 years, the annual depreciation charge is:

    **a** £7,500
    **b** £9,000
    **c** £1,500
    **d** £6,000.

**17** If a fixed asset cost £50,000, has a scrap value of £2,000 and a life of 12 years, the net book value after 4 years is:

a £16,000
b £42,000
c £34,000
d £33,330.

**18** Net current assets on the balance sheet represent:

a fixed assets plus creditors due within 12 months
b current assets plus creditors due within 12 months
c fixed assets less creditors due within 12 months
d current assets less creditors due within 12 months.

**19** On the balance sheet of a sole trader:

a capital is shown with profit and drawings added
b capital is shown with profit added and drawings deducted
c capital is shown with profit and drawings deducted
d capital is shown with profit deducted and drawings added.

**20** If a business has an additional income from renting part of the premises, it is shown in the profit and loss account as:

a a deduction from sales
b an addition to net profit
c an addition to gross profit
d a deduction from gross profit.

Practice questions:

**21** Naomi Cameron has opened a health and beauty salon called Top-to-Toe, offering a range of slimming and beauty treatments. She is renting the property and sublets one of the rooms 2 days per week to an aromatherapist. The trial balance for the first year of business is as follows:

**Top-to-Toe**
**Trial balance as at 31 December 1998**

|  | £ | £ |
|---|---|---|
| Sales |  | 72,100 |
| Purchases | 11,160 |  |
| Wages | 12,000 |  |
| Rent | 18,000 |  |
| Insurance | 7,400 |  |
| Electricity | 1,840 |  |
| Advertising | 3,860 |  |
| Telephone | 1,450 |  |
| Administration expenses | 1,250 |  |
| Rental income |  | 1,500 |
| Equipment | 15,000 |  |
| Debtors | 1,200 |  |
| Creditors |  | 1,620 |
| Bank | 1,060 |  |
| Capital |  | 15,000 |
| Drawings during year | 16,000 |  |
|  | 90,220 | 90,220 |

*Notes*:
The stock at the end of the year is valued at £790
Advertising paid in advance is £260
It has been decided to depreciate the equipment by 25%
The following accruals should be allowed:
    administration expenses £160; telephone £290;
    electricity £540
A provision for doubtful debts of 20% of debtors should
be made.

Prepare the profit and loss account for Top-to-Toe for the year ending 31
December 1988.

**22** Using the Top-to-Toe information in Question **21**, prepare a balance sheet for
the business as at 31 December 1998.

**23** Rob Walters has a business called Walters Watches which has the following
items in its balance sheet as at 31 March 1998:

| | £ |
|---|---|
| Capital | 85,000 |
| Creditors | 5,000 |
| Bank loan | 15,000 |
| Fixtures and fittings | 45,000 |
| Stocks | 24,000 |
| Debtors | 17,000 |
| Bank balance | 19,000 |

During the first week of April, the business:

- bought more stock on credit for £7,000;
- repaid the bank loan in full;
- collected a cheque for £7,000 from a debtor;
- bought more fixtures and fittings, paying £5,000 for them by cheque;
- paid one of its creditors £3,000 by cheque.

Draw up a balance sheet for Walters Watches as at 7 April, after all the above
transactions have been taken into account.

**24** Write a letter to Rob Walters explaining the purpose of a balance sheet and
the structure and information content of the balance sheet you have prepared
in Question **23**.

**25** Draw up final accounts for Back Up Business Services from the following
trial balance:

**Back Up Business Services**
**Trial balance as at 31 December 1998**

| | Debit £ | Credit £ |
|---|---|---|
| Capital | | 55,500 |
| Premises | 55,000 | |
| Equipment | 20,000 | |
| Car | 9,000 | |
| Provision for depreciation: | | |
| Equipment | | 3,000 |
| Car | | 3,000 |

| | | |
|---|---:|---:|
| Stock at 1 January 1999 | 500 | |
| Purchases | 2,600 | |
| Sales | | 42,800 |
| Wages | 15,600 | |
| Rental income | | 350 |
| Lighting and heating | 2,000 | |
| Postage and stationery | 550 | |
| Insurance | 1,250 | |
| Telephone | 950 | |
| Debtors | 7,000 | |
| Creditors | | 11,750 |
| Bank | 1,950 | |
| | 116,400 | 116,400 |

*Notes*:

Stock at 31 December is valued at £560

Amount accrued for lighting and heating is £750

Rental income outstanding is £150

Equipment is depreciated at 15% of cost; car at $33\frac{1}{3}\%$

Provision of £450 will be made for doubtful debts.

(Answers on pp. 325–8)

# 9 The Accounts of a Partnership

## 9.1 Introduction

*Partnerships* are a form of business organisation commonly adopted by businesses offering professional or other personal services, such as solicitors, accountants, doctors and dentists. As its name implies, a sole trader business has only one owner, but a partnership is a larger business because it has two or more owners. However, like the sole trader, the partners have unlimited liability and in this respect both differ from limited companies.

The profit and loss account and balance sheet of partnerships are very similar to those of sole traders. In sole trader accounts, all the profits and drawings made by the sole trader can be entered into a single capital account, but in partnership accounts we need to show the financial relationship of each partner with the business by opening separate accounts for them. In this chapter we explain how the net profit of a partnership is adjusted to allow for any agreed benefits the individual partners may receive, before any balance of profit is divided among the partners. These transactions are entered into an *appropriation account* which is added to the partnership profit and loss account. Each partner has a *capital account* and a *current account* where their regular transactions with the business are recorded, and both these accounts appear on the partnership balance sheet.

During the lifetime of the partnership it may be decided to admit a new partner to the business and we describe the accounting procedures that this entails. We also show how the accounts are closed and the assets distributed when a partnership ceases to trade.

## 9.2 Main Features

A *partnership* can be defined as a form of business organisation in which *two or more* people join together to carry on a business with a view to making a profit. The major legislation governing partnerships is the *Partnership Act 1890*. Some features of a partnership which have a direct effect on the accounting records, the profit and loss account and the balance sheet are as follows:

- The partners may not contribute equal amounts of *capital* to the business and may wish this to be recognised in some way.
- Partners can make *loans* to the business over and above the capital they have invested and may wish to receive interest on their loan.
- As with a sole trader, partners can make *drawings* during the course of the financial year in anticipation of profits. However, they may agree that drawings should be kept to a minimum and in order to encourage this, they may charge interest on drawings.
- Some of the partners may work full-time in the business and wish to receive a regular *salary* for this work.

As we stated in our definition, the objective of a partnership is to make a profit. It is up to the partners to decide how they will share the profits. The following are some of the methods commonly used to do this:

- *A fixed ratio* – Partners may agree to share the profits equally. However, if one partner has contributed more capital or spends more time working for the partnership, they may decide an alternative basis. For example, if there are three partners, it may be agreed that one partner receives 50% of the profits and the others receive 25% each.
- *A ratio based on capital balances* – If the partners have contributed unequal amounts of capital, they may agree to share the profits in the same ratio to reflect this.
- *Making allocations to partners and sharing the balance* – The partners may agree that interest will be paid on the capital contributed by the partners, that partners who spend a certain amount of time working in the business will receive a salary or that interest will be charged on any drawings. All these transactions will be allocations of the net profit earned by the business. Once these allocations have been made, any balance (whether a profit or a loss) will be shared amongst the partners in an agreed ratio.

In the absence of a *partnership agreement* on these matters, the *Partnership Act 1890* provides the following rules:

- *Profits and losses* – All partners are entitled to share equally in the capital gains and profits, and must contribute equally towards the losses, whether capital losses or otherwise, incurred by the firm.
- *Interest on capital* – Partners are not entitled to any interest on capital and therefore such interest cannot be deducted in ascertaining the profits of the business.
- *Interest on loans* – Partners are entitled to interest at 5% per annum on any loan capital contributed in excess of the agreed capital subscribed.
- *Salaries* – All partners are entitled to take part in the management of the business, but no partner is entitled to any remuneration for acting in the business of the partnership.

## Activity

Compare a partnership with a sole trader as a form of business organisation.

You may have thought of some of the following points:

- Whereas there are no legal formalities for a sole trader who wishes to start a business, there are some legal requirements that apply to partnerships.
- A partnership can raise more capital to start the business than a sole trader.
- A greater range of skills is likely to be available to run a partnership business than are available in a sole trader business because partnerships have more than one owner.
- In a partnership the pressures of managing the business are shared, whereas a sole trader must bear them alone.
- Any loss made by a partnership is shared among the partners, whereas a sole trader suffers the whole of any loss the business incurs.
- In a partnership responsibility for debts incurred by individual partners, or the business as a whole, are shared; a sole trader is responsible only for debts incurred by the business.
- In a partnership individual partners are responsible for the actions of the others; a sole trader has none of these worries.
- In a partnership no one has sole control and one partner's wishes may be overruled by the other partners; a sole trade has total control over the business.
- It can be more difficult to transfer interest in a partnership than in a sole trader business.

## 9.3 The Profit and Loss Account

All the basic rules covered so far with regard to the preparation of the profit and loss account of a sole trader also apply to the preparation of a *partnership profit and loss account*. The crucial difference is that the latter includes an *appropriation account*. It may not be headed as such, but it is merely a continuation of the type of profit and loss account we described for the sole trader. The appropriation account is an additional section that shows how the net profit is allocated to the partners. It contains such items as salaries and interest on capital before the division in the profit-sharing ratios of the remaining profit

The appropriation account is part of the *double-entry bookkeeping system*. If an entry is made to the appropriation account, such as interest paid on capital, a corresponding entry must be made to another account. In partnerships it is usual for a *current account* to be opened for each partner which will record the corresponding entries to the appropriation account. We consider current accounts in a moment. At this stage we will concentrate on the proper treatment of transactions in the appropriation account:

- *Salaries of partners* cannot be classified as an expense when arriving at the figure of profit and are shown in the appropriation account before calculating the profit division between the partners.
- *Interest on capital* is normally paid where partners have contributed different amounts of capital, or their profit-sharing ratio is unequal. Interest paid on capital is a charge against the profits available for appropriation and therefore, like salaries, it reduces the amount of profit shared among the partners.
- *Interest on drawings* may be charged to the partners in order to avoid cash flow problems which might be caused if they draw substantial amounts in anticipation of profits. This encourages partners to keep drawings to a minimum or not to make drawings until profits are calculated. Where interest is charged, the amounts received by the business are credited to the profit and loss appropriation account as income to the business and charged to the partners through their current accounts.
- *Interest on loans* provided by the partners in excess of their agreed capitals, unlike interest on partners' capitals, represents a normal business expense. The fact that the loans are provided by the partners is incidental; loans could equally be provided by outsiders to the partnership, in which case the interest paid would be deductible from the normal trading profits.

We can demonstrate these transactions with an example. Rob and John Rennie are in partnership selling cast iron fireplaces, cookers and wood-burning stoves, and call their business Hearth & Home. Their net profit for the year ending 31 December 1998 was £228,000. The two partners' annual salaries were: Rob £44,000, John £40,000. Interest was paid on capital as follows: Rob £27,000, John £13,000. Rob was charged interest on drawings for the year of £4,000. The remaining profit is to be shared equally. We can now draw up the profit and loss appropriation account.

**Hearth & Home**
**Profit and loss appropriation account for the year ending 31 December 1998**

|  |  | £000 | £000 | £000 |
|---|---|---|---|---|
| **Net profit available for appropriation** |  |  |  | 228 |
| *Add* Interest on drawings |  |  |  | 4 |
|  |  |  |  | 232 |
| *Less* Interest on capital | Rob | 27 |  |  |
|  | John | 13 | 40 |  |
| *Less* Salaries | Rob | 44 |  |  |
|  | John | 40 | 84 | 124 |
| **Balance of profits to be shared** |  |  |  | 108 |
|  | Rob 50% |  | 54 |  |
|  | John 50% |  | 54 | 108 |

The main item to note is that the interest on drawings is added to profit because it is a credit to the profit and loss account as a source of income. The debit balance will go to the partner's current account. The actual drawings made by the partners must also be entered in each partner's current account as a debit entry. Note that the credit entry for drawings is to the bank account and not to the appropriation account.

## Activity

Jenny, Sally and Patrick are in partnership and own a dance and fitness studio called Upbeat. They each receive a salary of £8,000 per annum from the business and are paid interest of 10 per cent on their capital. They share profits as follows: Jenny 60 per cent; Sally and Patrick 20 per cent each. Their capital balances are: Jenny £10,000, Sally £6,000, Patrick £2,000. The net profit for the year ending 31 December 1998 was £28,300. Draw up the appropriation account for the partnership.

The main difference in this activity compared with the Hearth & Home example in the text is that the profit is shared between three partners with Jenny taking 60%. Your completed answer should look like this:

**Upbeat**
**Profit and loss appropriation account for the year ending 31 December 1998**

|  |  | £ | £ | £ |
|---|---|---:|---:|---:|
| **Net profit available for appropriation** |  |  |  | 28,300 |
| *Less* Interest on capital |  |  |  |  |
|  | Jenny | 1,000 |  |  |
|  | Sally | 600 |  |  |
|  | Patrick | 200 | 1,800 |  |
| *Less* Salaries |  |  |  |  |
|  | Jenny | 8,000 |  |  |
|  | Sally | 8,000 |  |  |
|  | Patrick | 8,000 | 24,000 | 25,800 |
| **Balance of profits to be shared** |  |  |  | 2,500 |
|  | Jenny 60% |  | 1,500 |  |
|  | Sally 20% |  | 500 |  |
|  | Patrick 20% |  | 500 | 2,500 |

## 9.4 The Balance Sheet

With the entries made to the *appropriation account*, it would be possible to make the corresponding entry to the *capital account* of each partner. However, this can be slightly confusing, particularly where interest is paid on capital invested by the partners. The usual system is to maintain a capital account for each partner which shows any capital subscribed and withdrawn, and a *current account* for each partner showing salaries, interest on capital, interest on drawings, share of profit and any drawings may by the partners. A *capital account* is shown in the balance sheet for each partner. The balance on each capital account represents the agreed fixed capital invested in the business by the partner. The fixed capital changes only when additional capital is introduced or some capital is withdrawn by agreement.

Unlike sole trader accounts, where profits or losses for the period adjust the capital accounts of the owner, in partnership accounts the profits or losses for the period adjust each partner's *current account*. The current account is part of the double-entry bookkeeping system, with the appropriation account containing the other entries. When an entry is made to the appropriation account for salaries, interest or share of profits, it appears as a debit entry. The corresponding entry will go the credit side of the current account of each partner. For example, the above entries in the current accounts of Rob and John Rennie would look as follows:

### Current account: Rob Rennie

|  | £ |  | £ |
|---|---|---|---|
| Interest on drawings | 4,000 | **Appropriation account** |  |
|  |  | Interest on capital | 27,000 |
|  |  | Salary | 44,000 |
|  |  | Share of profit | 54,000 |
|  |  |  |  |

### Current account: John Rennie

|  | £ |  | £ |
|---|---|---|---|
|  |  | **Appropriation account** |  |
|  |  | Interest on capital | 13,000 |
|  |  | Salary | 40,000 |
|  |  | Share of profit | 54,000 |
|  |  |  |  |

Note that the charge for interest on drawings is a debit balance to the current account because it is a cost to be borne by the partner. The entry on the appropriation account is a credit entry and is shown as an addition to the net profit. The closing balance on the current account for each partner is shown in the balance sheet. The balance on the account represents the amount due to or from the partner at the date of the balance sheet.

## Activity

Linda, Alan and David are partners in LAD Renovations and agree to share profits 30%, 60% and 10%, respectively. Their partnership agreement states that the partners are entitled to receive interest on capitals at 10% per annum; 10% per annum interest is charged on drawings; David and Linda are both entitled salaries of £5,000 per annum. The agreed balances on the capital and current accounts at the beginning of the year were as follows:

|  | Capital account £ | Current account £ |
|---|---|---|
| Linda | 78,000 | 2,000 |
| Alan | 156,000 | 13,000 |
| David | 6,000 | 1,000 |

The net profit for appropriation for the year ending 31 December 1998 was £150,000 and the partners' drawings for the year were: Linda £10,000, Alan £10,000, David £60,000.

Draw up the profit and loss appropriation account for LAD Renovations for the year ending 31 December 1998, the entries in the current accounts of the three partners and how they would appear on the balance sheet.

If you followed the correct procedures, your answer should be as follows:

**LAD Renovations**
**Profit and loss appropriation account for the year ended 31 December 1998**

|  |  | £ | £ | £ |
|---|---|---|---|---|
| **Net profit available for appropriation** |  |  |  | 150,000 |
| *Add* Interest on drawings | Linda | 1,000 |  |  |
|  | Alan | 1,000 |  |  |
|  | David | 6,000 |  | 8,000 |
|  |  |  |  | 158,000 |
| *Less* Interest on capital | Linda | 7,800 |  |  |
|  | Alan | 15,600 |  |  |
|  | David | 600 | 24,000 |  |
| *Less* Salaries | Linda | 5,000 |  |  |
|  | David | 5,000 | 10,000 | 34,000 |
| **Balance of profits to be shared** |  |  |  | 124,000 |
|  | Linda 30% | 37,200 |  |  |
|  | Alan 60% | 74,400 |  |  |
|  | David 10% | 12,400 | 124,000 |  |

## Current accounts

|  |  | Linda | Alan | David |
|---|---|---|---|---|
|  |  | £ | £ | £ |
|  | **Opening balance** | 2,000 | 13,000 | 1,000 |
| *Add* |  |  |  |  |
|  | Interest on capital | 7,800 | 15,600 | 600 |
|  | Salary | 5,000 | – | 5,000 |
|  | Share of profits | 36,000 | 72,000 | 12,000 |
|  |  | 50,800 | 100,600 | 18,600 |
| *Less* |  |  |  |  |
|  | Interest on drawings | 1,000 | 1,000 | 6,000 |
|  | Drawings | 10,000 | 10,000 | 60,000 |
|  | **Closing balance** | 39,800 | 89,600 | (47,400) |

## LAD Renovations
### Balance sheet as at 31 December 1998 (extract)

|  |  | £ | £ |
|---|---|---|---|
| Capital accounts | Linda | 78,000 |  |
|  | Alan | 156,000 |  |
|  | David | 6,000 |  |
|  |  |  | 240,000 |
| Current accounts | Linda | 39,800 |  |
|  | Alan | 89,600 |  |
|  | David | (47,400) | 82,000 |
|  |  |  | 322,000 |

It is clear from this that David is in a very poor position. He has a debit balance of £47,400 on his current account. This means that he owes this amount to the business. Unfortunately, his debt is not covered by the balance in his capital account. Later on in this chapter we will see what effect this has on David and the business.

Having looked at the separate elements making up the appropriation account and the balance sheet, we can now put these together to do the final accounts for a partnership using the trial balance. To do this we will return to our example of Rob and John Rennie's business, Hearth & Home, as we have already calculated some of the figures we need. The trial balance drawn up from the partnership books is as follows:

## Hearth & Home
### Trial balance as at 31 December 1998

|  | £ | £ |
|---|---|---|
| Premises | 300,000 |  |
| Furniture and fittings | 60,000 |  |

| | | £ | £ |
|---|---|---:|---:|
| Debtors | | 198,000 | |
| Creditors | | | 37,000 |
| Stock as at beginning of the year | | 96,000 | |
| Purchases and sales | | 245,000 | 532,000 |
| Administration expenses | | 43,000 | |
| Wages | | 67,000 | |
| Provision for doubtful debts | | | 1,000 |
| Capital accounts | Rob | | 270,000 |
| | John | | 130,000 |
| Current accounts | Rob | | 7,000 |
| | John | | 6,000 |
| Drawings | Rob | 40,000 | |
| | John | 27,000 | |
| Bank | | | 93,000 |
| | | 1,076,000 | 1,076,000 |

The following information is also available:

- Stock at 31 December 1998 was valued at £148,000
- The provision for doubtful debts is to be set at £2,000
- Rob Rennie receives a salary of £44,000 and John Rennie a salary of £40,000
- Interest on capital is allowed at 10% per annum
- Interest on drawings charged to Rob Rennie is £4,000

We can now prepare a partnership trading, profit and loss account, including an appropriation section, for the year ending 31 December 1998 and a partnership balance sheet as at 31 December 1998. We can also show the movements on the partners' current accounts for the year and the balances outstanding at the end of the year:

---

**Hearth & Home**
**Trading, profit and loss account for the year ending 31 December 1998**

| | | £000 | £000 | £000 |
|---|---|---:|---:|---:|
| | Sales | | | 532 |
| | Opening stock | | 96 | |
| *Add* | Purchases | | 245 | |
| | | | 341 | |
| *Less* | Closing stock | | 148 | 193 |
| | **Gross profit** | | | 339 |
| *Less* | **Expenses** | | | |
| | Administration | | 43 | |
| | Wages | | 67 | |
| | Provision for doubtful debts | | 1 | 111 |
| | Net profit available for appropriation | | | 228 |
| *Add* | Interest on drawings | | | 4 |
| | | | | 232 |

|  |  | £000 | £000 | £000 |
|---|---|---|---|---|
| *Less* Interest on capital | Rob | 27 | | |
| | John | 13 | 40 | |
| | | | | |
| *Less* Salaries | Rob | 44 | | |
| | John | 40 | 84 | 124 |
| **Balance of profits to be shared** | | | | 108 |
| | Rob 50% | | 54 | |
| | John 50% | | 54 | 108 |

## Current accounts

| | | Rob Rennie £000 | John Rennie £000 |
|---|---|---|---|
| | **Opening balance** | 7 | 6 |
| *Add* | | | |
| | Interest on capital | 27 | 13 |
| | Salary | 44 | 40 |
| | Share of profits | 54 | 54 |
| | | 132 | 113 |
| *Less* | | | |
| | Drawings | 40 | 27 |
| | Interest on drawings | 4 | |
| | **Closing balance** | 88 | 86 |

## Hearth & Home
## Balance sheet as at 31st December 1998

| | | £000 | £000 | £000 |
|---|---|---|---|---|
| **Fixed assets** | | | | |
| Premises | | | 300 | |
| Equipment | | | 60 | 360 |
| **Current assets** | | | | |
| Stock | | | 148 | |
| Debtors | | | 196 | |
| | | | 344 | |
| *Less* **Creditors: amounts due within one year** | | | | |
| Creditors | | 37 | | |
| Bank overdraft | | 93 | 130 | 214 |
| | | | | 574 |
| | | | | |
| Capital accounts | Rob | | 270 | |
| | John | | 130 | 400 |
| | | | | |
| Current accounts | Rob | | 88 | |
| | John | | 86 | 174 |
| | | | | 574 |

## 9.5 Admission of a New Partner

If a business is expanding and requires additional capital or new management skills, the existing partners may decide to admit a new partner. This might be a relative of one of the partners, perhaps a spouse or a sibling. If a new partner were to join the partnership, the existing partners would expect him or her to invest in the partnership. The amount of capital the new partner invests would then reflect his or her share in worth of the business.

From an accounting point of view, the admission of a new partner is relatively simple. There are two points you need to remember. First, you need to rearrange the accounting equation you met in previous chapters to read: total assets *less* the total liabilities of the business gives the net assets (the net worth) of the business. This is written as:

$$\text{Assets} - \text{Liabilities} = \text{Capital}$$
$$\text{or}$$
$$\text{Net assets} = \text{Capital}$$

Second, over the years the business may have developed *goodwill*. This can be difficult to define and measure, but is made up of such things as the business' name and reputation, the loyalty of its workforce, its customer base and its links with suppliers. The existing partners will consider the goodwill of the business as an asset and expect the new partner to recompense them for acquiring a share of it.

We can now show how the accounts look on admission of a new partner. Charlie Wye and Helen Knott are partners in the Wye Knott Café and share profits equally. Their existing capital accounts each show a balance of £60,000. They decide to allow Jonathan Letts join the partnership and he will invest capital of £100,000 in the business and receive a one-third interest in return. They agree that goodwill will be recorded as an asset of the business.

The first step is to draw up the *goodwill account*, the bank account and the partners' capital accounts to show the admission of the new partner. As Jonathan Letts has agreed to invest £100,000 for a one-third interest in the partnership the new capital will be £100,000 × 3 = £300,000. Using the accounting equation, if the capital is £300,000 then the net assets must be the same amount. Therefore the amount for goodwill is as follows:

|  | £ |
|---|---|
| Total net assets of the new partnership | 300,000 |
| Identifiable net assets of the old partnership (£60,000 × 2 = £120,000) | |
| *plus* the investment by the new partner (£100,000) | 220,000 |
| Difference (goodwill) | 80,000 |

This difference of £80,000 represents goodwill which it has been agreed will be recorded in the books of accounts as follows:

### Goodwill account

|       | £      |  | £ |
|-------|--------|--|---|
| Knott | 40,000 |  |   |
| Wye   | 40,000 |  |   |
|       |        |  |   |

### Bank account

|               | £       |  | £ |
|---------------|---------|--|---|
| Capital: Letts | 100,000 |  |   |
|               |         |  |   |

### Capital account: Letts

|  | £ |              | £       |
|--|---|--------------|---------|
|  |   | Bank account | 100,000 |
|  |   |              |         |

### Capital account: Wye

|  | £ |                 | £      |
|--|---|-----------------|--------|
|  |   | Opening balance | 60,000 |
|  |   | Goodwill        | 40,000 |
|  |   |                 |        |

### Capital account: Knott

|  | £ |                 | £      |
|--|---|-----------------|--------|
|  |   | Opening balance | 60,000 |
|  |   | Goodwill        | 40,000 |
|  |   |                 |        |

You will see that after admission of the new partner the balances in the old partners' capital accounts stand at £100,000 each; they have both benefited by £40,000. This is recognised by the opening of a goodwill account. It is usual to leave the goodwill account in the books. It can either be written off immediately in the partners' agreed profit-sharing ratios and their capital accounts debited, or it can be written off over a number of years in the profit and loss account.

## 9.6 Cessation of a Partnership

When a partnership ceases to trade we refer to it as the *cessation* or *dissolution* of the partnership. There are a number of reasons for the cessation of a partnership; for example, one of the partners might want to retire or move away, or one of them might die. When the partnership ceases the accounts must be closed and the assets of the business realised by opening a *realisation account*, which is part of the double-entry bookkeeping system. The accounting steps involved in dealing with the cessation of a partnership are as follows:

1 Open a realisation account.
2 Debit the realisation account with the book value of the assets of the business.
3 Debit the realisation account, thus closing them, and credit the bank account with the expenses of dissolving the partnership.
4 Credit the realisation account and debit the bank account with the cash proceeds from the sale of the assets of the business.
5 Credit the bank account and debit the liability accounts (e.g. creditors) as they are paid.
6 Distribute the profit or loss on the realisation account among the partners according to the agreed ratios.
7 Pay cash to the partners by crediting the bank account and debiting each partner's current and capital account.

To illustrate the cessation of a partnership we will use the example of Rob and John Rennie's business, Hearth & Home, again. At the end of Section 9.4 we drew up the balance sheet as at 31 December 1998. However, Rob and John have decided to dissolve the partnership and on 1 January 1999 the following events occurred: the premises were sold for £260,000 and the equipment for £54,000. The debtors paid £193,000 and the stock was sold for £141,000. The creditors were paid in full. Before we proceed, we will revise the steps we need to take.

1 We need to open an account for all of the items shown on the balance sheet and enter the balances.
2 Next we will close off the fixed assets, stock and debtor accounts by crediting them and entering the corresponding entries on the debit side of the realisation account.
3 Then we can pay off the creditors in full, credit the bank account and debit the creditors' accounts.

**4** At this stage the only accounts which have balances on them are the realisation account, the bank account and the partners' capital accounts. We will total both sides of the realisation account. If the balancing figure has to be added on the debit side to make the totals agree we will know that there is a profit on realisation. In our example, the balancing figure has to go on the credit side, so there is a loss which must be shared equally among the partners. Therefore we will debit their capital accounts with this amount.

**5** The next step is to calculate the balancing figures on the partners' capital accounts. In both cases we have debit balances and these are the proceeds they are due. We will debit the partners' capital accounts to close them and credit the bank account.

**6** Finally, we will total both sides of the bank account. If they do not agree, it will be necessary to work through the example again to find the error.

We will now carry out these steps using the data in the example.

### Premises account

|  | £ |  | £ |
|---|---|---|---|
| Opening balance | 300,000 | Realisation account | 300,000 |
|  |  |  |  |

### Equipment account

|  | £ |  | £ |
|---|---|---|---|
| Opening balance | 60,000 | Realisation account | 60,000 |
|  |  |  |  |

### Stock account

|  | £ |  | £ |
|---|---|---|---|
| Opening balance | 148,000 | Realisation account | 148,000 |
|  |  |  |  |

### Debtors' account

|  | £ |  | £ |
|---|---|---|---|
| Opening balance | 196,000 | Realisation account | 196,000 |
|  |  |  |  |

### Creditors' account

|  | £ |  | £ |
|---|---|---|---|
| Bank | 37,000 | Opening balance | 37,000 |
|  |  |  |  |

### Realisation account

|  | £ |  | £ |
|---|---|---|---|
| Premises | 300,000 | Bank: Sale of premises | 260,000 |
| Equipment | 60,000 | Bank: Sale of equipment | 54,000 |
| Stock | 148,000 | Bank: Sale of stock | 141,000 |
| Debtors | 196,000 | Bank: Debtors realised | 193,000 |
|  |  | Loss on realisation: Rob | 28,000 |
|  |  | John | 28,000 |
|  | 704,000 |  | 704,000 |
|  |  |  |  |

### Bank account

|  | £ |  | £ |
|---|---|---|---|
| Realisation: Premises | 260,000 | Opening balance | 93,000 |
| Realisation: Equipment | 54,000 | Creditors | 37,000 |
| Realisation: Stock | 141,000 | Capital accounts: Rob | 330,000 |
| Realisation: Debtors | 193,000 | John | 188,000 |
|  | 648,000 |  | 648,000 |
|  |  |  |  |

### Capital account: Rob Rennie

|  | £ |  | £ |
|---|---|---|---|
| Loss on realisation | 28,000 | Opening balance | 270,000 |
| Bank | 330,000 | Current accounts | 88,000 |
|  | 358,000 |  | 358,000 |
|  |  |  |  |

### Capital account: John Rennie

|  | £ |  | £ |
|---|---|---|---|
| Loss on realisation | 28,000 | Opening balance | 130,000 |
| Bank | 188,000 | Current account | 86,000 |
|  | 216,000 |  | 216,000 |
|  |  |  |  |

In this example the liabilities of the business, the creditors, were paid off in full. If this had not been the case, the entries would have been put through the realisation account. First, the creditors' account would have been closed by debiting with the final balance and crediting the realisation account. When the agreed amount was paid, the bank would have credited and the realisation account would have been debited.

The realisation account shows that a loss has been made of £56,000 and this has been shared equally between the two partners by crediting the realisation account and debiting their capital accounts. Their current accounts are then closed by transferring the outstanding balances to their respective capital accounts. The capital accounts are closed by entering the difference between the debit and credit entries. In both cases this is a debit entry which represents the amount of money owed by the business to the partner. The corresponding credit entries are entered into the bank account to represent the money paid to the partners. The two sides of the bank account should now agree. If they do not balance, you have made an error and need to work through the procedures again until you find it.

There is one occasion when the above procedures are not used. This is when one (or more) of the partners becomes *insolvent*. In this case, there will be a debit balance on the relevant partner's account. If the partner had money and paid this into the partnership, you would debit the bank account and close the partner's account by crediting it. However, if the partner has no cash, the capital account will show a deficit which must be shared among the other partners in the ratio of their capital accounts. This provision was set out in a famous legal case, *Garner* v. *Murray* (1904). To demonstrate the accounting procedures when one partner is insolvent we will return to our example of LAD Renovations, the business owned by Linda, Alan and David. On 31 December their balance sheet was as follows (*see page 129*).

The partnership was dissolved on 1 January 1999 and the premises were sold for £156,000, plant and equipment for £80,900. The stock was sold for

## LAD Renovations
## Balance Sheet as at 31 December 1998

|  | £ | £ | £ |
|---|---|---|---|
| **Fixed assets** | | | |
| Premises | | 172,000 | |
| Plant and equipment | | 84,500 | 256,500 |
| **Current assets** | | | |
| Stock | | 44,800 | |
| Debtors | | 84,300 | |
| | | 129,100 | |
| *Less* **Creditors: amounts due within one year** | | | |
| Creditors | 38,100 | | |
| Bank overdraft | 19,500 | 57,600 | 71,500 |
| | | | 328,000 |
| Capital accounts | Linda | 78,000 | |
| | Alan | 156,000 | |
| | David | 6,000 | 240,000 |
| Current accounts | Linda | 39,800 | |
| | Alan | 89,600 | |
| | David | (41,400) | 88,000 |
| | | | 328,000 |

£42,600 and the debtors realised £72,100. Creditors were settled for £37,100. David was unable to make any contribution to the dissolution of the partnership. These accounting transactions are shown as follows:

### Realisation account

|  | £ |  | £ |
|---|---|---|---|
| Premises | 172,000 | Creditors | 38,100 |
| Plant and equipment | 84,500 | Bank: Sale of premises | 156,000 |
| Stock | 44,800 | Bank: Sale of plant and equipment | 80,900 |
| Debtors | 84,300 | Bank: Sale of stock | 42,600 |
| Payment of creditors | 37,100 | Bank: Debtors realised | 72,100 |
| | | Loss on realisation: Linda | 99,000 |
| | | Alan | 19,800 |
| | | David | 3,300 |
| | 422,700 | | 422,700 |

**Bank account**

| | £ | | £ |
|---|---|---|---|
| Realisation: Premises | 156,000 | Opening balance | 19,500 |
| Realisation: Plant and equipment | 80,900 | Creditors | 37,100 |
| Realisation: Stock | 42,600 | Payment to Linda | 95,000 |
| Realisation: Debtors | 72,100 | Payment to Alan | 200,000 |
| | 351,600 | | 351,600 |
| | | | |

**Capital accounts**

| | Linda | Alan | David | | Linda | Alan | David |
|---|---|---|---|---|---|---|---|
| | £ | £ | £ | | £ | £ | £ |
| Current account | | | 41,400 | Opening balance | 78,000 | 156,000 | 6,000 |
| Loss on realisation | 9,900 | 19,800 | 3,300 | Current accounts | 39,800 | 89,600 | |
| David* | 12,900 | 25,800 | | Linda* | | | 12,900 |
| Bank | 95,000 | 200,000 | | Alan* | | | 25,800 |
| | 117,800 | 245,600 | 44,700 | | 117,800 | 245,600 | 44,700 |

* *Garner* v. *Murray* (1904).

David's deficit is £38,700 which must be shared by Linda and Alan in the same proportions as their share of capital: 30% and 60% respectively. The balances outstanding on Linda and Alan's capital accounts are settled by payments from the bank which closes that account.

## 9.7 Conclusions

The partnership profit and loss account is similar to that of a sole trader, except that the figure for net profit is transferred to an additional section known as the appropriation account. This shows the financial transactions of each partner separately and is part of the double-entry bookkeeping system. Interest on capital, salary and share of profit are shown as debit entries; interest on drawings is shown as a credit entry.

Corresponding entries appear in the partnership balance sheet, which shows the closing balances of each partner's capital and current accounts.

When a new partner is admitted a goodwill account is opened so that the existing partners can benefit from the goodwill they have generated. This can be written off immediately or over a period of time. When a partnership is dissolved a realisation account is opened which allows the profit to be calculated and shared among the partners in their agreed profit-sharing ratios. However, if the cause of the cessation of the business is due to the insolvency of one of the partners, under the rules of Garner v. Murray (1904) the other partners must bear the loss in the ratio of their capital accounts.

Having completed this chapter, you should now be able to:

- describe the main features of partnership accounts;
- construct a partnership profit and loss account;
- construct a partnership balance sheet;
- account for the admission of a new partner;
- close the accounts in a number of different circumstances when a partnership ceases.

## Exercises

Complete the following sentences:

**1** Partners are entitled to a salary if ........................................................................

**2** In the absence of a specific agreement between the partners .........................

**3** The value of any goodwill is considered to be ...............................................

**4** Profits on the realisation of a partnership are ..............................................

**5** The main disadvantage of a partnership compared to a limited company is .....

........................................................................................................................

Are the following statements true or false?

**6** Interest on drawings are shown on the debit side of the appropriation account.

**7** The current accounts of partners do not show interest on capital.

**8** Partners must always pay interest on drawings.

**9** If a partner is insolvent any deficit on the capital account is borne by the bank.

**10** A realisation account is part of the double-entry system.

You may wish to read more widely than this book to answer the following questions fully, but you can check the main points by referring to the appropriate sections in this chapter.

**11** Describe the main features of a partnership. (Section 9.2)

**12** Outline the items you would expect to find in a partnership appropriation account. (Section 9.3)

**13** Summarise the accounting procedures which must be followed when dealing with the cessation of a partnership. (Section 9.6)

**14** Explain the importance of *Garner* v. *Murray* (1904) (Section 9.6)

Multiple choice questions (more than one answer may apply):

**15** A partnership:

  **a** is limited to a maximum of 10 partners
  **b** has legal status separate from its owners
  **c** must prepare proper books of account
  **d** is governed by the Companies Act

**16** In the absence of any other agreement the rules of the Partnership Act 1890 state that:

  **a** all partners are entitled to a salary
  **b** losses and profits are shared equally
  **c** partners must contribute equal amounts of capital
  **d** interest must be charged on drawings.

**17** Salaries paid to partners are:

  **a** deducted as a cost before calculating net profit
  **b** shown as a credit on the appropriation account
  **c** shown as a debit on the appropriation account
  **d** shown as a credit to the profit and loss account.

**18** Normally a balance sheet for a partnership shows:

  **a** the capital accounts only
  **b** the current accounts only
  **c** both the capital and current accounts
  **d** neither the capital or current accounts.

**19** Partners can only receive a salary if:

  **a** the business has made a profit
  **b** they work full-time in the business
  **c** the partnership agreement states they can
  **d** they have not contributed any capital.

**20** If there is a loss on the realisation account it is:

  **a** debited to the bank account in the partners profit-sharing ratios
  **b** debited to the capital accounts in their capital-balance ratios
  **c** debited to the capital accounts in their profit-sharing ratios
  **d** credited to the capital accounts in their capital-balance ratios.

Practice questions:

**21** Two brothers, Harold and George Cobb, are in partnership trading as H&G Tool Hire. The following information is available for the year ending 31 December 1998:

| | Harold | George |
|---|---|---|
| Capital accounts | £20,000 | £60,000 |
| Drawings | £35,000 | £32,000 |
| Interest on drawings | £1,500 | £1,000 |
| Salaries | £15,000 | £10,000 |
| Profit share | 60% | 40% |

The net profit available for appropriation is £95,000 and the partners receive 5 per cent interest on their capital. Prepare the appropriation account.

**22** Using the information from Question **21**, show the current accounts for Harold and George Cobb for the year ending 31 December 1998.

**23** Jarvis and Berry are in partnership and call their business J&B Services. Their capital accounts each show a balance of £120,000. They agree to let Lindsay join if he agrees to pay £200,000. For this he will receive a one-third interest in the business. Draw up a goodwill account and the partners' capital accounts.

**24** On 1 January 1998 the capital and current accounts of the partners in Page & Partners were as follows:

|         | Capital account | Current account |
|---------|-----------------|-----------------|
| Page    | 50,000          | 4,500           |
| Jones   | 75,000          | 2,000           |
| Beattie | 85,000          | 5,000           |

During the year the following transactions took place:

|         | Salaries | Drawings |
|---------|----------|----------|
| Page    | 15,000   | 55,000   |
| Jones   | 10,000   | 20,000   |
| Beattie | 10,000   | 28,000   |

The net profit for the year was £131,950. Interest on capital is paid at 10% and interest on drawings is charged at 5%. The partners share the profits equally. Prepare the appropriation account and show the partners' current accounts.

**25** Mourne, Noonan & Knight are in partnership, sharing profits equally. The partnership balance sheet as at 30 June 1998 is as follows:

**Mourne, Noonan & Knight**
**Balance Sheet as at 31 December 1998**

|                                          |           | £      | £       | £      |
|------------------------------------------|-----------|--------|---------|--------|
| **Fixed assets**                         |           |        |         |        |
| Premises                                 |           |        |         | 50,000 |
| **Current assets**                       |           |        |         |        |
| Stock                                    |           |        | 48,600  |        |
| Debtors                                  |           |        | 28,200  |        |
|                                          |           |        | 76,800  |        |
| *Less* **Creditors: amounts due within one year** |   |        |         |        |
| Creditors                                |           | 78,300 |         |        |
| Bank overdraft                           |           | 28,700 | 107,000 | 30,200 |
|                                          |           |        |         | 19,800 |
| Capital accounts                         | Mourne    |        | 8,000   |        |
|                                          | Noonan    |        | 6,000   |        |
|                                          | Knight    |        | 2,000   | 16,000 |
| Current accounts                         | Mourne    |        | 2,000   |        |
|                                          | Noonan    |        | 1,400   |        |
|                                          | Knight    |        | 400     | 3,800  |
|                                          |           |        |         | 19,800 |

The partnership was dissolved on 1 July 1998 and the fixed assets were sold for £47,500, stock for £41,100. On the same date, debtors realised £26,800 and creditors were paid in full. However, Knight is insolvent. Prepare accounts to close the partnership.

(Answers on pp. 323–32)

# 10 Financial Reporting by Limited Companies

## 10.1 Introduction

*Financial reporting* is the communication of the financial statements of an organisation to interested parties. All forms of organisations produce some form of annual report on their financial progress and position. For sole traders and partnerships the circulation of these reports is usually restricted to the owners of the business and those with a direct interest, such as the bank and the Inland Revenue. However, the financial reports of limited companies are public documents and because of the importance of such companies in the economy, in this chapter we will focus on financial reporting by *limited companies*. This does not mean that you need to know how to draw up a full set of company accounts which comply with every aspect of the regulations as accountants do, but you do need to be able to read, analyse and interpret company accounts. To do this, you must be familiar with the main features of limited liability companies and understand the regulations that control their accounting activities.

In this chapter we start by looking at those aspects of companies that are of particular importance from an accounting perspective. This is followed by a discussion of the *regulatory framework* under which sole traders, partnerships and companies operate. The regulatory framework comprises the Companies Act 1985, as amended by the Companies Act 1989, which applies to all companies; accounting standards, which apply to all entities whose accounts are intended to give a true and fair view; and Stock Exchange regulations which apply solely to public limited companies listed on the London Stock Exchange (LSE). The chapter concludes with an examination of the main elements of the financial reports of limited companies and a discussion of an increasingly important topic: international harmonisation.

## 10.2 Limited Companies

We looked at the different types of business organisation in Chapter 2, but so far we have described only the accounts of sole traders and partnerships.

Because a sole trader's business is relatively small, the financial statements are fairly easy to understand. To a large extent the financial statements of a partnership are similar to those of a sole trader. However, by far the most important financial statements are those of a *limited company*.

The main advantages limited companies have over sole traders and partnerships are as follows:

- Limited companies can raise more capital.
- They continue even if the owners die.
- The owners' liability is limited to the capital they have agreed to invest in the company.

Limited companies can be divided into *public limited companies (plcs)*, which are often referred to as *listed companies*, and *private limited companies*, which are also referred to as *unlisted companies*.

There are approximately 2,000 public limited companies, many of which are well known high street names. For example, stores such as W. H. Smith, Marks & Spencer, Tesco and J Sainsbury, or banks such as Barclays, Lloyds, Halifax, Midland and National Westminster. Other well known companies are in the food and drinks sector such as RHM, Unigate, Bass, Grand Metropolitan and Guinness. If you look in any broadsheet newspaper, such as the *Independent*, *The Times* or the *Financial Times*, you will find the names and share prices listed of the major public limited companies. Because of their importance to the economy in terms of the numbers they employ and their products and services, information on public limited companies is by far the easiest to obtain. Their activities are reported in the press and they make information about themselves readily available, in particular, their annual report and accounts.

It is an offence for a private limited company to offer its shares to the public, but under the legislation one person alone may form a private company by completing all the formalities. There are approximately 1 million private limited companies in Great Britain. However, some of them are very small with only a handful of employees. As far as reporting requirements are concerned, private companies and public limited companies not listed on the LSE, do not have to comply with Stock Exchange requirements. In addition, there are a number of exceptions and exclusions for private companies relating to the financial information they have to publish.

## Activity

What do you think the main differences are between private and public limited companies?

The most obvious differences are their names and the fact that public limited companies can offer their shares to the public, but there are other dissimilarities. It is usually easier for public companies to raise large amounts of finance because they can offer their shares to the public. Considerable sums of capital are required for some business activities and therefore the company needs to be able to offer its shares to the public. Public limited companies also have a higher public profile and often, but not always, are familiar names and have a good reputation. They can often pay high salaries to attract the best staff and negotiate favourable terms for many of their transactions because of their size and status.

Private limited companies have some advantages over public limited companies. As mentioned above, they do not have to disclose so much information publicly and the formalities for setting up a private limited company are somewhat easier. In fact, companies are normally started as private limited companies. If they are successful and grow, the owners may decide to float the company. This is sometimes referred to as a *floatation* or *going public* because it means that the owners will turn the company into a public company and seek a listing on the LSE. Part of the proceeds from the (new) issue of shares to the public goes to the original owners, who inevitably lose some control of the company. However, they are handsomely paid for the interests they are relinquishing, and could become millionaires.

## 10.3 **The Regulatory Framework**

Financial reporting by limited liability companies is controlled by legislation and a number of different regulations. This is known as the *regulatory framework*. The key elements of the regulatory framework are:

- the *Companies Acts*, the most recent of which is the *Companies Act 1989* which added to and amended the *Companies Act 1985*;
- the pronouncements of the *Accounting Standards Committee (ASC)* in the form of *Statements of Standard Accounting Practice (SSAPs)* and its successor the *Accounting Standards Board (ASB)* in the form of *Financial Reporting Standards (FRSs)*;
- the requirements of the *LSE*, which apply to listed companies only.

The Companies Acts 1985 and 1989 lay down the broad requirements of the financial information which must be disclosed by limited companies, but the details of how and what financial information should be disclosed are contained in accounting standards. The main requirements placed on every limited company by the Companies Acts are as follows:

- All limited companies must register with the *Registrar of Companies.*
- They must file a *memorandum of association*, which defines the company's constitution and objects, and *articles of association*, which contain the internal regulations of the company, with the Registrar of Companies.

- They must keep *accounting records* which show and explain the company's transactions.
- All limited companies must prepare final accounts comprising a *profit and loss account, balance sheet, auditors' report* and *directors' report* in respect of each financial year of the company and lay them before the shareholders (or members) in a general meeting. This forms the basis of the *annual report and accounts* which must also be delivered to the Registrar of Companies and thus becomes a public document.
- Under the Companies Act 1985 external *auditors* must report on all the published accounts of companies and are required to form an opinion as to whether the accounts they audit show a *true and fair view* of the organisation's affairs. This is an important concept in the UK and may be used as an override to depart from legal requirements. Despite its importance, there is no legal definition of the term.

Prior to 1970, financial reporting was governed only by legislation and, for listed companies, the LSE. This basic framework was insufficient for the complexities of business and there were a number of highly publicised cases of companies reporting profits which were misleading. The main problems concerned the amount of flexibility permitted to companies in the way that they could account for transactions and the minimum amount of information they could disclose.

As an answer to these problems, the accounting profession set up the *Accounting Standards Committee (ASC)* with the objective of reducing the flexibility allowed in accounting. In its lifetime, the ASC issued 25 *Statements of Standard Accounting Practice (SSAPs)* dealing with a number of issues. For example, SSAP 12 sets out how companies should account for depreciation, SSAP 2 is concerned with the disclosure of accounting policies and SSAP 24 is concerned with accounting for pension costs.

Although the ASC did much to improve the quality of financial reporting, it never had sufficient authority or resources to deal with all the problems arising. In 1990 it was replaced by the *Accounting Standards Board (ASB)*. This has more financial resources and there is now legal backing attached to accounting standards. The *Urgent Issues Task Force (UITF)* is an offshoot of the ASB and deals with urgent matters. The ASB has issued a number of important accounting standards which are known as *Financial Reporting Standards (FRSs)*. For example, FRS 1 requires companies to provide a cash flow statement in addition to the profit and loss account and balance sheet required by legislation.

It is important to remember that accounting standards apply to all accounts that are intended to give a *true and fair view*. This includes the accounts of sole traders and partnerships. Because of the organisational structure of large, limited companies and the complexity of activities, accounting standards are most important for them.

## Activity

What do you consider are the advantages and disadvantages of having accounting standards?

Looking first at the *advantages*, accounting standards offer a number of benefits to the users and preparers of accounts. The preparers have an authoritative guide to the most appropriate method for accounting for many of the important activities undertaken by companies. The users have additional financial information than that required by legislation alone, as well as information about the basis on which the accounts have been drawn up. This allows comparison of a company's results with other companies and between one year and another.

The main *disadvantage* of accounting standards is that they impose additional work, and therefore additional costs, on companies. This can be a considerable burden on smaller companies. There is also the difficulty of deciding which accounting method would be appropriate for all companies in all industries and in all circumstances.

The requirements of the LSE do not affect accounting in companies as much as the legislation and accounting standards do. The aspects of the Stock Exchange requirements which are most relevant to financial accounting are those concerned with the information that listed companies must disclose. As well as requiring some information to be given in the annual report and accounts, the Stock Exchange requires all listed companies to issue *interim reports* (also known as *interim accounts* or *interim financial statements*) and *preliminary announcements*. Neither of the latter two documents is covered by legislation or accounting standards.

Interim reports must be published at the end of the first 6 months of every financial year and are very much shorter than the annual report and accounts. Essentially they provide only profit-related information, together with an explanatory statement on the company's performance during the half-year. The aim is to give shareholders an overview of the company's progress and therefore the interim financial statement must either be sent to them or advertised in at least one national newspaper no later than 4 months after the end of the period to which the statement relates.

Preliminary announcements of a company's profit or loss must be made prior to the annual report and accounts being issued. The financial information required is similar to that given in the interim statement, but the objective is to ensure that the key financial results for the year are made public as soon as possible to prevent *insider dealing*. This is where individuals, who are in possession of information that can affect the share price of a company, attempt to take advantage of their knowledge by buying or selling shares. Unlike interim reports, companies need lodge the preliminary announcement only with the Stock Exchange; they need not send them to their shareholders.

## 10.4 **The Annual Report and Accounts**

The *annual report and accounts* is the most useful source of financial information issued by limited companies. The document discloses information required by the regulatory framework as well as information on other issues. Anyone can inspect the annual report and accounts filed with the Registrar of Companies on payment of a small fee. Public limited companies make their annual report and accounts freely available and a copy can be obtained by telephoning or writing to the company; using the service offered by the *Financial Times*; or by becoming a shareholder, which means that the company is legally required to send you a copy. In addition, you may be able to find copies for reference purposes in your library.

---

## Activity

Obtain a copy of the annual report and accounts for three different listed companies and identify the main disclosures of information under the three elements of the regulatory framework.

---

In addition to the information that a company must provide, additional material is often provided voluntarily. This may be information about its products, its employees, the environment or any charitable or community work it is involved in. Because companies differ in their activities and the amount of information they volunteer, no two annual reports and accounts are exactly the same. However, the following list shows the type of information you are likely to find:

- chairman's statement;
- highlights of the main financial results;
- operating and financial review;
- corporate governance statement;
- environmental and community issues;
- profit and loss account;
- balance sheet;
- cash flow statement;
- directors' report;
- auditors' report;
- statement of accounting policies;
- notes to the accounts.

In some annual accounts you may find that the profit and loss account and balance sheet are headed '*consolidated*'. This is because the financial statements are for a group of companies, normally a *holding company* and a number of *subsidiary companies*. To allow shareholders to appreciate the activities of the entire group, the individual companies' financial statements are added together to form the consolidated accounts.

Financial reporting is a dynamic and expensive activity. As new corporate issues, such as the environment, directors' remuneration and corporate governance, for example, are raised as areas of public interest, so companies must attempt to address them in their annual report and accounts, either voluntarily or mandatorily. This has resulted in the annual report and accounts of major companies expanding greatly; some now exceed 100 pages. In addition to publishing printed copies of their annual report, some companies provide Braille, audio and video versions. Recently, the Internet has become another medium through which companies communicate their annual results. The cost of these activities, together with the cost of posting the annual report and accounts (and possibly the interim financial statements as well) to all shareholders, is an expensive exercise.

To help reduce this burden and the size and complexity of the annual report and accounts for private shareholders, since April 1990 listed companies have been able to issue *summary financial statements* instead of the full report and accounts, providing certain conditions are met. A summary financial statement need only contain a minimum amount of financial information, taking up some three or four pages, but many companies have chosen to incorporate it in a larger document often referred to as an *annual review*. The annual review also contains voluntarily provided information, usually concerning the company's products, progress and activities, in an attractive and easy-to-digest format. However, if a company's shareholders choose to receive the summary financial statements instead of the full report and accounts, the company must still prepare the full report and accounts and send them to the Registrar of Companies.

In addition to the legal provisions to reduce the burden of financial reporting by large companies, there are some which affect financial reporting by smaller companies. If a company meets certain size conditions relating to turnover, total assets and number of employees, it qualifies as either 'small' or 'medium-sized'. This allows the company to file *abbreviated accounts* with the Registrar of Companies instead of the full report and accounts. However, the company must continue to send the full report and accounts to its shareholders.

## 10.5 International Harmonisation

As companies have become larger and increasingly more multinational in their activities and ownership, pressure for *international harmonisation* of financial regulation has grown. In the past, financial regulations have been country-specific; thus, the Companies Act 1985 and UK accounting standards have applied only to UK companies. Other countries have developed their own regulatory systems. Some countries in the developing world have minimal legislation, whilst other countries, such as the USA, have a very highly developed and prescriptive system of regulation.

Not surprisingly, with most countries having separate regulatory frameworks, there have been some significant differences in accounting treatments. These are emphasised when a company seeks a listing on a Stock Exchange in another country; for example, a UK company wanting its shares to be traded on the New York Stock Exchange (NYSE) as well as on the LSE. In such circumstances the company must prepare two sets of accounts: one complying with UK requirements, the other complying with US requirements. This usually results in different figures for profit in the two sets of accounts, and this can mean that a UK or other European company might report a profit in their own country, but a loss in the USA.

In an attempt to resolve this confusing state of affairs, the *International Accounting Standards Committee (IASC)* was established in 1973. Their task has been particularly hard as countries are understandably reluctant to change their own standards which have been developed in the context of their own accounting practices. They have also found it difficult to agree the regulations that would be appropriate for all companies in all countries and in all circumstances. In recent years the problems facing multinational companies, auditors, investors and national regulators have escalated and in 1987 the *International Organisation for Securities' Commissions (IOSCO)* was formed to establish internationally agreed accounting standards to aid in multinational share offering by companies. Although critical of the international accounting standards issued by the IASC in the past, IOSCO is now actively cooperating in improving them. It is too early to predict how close we are to harmonising international accounting standards. However, there is every indication of close collaboration between the major countries' national standard-setters, including the UK's ASB, and it is likely that within a few years a set of international accounting standards will have been agreed. This would mean that multinational companies would need only prepare one set of accounts which would be acceptable to Stock Exchanges in different countries.

## 10.6 **Conclusions**

In this chapter we have looked at the various sources of information on limited liability companies and the importance of one of the main sources: the annual report and accounts. We have examined the impact of the regulatory framework on the information published by limited companies and the nature of information disclosed in the annual report and accounts. We have also considered the possibility of the international harmonisation of accounting standards.

Having completed this chapter, you should now be able to:

- describe the main features of limited companies;
- explain the principal regulations affecting financial reporting by limited companies;

- describe the information contained in the annual report and accounts of a limited company;
- evaluate the information contained in an annual report and accounts;
- discuss the international harmonisation of accounting standards.

## Exercises

Complete the following sentences:

**1** With limited companies, the shareholders' liability is ......................................
.............................................................................................................................

**2** The three elements of the regulatory framework are ....................................
.............................................................................................................................

**3** The Accounting Standards Committee (ASC)was replaced in 1990 by ..........
.............................................................................................................................

**4** A summary financial statement is ................................................................

**5** The two bodies working together to achieve international harmonisation of accounting standards are .............................................................................

Are the following statements true or false?

**6** Only public limited companies can be listed on the Stock Exchange.

**7** Private limited companies do not have to send their annual report and accounts to shareholders.

**8** Under the Companies Act 1985, all accounts must give a true and fair view.

**9** Interim reports are required under Stock Exchange regulations.

**10** All limited companies must publish preliminary announcements.

You may wish to read more widely than this book to answer the following questions fully, but you can check the main points by referring to the appropriate sections in this chapter.

**11** What are the main advantages of a limited company compared with a sole trader? (Section 10.2)

**12** What are the main requirements for financial reporting by a limited company? (Section 10.3)

**13** Which companies must comply with Stock Exchange regulations? (Section 10.3)

**14** What are the benefits of international harmonisation? (Section 10.5)

Multiple choice questions (more than one answer may apply):

**15** The memorandum of association provides information concerning:

   **a** accounts and audit
   **b** meetings and voting rights
   **c** the objects of the company
   **d** the powers and duties of directors.

**16** A limited liability company:

   **a** must have at least three shareholders
   **b** must be quoted on the Stock Exchange
   **c** must have the letters 'plc' after its name
   **d** is a company where the liability of its shareholders is limited to the amount that they have agreed to invest.

**17** A private limited company must have:

    **a** a minimum of 30 shareholders
    **b** a maximum of 30 shareholders
    **c** a minimum of 2 and a maximum of 30 shareholders
    **d** none of these.

**18** Accounting standards issued by the Accounting Standards Board (ASB) apply:

    **a** to all companies world-wide
    **b** to all accounts of UK companies intended to give a true and fair view
    **c** to the accounts of public limited companies only
    **d** only if the company employs a qualified accountant.

**19** Interim statements issued by companies are required by:

    **a** The Companies Act 1985
    **b** Stock Exchange regulations
    **c** accounting standards
    **d** all of these.

**20** If the owners of a private limited company decide to float it on the Stock Exchange, this means that:

    **a** the company is going into liquidation
    **b** the accounts will not comply with accounting standards
    **c** the company will be listed on the Stock Exchange
    **d** the company will be multinational.

Practice questions:

**21** Describe the main contents of the annual report and accounts of a listed company.
**22** Describe the different types of financial report that listed companies are required to publish.
**23** Explain the standard-setting structure in the UK.
**24** Describe the main features of the regulatory framework for listed companies.
**25** Do you consider that accounting standards have improved financial reporting in the UK and, if so, how?

(Answers on pp. 332–3)

# 11 The Financial Statements of a Limited Company

## 11.1 Introduction

The financial statements of a *limited company* form the key contents of the annual report and accounts. They differ significantly from those of sole traders and partnerships, mainly because the former are more likely to be undertaking activities which are regulated by accounting standards. We start by considering the *profit and loss account* and *balance sheet* of limited companies, both of which are required by company legislation. We then go on to look at the *cash flow statement* and the *statement of total recognised gains and losses*, which are required by accounting standards. At an introductory level you do not need a detailed knowledge of these last two statements, but merely to appreciate their purpose and general content.

Throughout the chapter we use *consolidated statements* to illustrate the financial statements of limited companies. A consolidated statement is one in which the information contained in the individual financial statements of a group of companies has combined, subject to any consolidation adjustments.

## 11.2 The Published Profit and Loss Account

When you first look at the *profit and loss account* of a limited company you will see that it differs in many ways from that of the sole trader. One major difference is that you do not find the detailed information on costs. The reason for this is that limited companies are not obliged to disclose this information. Because of the different types and sizes of limited companies, and the diverse nature of their business transactions, their profit and loss accounts look different. However, there are always a considerable number of similarities because of the requirements of the regulatory framework we discussed in Chapter 10. The following simple example shows a consolidated profit and loss account:

**RWJ Group plc**
**Consolidated profit and loss account for the year**
**ending 30 June 1998**

|  | £000 |
|---|---|
| **Turnover** | 1,000 |
| Cost of sales | (500) |
| Gross profit | 500 |
| Other operating costs | (300) |
| **Operating profit** | 200 |
| Net interest payable | (30) |
| **Profit on ordinary activities before taxation** | 170 |
| Tax on profit on ordinary activities | (70) |
| **Profit on ordinary activities after taxation** | 100 |
| Minority interests | (20) |
| **Profit on ordinary activities attributable to shareholders** | 80 |
| **Dividends** | (40) |
| **Retained profit for the year** | 40 |
| Earnings per share | 25p |

If you compare our simple example with a published example from a company's annual report and accounts, you will see that one of the main differences is that the published example also gives the *previous year's figures*. This is a requirement of the Companies Act 1985. You will also find that the published profit and loss account makes reference to various *notes*. This is additional information which is not included on the face of the profit and loss account, but in the notes which follow the financial statements.

There are a number of items in our example that you will also find in most published profit and loss accounts and these require some explanation. Because it is important to appreciate how a limited company is financed and the cost of borrowing money, the figure of operating profit is shown before any *interest* is charged. Then, since limited companies are subject to *tax*, this figure is also shown.

The next unusual term is *minority interests*. As already mentioned, all the profit and loss accounts for the group of companies have been added together resulting in a consolidated profit and loss account. However, in some of the subsidiary companies there may be a few other shareholders who are entitled to a share of the profit. Therefore these minority interests are deducted next from the profit.

After interest, tax and minority interests, the remaining *profit* belongs to the shareholders. Some will be paid to them in the form of dividends in return for their investment and some will be retained for reinvestment in the company to make it grow.

The final figure shows the *earnings per share (EPS)*. This is a performance measure on which many shareholders place considerable weight. Normally a company pays out only a proportion of the profit on ordinary activities to shareholders in the form of a dividend. The remainder is retained in the company to help it grow, as in our example. This retained profit still belongs to the shareholders and therefore the dividend they receive is only part of the return on their investment. The EPS figure shows the total return. In general terms it is calculated by dividing the profit on ordinary activities attributable to ordinary shareholders by the number of ordinary shares issued. In our example the company has issued 32,000 ordinary shares. Thus:

$$\text{EPS} = \frac{\pounds 8,000}{32,000} = 25\text{p}$$

The figure for EPS is not required by law, but was originally introduced by *SSAP 3, Earnings Per Share*. Because there are a number of different ways of calculating EPS, you will find that some companies give two or three different figures. One must be calculated according to SSAP 3; the others are calculations which the company has decided are relevant to its own circumstances.

Some companies provide a detailed analysis of certain figures, breaking them down into *continuing operations, acquisitions* and *discontinued operations.* This is the result of *FRS 3, Reporting Financial Performance,* which was issued in 1992 to assist investors to appreciate the underlying trend of the company's financial performance and any significant changes in its operation. FRS 3 requires companies to provide a breakdown of turnover and operating profit by continuing operations, acquisitions and discontinued operations on the face of the profit and loss account. A similar analysis must be made for the items between turnover and operating profit, but this can be shown either on the face of the profit and loss account or as a note to the accounts. If the company has disposed of a significant part of its activities during the year, this allows investors to see what contribution to financial performance was made by operations that will be continued. Conversely, if the company has made any acquisitions during the year, investors can see what contribution they have made to financial performance.

## Activity

Find the profit and loss account in the annual reports you have obtained and identify the items described in Section 11.2.

## 11.3 The Published Balance Sheet

The *balance sheet* of a limited company looks very similar to the vertical format balance sheet of a sole trader. However, there may be some terms with which you are not familiar. The main terms are as follows:

- *Share capital* – This is the money invested by the owners of the business. Most shares are in denominations of 25p. This is the nominal or face value of the share. For example, a company may have issued 4 million 25p shares. The amount shown on the balance sheet will be £1 million (4 million × 25p). However, if you wanted to buy or sell one of the company's shares, you would need to know the *market price*, which is likely to be very different and depends on a number of different factors.
- *Debentures* – These are long-term loans to the company, usually made by financial institutions. They are not part of share capital and debenture holders receive interest rather than a dividend.
- *Minority interests* – As explained already, these represent the interests of individual shareholders in subsidiary companies who are entitled to receive a share of the profits of the holding company in the form of dividends.
- *Reserves* – A company may identify a number of different reserves which may have arisen for a variety of reasons. Normally the largest reserve represents the profit which has been earned in previous years, but which has been kept in the business to help it grow.

The balance sheet of a limited company is made up of three sections:

- *Assets* – *Fixed assets* are assets which are held in the business on a continuing basis. They include *tangible assets*, such as land, factories and machines, and *intangible assets*, such as spending on research and development (R&D), and goodwill. *Current assets* are assets which are expected to be converted into cash within the next 12 months. They include, in order of liquidity, stocks, debtors and cash.
- *Creditors* – *Creditors: amounts falling due within one year* are current liabilities. These are debts where repayment is due within 1 year, such as overdrafts or goods bought on credit. Current liabilities are subtracted from current assets to give *net current assets* or *working capital*. The value of fixed assets can then be added to give *total assets less current liabilities*. *Creditors: amounts falling due after more than one year* are long-term liabilities. These are debts on which repayment is due after 1 year, such as long-term bank loans. This figure can be subtracted from *total assets less current liabilities* to give *net assets*.
- *Capital and reserves* – The company's issued share *capital*, which is the value of shares (based on their nominal value rather than on their current market price) is added to the company's reserves or retained profit to give *capital employed*. This must balance with the figure for net assets.

The following simple example shows a consolidated balance sheet.

**RWJ Group plc**
**Consolidated balance sheet as at 30 June 1998**

|  | £000 |
|---|---:|
| **Fixed assets** | |
| Tangible assets | 60 |
| Investments | 40 |
|  | 100 |
| **Current assets** | |
| Stock | 30 |
| Debtors | 30 |
| Cash | 30 |
|  | 90 |
| **Creditors: amounts falling due within one year** | |
| Trade creditors | (40) |
| Overdraft | (10) |
| **Net current assets** | 40 |
| **Total assets *less* current liabilities** | 140 |
| **Creditors: amounts falling due after more than one year** | (25) |
| **Provisions for liabilities and charges** | (25) |
| **Minority interests** | (5) |
| **Total net assets** | 85 |
| **Capital and reserves** | |
| Called-up share capital | 45 |
| Profit and loss account | 40 |
| **Shareholders' funds** | 85 |

## Activity

Find the balance sheet in the annual reports you have obtained and identify the items described in the above example.

## 11.4 The Published Cash Flow Statement

The published *cash flow statement* is required by *FRS 1, Cash Flow Statements,* which was introduced in 1991 and amended in 1996. This reporting standard contains some specialist terms and definitions, but essentially the statement is a summary of the cash going in and out of the business. It is designed to show the relationship between profit ability and cash-generating ability and thus the quality of the profit earned. The following simple example shows a consolidated cash flow statement:

## RWJ Group plc
## Consolidated cash flow statement for the year ending 30 June 1998

|  | £000 | £000 |
|---|---:|---:|
| **Cash flow from operating activities** |  | 8,000 |
| **Returns on investments and servicing of finance** |  |  |
| Interest received | 250 |  |
| Interest paid | (1,000) |  |
| Preference dividends paid | (200) |  |
| **Net cash outflow for returns on investments and servicing of finance** |  | (1,050) |
| **Taxation** |  | (1,100) |
| **Capital expenditure and financial investment** |  |  |
| Purchase of tangible fixed assets | (1,750) |  |
| Sale of plant and machinery | 1,300 |  |
| **Net cash outflow for capital expenditure and financial investment** |  | (450) |
| **Acquisitions and disposals** |  |  |
| Purchase of subsidiary undertaking | (11,000) |  |
| Sale of business | 2,100 |  |
| **Net cash outflow for acquisitions and disposals** |  | (8,900) |
| **Equity dividends paid** |  | (1,300) |
| Cash outflow before use of liquid resources and financing |  | **(4,800)** |
| **Management of liquid resources** |  |  |
| Purchase of government securities | (2,500) |  |
| Sale of government securities | 2,100 |  |
| Sale of corporate bonds | 1,100 |  |
| **Net cash inflow from management of liquid resources** |  | 700 |
| **Financing** |  |  |
| Issue of shares | 300 |  |
| Increase in debt | 1,200 |  |
|  |  | 1,500 |
| **Decrease in cash in the period** |  | **(2,600)** |

## Activity

Find the cash flow statements in the annual reports you have obtained and identify the items described in the above example.

## 11.5 Statement of Total Recognised Gains and Losses

The *statement of total recognised gains and losses* for limited companies was introduced by *FRS 3, Reporting Financial Performance*, to enable users of company financial statements to consider all recognised gains and losses. It not only includes the profit or loss for the period from the profit and loss account, but also all other recognised gains and losses which may have occurred during the period, which are normally transferred direct to the reserves on the balance sheet.

For example, a company decides that the property it owns has increased in value over the years. The property is currently shown in the balance sheet at its historic cost, but the company wants to show it at its new value so that shareholders can appreciate the value of what they own. To show this increased value or gain, the company increases the assets in the balance sheet. However, it must make a corresponding entry to make the balance sheet balance. It cannot put the surplus through the profit and loss account because, although the increase has been recognised, the company has not sold the property and therefore no profit has been realised. Instead, the company creates a *revaluation reserve* which is placed under the 'capital and reserves' heading in the balance sheet.

Although the statement of total recognised gains and losses is not significant for most companies in terms of the number of items it contains, the amounts involved may be highly significant and can be larger than the realised profit for the period. For this reason it must be given the same prominence as the profit and loss account, the balance sheet and the cash flow statement. If a company does not have any recognised gains or losses other than the profit or loss for the period, no statement need be provided, but a note to this effect must be given immediately after the profit and loss account.

The following example shows most items that could appear in a consolidated statement of total recognised gains and losses. As it is purely an illustrative example, no figures are shown:

---

**RWJ Group plc**
**Consolidated statement of total recognised gains and losses**
**for the year ending 30 June 1998**

|  | 1998 £m | 1997 £m |
|---|---|---|
| Profit for the year | X | X |
| Unrealised surplus on revaluation of properties | X | X |
| Unrealised (loss)/gain on trade investments | (X) | X |
|  | X | X |
| Currency translation differences on foreign currency net investments | (X) | X |
| Total recognised gains and losses relating to the year | X | X |

---

Before FRS 3 was introduced, recognised gains and losses of this nature were shown in the reserves. However, they were often missed or their significance not fully appreciated. The statement of recognised gains and losses brings these factors to the attention of the investor and shows the gains and losses attributable to the shareholder.

## Activity

Find the statement of total recognised gains and losses in the annual reports you have obtained and identify the items described in the above example.

## 11.6 Conclusions

In this chapter we have examined the consolidated profit and loss account, balance sheet and cash flow statement, as well as the statement of total recognised gains and losses published by limited companies. These four financial statements form the key components of the annual report and accounts of limited companies. We have also looked at the terminology and structure of these financial statements and the regulatory framework under which they are required.

Having completed this chapter, you should now be able to:

- describe the published profit and loss account;
- describe the published balance sheet;
- describe the published cash flow statement;
- describe the statement of total recognised gains and losses of a limited company.

## Exercises

Complete the following sentences:

**1** Minority interests represent ...................................................................................
**2** Debentures are ...........................................................................................................
**3** Share capital is calculated by ...............................................................................
**4** FRS 1 requires companies to produce a ...............................................................
**5** The statement of total recognised gains and losses is intended to show

.......................................................................................................................................

Are the following statements true or false?

**6** A company's profit and loss account shows interest before operating profit is calculated.
**7** Earnings per share is the same as dividends.
**8** The balance sheet of a limited company does not show fixed assets.
**9** Cash flow statements are required by FRS 3.
**10** The statement of total recognised gains and losses gives the cash position of the company.

You may wish to read more widely than this book to answer the following questions fully, but you can check the main points by referring to the appropriate sections in this chapter.

**11** What are the main changes FRS 3 has made to the profit and loss account? (Section 11.2)

**12** What are the calculations for arriving at the figure for earnings per share? (Section 11.2)

**13** What are the items which comprise net current assets on the balance sheet? (Section 11.3)

**14** What is the purpose of the statement of total recognised gains and losses? (Section 11.5)

Multiple choice questions (more than one answer may apply):

**15** If a company has 100,000 ordinary shares and during the year pays dividends of £3,000 and has a retained profit of £5,000, earnings per share figure is:

  **a** 3p
  **b** 5p
  **c** 8p
  **d** 50p.

**16** If the net current assets of a company are £58,000 and current creditors are £22,000, the current assets are:

  **a** £80,000
  **b** £36,000
  **c** £116,000
  **d** £44,000.

**17** Minority interests in the profit and loss account represent:

  **a** interest paid to lenders of finance
  **b** a charge made by the holding company of the group of companies
  **c** amounts set aside for tax
  **d** shareholdings which are external to the group of companies.

**18** The number of shares in a company is 50,000 and the denomination of each share is 25p. A dividend of 15% has proposed. Therefore, the total amount of the proposed dividend is:

  **a** £750
  **b** £7,500
  **c** £1,875
  **d** £187.50.

**19** The net profit this year is £9,876 and the net profit brought forward from last year is £1,234. £3,654 was transferred to reserves and a provision of £3,456 made for corporation tax. The proposed dividend is £1,432. Therefore, the net balance on the profit and loss account carried forward to next year will be:

  **a** £100
  **b** £2,568
  **c** £19,652
  **d** £5,432.

**20** A statement of total recognised gains and losses is:

  **a** only required if a cash flow statement is not prepared
  **b** not required if there are no recognised gains or losses
  **c** only required for multinational companies
  **d** a reconciliation between the balance sheet and the cash flow statement.

Practice questions:

**21** Explain the main items you would expect to find on the profit and loss account of a limited company which are not present on the profit and loss account of a sole trader.

**22** Explain the main items you would expect to find on the balance sheet of a limited company which are not present on the balance sheet of a sole trader.

**23** Describe the disclosure requirements in respect of the profit and loss account under FRS 3.

**24** Explain what is meant by the term 'earnings per share' and why it is of interest to investors.

**25** Describe the main items in a consolidated cash flow statement.

(Answers on p. 333)

# 12 Interpretation of Financial Statements

## 12.1 Introduction

Being able to read and understand the financial statements of a limited company is an achievement worth striving for. It is even more valuable if you can also *analyse* and *interpret* them, because you can then identify the company's financial strengths and weaknesses, and compare them with other companies or with the industry as a whole.

In this chapter we look at how financial performance can be assessed and how the financial stability of a company can be evaluated using a technique known as *ratio analysis*. This technique is widely used by managers, investors, financial journalists and others interested in a company's financial performance. The main data required for ratio analysis comes from the business's financial statements. Although we use a simple example of a sole trader, the same principles apply to partnerships and limited companies.

## 12.2 Purpose of Ratios

*Ratio analysis* is a technique used to describe and interpret the relationships of certain data in the financial statements which would otherwise be devoid of meaning. It allows a comparison to be made between the same company over a period of time, companies of different sizes and a particular company and the industry average. It can be used for the following *purposes*:

- to assess a company's financial performance;
- to evaluate the financial stability of a company;
- to predict the future performance and stability of a company.

To demonstrate the ratios we are going to use the profit and loss account and balance sheet of Harvest Bakery, a business which has been trading in health foods for a number of years. You can assume that Harvest Bakery is a sole trader, but the principles and ratios we describe can also be applied to the financial statements of other forms of business:

155

**Harvest Bakery**
**Profit and loss account for the year ending 31 December 1998**

|  | | £000 | £000 |
|---|---|---:|---:|
| | **Sales** | | 500 |
| *Less* | **Cost of sales** | | 375 |
| | **Gross profit** | | 125 |
| *Less* | **Expenses** | | |
| | Salaries | 30 | |
| | Rent | 10 | |
| | Administration | 9 | |
| | Depreciation | 20 | |
| | Interest | 5 | 74 |
| | **Profit before tax** | | 51 |

**Harvest Bakery**
**Balance sheet as at 31 December 1998**

| | | £000 Cost | £000 Depreciation | £000 Net book value |
|---|---|---:|---:|---:|
| | **Fixed assets** | | | |
| | Fixtures and fittings | 140 | 86 | 54 |
| | **Current assets** | | | |
| | Stock | | 78 | |
| | Debtors | | 46 | |
| | Cash | | 6 | |
| | | | 130 | |
| *Less* | **Creditors: amounts due within one year** | | | |
| | Trade creditors | | 63 | 67 |
| | **Total net assets** | | | 121 |
| | Capital at beginning of year | | 70 | |
| *Add* | Profit | | 51 | |
| | | | 121 | |
| *Less* | Drawings | | 50 | 71 |
| *Add* | Loan | | | 50 |
| | | | | 121 |

The main points to note are as follows:

- The *cumulative depreciation* shown in the balance sheet is all the depreciation that has been charged for the fixed assets since they were acquired. It includes the annual depreciation charge of £20,000 charged in the profit and loss account for 1998.

- The amount of *capital* shown in the balance sheet has increased over the years because the owner has not withdrawn all the profit, but has left some in the business to fund growth.
- In 1998 the owner of the business withdrew £50,000 from the business. This is not shown as a salary because it is the owner withdrawing part of the profit. The *drawings* are therefore shown on the balance sheet as a reduction in the profit.
- To make the exercise easier, *taxation* has been ignored.

## 12.3 **Performance Ratios**

There are a number of ratios which can be used to assess performance. Because the terms used in the ratios can be defined in several different ways, it is important to state the precise meaning of the terms you are using. We will use the following definitions:

- *Return* is defined as profit before interest and tax.
- *Capital employed* is defined as fixed assets, plus current assets, less current liabilities (creditors: amounts due within one year).

Since there are no standard definitions of the above terms, it is important to find out what definitions have been used in any ratios quoted, in order to fully understand what is being referred to and the implications of the ratio calculated. We have defined the term *return* as profit before interest and tax. You should be able to find this figure on the profit and loss account of a business. In the accounts of a limited company it may be labelled *operating profit*.

There are five main profitability ratios:

- *return on capital employed (ROCE)*, also known as the *prime ratio*;
- *profit margin*, also known as the *return on sales (ROS)*;
- *capital turnover*;
- *gross profit mark up*;
- *gross profit margin*, also known as the *gross profit percentage*.

*ROCE* or the *prime ratio* measures the percentage total return on the investment of funds (i.e. capital plus loans). The formula is:

$$\frac{\text{Profit before interest and tax}}{\text{Capital employed}} \times 100$$

Using the data given in the financial statements of Harvest Bakery, we will now calculate the return on capital employed. The first step is to find the figure for profit before interest and tax. On the profit and loss account no figure for tax is shown. The figure of £51,000 profit is therefore before tax.

However, if you look at the costs, you will see that the organisation had to pay interest of £5,000 on a loan. As we want the figure of profit before interest, we must add the figure of £5,000 to the profit of £51,000 (£56,000). Next, find the figure for capital employed, which we defined as fixed assets (£54,000) plus current assets (£130,000) less creditors: amounts due within one year (£63,000). This results in a figure of £121,000. Substituting the figures in the formula, the answer is:

$$\frac{£56,000}{£121,000} \times 100 = 46.3\%$$

The resulting percentage should reflect the element of *risk* in the investment and can be compared with interest rates for other investments where there is barely any risk, such as building society interest rates. It is also useful to compare the prime ratio over time. However, if we want to know how this profitability has been achieved or how it can be improved, we need to look at two subsidiary ratios.

The *profit margin* or *ROS* measures the percentage return on sales (net profit per £1 of sales). The formula is:

$$\frac{\text{Profit before interest and tax}}{\text{Sales}} \times 100$$

We will now calculate the profit margin for Harvest Bakery. We have already found the figure for profit before interest and tax, so now we need to identify the figure for sales which is also on the profit and loss account. Substituting the figures in the formula, the answer is:

$$\frac{£56,000}{£500,000} = 11.2\%$$

Profit margin can be improved by increasing the selling prices and/or reducing costs.

*Capital turnover* measures the level of activity in the business as reflected by sales in relation to the capital employed. In other words, it measures the number of times the assets (the capital employed) are utilised or turned over to achieve those sales. It is usually expressed as the number of times rather than a percentage. The formula is:

$$\frac{\text{Sales}}{\text{Capital employed}}$$

We will now calculate the capital turnover for Harvest Bakery. We used the figures for sales and capital employed when calculating the two previous ratios, so we simply have to substitute them in the formula to arrive at the answer:

$$\frac{£500,000}{£121,000} = 4.13 \text{ times}$$

The level of activity should be as high as possible for the lowest level of investment. Capital turnover can be improved by increasing sales activity or decreasing capital employed (perhaps by reducing loans), or by selling off fixed assets which are no longer used.

These three ratios are interrelated:

Profit margin × Capital turnover = Return on capital employed

We can test this using the Harvest Bakery data:

$$11.2\% \times 4.13 = 46.3\%$$

A business can improve its prime ratio by reducing costs and/or raising prices, which will improve its profit margin. Alternatively, it can increase its sales volume and/or reduce its capital employed, which will improve its capital turnover.

## Activity

Which of the following methods would you suggest Harvest Bakery uses to try to improve the capital turnover:

**a** Decrease the sales volume?
**b** Increase the sales volume?
**c** Reduce the capital invested in the business?
**d** Keep the capital invested in the business at the same level?

What the owners of Harvest Bakery need to do is to increase the sales volume and at the same time keep the capital invested at the same level or, if possible, reduce it. Therefore all the answers are correct except **a**. In some profit and loss accounts you may also be given the figure for gross profit, as in the Harvest Bakery example. In some industries, retailing in particular, the gross profit figure is considered to be an essential feature of management control and a guide to pricing and purchasing policies.

The *gross profit mark up* measures gross profit as a percentage of cost of sales. The formula is:

$$\frac{\text{Gross profit}}{\text{Cost of sales}} \times 100$$

We will now calculate the gross profit mark up for Harvest Bakery. We need to look at the profit and loss account to find the figures for gross profit and cost of sales. Substituting the figures in the formula, the answer is:

$$\frac{£125}{£375} \times 100 = 33.3\%$$

The *gross profit margin* or the *gross profit percentage* measures gross profit as a percentage of sales. The formula is:

$$\frac{\text{Gross profit}}{\text{Sales}} \times 100$$

We will now calculate the gross profit margin for Harvest Bakery. We used the figure for gross profit in the last ratio, so you need only look up the sales figure in the profit and loss account. Substituting the figures in the formula, the answer is:

$$\frac{£125}{£500} \times 100 = 25\%$$

As with the other profitability ratios, trends and inter-company comparisons are useful when interpreting gross profit mark up and gross profit margin.

## 12.4 Liquidity Ratios

*Liquidity ratios* reflect the financial stability of a business and show how effectively the business is managing its working capital. There are four main ratios:

- the *current test ratio*, also known as the *working capital ratio*;
- the *acid test ratio*, also known as the *quick ratio* or the *liquid capital ratio*;
- the *debt collection period* or *credit ratio*;
- the *credit period ratio*.

The *current test ratio* or *working capital ratio* gives an overall view of the financial stability of a company. *Working capital* or *net current assets* is the term used for current assets less creditors: amounts due within one year. The current test ratio is usually expressed as a ratio of $x:1$ rather than a percentage. The formula is:

$$\frac{\text{Current assets}}{\text{Creditors: amounts due within one year}}$$

Using the data given in the financial statements of Harvest Bakery, we will now calculate the current test ratio. We need to look at the balance sheet to obtain the figures for this ratio. Substituting the figures in the formula, the answer is:

$$\frac{£130,000}{£63,000} = 2.1:1$$

It is useful to consider what the ratio 2.1:1 means. In simple terms we are saying that the business has £2.10 of current assets for every £1 of current liabilities. Therefore, if the creditors had to be paid, the business should have enough current resources to do so without having to obtain a loan or sell off its fixed assets. In many industries there are benchmarks of what is considered to be a good current test ratio. Generally, if the ratio drops below 1.5:1 it may indicate a lack of liquidity; a ratio of above 2:1 could indicate poor management of working capital. A ratio of 0.9:1 would indicate that the business would be unable to pay its creditors. However, it is essential to relate the ratio to the type of business and its trend over a period of time.

The *acid test ratio, quick ratio* or *liquid capital ratio* is a more stringent test of liquidity than the current test ratio. It is similar to the current ratio except that it excludes stock. It shows the relationship between the business's liquid assets and its current liabilities. The acid test ratio is usually expressed as a ratio of $x:1$ rather than a percentage. The formula is:

$$\frac{\text{Current assets} - \text{Stock}}{\text{Creditors: amounts due within one year}}$$

which, for Harvest Bakery, is the same as:

$$\frac{\text{Debtors} + \text{Cash}}{\text{Creditors: amounts due within one year}}$$

Using the Harvest Bakery data, we will now calculate the acid test ratio.

$$\frac{\text{Current assets} - \text{Stock}}{\text{Creditors: amounts due within one year}} = \frac{£130,000 - £78,000}{£63,000} = 0.8:1$$

or

$$\frac{\text{Debtors} + \text{Cash}}{\text{Creditors: amounts due within one year}} = \frac{£46,000 + £6,000}{£63,000} = 0.8:1$$

Generally the ratio should not fall below 1:1. However, this would not be true of all businesses. For example, some businesses collect from debtors weekly, but pay their creditors monthly. This results in a low level of debtors and higher level of creditors, varying according to the time of the month. It is hard to generalise about ideal levels of liquidity, but trends and inter-firm comparisons make this an important ratio to use as a measure of liquidity.

The *debt collection period ratio*, or *credit ratio*, measures the average time in days (or months) that debtors take to settle their accounts. It attempts to give an indication of the effectiveness of working capital management. The formula is:

$$\frac{\text{Debtors at the end of the year}}{\text{Sales}} \times 365 \text{ days (or 12 months)}$$

We will now calculate the debt collection period for Harvest Bakery. We need to look at the balance sheet to obtain the figures for this ratio. Substituting the figures in the formula, the correct answer is:

$$\frac{£46,000}{£500,000} \times 365 = 34 \text{ days} \qquad \text{or} \qquad \frac{£46,000}{£500,000} \times 12 = 1.1 \text{ months}$$

This means that, on average, Harvest Bakery' customers take 34 days or 1.1 months to pay. If company policy or the industry average is 1 month's credit, then 45 days (the average length of the credit period) is what we would expect. Therefore, 34 days indicates good management; 76 days, for example, would indicate bad management. It appears that the managers of Harvest Bakery are very efficient in collecting money that is owed to the business, although we would want to make comparisons to ensure that we are drawing the correct conclusions.

The *credit period ratio* measures the average time in days (or months) that the business takes to settle accounts with their creditors. The formula is:

$$\frac{\text{Creditors}}{\text{Purchases}} \times 365 \text{ days (or 12 months)}$$

Sometimes we do not know the figure for purchases and have to use the cost of sales figure. This is not quite such a good measure, because it is affected by changes in stock levels. However, as long as we are consistent, it is possible to draw conclusions from it.

Using the Harvest Bakery data, we will now calculate the credit collection period. We need to look at the balance sheet to obtain the figures for this ratio. Substituting the figures in the formula, the answer is:

$$\frac{£63,000}{£375,000} \times 365 = 61 \text{ days} \qquad \text{or} \qquad \frac{£63,000}{£375,000} \times 12 = 2.016 \text{ months}$$

## Activity

It would appear that the management of Harvest Bakery takes twice as long to pay the money the business owes than they do to collect their debts. Does this indicate efficient or inefficient cash management?

Although some people do not like debts and prefer to pay them on receipt rather than wait until they are due, this is not a good way of managing cash in an organisation. If the business receives goods on credit, it is the equivalent of having an interest-free loan. If the supplier does not give credit, the business may have to go into overdraft to pay for the goods. This does not mean that a business should wait until they receive a solicitor's letter or risk supplies being cut off, but from a business point of view they should take the maximum time allowed to pay their creditors whilst at the same time collect payment from their debtors as quickly as possible. This is what Harvest Bakery appears to be doing and, therefore, the management is efficient at managing cash.

## 12.5 Limitations of Ratios

Ratio analysis suffers from a number of *limitations*. The main problems are as follows:

- There are no agreed definitions of the terms used.
- Data drawn from different sources may not be comparable.
- The figures needed to construct the ratios may not be available and less precise alternatives may have to be used.
- If there is high inflation, the figures in the financial statements may be misleading.
- The business may have used an unusual accounting treatment, the effect of which is not apparent.
- Not all aspects of a business which should be taken into account are shown in the figures in the financial statements. For example, a company's products may have a good reputation or it may suffer from poor industrial relations.

Despite these drawbacks, ratio analysis is an invaluable method for interpreting the financial statements of an organisation. You should not treat ratios as absolute answers, but as an indication of where your investigations should be directed to find out the underlying reasons for the financial performance.

## Activity

Calculate the profitability ratios for Harvest Bakery using profit after interest instead of profit before interest and comment on the differences.

Check your calculations against the following figures:

| Profitability ratio | Using profit after interest | Using profit before interest |
|---|---|---|
| Capital employed | £121,000 | £121,000 |
| Return | £51,000 | £56,000 |
| ROCE | 42.1% | 46.3% |
| Profit margin | 10.2% | 11.2% |
| Capital turnover | 4.13 times | 4.13 times |

In this activity, *return* has been defined as *profit after interest* which is lower than when it is defined as *profit before interest*. Therefore, it is no surprise that the profit margin has decreased from 11.2% to 10.2%. Capital turnover is unaffected, but the ROCE is also slightly lower. If you consider the relationship of the figures, you will see that there is a good argument for not using capital employed when return is defined as profit after interest. This is because Harvest Bakery has a loan of £50,000 on which interest is paid. If return is defined as profit after interest, it is more logical to use the owner's investment only, and exclude the loan.

## 12.6 Conclusions

In this chapter we have examined a technique for assessing financial performance known as ratio analysis. We have calculated the five main profitability ratios, considered the relationship between them and identified the role of management in bringing about improvements in the financial performance of an organisation. We have also calculated and interpreted four liquidity ratios and considered the main limitations of ratio analysis. Despite some drawbacks, this method of interpreting financial statements is one of the most useful and commonly used techniques in the financial world.

Having completed this chapter, you should now be able to:

- identify the purposes of ratios;
- calculate the main performance ratios;
- calculate the main liquidity ratios;
- interpret the meaning of these ratios and recognise their limitations.

# Exercises

Complete the following sentences:

**1** Return can be defined as ................................................................

**2** The prime ratio is calculated by ......................................................

**3** Ratios may be misleading if ............................................................

**4** The definition of capital employed is .............................................

**5** Capital turnover measures .............................................................

Are the following statements true or false?

**6** If a business gives 1 month's credit, the average collection period will be 30 days.

**7** The profit margin ratio can be improved by increasing sales volume.

**8** Capital turnover can be improved by increasing sales volume.

**9** The profit margin can be improved by increasing selling prices.

**10** A good current test ratio is 0.8:1.

You may wish to read more widely than this book to answer the following questions fully, but you can check the main points by referring to the appropriate sections in this chapter.

**11** What are the main purposes of ratio analysis? (Section 12.2)

**12** What does the prime ratio tell you? (Section 12.3)

**13** Give three examples of a liquidity ratio. (Section 12.4)

**14** What are the limitations of ratio analysis? (Section 12.5)

Multiple choice questions (more than one answer may apply):

**15** Capital employed is calculated by:

**a** adding fixed and current assets

**b** adding back interest on loans

**c** adding fixed assets and net current assets

**d** adding fixed assets and net current assets and deducting long-term loans.

**16** The prime ratio results from multiplying:

**a** profit before interest and tax by capital employed

**b** the gross profit ratio by the capital turnover ratio

**c** the profit margin ratio by the capital turnover ratio

**d** the capital turnover ratio by the current test ratio.

**17** If debtors are £20,000, creditors £7,000, cash £6,000 and overdraft £6,000, then:

**a** the current test ratio is 1.54:1

**b** the current test ratio is 2.25:1

**c** the acid test ratio is 1.54:1

**d** the acid test ratio is 2:1.

**18** If sales are £80,000, purchases £60,000 and gross profit £20,000, then gross profit mark up is:

**a** 25%

**b** 50%

**c** 33.3%

**d** 20%.

**19** The collection period in days is calculated by:

   **a** dividing debtors by purchases and multiplying by 365
   **b** adding debtors to sales and multiplying by 365
   **c** dividing debtors by sales and multiplying by 365
   **d** dividing creditors by sales and multiplying by 365.

**20** If return is defined as profit after interest, when calculating the prime ratio it is preferable to use:

   **a** capital employed
   **b** long-term liabilities
   **c** owners' interest
   **d** owners' interest plus long-term liabilities.

Practice questions:

**21** Speedo Bikes Ltd has sales of £145,000 and the cost of sales is £106,000. Calculate the gross profit margin and the gross profit mark up.

**22** Calculate the return on capital employed (ROCE), profit margin and capital turnover from the following key figures which have been taken from the profit and loss account and balance sheet of Fat Cats Company Ltd.

|  | £ |
|---|---|
| Capital employed | 850,000 |
| Sales | 490,000 |
| Profit before interest and tax | 74,500 |

**23** The following figures have been taken from the balance sheet of Chepstow Storage Ltd. Calculate the current test and acid test ratios and comment on your results.

|  | £ |
|---|---|
| **Current assets** | |
| Stock | 86,100 |
| Debtors | 32,800 |
| Bank | 4,500 |
|  | 123,400 |
| **Current liabilities** | |
| Creditors | 72,700 |

**24** The following figures have been extracted from the financial statements of two companies. Calculate the main profitability ratios for both companies and suggest reasons for any differences you find.

|  | Adams Ltd £ | Evelyn Ltd £ |
|---|---|---|
| Capital employed | 281,000 | 596,000 |
| Profit before interest and tax | 29,500 | 41,500 |
| Gross profit | 71,400 | 156,200 |
| Sales | 354,900 | 706,260 |

**25** The following financial statements have been taken from the annual report and accounts of Parva Vine Products Ltd. Calculate as many ratios as possible.

---

### Parva Vine Products Ltd
### Profit and loss account for the year ending
### 31 December 1998

|      |                               | £      | £      |
|------|-------------------------------|--------|--------|
|      | **Sales**                     |        | 75,220 |
| Less | **Cost of sales**             |        |        |
|      | Opening stock                 | 18,300 |        |
| Add  | Purchases                     | 24,300 |        |
|      |                               | 42,600 |        |
| Less | Closing stock                 | 21,000 | 21,600 |
|      | **Gross profit**              |        | 53,620 |
| Less | **Operating expenses**        |        |        |
|      | Salaries and wages            | 26,400 |        |
|      | Rent                          | 1,200  |        |
|      | Lighting and heating          | 820    |        |
|      | Miscellaneous expenses        | 1,400  |        |
|      | Depreciation: Plant and machinery | 2,300 | 32,120 |
|      | **Net profit**                |        | 21,500 |

---

### Parva Wine Products Ltd
### Balance sheet as at 31 December 1998

|      |                                | £ Cost | £ Depreciation | £ Net book value |
|------|--------------------------------|--------|---------------|------------------|
|      | **Fixed assets**               |        |               |                  |
|      | Plant and machinery            | 85,000 | 9,700         | 75,300           |
|      | **Current assets**             |        |               |                  |
|      | Stock                          |        | 21,000        |                  |
|      | Debtors                        |        | 27,600        |                  |
|      | Bank                           |        | 1,200         |                  |
|      |                                |        | 49,800        |                  |
| Less | **Creditors: amounts due within one year** |        |               |                  |
|      | Trade creditors                |        | 13,600        | 36,200           |
|      | **Total net assets**           |        |               | 111,500          |
|      | Capital at beginning of year   |        | 90,000        |                  |
| Add  | Profit                         |        | 21,500        | 111,500          |

---

(Answers on pp. 333–4)

# Part III
# Management Accounting

# 13 Cost Classification

## 13.1 Introduction

In order to run a business successfully, managers need to know the *cost* of making the products or supplying the services. This information is required in some detail so that the cost of materials, wages and other items can be identified separately. The cost of an item can be very hard to determine and it is made more difficult by our differing perspectives, which vary according to whether we are buying or selling. There are also problems concerned with the meaning attached to the term *cost* which can be used as a verb, a noun or an adjective.

The financial accounts we considered in Part II of this book are rarely suitable for calculating the cost of making a product or supplying a service, particularly if the business offers more than one type of product or service. As you will remember, financial accounts are intended to give information about the entire organisation to external users and their format and content are strictly regulated. In Part III of this book we focus on management accounting, the purpose of which is to provide useful and timely information to management.

In this chapter we look at the detailed elements of a company: the individual products and services and the various departments. We begin by clarifying what we mean by the term *cost*, before going on to describe *cost units* and *cost centres*. We then examine the various ways in which cost can be classified and the reasons for using them in organisations, before going on to describe the *elements of cost*.

## 13.2 Definition of Cost

Before we look at what is meant by the term *cost*, it is useful to consider why a business might want to know the cost of making its products. Although we are going to use the example of a manufacturing company, the reasons also apply to other types of organisation. The main reasons a company might want to know the cost of making its products are:

- *To establish the selling price* – If the managers do not know the cost of making the company's products, they cannot decide on the selling price. If the market is very buoyant, the company may be able to charge a very high price, but it is still important to ensure that this covers the cost. If competition is very intensive, the company may wish to know how far the selling price of the product can be reduced before a loss is made.
- *To plan production* – It would be very difficult to determine the best way to plan production without knowing the relevant costs. It is necessary to know the cost of all the items making up the production process and the funds required to support them. Such costs are not confined to materials and labour, but also include machinery, buildings, transport, administration, maintenance and many other items.
- *To maintain control* – Managers have no control if they do not know the costs incurred and are unable to compare them with the original plan. This would lead to the resources used by the organisation being employed inefficiently, resulting in waste and, in the worst circumstances, to the complete failure of the organisation.
- *To aid decision-making* – Managers are constantly making decisions and it is often imperative that they have knowledge of costs for the correct decisions to be taken. For example, it is impossible to decide whether it would be worthwhile investing in new manufacturing machinery without having financial information. It is also necessary to know costs so that alternative ways of carrying out various activities can be evaluated.

Although it is important to know the costs involved in making a product or providing a service, they are not always easy to identify. Let us take a simple example. You go into a shop one Friday and buy a box of 10 floppy disks for your computer for £15. On Sunday your friend asks you to sell him one for some urgent work he is doing. You know that if you were to replace that disk on Monday it would cost you £2.00.

## Activity

What do you think is the cost of the disk?

**a** £1.50
**b** £2.00
**c** Both these figures
**d** Neither of these figures.

You may have answered this by taking the original cost of 10 disks (£15) and dividing it by the number of disks to reach the answer of £1.50, or you may have decided that the cost is Monday's price of £2.00. You may be surprised to know that in some senses all the answers are correct.

However, in order to decide which is the most appropriate answer, we need to define the word *cost* precisely and put it in a context. As you can see, one difficulty we have is that our view of cost is determined by our different perspectives, depending on whether we are buyers or sellers, the context in which we are making our calculations, and our reasons for wanting the information. In addition, we need to consider the grammatical sense in which the term *cost* is being used. It can be used as a verb, meaning to calculate the cost of a specific thing or activity, as in 'I shall need you to cost this product/service for me as soon as possible'. It can also be used as a noun, meaning the amount of actual or notional expenditure incurred on or attributable to a specific thing or activity, as in 'I have now calculated the total cost of this product/service'. Finally, it can be used as an adjective to describe a noun, as in 'I have decided that the most appropriate cost classification for this product/service is by function'.

## 13.3 Cost Units

The above definitions include the phrase 'a specified thing or activity'. All organisations provide an identifiable output which may be in the form of a service, a product or both. The output of a business can be measured by devising some form of *cost unit*. A cost unit can be defined as a quantitative unit of the product or service to which costs are allocated. The type of cost unit depends on the type of industry. In a manufacturing industry there may be a large number of identical products. A brick works, for example, may have a cost unit of 1,000 bricks, because the cost of one brick is so small that it would be difficult to measure. In a service industry the cost unit may be of a more abstract nature. In a hospital, for example, the cost unit may be a patient-bed-occupied.

## Activity

Suggest appropriate cost units for the following businesses:

A car manufacturer
A carrier bag manufacturer
A transport company
A plumber
A sports and leisure centre
A hairdresser.

Some of these businesses may have been more difficult than others to find suitable cost units for, particularly if you are not familiar with the industries. However, you may have identified some of the following types of cost unit.

- A car manufacturer producing a range of different models could use each model as a cost unit. If the same organisation manufactures the engine, gearbox, body and electrical system, these could also be treated as separate cost units.
- A carrier bag manufacturer has the same problems as a brick manufacturer: the costs identified with manufacturing one carrier bag are so small that they cannot be measured. Therefore, a suitable cost unit would be 1,000 bags of each type produced.
- A transport company is a bit more difficult. You need to consider what information the company would find useful. This might be the costs associated with moving 1 tonne of goods over 1 mile. Therefore, the cost unit will be 1 tonne/mile.
- Plumbers often work on a number of small jobs which may vary from fitting a bathroom suite to replacing a tap washer. The plumber needs to know the cost of each job and so a suitable cost unit would be each job.
- In the case of a sports and leisure centre the management needs to know the separate cost of supplying badminton, squash, swimming, table tennis, keep fit, etc. for a period of time. Therefore, a suitable cost unit would be each activity for an hour.
- A hairdresser is likely to offer a number of standard services, such as cut and blow dry, restyling, colouring, etc. Therefore, a suitable cost unit would be each standard service.

As you can see from these examples, many businesses offer a range of different products or services. Before the cost of each product or service can be calculated, a quantitative unit must be identified to which costs can be allocated.

## 13.4 Cost Centres

As well as calculating the costs for each cost unit, an organisation will probably also need to know the costs for particular *cost centres*. A cost centre is an identifiable part of an organisation for which costs can be collected. It may be a single factory, a department or section, a single machine or group of machines, an individual or a group of individuals.

## Activity

Tick which of the following might be cost centres in the two examples below:

| Toy manufacturer | Hotel |
|---|---|
| Assembly department | Kitchen |
| Stores department | Cost of drinks sold |
| Sales team | Reception area |
| Specialised moulding machine | Laundry |
| Clerical salaries. | Restaurant. |

You may not know anything about the manufacture of toys, but the definition of a cost centre given above should have helped you to identify the first four of these as possible cost centres. Clerical salaries are usually an expense, not a cost centre. The specialised moulding machine may be a cost centre if it is sufficiently important and complex to allow a number of costs to be identified with that particular activity. Of course, not all toy manufacturers would use the above cost centres, but they are all areas of activity where managers may need to know the costs. As far as the hotel is concerned, the cost of drinks sold is an item of expense, but all the others are potential cost centres.

Some organisations do not formally identify their cost centres and/or cost units, but answering the following questions should help you to identify them:

- What can be regarded as the cost centres and cost units in the organisation?
- What financial information is generated in respect of the possible cost centres and cost units?
- Does someone have direct responsibility for any of them or is able to influence them?

In a manufacturing organisation it should be fairly easy to identify the cost units as being the products made. In a service organisation there may not be any identifiable cost units. In a hotel the cost unit used might be the room occupancy; in a distribution company a cost unit might be a tonne/mile (the cost involved in moving 1 tonne of goods 1 mile); in a funeral business it may be the cost of conducting a standard cremation.

Identifying cost centres is relatively easy as they are usually clearly defined. One example is that of a works canteen or a college refectory. In manufacturing companies departments may be referred to as shops – for example, the machine shop. The sort of financial information that would be available are staff wages, heating, lighting, food, etc. and the meals may be used as the cost units. The degree of financial sophistication in the organisation will determine whether they are treated as such.

## 13.5 Cost Classification

Although it may be useful to know the total costs of an organisation for a financial period or the total cost of one cost unit, it is even more useful if the costs are *classified*. By classifying costs we can obtain more detailed information and use it in a variety of ways for planning, controlling and decision-making. Classifying costs helps us to understand better what is meant by the term *cost*. The main classifications are:

- *product costs*, which can be identified with the goods produced or purchased for retail and are part of the value of stock, and *period costs*, such as selling and administration costs, which are deduced as expenses in the current period without being included in the value of stock;

- *direct costs*, which can be identified with a specific product or saleable service, such as materials used in production or the salaries of staff providing the service, and *indirect costs* which cannot be identified with any particular product or service but are shared, such as managers' salaries;
- *fixed costs*, which tend to remain the same in total irrespective of changes in the level of activity, and *variable costs* which tend to change in total in direct proportion to changes in the level of activity;
- by the *nature* of costs, such as material, labour and expenses, which can be further divided into raw materials, maintenance materials, etc.;
- by the *function* of costs, such as production, administration, selling and distribution costs.

## Activity

Which of the costs in the following list are normally classified as direct costs, indirect costs, fixed costs or variable costs in a manufacturing organisation?

Materials used in the product
Rent of the factory
Insurance of the factory
Depreciation
Maintenance of machinery
Canteen
Supervisors' salaries
Production workers' wages
Accountants' salaries.

Even if you do not have any experience of working in a manufacturing environment, you should have been able to work out the answers from the definitions of direct and indirect costs. Materials and production workers' wages can be identified with the product and are therefore *direct costs*. Rent, insurance, maintenance of machinery, canteen, supervisors' salaries and accountants' salaries cannot be identified with a single product, but must be shared over a number of products; therefore, these are *indirect costs*. In a service industry the same principles apply.

You may have had more difficulty in distinguishing between *fixed* and *variable costs*. One thing you may have noticed is that direct costs are always variable costs. For example, the materials used in the product can be directly identified with it and the more products made, the higher the total material costs will be. Therefore, these are variable costs. In the above list the indirect costs are also all fixed costs, but in certain situations some indirect costs may be variable costs.

We will now look more closely at the difference between fixed and variable costs using an example. Sam Reeves has a taxi business. The average mileage by a taxi in 1 quarter is 15,000 miles and the costs, analysed by nature, are as follows:

| Expense | Total for quarter £ |
|---|---|
| Driver's salary | 2,670 |
| Petrol and oil | 1,050 |
| Annual service | 450 |
| Tax and insurance | 1,110 |
| Depreciation | 870 |

We can use the details of Sam's business expenses as the basis for calculating further cost information. For example, we can add up the costs so that Sam can find out that the total costs for 1 vehicle for 1 quarter are £6,150. From this we can calculate the total cost per mile:

$$\frac{\text{Total costs}}{\text{Total mileage}} = \frac{£6,150}{15,000} = 41\text{p per mile}$$

We can now calculate the cost per mile for each of the expenses:

| Expense | Total for quarter £ | Cost per mile Pence |
|---|---|---|
| Driver's salary | 2,670 | 17.8 |
| Petrol and oil | 1,050 | 7.0 |
| Annual service | 450 | 3.0 |
| Tax and insurance | 1,110 | 7.4 |
| Depreciation | 870 | 5.8 |
| Total | 6,150 | 41.0 |

Sam now has a considerable amount of information, including the total cost per unit (in this example a cost unit is 1 mile), and this total cost is further analysed by the nature of the expense. However, there are some problems if Sam tries to use this cost information without understanding the difference between fixed and variable costs. For example, he may want to know what the cost is per mile if the taxi travelled 30,000 miles in 1 quarter. Your immediate response may be to say that the cost per mile would remain at 41p. However, on consideration, you may have seen that the cost per mile is likely to be lower. This is because the *total fixed costs* – that is, the cost of the driver's salary, taxation, insurance and depreciation – tend to remain the same, even though the mileage has doubled. On the other hand, the *total variable costs* – that is, the cost of petrol and oil – tend to change in direct proportion to the change in the level of activity. This means that if activity doubles (in our example, if mileage doubles), the variable costs will tend to double.

We shall be looking at the importance of fixed and variable costs again in Chapter 18, but for the moment you need to remember that calculating the average total cost per unit can be misleading if there are significant changes in the activity level of the business.

## 13.6  Elements of Total Cost

The total cost of a product or service is built up from a number of *elements of cost*. In a manufacturing organisation, *direct materials* (which become part of the finished goods) plus *direct labour* (which converts direct materials into the finished goods), plus *direct expenses* (such as subcontracted work or special tools) gives *prime cost*. If you then add the *production overheads*, which are the indirect costs arising from the provision of the production resources, you arrive at the *production cost*. By adding *administration, sales overheads* and *distribution overheads* (which are the indirect costs analysed by function), you arrive at the *total product cost*. These calculations can be worked out using the following layout:

**Elements of total cost**

|     |                         | £ | £ |
|-----|-------------------------|---|---|
|     | **Direct costs**        |   |   |
| *Add* | Direct materials      | X |   |
|     | Direct labour           | X |   |
|     | Direct expenses         | X |   |
|     | **Prime cost**          |   | X |
| *Add* | Production overheads   |   | X |
|     | **Production cost**     |   | X |
| *Add* | **Indirect costs**     |   |   |
|     | Administration          | X |   |
|     | Sales overheads         | X |   |
|     | Distribution overheads  | X | X |
|     | **Total product cost**  |   | X |

A system is needed to charge the *direct materials, direct labour* and *direct expenses* to the cost unit. *Direct materials* can be charged to the cost unit by the production department using a materials requisition or stores issue note. These are documents which show the quantity and cost of the materials to be charged to the cost units. These documents are passed to the accounts department which maintains the costing records. The direct materials become part of the finished goods. *Direct labour* converts the direct materials into the finished goods. The time spent on cost units can be calculated from time sheets, job cards or computerised records. *Direct expenses* are not always present. They may include such items as subcontract work, or special tools or equipment bought for a particular job. The accounts department may use the invoices to charge the cost to the appropriate cost units.

*Production overheads* are the indirect costs of production that cannot be traced directly to the product or cost unit, such as depreciation of machinery, factory rent and business rates, factory insurance, cleaning materials, maintenance expenses and canteen costs. *Administration overheads* are the indirect costs that arise from the provision of the administrative function. *Sales overheads* are the indirect costs that arise from the sale of the cost unit, such as advertising and the salaries of the sales force. *Distribution overheads* are the indirect costs that arise from the activity of getting the cost unit to the customer, such as packing and transport costs.

## Activity

Select any ordinary household item and describe the various elements of cost that may have been incurred in arriving at the total cost.

Even if you have selected a simple item you will be surprised by how complex the activities involved in its manufacture are, and therefore how difficult it is to ascertain the elements of cost. For example, in the case of a small business bottling spring water, the following elements may be found:

**Direct materials**
    Plastic bottles and lids
    Water
    Labels
**Direct labour**
    Bottling plant wages
**Production overheads**
    Factory rent and rates
    Heat, light and power
    Depreciation of machinery
    Supervisors' salaries
    Maintenance and cleaners' wages
    Packaging materials
**Sales overheads**
**Distribution costs**
**Administration overheads**

In this example the cost unit may be a crate of bottles, rather than an individual bottle. Direct materials and direct labour have to be identified with each individual cost unit. To do this, the business needs good procedures for controlling and recording the costs and we consider these in Chapter 14.

## 13.7 Conclusions

In this chapter we have looked at what is meant by the term 'cost' and considered the reasons why cost is important to a business. In addition, we have described how you can identify potential cost units and cost centres. We have also examined the different ways in which costs can be classified, distinguishing between direct costs and indirect costs, fixed costs and variable costs, the nature of costs and the function of costs. In this way we have shown how they can be used to provide information which is useful to managers.

Having completed this chapter, you should now be able to:

- explain what is meant by cost, cost units and cost centres;
- identify the cost units appropriate to different organisations;
- classify costs in a number of different ways.

## Exercises

Complete the following sentences:

**1** A cost unit can be defined as ....................................................................................
**2** Direct costs can be identified with .......................................................................
**3** In the short term, fixed costs tend to .................................................................
**4** A cost centre is .......................................................................................................
**5** Production overheads are .......................................................................................

Are the following statements true or false?

**6** Total variable costs stay the same when activity increases.
**7** Fixed costs per unit decrease as activity increases.
**8** Directors' costs are always fixed.
**9** Supervisors' salaries are an indirect cost.
**10** Direct materials plus direct wages plus direct expenses equals prime cost.

You may wish to read more widely than this book to answer the following questions fully, but you can check the main points by referring to the appropriate sections in this chapter.

**11** Why is it important to know the cost of providing a service of making a product? (Section 13.2)
**12** What is meant by a cost unit? (Section 13.3)
**13** Describe the main classifications of cost. (Section 13.4)
**14** What are the main elements of cost? (Section 13.5)

Multiple choice questions (more than one answer may apply):

**15** An example of a direct cost is:

**a** subcontract work
**b** factory foreman's wages
**c** electricity to power a grinding machine
**d** none of these.

**16** An example of a production overhead is:

**a** subcontract work
**b** piecework
**c** depreciation of the managing director's Jaguar
**d** factory cleaning costs.

**17** If a cost is described as fixed, when activity doubles the cost per unit:

**a** remains constant
**b** doubles
**c** halves
**d** none of these.

**18** If a cost is described as variable, when activity doubles the cost per unit:

**a** remains constant
**b** doubles
**c** halves
**d** none of these.

**19** A hotel bar may be considered as a:

**a** cost unit
**b** production centre
**c** cost centre
**d** none of these.

**20** The prime cost is:

**a** all direct costs
**b** all direct costs plus production overheads
**c** all overheads
**d** production overheads only.

Practice questions:

**21** Explain why it is important to classify costs.
**22** Explain the difference between cost centres and cost units
**23** Distinguish between product costs and period costs.
**24** Indicate which of the following costs that are incurred in a manufacturing company are production costs, selling and distribution costs or administration costs:

> Motor vehicles' licences
> Depreciation of factory machinery
> Commission paid to sales team
> Salary of finance director's secretary
> Salary of factory security guard
> Fees to advertising agency
> Buildings' insurance
> Lubricants for factory machinery
> Depreciation of fork lift truck
> Accounting software
> Bonuses for factory staff
> Training course for clerical staff

**25** Julie's Jardinières manufactures a range of ornamental plant pots. The business plans to produce 2,000 units over the next month. Each variety takes about the same amount of materials and time to produce. Costs for the month are as follows:

|  | £ |
|---|---|
| Rent: | |
| Factory | 500 |
| Office | 100 |
| Rates: | |
| Factory | 300 |
| Office | 100 |
| Sand | 1,000 |
| Power | 700 |
| Light and heat: | |
| Factory | 2,000 |
| Office | 1,300 |
| Wages: | |
| Operators | 10,000 |
| Maintenance staff | 1,500 |
| Canteen staff | 2,500 |
| Cement | 5,000 |
| Depreciation: | |
| Office equipment | 500 |
| Moulds | 2,200 |
| Fixtures and fittings | 800 |
| Salesmen's salary and commission | 2,200 |
| Delivery expenses | 500 |
| Office salaries | 1,800 |
| Cement mixer repairs | 900 |
| Salesmen's car expenses | 1,100 |
| Finishing paint | 200 |
| Packing | 800 |

Julie, the owner of the business, finds the list of information somewhat confusing and asks if you can draw it up in a more structured format, identifying important figures and explaining what they mean. Prepare a report for Julie's Jardinières which provides the following financial information for the costs in total and per pot, and explain any terms used:

**a** Prime cost
**b** Production cost
**c** Total cost
**d** Administration overheads
**e** Selling overheads
**f** Distribution overheads.

(Answers on pp. 334–5)

# 14 Cost Control Procedures

## 14.1 Introduction

In Chapter 13 we identified direct costs as one of the key elements of the total cost of a product or service. In this chapter we are going to examine how cost control can be exercised over *direct materials* and *direct labour*. Even in a very small business the minimum information required is the total cost of direct materials and the total cost of direct labour. In most businesses management needs a more detailed breakdown of these total costs by activity for each product or service so that they can plan and control costs, and make decisions. For example, they need to know the labour costs in the canteen, the materials cost of making one product and the labour cost in the maintenance department. Once systems have been established to collected this detailed information, the total direct materials and total direct labour cost of a particular product or service can be calculated. For example, a car manufacturer can establish the total direct materials and labour costs of producing one particular model; a civil engineering company the labour costs of constructing a particular building; a plumber the total direct materials and labour costs of a particular job.

In this chapter we start with *costing for materials*, which involves setting up procedures, together with suitable documentation, for the purchase and receipt of materials used in each part of the production process. If the materials are to be stored, stores records must be kept to maintain an adequate level of stock. For proper control it is essential that period stock-taking takes place and that a suitable method for pricing issues of materials is adopted. We then go on to examine *costing for labour*, where the principles are similar, since procedures and documentation to record the costs of each activity must be set up. The techniques used are related to the methods of remuneration the business uses.

## 14.2 **Costing for Materials**

In many businesses, particularly in the manufacturing sector, *materials* represent a substantial cost. Some organisations have introduced just-in-time (JIT) manufacturing systems in which parts are produced just in time to meet manufacturing requirements rather than by the traditional approach which produces parts just in case they are needed. This greatly reduces or eliminates the need for stocks of raw materials. However, whatever system is used, management requires information to establish costs. The procedure for *costing for materials* should ensure that:

- the correct materials are delivered;
- materials are correctly stored and issued only with proper authorisation;
- production is charged with the cost of materials used;
- stored materials are correctly valued.

Stores departments often carry many hundreds of different types of materials and therefore require an efficient and accurate system for recording and controlling the cost of materials. This can be either a manual or a computer system. Although firms devise systems and procedures to suit their own particular type of business, there are some standard terms for the documents most commonly used and the main stages are as follows:

1 A *purchase requisition note* is sent to the purchasing department by the production department or stores department specifying the *type* and *quantity* of materials required.
2 The buyer sends a *purchase order* to the supplier.
3 The supplier sends the materials with a *goods received note (GRN)*. The GRN is checked against the materials received and compared with the original order.
4 The materials are taken to the stores department and added to the stock. The quantity is added to the stock level shown on the *bin card.*
5 The production department requiring the materials sends a *materials requisition note* to the stores department. The stores department issues the materials and deducts the quantity from the stock level shown on the bin card.

Although adequate records may be maintained, proper control is exercised through a physical examination and count of the stored materials known as *stock-taking*. This may be periodic or continuous. In a perpetual inventory system, a *stores record card* is maintained to give the balance of each item in store after each issue or receipt of materials has been physically checked.

## **Activity**

Draw a diagram showing the flow of documents used to control the movement of materials.

The design of your diagram will depend on your creative abilities and the assumptions you have made, but you should have shown a logical flow of information. One thing to bear in mind is that copies of the documents will be sent to the accounts department so that they can ensure that goods have been properly ordered and received before paying the supplier's invoice. The accounts department also maintains costing records so that it is possible to calculate the *cost of a unit*.

## 14.3  Pricing Materials Issues

Having looked at the procedures and documents for purchasing, storing and issuing materials to production, we now need to consider the *price* at which they are issued from stores. This is more complex than it first appears. It is highly likely that the materials in store will have been received on different dates and perhaps at a number of different purchase prices. In addition, it may not be possible to identify each issue of materials with the corresponding receipt into stores.

The main methods for pricing materials issues are:

- *first in, first out (FIFO)*, which uses the price of the first delivery of materials for all issues from store until that particular consignment has been exhausted, followed by the price of the subsequent consignment;
- *last in, first out (LIFO)*, which uses the price of the last delivery of materials for all issues from store until that particular consignment has been exhausted, followed by the price of the previous consignment;
- *average price method*, which uses either a simple average or a weighted average price for all issues from store;
- *replacement price method*, which uses the replacement price on the day of issue to value materials issued from store;
- *standard price method*, which uses a predetermined standard price for all issues and returns of materials from store.

We will now illustrate some of these methods. A stores department has a record of the following receipts and issues of materials:

> 1 January received 1,000 kg of materials at £2.00 per kg
> 2 January received 1,000 kg of materials at £2.20 per kg
> 3 January issued 500 kg to production

We will now try to calculate the cost of the 500 kg of stock issued to production using as many different methods as possible. From the information given, we can only use the first three methods and the calculations are as follows:

> FIFO: 500 kg @ £2.00 per kg = £1,000
> LIFO: 500 kg @ £2.20 per kg = £1,100
> Average price: 500 kg @ £2.10 per kg = £1,050

As you can see, the cost of materials used in production varies according to the method used. All these methods are correct and other methods which organisations use may also be acceptable. Each method has advantages and disadvantages. Of the three described above, FIFO makes sense in that most organisations tend to issue the materials from the stores department that have been stored the longest. This method is also acceptable to accountants and the Inland Revenue, whereas LIFO is not recommended by accountants and is not normally acceptable to the Inland Revenue.

The method used to price the issues of materials from stores also determines the value of the materials remaining in the stores department. In some organisations the value of materials remaining in stores is very high. The materials must be kept safe and secure, and in a position where they can be issued conveniently to production. Records should be maintained of the quantity of goods in store at any one time. Because of the possibility of errors and theft, it is essential that a physical count of items in store is taken at regular intervals. Some organisations carry out *periodic stock-taking*, with a physical count of all materials at a given date. This is done at least annually and requires a substantial amount of work and organisation. It can be very disruptive. Some organisations use *continuous stock-taking*, where staff are employed to check a few items every day so that all stock is checked at least once a year. Whichever method of counting the physical quantity is used, the method used for pricing the issue of materials affects the value of the materials remaining in store.

## Activity

Calculate the value of the remaining 1,500 kg of materials in stock using the three methods, FIFO, LIFO and average price.

The answer is as follows:

| *FIFO* | | £ |
|---|---|---|
| **Receipts** | | |
| 1 January | 1,000 kg at £2.00 per kg | 2,000 |
| 2 January | 1,000 kg at £2.20 per kg | 2,200 |
| Total stock | 2,000 kg | 4,200 |
| **Issues of materials** | | |
| 3 January | 500 kg at £2.00 | 1,000 |
| Value of remaining stock | (1,500 kg) | 3,200 |
| *LIFO* | | £ |
| **Receipts** | | |
| 1 January | 1,000 kg at £2.00 per kg | 2,000 |
| 2 January | 1,000 kg at £2.20 per kg | 2,200 |
| Total stock | 2,000 kg | 4,200 |

**Issues of materials**

| | | |
|---|---|---|
| 3 January | 500 kg at £2.20 | 1,100 |
| Value of remaining stock | (1,500 kg) | 3,100 |

| *Average price* | | £ |
|---|---|---|
| **Receipts** | | |
| 1 January | 1,000 kg at £2.00 per kg | 2,000 |
| 2 January | 1,000 kg at £2.20 per kg | 2,200 |
| Total stock | 2,000 kg | 4,200 |
| **Issues of materials** | | |
| 3 January | 500 kg at £2.10 | 1,050 |
| Value of remaining stock | (1,500 kg) | 3,150 |

Once again, all these values are correct, depending on the method the organisation uses. It is clearly important that the organisation uses the same method consistently and does not change it unless there is a very good reason.

To make certain that you understand the three methods, we will use the information above but add to it. On 4 January a further 600 kg of materials are issued from stores. We can now use the three different methods to find out the cost of the materials issued to production and the value of the stock remaining in store:

| *FIFO* | | £ |
|---|---|---|
| **Receipts** | | |
| 1 January | 1,000 kg at £2.00 per kg | 2,000 |
| 2 January | 1,000 kg at £2.20 per kg | 2,200 |
| Total stock | 2,000 kg | 4,200 |
| **Issues of materials** | | |
| 3 January | 500 kg at £2.00 | 1,000 |
| Value of remaining stock | (1,500 kg) | 3,200 |
| **Issues of materials** | | |
| 4 January | 500 kg at £2.00 | |
| | 100 kg at £2.20 | 1,220 |
| Value of remaining stock | (900 kg) | 1,980 |

| *LIFO* | | £ |
|---|---|---|
| **Receipts** | | |
| 1 January | 1,000 kg at £2.00 per kg | 2,000 |
| 2 January | 1,000 kg at £2.20 per kg | 2,200 |
| Total stock | 2,000 kg | 4,200 |
| **Issues of materials** | | |
| 3 January | 500 kg at £2.20 | 1,100 |
| Value of remaining stock | (1,500 kg) | 3,100 |
| **Issues of materials** | | |
| 4 January | 500 kg at £2.20 | 1,100 |
| | 100 kg at £2.00 | 1,300 |
| Value of remaining stock | (900 kg) | 1,800 |

| *Average price* | | £ |
|---|---|---|
| **Receipts** | | |
| 1 January | 1,000 kg at £2.00 per kg | 2,000 |
| 2 January | 1,000 kg at £2.20 per kg | 2,200 |
| Total stock | 2,000 kg | 4,200 |
| **Issues of materials** | | |
| 3 January | 500 kg at £2.10 | 1,050 |
| Value of remaining stock | (1,500 kg) | 3,150 |
| **Issues of materials** | | |
| 4 January | 600 kg at £2.10 | 1,260 |
| Value of remaining stock | (900 kg) | 1,890 |

It must be remembered that the profit and loss account and balance sheet that we examined in Part II of this book are regulated in the area of stock valuation by *SSAP 9, Stock Valuation*. This accounting standard states that stock should be valued at the lower of cost or net realisable value. 'Cost' means the total cost incurred in bringing the product to its present location and condition, including an appropriate proportion of production overhead costs.

## 14.4  Costing for Labour

*Labour costing* is closely related to the method of remuneration operated by the organisation. The methods for costing for labour include:

- *time-based schemes*, which are used when workers are paid a basic rate per time period;
- *piecework schemes*, which are used when workers are paid an agreed amount for each unit produced or piecework time is paid for each unit produced;
- *bonus/incentive schemes*, which are used when a time allowance is given for each job and a bonus is paid for any time saved.

Calculating pay for time-based schemes is straightforward. A system is required to ensure that the employee is properly appointed and, if necessary, a procedure is in place to record the employee's attendance at the workplace. In most clerical jobs it is assumed that the employee is present unless absence is specifically reported. In some organisations it is necessary for employees to record their attendance.

In a piecework scheme wages are often calculated using the following formula:

$$\text{Wages} = \text{Units produced} \times \text{Rate of pay per unit}$$

For example, if an employee is paid £1.50 per unit and produces 60 units in a week, his or her pay will be £90. This method works only where all units are identical and if the employee produces a number of units a conversion factor must be applied. As a piecework system is based on time spent on production, a standard time allowance is given for each unit to arrive at a total of piecework hours. For example, an employee may be allowed 15 minutes to produce 1 unit of product *A* (a simple electronic circuit board) and 30 minutes to produce 1 unit of product *B* (a more complex electronic circuit board). If the employee produces 60 units of *A* and 60 units of *B* in a week, his or her pay can be calculated as follows:

| Product | Number of units | Time allowance per unit | Total piecework hours |
|---------|-----------------|-------------------------|-----------------------|
| *A*     | 60              | 0.25                    | 15                    |
| *B*     | 60              | 0.50                    | 30                    |
|         |                 |                         | 45                    |

The employee will therefore be paid for 45 hours at the agreed hourly rate.

Bonus/incentive schemes are usually introduced where workers are paid under a time-based scheme. There are various types of scheme in operation, but most are based on setting a target for output and actual performance is compared with the target. If actual performance exceeds target, employees receive a payment for their efficiency. This payment is a proportion of the savings made by the business because of the increased efficiency and therefore the labour cost per unit should be lower.

The documents used in labour costing depend largely on the method of payment used. The main documents are:

- *clock cards*, which record attendance time;
- daily or weekly *time sheets*, countersigned by a supervisor, which record how workers have spent their time;
- *job cards*, which refer to a batch or single job and record how long each activity takes to pass through the production process;
- *piecework tickets*, which refer to each stage of manufacture.

## Activity

Describe two work situations where you consider it would be preferable to adopt the time-based method of remuneration rather than an performance-based scheme.

It would be impossible to use a performance-based scheme if the output cannot be measured reliably. It is preferable to adopt a time-based method of remuneration where quality is important, even if the output can be measured. This avoids the obvious danger of the quality of output suffering if workers have a monetary incentive to achieve high outputs.

You should not be misled into thinking that costing for labour is used only in manufacturing businesses. In all organisations it is necessary to have a system to ensure that staff are properly remunerated for their contribution. In service organisations some form of bonus or profit-sharing scheme is likely to exist and this requires more detailed information to be kept. For example, even professionals such as solicitors and accountants usually complete time sheets so that their individual clients can be properly billed for the services they receive.

Sometimes students find it difficult to decide which are direct labour costs and which are indirect when trying to classify the elements of cost to arrive at the prime cost. Basically, direct labour costs are those which can conveniently be identified with a *cost unit*. To do this a documentation system, as described in this chapter, is needed.

Indirect labour costs are the wages of indirect workers, such as supervisors and maintenance staff, plus the wages of direct workers when working on indirect tasks, such as cleaning machinery and setting up production lines. Overtime is classified as a direct cost if the overtime is worked at the specific request of a customer; otherwise it is an indirect cost.

## 14.5 **Conclusions**

In this chapter we have examined a number of methods for pricing materials and labour which allow these two direct costs to be calculated. In addition, we have described the key documents and procedures involved. We have also discussed some of the reasons why different methods of costing for materials might be adopted in an organisation and how the method of labour costing is related to the method of remuneration operated.

Having completed this chapter, you should now be able to:

- describe the procedure and documents used when costing for materials;
- price issues of materials using a number of different methods;
- describe the methods used for costing for labour;
- describe the documents used in labour costing.

## **Exercises**

Complete the following sentences:

**1** A purchase requisition note is sent to ........................................................................
**2** The average price method of pricing issues of materials uses ...........................
...............................................................................................................................................
**3** Piecework tickets are used for ...............................................................................
**4** Job cards record ........................................................................................................
**5** Labour costing is closely related to ......................................................................

Are the following statements true or false?

**6** The supplier sends the purchase order to the customer.

**7** Clock cards record the time spent on each job.

**8** LIFO is an acceptable method for pricing material issues.

**9** A goods received note is normally checked against the original purchase order.

**10** An incentive payment scheme is best where high quality in production is essential.

You may wish to read more widely than this book to answer the following questions fully, but you can check the main points by referring to the appropriate sections in this chapter.

**11** Describe the procedures for costing materials. (Section 14.2)

**12** Explain the main methods for pricing issues of materials. (Section 14.3)

**13** Explain the significant differences between FIFO and LIFO for pricing issues of materials. (Section 14.3)

**14** Outline the main methods of remuneration which may be used in an organisation. (Section 14.4)

Multiple choice questions (more than one answer may apply):

**15** On receiving a materials requisition note the stores department will:

   **a** add the quantity to the stock level on the bin card

   **b** deduct the quantity to the stock level on the bin card

   **c** issue a goods received note

   **d** none of these.

**16** If materials are issued from stores using the price of the most recent delivery, this is an example of:

   **a** FIFO

   **b** replacement price method

   **c** average price method

   **d** LIFO.

**17** If prices of raw materials are rising using LIFO will mean that the value of materials in store are:

   **a** close to the most recent price

   **b** higher than the most recent price

   **c** lower than the most recent price

   **d** the average of all prices.

**18** If prices of raw materials are rising using FIFO will mean that the prices of materials issued to production are:

   **a** close to the most recent price

   **b** higher than the most recent price

   **c** lower than the most recent price

   **d** the average of all prices.

**19** A goods received note is used to:

   **a** issue materials from store

   **b** check the goods sent by the supplier

   **c** price the issue of material used in production

   **d** return unwanted materials to the supplier

**20** Job cards record:

    **a** how long each activity takes to pass through the production process
    **b** the total time spent at work by an employee
    **c** how employees have spent their time
    **d** the amount of bonus to be paid.

Practice questions:

**21** Describe the main documents used in costing for materials.
**22** Explain the difference between LIFO and FIFO.
**23** Describe the main methods for costing for labour.
**24** What problems might arise in recording direct labour costs and how would you attempt to remedy them?
**25** Janet is paid £5 per piecework hour produced. Calculate her pay if in a 36-hour-week she produced the following:

| Product | Number of units | Time allowance per unit |
|---------|-----------------|-------------------------|
| A | 12 | 0.8 hours |
| B | 30 | 0.6 hours |
| C | 24 | 0.5 hours |

(Answers on pp. 335–6)

# 15 Absorption Costing

## 15.1 Introduction

In Chapter 14 we looked at the methods that allow us to calculate the direct materials and direct labour costs for each cost unit. However, these figures alone are not sufficient, as management needs to know the total costs, including all the indirect costs. *Absorption costing*, which is also known as *total costing* or *total absorption costing*, is a method which gathers together all the *direct costs* and the *indirect costs* to arrive at a total cost for a product. The indirect costs comprise the production, selling, distribution and administration overheads. In many businesses the overheads are extremely high and therefore it is essential to find a suitable method for charging them to each cost unit.

In this chapter we are going to focus on how to allocate and apportion the indirect costs to the cost centres and cost units so that the total cost of an individual cost unit can be calculated. To do this, we will be working out the total costs of the organisation. This information should be similar to that in the financial accounts. However, there are differences. In management accounting the total costs are required on a monthly basis or, in some cases, as forecasts. Therefore, such costs may be less accurate than those in the financial accounts, but more timely. In addition, more detailed information is required in a management accounting system than is needed for financial accounting. However, at the end of the financial year we would expect the total costs for the business shown in the financial accounts to be very similar to the aggregated costs in the management accounts.

## 15.2 Calculating Total Costs

In Chapter 13 we looked at a number of ways in which costs can be classified and you will remember that one way is to divide them into *direct costs* and *indirect costs*. The following activity allows us to examine this in more detail.

## Activity

Country Pine is a small business in the Forest of Dean that manufactures pine tables. It has one production department and makes only one style of table. Materials for the table cost £25. Labour costs are £18. The company manufactures 1,000 tables per annum and production overheads are £36,000. What is the total production cost of each table?

You should have had no problem in deciding that the total direct costs are £43, made up of £25 for materials and £18 for labour. However, the total cost must include a fair share of the production overheads, but what is a 'fair share'? As the organisation is making only tables and they are all the same, a fair method would be to divide the total overhead cost by the total number of units produced:

$$\frac{£36,000}{1,000} = £36$$

The following statement draws these calculations together to show the total production cost of one table.

| Production cost of one table | | |
|---|---|---|
| | £ | £ |
| **Direct costs** | | |
| *Add*    Materials | 25 | |
| Labour | 18 | |
| **Prime cost** | | 43 |
| *Add*   Production overhead | | 36 |
| **Production cost** | | 79 |

Unfortunately, it is often not possible to use this method as businesses are rarely as simply as this. Usually there are a number of different departments with a range of activities; some departments may not be production departments but service departments which provide maintenance facilities, storage facilities, administrative support, selling and distribution or canteen facilities. In addition, there may be a range of goods, rather than a single product, with each product spending different lengths of time in the production department and making unequal demands on resources. In such a situation, the above method is not a fair way of sharing overheads over production.

## 15.3 **Allocating and Apportioning Production Overheads**

To overcome this difficulty we can use a technique called *absorption costing*. This allows us to charge overheads to cost units by means of rates calculated separately for different cost centres. The technique seeks to provide answers to two problems:

- how to share the total overheads of the organisation over the various production departments; and
- how to share the overheads for a particular production department over the various products passing through it.

---

## Activity

In the previous example of Country Pine Ltd, was the method used a solution to the first or the second of these problems?

---

The method used was a solution to the second problem because we were looking at a small organisation which had only one production department. By dividing the total overhead by the number of tables, we shared the overheads over the products passing through the production department.

Usually we have to solve the first problem before we can tackle the second. You will remember from Chapter 13 that overheads can be classified by *nature*, such as rent, wages and depreciation. When overheads are classified in this way, they fall into two main groups. The first group is those which can be wholly identified with one particular cost centre; for example, all the depreciation charge on machinery may be due to only one particular production department. This process of charging to one particular cost centre is called *cost allocation*. The second group of overheads is those which cannot be identified with a single cost centre, but must be shared or *apportioned* over all the cost centres benefiting from them. This process is known as *cost apportionment* – for example, factory rent might be apportioned over the cost centres on the basis of the space that they occupy.

To charge overheads to cost centres by allocation and apportionment an *overhead analysis* is prepared. This classifies the overheads by nature and shows the total cost of each. The various costs centres are shown at the top of the analysis. We will use an activity to illustrate this.

---

## Activity

Jarvis Jackets Ltd makes leather jackets. It has a Cutting Department where the jackets are cut out by machine and a Stitching Department where they are sewn and finished by machinists. Some of the overheads have been allocated from information available within the business; others must be apportioned. The following information should help you decide what would be a fair way of sharing them over the two cost centres:

|  | **Cutting Dept** | **Stitching Dept** |
|---|---|---|
| Production area | 250 sq metres | 150 sq metres |
| Number of employees | 5 | 15 |
| Value of machinery | £100,000 | £20,0000 |
| Value of stock | £40,000 | £80,0000 |

In order to complete the following overhead analysis, you need to decide on the basis of apportionment and calculate the portion of the total overhead to be borne by each cost centre. Of the overhead costs, indirect materials and labour have been allocated and entered for you. The rent has also been apportioned to show you the method. Rent is best apportioned on the basis of the area occupied. The total area is $250 + 150 = 400$ sq metres and the rent is £12,000. Therefore the rent can be apportioned as follows:

Cutting Department: $\dfrac{250}{400} \times £12,000 = £7,500$

Stitching Department: $\dfrac{150}{400} \times £12,000 = £4,500$

**Jarvis Jackets Ltd**
**Overhead analysis**

| Overhead | Total cost £ | Basis of apportionment | Cutting Dept £ | Stitching Dept £ |
|---|---|---|---|---|
| Indirect materials | 40,000 | Allocated | 17,500 | 22,500 |
| Indirect labour | 17,100 | Allocated | 4,200 | 12,900 |
| Rent | 12,000 | Area | 7,500 | 4,500 |
| Electricity | 4,000 |  |  |  |
| Depreciation on machinery | 9,000 |  |  |  |
| Supervisors' salaries | 22,000 |  |  |  |
| Stock insurance | 900 |  |  |  |
| Total | 105,000 |  |  |  |

After deciding a fair way of apportioning the overheads, the calculations should not have presented any great problems. Check your completed overhead analysis against the following:

**Jarvis Jackets Ltd**
**Overhead analysis**

| Overhead | Total cost £ | Basis of apportionment | Cutting Dept £ | Stitching Dept £ |
|---|---|---|---|---|
| Indirect materials | 40,000 | Allocated | 17,500 | 22,500 |
| Indirect labour | 17,100 | Allocated | 4,200 | 12,900 |
| Rent | 12,000 | Area | 7,500 | 4,500 |
| Electricity | 4,000 | Area | 2,500 | 1,500 |
| Depreciation on machinery | 9,000 | Value of machinery | 7,500 | 1,500 |
| Supervisors' salaries | 22,000 | Number of employees | 5,500 | 16,500 |
| Stock insurance | 900 | Value of stock | 300 | 600 |
| Total | 105,000 |  | 45,000 | 60,000 |

If your analysis differs from the above, it may be because you decided to use different bases of apportionment, so we will look at the reasons for the choices we made. Both rent and electricity would seem to be best shared on the basis of the area occupied by each cost centre. Depreciation is clearly related to the value of the machinery used in each cost centre. Deciding on the best way to apportion the supervisors' salaries is more difficult. In the absence of any other information, we have assumed that their salaries are related to the number of employees. You might argue that they could be related to floor space and in some circumstances you would be right. Finally, the stock insurance is clearly based on the value of the stock and therefore it has been allocated on that basis.

Agreeing on a fair way to apportion overheads is a major problem in many organisations, but the guiding principle is to be consistent and to choose a method that appears to be fair from the information provided. Later in this chapter we will be looking at the problem of service cost centres, but at this stage we will concentrate on our two production departments.

## 15.4 Overhead Cost Absorption

We now know that the total overhead cost is £45,000 for the Cutting Department and £60,000 for the Finishing Department. Next we must decide how we are going to share these overheads between all the jackets passing through the two departments. At the beginning of this chapter we stated that if all the products were the same, we could simply divide the total overhead costs by the number of cost units. The method of charging overheads to cost units is known as the *overhead absorption rate* or *overhead recovery*. If it is calculated on the number of units, as in the Country Pine example, we are using the cost unit overhead absorption rate. The most appropriate overhead absorption rate depends on the resources used and the way we measure them.

There are a number of methods used to charge overheads to the cost unit. Using the cost unit itself as the basis for the calculation is the simplest way. This is done by dividing the production overheads for each production department by the number of cost units passing through them. This gives an overhead absorption rate for each department.

Continuing with our example, Jarvis Jackets Ltd, the company makes two styles of jacket: the classic and the designer. In one year, 4,000 classic jackets are made and 1,000 designer jackets. We can now calculate the total overhead cost for each jacket using the cost unit overhead absorption rate. This needs some care. We need to remember that each jacket must pass through the Cutting Department and the Stitching Department. Therefore, the overhead absorption rate must be calculated separately for each department and then added together as follows:

| Overhead absorption rate | Cutting Dept | Stitching Dept |
|---|---|---|
| Cost units | $\dfrac{£45,000}{5,000} = £9$ per cost unit | $\dfrac{£60,000}{5,000} = £12$ per cost unit |

The total overhead cost is therefore $£9 + £12 = £21$ per cost unit.

Although using cost units is the easiest method, it would be unfair to charge the same overhead to the different styles of jackets if the more expensive jackets use up more of the resources. It is fairer to make sure that the product which uses up more of the resources bears more of the overhead. For example, if you took your car to the garage merely to have the brakes adjusted and you were charged the same overhead charge as someone who had had a full service, you would be very upset. It would not help if the garage owner told you that he had worked out his overhead charge by dividing his total overheads by the number of cars repaired.

So what other basis might he use for charging overheads on the work done? You may consider that the overheads should be charged on a time basis. Garages usually charge an hourly rate for repairs, as do many other businesses, such as plumbers and electricians. The hourly rate can be calculated on the basis of the time an employee spends working on the product, the direct labour hour rate, or on how long the product is on a machine, the machine hour rate.

## Activity

Returning to our example of Jarvis Jackets Ltd, calculate an hourly overhead rate for each department based either on direct labour hours or machine hours. The following table gives details of how many direct labour hours and machine hours are required in each department to make the 5,000 jackets:

| Overhead absorption rate | Cutting Dept | Stitching Dept |
|---|---|---|
| Direct labour hours | 10,000 | 30,000 |
| Machine hours | 40,000 | 5,000 |

You may have found this difficult. You should have divided the overheads for each department first by the total number of direct labour hours and then by the total number of machine hours to give the absorption rates:

| Overhead absorption rate | Cutting Dept | Stitching Dept |
|---|---|---|
| Direct labour hours | $\dfrac{£45,000}{10,000} = £4.50$ | $\dfrac{£60,000}{30,000} = £2.00$ |
| Machine hours | $\dfrac{£45,000}{40,000} = £1.13$ | $\dfrac{£60,000}{5,000} = £12.00$ |

We have now calculated three different overhead absorption rates for each department. The overhead absorption rate gives us a method of charging the total overheads of the department to all the cost units passing through it. The *cost unit overhead absorption rate* was calculated by dividing the overheads for the department by the total number of cost units. The *direct labour hour overhead absorption rate* was calculated by dividing the overheads for the department by the total number of direct labour hours. Finally, the *machine hour overhead absorption rate* was calculated by dividing the overheads for the department by the total number of machine hours. There are other types of overhead absorption rates which are used, often based on a percentage calculation, but we will concentrate on these three as they are frequently used and illustrate the main principles.

The following table summarises the information we have so far:

|  | Cutting Dept | Stitching Dept |
| --- | --- | --- |
| Total overheads | £45,000 | £60,000 |
| Number of cost units | 5,000 | 5,000 |
| Direct labour hours | 10,000 | 30,000 |
| Machine hours | 40,000 | 5,000 |
| **Overhead absorption rate** | | |
| Cost unit | £9.00 | £12.00 |
| Direct labour hour | £4.50 | £2.00 |
| Machine hour | £1.13 | £12.00 |

For illustrative purposes we have calculated three types of overhead rate, but only one will be used in each department. Now we need to select the fairest rate for each department for charging the overhead to each jacket, bearing in mind that the same rate need not be used in both departments. As already pointed out, it would be unfair to use the cost unit absorption rate because the two types of jacket use unequal amounts of resources. With the other two rates you should have considered the main resources being provided in each department by the expenditure on overheads. You will see that in the Cutting Department the overheads have been incurred mainly in the supply of machine hours. Therefore, this is the most appropriate basis for calculating the overhead absorption rate. In the Finishing Department the work is mainly manual and therefore the direct labour hour rate would be the most appropriate overhead absorption rate.

## 15.5 Calculating the Total Unit Cost

We have now reached the final and most important stage of our calculations, which is to calculate the total cost of making each classic jacket and each designer jacket. Although we have spent some time learning how the overheads are calculated, we must not forget to charge for the direct materials and direct labour. The following information is available:

|                                         | Classic jacket | Designer jacket |
|-----------------------------------------|:--------------:|:---------------:|
| Direct materials                        | £50            | £80             |
| Direct labour                           | £20            | £40             |
| Cutting Department machine hours         | 7              | 12              |
| Stitching Department direct labour hours | 5              | 10              |

**Total cost of one jacket**

|                                                    | Classic jacket | Designer jacket |
|----------------------------------------------------|:--------------:|:---------------:|
|                                                    | £              | £               |
| **Direct costs**                                   |                |                 |
| Direct materials                                   | 50.00          | 80.00           |
| Direct labour                                      | 20.00          | 40.00           |
| **Production overheads**                           |                |                 |
| Cutting Dept (£1.13 per machine hour)              | 7.91           | 13.56           |
| Stitching Dept (£2.00 per direct labour hour)      | 10.00          | 20.00           |
| **Production cost**                                | 87.91          | 153.56          |

You may consider that calculating a different overhead absorption rate for each production department is a complex activity: it would be far simpler to calculate a factory-wide absorption rate. Thus, if a factory had total overheads of £1m and there were 250,000 direct labour hours worked during the period, the overhead absorption rate would be £4 per hour in all the separate departments. Although this method is simple and inexpensive to apply, it is likely to generate incorrect data, except in the most straightforward production systems. If there are a number of departments and products do not spend an equal time in each department, separate departmental overhead absorption rates must be calculated. If this is not done, some products will receive a higher overhead charge than they should fairly bear and others a lower charge. This will make it difficult for management to control costs and make decisions on pricing and alternative production systems.

## 15.6 Service Cost Centres

So far, we have considered only production cost centres. However, most businesses also have *service cost centres*. Examples include departments which are associated with the production areas, such as maintenance, stores and canteen, and others which are not, such as administration, sales and distribution. The first stage is to calculate the total production cost as before, but this time we will include the service cost centres associated with the production area. We will deal with other overheads later. The same procedure is used; the different types of production overheads are allocated and apportioned, and subtotalled. Then the subtotal of the service cost centres is apportioned to the production cost centres on a fair basis.

# Activity

Country Pine Ltd, the business we looked at earlier in this chapter, has expanded and now makes quality bookcases of different sizes. The following information is available:

| | Joinery Dept | Finishing Dept | Maintenance Dept |
|---|---|---|---|
| Area | 200 sq metres | 200 sq metres | 100 sq metres |
| Number of employees | 12 | 16 | 4 |
| Value of machinery | £250,000 | £100,000 | £50,000 |

Complete the following overhead analysis by showing the basis of apportionment and the total overhead to be borne by each of the three production cost centres. The allocated overhead costs have been entered for you. Once you have arrived at a subtotal for all three cost centres, you must apportion the total for the Maintenance Department (a service department) over the two production departments on whatever basis you consider appropriate:

**Country Pine Ltd**
**Overhead analysis**

| Overhead | Total cost | Basis of apportionment | Joinery Dept | Finishing Dept | Maintenance Dept |
|---|---|---|---|---|---|
| | £ | | £ | £ | £ |
| Indirect materials | 10,000 | Allocated | 6,000 | 3,000 | 1,000 |
| Indirect labour | 31,500 | Allocated | 4,000 | 8,000 | 19,500 |
| Rent | 20,000 | | | | |
| Electricity | 5,000 | | | | |
| Depreciation on machinery | 40,000 | | | | |
| Supervisors' salaries | 36,000 | | | | |
| Subtotal | 142,500 | | | | |
| Apportioned service cost centre | – | | | | |
| Total | 142,500 | | | | |

Your completed overhead analysis should look like this:

**Country Pine Ltd**
**Overhead analysis**

| Overhead | Total cost | Basis of apportionment | Joinery Dept | Finishing Dept | Maintenance Dept |
|---|---|---|---|---|---|
| | £ | | £ | £ | £ |
| Indirect materials | 10,000 | Allocated | 6,000 | 3,000 | 1,000 |
| Indirect labour | 31,500 | Allocated | 4,000 | 8,000 | 19,500 |
| Rent | 20,000 | Area | 8,000 | 8,000 | 4,000 |
| Electricity | 5,000 | Area | 2,000 | 2,000 | 1,000 |
| Depreciation on machinery | 40,000 | Value of machinery | 25,000 | 10,000 | 5,000 |
| Supervisors' salaries | 36,000 | Number of employees | 13,500 | 18,000 | 4,500 |
| Subtotal | 142,500 | | 58,500 | 49,000 | 35,000 |
| Apportioned service cost centre | – | Value of machinery | 25,000 | 10,000 | (35,000) |
| Total | 142,500 | | 83,500 | 59,000 | – |

The subtotal of the Maintenance Department has been apportioned to the two production departments on the basis of the value of the machinery in the Production Department. The value of the machinery in the Maintenance Department itself is excluded from the calculations.

Continuing this example, the overhead absorption rate in the Joinery Department is based on 10,000 machine hours and in the Finishing Department on 30,000 direct labour hours. We can now calculate the two overhead absorption rates in the Joinery and Finishing Departments. This is done by dividing the total cost centre overhead for the period by the number of units of the basis of absorption; in this case, machine hours in the Joinery Department and direct labour hours in the Finishing Department:

$$\text{Joinery Department:} \quad \frac{£83,500}{10,000} = £8.35 \text{ per machine hour}$$

$$\text{Finishing Department:} \quad \frac{£59,000}{30,000} = £1.97 \text{ per direct labour hour}$$

Supposing a customer puts in an order for a bookcase for which the direct costs are direct materials £80.00 and direct labour £50.00. It is estimated that the bookcase will require 8 machine hours in the Joinery Department and 10 labour hours in the Finishing Department. We can calculate the total production cost as follows:

|  | £ | £ |
|---|---|---|
| **Direct costs** | | |
| Direct materials | 80.00 | |
| Direct labour | 50.00 | |
| **Prime cost** | | 130.00 |
| **Production overheads** | | |
| Joinery Dept (8 hours @ £8.35) | 66.80 | |
| Finishing Dept (10 hours @ £1.97) | 19.70 | 86.50 |
| **Production cost** | | 216.50 |

What we have just calculated is the production cost, but you will remember from Chapter 13 that in order to find out the total product cost, we need to add a proportion of the indirect costs, which are as follows:

| Administration overheads | £18,250 |
|---|---|
| Selling and distribution overheads | £27,750 |
| Production costs | £230,000 |

The formula is:

$$\frac{\text{Administration overhead} + \text{Selling overheads}}{\text{Production costs}} \times 100$$

Substituting the figures in the formula:

$$\frac{£18,250 + £27,750}{£230,000} \times 100 = 20\%$$

So, the total indirect cost is 20% of the production cost:

$$£216.50 \times 20\% = £43.30$$

Now we have all the figures we need to calculate the total product cost of the bookcase:

|  |  | £ | £ |
|---|---|---|---|
| | **Direct costs** | | |
| *Add* | Direct materials | 80.00 | |
| | Direct labour | 50.00 | |
| | **Prime cost** | | 130.00 |
| *Add* | Production overheads | | 86.50 |
| | **Production cost** | | 216.50 |
| *Add* | **Indirect costs** | | 43.30 |
| | **Total product cost** | | 259.80 |

## 15.7 Predetermined Overhead Absorption Rates

So far, we have implied that the absorption rates are based on actual costs, but in practice these costs are predetermined. Before the start of a financial period, which may be as short as a month or as long as a year for this purpose, decisions will be made on the likely level of activity and the probable costs which will be incurred during the period. In Chapter 21 we will be looking at *budgetary control*, which is the process of establishing financial plans, in detail.

Once the likely level of activity has been decided, the amount of machine hours, labour hours and overheads which are likely to incurred can be determined. This allows a *predetermined overhead absorption rate* to be calculated at the beginning of a period and applied throughout. The actual costs are not used because the collection, analysis and absorption of overheads to products or jobs takes a considerable time, and the actual figures may not be available until after the end of the financial period. Naturally it would be impossible to wait until then to invoice customers, submit estimates, make decisions on production methods or carry out any other management task.

## Activity

What problems do you think might arise from using a predetermined overhead rate instead of an actual rate?

The main problems are as follows:

- The actual overheads are very likely to differ from those budgeted.
- The actual base of absorption may differ from that used in the budget.
- A combination of both these factors.

These problems can have serious consequences. If an organisation has been invoicing customers on a predetermined overhead rate which is wrong, it could have a significant impact on profits. Where the overheads charged to production are higher than the actual overheads for the period, the variance is known as *overabsorption*. In other words, too much overhead has been charged to production. Where the overheads charged to production are lower than the actual overheads, the variance is known as *underabsorption*.

Although we have used the manufacture of furniture and jackets in this chapter as examples, the same principles of allocating, apportioning and absorbing overheads apply in all organisations where management wants to know the total cost of a product, service or department.

## 15.8 Conclusions

In this chapter we have looked at the methods used to calculate the total cost of a product or service. We have explained how an overhead analysis is drawn up and how overheads are either allocated or apportioned to cost centres. We have examined the various methods for charging the overheads of a cost centre to the cost units passing through it and calculated the total cost of a product. In addition, we have discussed the practical problems which may arise and how they can be resolved.

Having completed this chapter, you should now be able to:

- describe the various stages in costing overheads;
- complete an overhead analysis;
- discuss the problems associated with costing overheads;
- calculate the total cost of a product or service.

## Exercises

Complete the following sentences:

**1** Cost apportionment is ...........................................................................................................
**2** An overhead analysis allows ...........................................................................................

**3** The overhead absorption rate is the method for ....................................................

**4** The overheads for service cost centres must be .................................................

**5** The direct labour hour absorption rate is calculated by .......................................

Are the following statements true or false?

**6** Cost allocation is a technique for charging overheads to cost units.

**7** Cost apportionment is the process of sharing overhead costs between two or more cost centres in proportion to the benefit they receive.

**8** Absorption costing can be used where the cost centre caused the overhead to be incurred and the exact amount is known.

**9** It is always best to use the direct labour hour absorption rate.

**10** The overheads of service cost centres are not part of the total cost of a unit.

You may wish to read more widely than this book to answer the following questions fully, but you can check the main points by referring to the appropriate sections in this chapter.

**11** Draw up a list of the main stages in finding out the total cost of a product. (Sections 15.3 and 15.4)

**12** What are the two main problems in charging overheads to cost units? (Section 15.3)

**13** Describe three overhead cost absorption rates. (Section 15.4)

**14** What are predetermined overhead absorption rates? (Section 15.7)

Multiple choice questions (more than one answer may apply):

**15** Costs must be allocated to a cost centre or cost unit if they are:

    **a** indirect costs
    **b** direct costs
    **c** production overheads
    **d** other overheads.

**16** The reasons for charging costs to cost centres are:

    **a** to determine the costs of operating a cost centre
    **b** to enable overheads to be charged to products
    **c** neither of these
    **d** both of these.

**17** A cost unit can be:

    **a** a complete product
    **b** a subassembly
    **c** a unit of production
    **d** none of these.

**18** A cost centre can be:

    **a** a department
    **b** a factory
    **c** neither of these
    **d** both of these.

**19** When calculating total unit cost, service cost centres in the factory are best:

    **a** ignored completely
    **b** added to selling and distribution overheads
    **c** apportioned to production cost centres
    **d** charged to cost units.

**20** An overhead analysis is prepared:

  **a** to apportion and allocate overheads to cost centres
  **b** to apportion and allocate direct costs
  **c** to calculate the total cost of cost unit
  **d** to calculate the direct costs.

Practice questions:

**21** In what circumstances would you recommend the use of the machine hour overhead absorption rate?

**22** Describe the treatment of administration, selling and distribution overheads in calculating total unit cost.

**23** What are the advantages and disadvantages of using a 'factory-wide' overhead absorption rate?

**24** Describe the most appropriate way of dealing with underabsorption or overabsorption of overheads.

**25** West Wales Windsurfers Ltd make two models of windsurfer. The company has two production departments: The Shaping Department and the Finishing Department. It also has a canteen which serves all the employees. The budgeted sales and costs for the next year are as follows:

|  | **Fun Wave** | **Hot Racer** |
|---|---|---|
| Selling price per unit | £600 | £700 |
| Sales/production volume | 2,000 units | 2,500 units |
| Material costs per unit | £80 | £50 |
| **Direct labour** | | |
| Shaping Dept (£3 per hour) | 50 hours per unit | 60 hours per unit |
| Finishing Dept (£2 per hour) | 40 hours per unit | 40 hours per unit |
| **Machine hours** | | |
| Shaping Dept | 30 hours per unit | 80 hours per unit |
| Finishing Dept | 10 hours per unit | |

|  | **Shaping Dept** £ | **Finishing Dept** £ | **Canteen** £ | **Total** £ |
|---|---|---|---|---|
| **Production overheads** | | | | |
| Variable | 260,000 | 90,000 | – | 350,000 |
| Fixed | 420,000 | 300,000 | 160,000 | 880,000 |
| Total | 680,000 | 390,000 | 160,000 | 1,230,000 |
| Number of employees | 150 | 90 | 10 | |
| Floor area (sq metres) | 40,000 | 10,000 | 10,000 | |

  **a** Advise the company on the method of overhead absorption which should be used for each department, giving reasons for your choice.
  **b** Calculate an appropriate overhead absorption rate for each production department.
  **c** Calculate the budgeted production cost per unit of each model of windsurfer.

(Answers on pp. 336–7)

# 16 Specific-order Costing

## 16.1 Introduction

You may remember from Chapter 1 that the different costing methods used for establishing actual costs can be divided in to two main groups according to the nature of production. Some businesses make products or provide services as *continuous operations* – such as a brewery producing cans of beer or a utility company providing electricity, gas or water – and we shall be looking at the costing methods used in these types of businesses in Chapter 17. Other businesses carry out their activities at the *specific order* of clients – such as a building firm that builds a house to meet the specific requirements of a client or an electrician who repairs a washing machine. In this chapter we shall be looking at the main specific-order costing methods used by these types of businesses.

*Specific-order costing* is a costing process that assesses the individual costs of performing each particular job. It is used in organisations where different products are manufactured and also in service organisations where the cost of each service provided is required. A *job* is an identifiable discrete piece of work carried out by an organisation. For costing purposes, a job is usually given a job number, which enables the costs to be charged to the number so that all the individual costs for a job can be collected. The costs incurred in carrying out a job are usually analysed into the constituent costs, such as direct materials costs, direct labour costs and overheads.

There are three main methods of costing for specific orders. Although they have much in common, each has its own specific requirements, depending on the nature of the industry. *Job costing* is used when customers specify their requirements and usually the job is short and small. Job costing is likely to be used by small businesses such as landscape gardeners, electricians, plumbers, decorators, small printing firms and small builders. Like job costing, *contract costing* is also used when customers specify their requirements. However, the job is normally long and large. Contract costing is likely to be used in civil engineering and road construction. *Batch costing* is used when a quantity of identical units are processed on the premises as a batch. The batch is treated as a single job and all the costs charged to it. The total costs for the batch may then be divided by the number of good units in the batch to give an average cost per unit, if this information is required.

It is not unusual for a business that is using job or batch costing to use *cost plus pricing* where the selling price is calculated by adding a fixed percentage (margin) to the cost of the job. This approach has a number of weaknesses as there is no incentive to control the cost of the job, it ignores market conditions and the total costs are dependent on the method of overhead recovery. However, it is simple to apply and where competitive pricing is not an issue, it allows the business to ensure that it recovers its costs.

## 16.2 **Job Costing**

*Job costing* is used when customers specify their requirements and the job is relatively small and short in duration. It is often carried out in the factory or workshop, although very small jobs may be carried out on the client's premises. The type of *job costing* adopted depends on the complexity of the organisation and the sophistication of its recording system, but in all forms of job costing rigorous costing procedures are needed. The main stages are as follows:

1 The customer informs the company of the *specific requirements.*
2 The estimating department prepares an *estimate*, quoting a selling price to the customer.
3 If the customer accepts the estimate and places an order, a *works order* with an identifying number is raised.
4 A *materials requisition note* is prepared so that materials can be drawn from the stores department.
5 A *purchase requisition note* is sent to the purchasing department for any special materials and equipment that may be required.
6 Traditionally, a *job card* is raised. This shows the written instructions for the operations to be carried out for the completion of a job. The instructions are now likely to be in the form of a computer printout.
7 If workers with special skills are needed, a *labour requirement note* is sent to the personnel department.
8 The job is entered into the *production schedule* with a starting date that will allow completion by the agreed delivery date.

Failure to maintain adequate records of all the costs relating to a specific job means that the profit or loss for the job cannot be calculated and future estimates based on past records will be inaccurate. All systems used to collect job costs concentrate on identifying the materials and labour for each job and recording them on a *job cost sheet*. Although many businesses have now adopted computerised systems, the principles remain the same.

Job costing is usually combined with *absorption costing* (see Chapter 15) and all the examples in this chapter are based on that assumption. A simple system for collecting costs has the following characteristics:

1  A *materials requisition note* is sent to the stores department identifying the materials required for the job. The materials requisition note is used to cost the materials to the job cost sheet.
2  A *job card* is given to the worker who is performing the first operation. The starting and finishing times for that operation are clocked onto the ticket and the same procedure is followed for subsequent operation. Finally, the job card is sent to the cost office where the time is costed and entered on the job cost sheet.
3  *Direct expenses* are entered on the job cost sheet from the invoices or an analysis of the cash book.
4  The cost of *direct materials* and *direct labour* as recorded on the *job cost sheet* is charged to the *job account*.
5  The job account is charged with an appropriate share of the *production overheads*, usually on the basis of predetermined overhead absorption rates.
6  If the job has not been completed at the end of an accounting period, it is valued at *production cost* on the balance sheet.
7  On completion of the job, an appropriate share of the administration, selling and distribution overheads are charged to the job account. This account now shows the *total cost* of the job.

If the business has a number of very small jobs it is not practical to keep a separate job cost sheet for each job. Instead, a general jobbing account is kept to which all the cost the jobs are charged.

We are now ready to calculate the cost of a job.

## Activity

Mayo Metalwork Ltd is a company in the jobbing industry. The firm uses absorption costing and the following information is available:

| Department | Budgeted overheads £ | Basis of absorption |
|---|---|---|
| Machine shop | 12,000 | 3,000 machine hours |
| Press shop | 7,000 | 2,000 labour hours |
| Assembly shop | 6,000 | 2,500 labour hours |

An order has been place for Job No 365 with a selling price of £5,200. The following information relates to the job:

| | |
|---|---|
| Direct materials | £1,415 |
| Direct labour: | |
| Machine shop | 50 hours @ £3.00 per hour |
| Press shop | 180 hours @ £2.50 per hour |
| Assembly shop | 100 hours @ £1.75 per hour |
| Time booked in machine shop | 210 machine hours |

Using the following pro forma, calculate the total cost of the job and the profit:

**Mayo Metalwork Ltd**
**Job No 365: Total cost**

|  |  | £ | £ |
|---|---|---|---|
| | **Direct costs** | | |
| | Direct materials | | |
| *Add* | Direct labour | | |
| | Machine shop | | |
| | Press shop | | |
| | Assembly shop | | |
| | **Prime cost** | | |
| *Add* | **Production overheads** | | |
| | Machine shop | | |
| | Press shop | | |
| | Assembly shop | | |
| | **Production cost** | | |
| *Add* | **Indirect costs** | | |
| | Administration and selling overheads | | |
| | **Total cost** | | |
| *Add* | Profit | | |
| | Selling price | | 5,200 |

The first step is to work out the overhead absorption rates:

$$\text{Machine shop} \quad \frac{£12,000}{3,000} = £4.00 \text{ per machine hour}$$

$$\text{Press shop} \quad \frac{£7,000}{2,000} = £3.50 \text{ per labour hour}$$

$$\text{Assembly shop} \quad \frac{£6,000}{2,500} = £2.40 \text{ per labour hour}$$

Your completed costing should look like this:

---

**Mayo Metalwork Ltd**
**Job No 365: Total cost**

|  |  | £ | £ |
|---|---|---:|---:|
| | **Direct costs** | | |
| | Direct materials | | 1,415 |
| *Add* | Direct labour | | |
| | Machine shop | 150 | |
| | Press shop | 450 | |
| | Assembly shop | 175 | 775 |
| | **Prime cost** | | 2,190 |
| *Add* | **Production overheads** | | |
| | Machine shop (210 × £4.00) | 840 | |
| | Press shop (180 × £3.50) | 630 | |
| | Assembly shop (100 × £2.40) | 240 | 1,710 |
| | **Production cost** | | 3,900 |
| *Add* | **Indirect costs** | | |
| | Administration and selling overheads | | 975 |
| | **Total cost** | | 4,875 |
| *Add* | Profit | | 325 |
| | Selling price | | 5,200 |

---

## 16.3 Batch Costing

A *batch* is a measure of production often used if the individual units of production are small or homogeneous. *Batch costing* is a form of costing that is particularly appropriate where the cost per unit of production would result in an infinitesimal unit cost and where homogeneous units of production can conveniently be collected together to form discrete batches; for example, because a customer orders a quantity of identical items or because replacement stock is required and an internal manufacturing order has been raised.

Costing a batch is very similar to costing a job. The same procedures are followed, but each batch treated as a separate, identifiable job. When the batch has been completed, the total batch cost is divided by the number of good units produced to give the *cost per unit*. Spoilt or scrap units are not included in the calculation.

---

## Activity

Shaws Ltd manufactures small pipe couplings and has the following budgeted overheads for the month based on normal capacity usage:

| Department | Budgeted overheads | Budgeted activity |
|---|---|---|
| Engineering Dept | £9,000 | 3,000 machine hours |
| Finishing Dept | £5,000 | 2,000 direct labour hours |

Selling and administration overheads are 10% of production costs. An order for 100 couplings made as Batch SB21 has the following direct costs:

| Materials | £5,000 |
|---|---|
| Labour: | |
| Engineering Dept | 60 hours @ £5 per hour |
| Finishing Dept | 150 hours @ £4 per hour |

The job takes 220 hours in the Engineering Department. Calculate the total cost of the batch and the cost per unit.

The first step is to work out the direct labour costs:

$$\text{Engineering Dept} \quad 60 \text{ hours} \times £5 = £300$$

$$\text{Finishing Dept} \quad 150 \text{ hours} \times £4 = £600$$

You also need to calculate the overhead absorption rates to work out the production overheads for the two departments:

$$\text{Engineering Dept} \quad \frac{£9,000}{3,000 \text{ hours}} = £3 \text{ per machine hour} \times 220 \text{ hours}$$

$$= £660$$

$$\text{Finishing Dept} \quad \frac{£5,000}{2,000} = £2.50 \text{ per labour hour} \times 150 \text{ hours}$$

$$= £375$$

Your completed costing should look like this:

**Shaws Ltd**
**Batch SB21: Total cost**

| | | £ | £ |
|---|---|---|---|
| **Direct costs** | | | |
| Direct materials | | | 5,000 |
| *Add* Direct labour | | | |
| Engineering Dept | | 300 | |
| Finishing Dept | | 600 | 900 |
| **Prime cost** | | | 5,900 |

| *Add* | **Production overheads** | | |
|---|---|---|---|
| | Engineering Dept | 660 | |
| | Finishing Dept | 375 | 1,035 |
| | **Production cost** | | 6,935 |
| *Add* | **Indirect costs** | | |
| | Administration and selling overheads (10%) | | 694 |
| | **Total cost** | | 7,629 |

$$\text{Cost per unit} = \frac{£7,629}{100} = £76.29$$

In both job costing and batch costing it is possible that the finished output is not of the standard required, but rather than scrapping the goods it may be possible to remedy the defects. The costs incurred in doing so are known are *rectification costs*. If it is unusual for this to happen and the costs can be traced to a specific job, the rectification costs should be charged to that job. If rectification is a normal occurrence, any costs incurred should be included in the production overheads.

## 16.4 Contract Costing

*Contract costing* is a costing technique applied to large, long-term contracts, such as construction and civil engineering projects, where the contract is conducted off the contractor's premises, in some cases abroad. The client appoints a contractor and a formal contract is drawn up which includes details of what work is to be carried out, the method and timing of payments and any financial penalties that can be invoked if the work is not completed to the required standard and in the agreed time. Contract costing allows the relevant costs for each contract to be identified and collected, and the profit or loss to be calculated on a contract at the end of a financial period. On uncompleted contracts at the end of the financial period, only a proportion of the profit is transferred.

The main characteristics of contract costing are as follows:

1 Each contract takes a long time to complete and may span more than one accounting period.
2 Most material is ordered specifically for each contract.
3 Most labour costs, including staff such as site clerks and security guards whose wages are normally regarded as indirect costs, are direct costs to the contract.
4 Most expenses, such as site electricity and telephones, are direct costs to the contract.
5 A method must be found to charge plant and machinery used on site to the contract and the most appropriate is usually a time basis.

6 Nearly all the overhead costs can be identified as head office costs.

7 An architect or surveyor inspects the work periodically and issues *certificates* to the contractor which detail satisfactorily completed work. Such work is valued at selling price and the contractor sends the certificate to the client with an invoice to obtain interim payments.

8 The contract often states that the client can withhold a proportion of the contract value for a period after final completion. This is know as *retention monies* and until the date when this is finally settle the contractor must make good any defects appearing in the work.

9 Because of the conditions on site and the involvement of non-clerical staff, great attention must be paid to collecting prime documentation and controlling costs.

The general procedure for contract costing is as follows:

1 A separate *account* for each contract is opened. This is charged with all the costs and credited with the contract price. Each contract account is regarded as a separate profit and loss account. The profit or loss on each account is transferred to the main profit and loss on contracts account.

2 *Materials* are charged either direct from the invoice or, if drawn from stores, from a materials requisition note. Any materials returned to stores from site are credited to the contract

3 All *labour* must be charged to each contract. If employees are working on a number of contracts at the same time, they must complete time sheets for each contract.

4 *Direct expenses* can be charged directly from invoices submitted to the company. In the construction industry a significant amount of the work may be completed by subcontractors, and these are regarded as direct expenses.

5 Any *plant and machinery costs* are charged to the contract in a number of different ways, depending on the circumstances. If it is hired, the cost is a direct expense. If it is owned, but on site short-term it is charged at an hourly rate for each item. If it is owned but is on site long-term the contract is charged with the value of the plant on arrival at the site and credited with its depreciated value when it is removed.

6 *Overhead costs* are usually added on the basis of a *predetermined overhead rate*. If a contract is unfinished at the end of the financial period, head office general costs are not added and only production overheads are included in the value of any work in progress.

7 The *contract price* is credited to the contract account from the *architect's certificate* and any profit or loss transferred to the profit and loss on contracts account. An agreed percentage should not be transferred until all defects have been remedied and *retention monies* received.

We can now use an example to illustrate the costing for a completed contract. Kennet Construction Ltd has just completed a terrace of houses for a client in the financial year and the period for retention monies has been satisfied. The following information is available at the end of the financial period:

---

**Kennet Construction Ltd**
**Contract 586: Worcester Place**

|  | £000 |
|---|---|
| Value of materials delivered to site | 230 |
| Wages | 250 |
| Subcontractors' charges | 30 |
| Site expenses | 20 |
| Plant transferred to site | 160 |
| Materials returned to stores | 30 |
| Plant removed from site (depreciation value) | 124 |
| Head office charges (10% of wages) | 25 |
| Value of work certified | 75 |

---

Using this information, we can now draw up a contract account for contract 586.

---

**Kennet Construction Ltd**
**Contract account 586**

|  | £000 |  | £000 |
|---|---|---|---|
| Materials | 230 | Materials to stores | 30 |
| Wages | 250 | Plant transferred | 124 |
| Plant to site | 160 | Cost of contract c/d | 561 |
| Subcontractors | 30 |  |  |
| Site expenses | 20 |  |  |
| Head office charges | 25 |  |  |
|  | 715 |  | 715 |
| Cost of contract b/d | 561 | Value of work certified | 750 |
| Profit on contract | 189 |  |  |
|  | 750 |  | 750 |

---

The profit on the contract of £189,000 will be transferred to the main profit and loss account. The value of the work certified of £750,000 will be debited to the client's account and this is shown as a debtor in the balance sheet until payment has been received.

However, a particular problem of long-term projects is the determination of annual profits to be taken to the profit and loss account when the contract is *incomplete*. This requires the valuation of *work in progress*

*(WIP)* at the end of the financial year. When work has been done, but has not yet been certified, it is valued at cost, without any profit element. The estimated profit for the entire contract is first calculated by deducting the total estimated costs of the contract from the total value of the contract. The total estimated costs of the contract comprise the actual costs incurred to date, the estimated costs to completion and the estimated future costs of any rectification and guarantee work. The amount of profit to be taken in the financial period is then calculated by applying the following formula:

$$\text{Profit to date} = \frac{\text{Cost of work completed}}{\text{Total estimated costs of contract}} \times \text{Estimated contract price}$$

If it is calculated that by deducting the total estimated costs from the value of the contract there is a loss rather than a profit, the loss should be shown in full in the accounts for the period.

We can now illustrate how a contact account is drawn up for an incomplete contract with another example taken from the books of Kennet Construction Ltd. The company has a long-term contract to construct a shopping mall called the Colonnades. At the end of the financial period, 31 December, the following information is available:

### Kennet Construction Ltd
### Contract 590: The Colonnades

|  | £ |
|---|---|
| Materials purchased for contract | 125,160 |
| Materials from stores | 22,240 |
| Operating costs of plant and machinery | 11,470 |
| Book value of plant to site 1 January | 96,420 |
| Wages | 43,120 |
| Subcontractors' charges | 20,000 |
| Site salaries | 10,000 |
| Site expenses | 16,200 |
| Materials returned to stores | 1,230 |
| Book value of plant removed from site | 10,640 |
| Materials on site at 31 December | 10,020 |
| Book value of plant on site at 31 December | 74,240 |
| Cost of work in progress not certified at 31 December | 32,580 |
| Total contract value | 500,000 |
| Value of work certified at 31 December | 250,000 |
| Estimated costs to complete contract | 220,000 |

Using this information, the contract account is drawn up as follows:

## Kennet Construction Ltd
## Contract account 590

| | £ | | £ |
|---|---|---|---|
| Materials purchased | 125,160 | Materials to stores | 1,230 |
| Materials from stores | 22,240 | Plant transferred | 10,640 |
| Plant operating costs | 11,470 | Materials on site c/d | 10,020 |
| Plant to site | 96,420 | Plant on site c/d | 74,240 |
| Wages | 43,120 | Work in progress c/d | 32,580 |
| Subcontractors' costs | 20,000 | Cost of work certified | 215,900 |
| Site salaries | 10,000 | | |
| Site expenses | 16,200 | | |
| | 344,610 | | 344,610 |
| Cost of work certified b/d | 215,900 | Value of work certified | 250,000 |
| Profit on contract to date | 16,718 | | |
| Profit in suspense c/d | 17,382 | | |
| | 250,000 | | 250,000 |
| 1 January | | | |
| Materials b/d | 10,020 | Profit in suspense b/d | 17,382 |
| Plant b/d | 74,240 | | |
| Work in progress b/d | 32,580 | | |

There are a number of calculations in the account which need explaining. The cost of work certified (£215,900) is the net balance on the first part of the contract account. The cost of work not certified (the work in progress of £32,580) is added to the cost of work certified (£215,900) to give the cost of all work done to date (£248,480). The profit for the period is calculated as follows:

| | £ | £ |
|---|---|---|
| Contract value | | 500,000 |
| Costs to date | 248,480 | |
| Estimated future costs | 220,000 | 468,000 |
| Estimated total profit | | 31,520 |

As the contract is not yet finished, it would be wrong to take the full amount of estimated profit of £31,520 and only a proportion should be recognised in the profit and loss account. There are a number of ways in which this can be calculated and the one used in this example uses costs as follows:

$$\text{Profit for period} = \frac{\text{Cost of work done}}{\text{Estimated total costs}} \times \text{Estimated total profit}$$

$$= \frac{£248,480}{£468,480} \times £31,520$$

$$= £16,718$$

The profit in suspense is calculated as follows:

|  |  | £ |
|---|---|---|
| | Value of work certified | 250,000 |
| *Less* | Cost of work certified | 215,900 |
| | | 34,100 |
| *Less* | Profit in period | 16,718 |
| | Profit in suspense | 17,382 |

## Activity

Kennet Construction Ltd started Contract LX24 on 1 March and completed on 31 August in the same accounting period. Draw up a contract account from the following information:

| | £ |
|---|---|
| Direct materials | 65,000 |
| Direct labour | 42,000 |
| Direct expenses | 13,000 |

The book value of plant charged to the contract on 1 March was £75,000. At the completion of the contract the plant was removed from site and had a written down value of £68,000. The company has the practice of charging overheads to contracts at the rate of £1,500 per month. The contract price was £150,000 and the final certificate has been issued.

Your completed contract account should look like this:

### Kennet Construction Ltd
### Contract account LX24

| | £ | | £ |
|---|---|---|---|
| Materials | 65,000 | Cost of sales (to profit and | 136,000 |
| Labour | 42,000 | loss account) | |
| Expenses | 13,000 | | |
| Plant costs (£75,000 – £68,000) | 7,000 | | |
| Overheads (£1,500 × 6 months) | 9,000 | | |
| | 136,000 | | 136,000 |

In the company's profit and loss account £150,000 will be included in the figure for turnover and £136,000 will be shown in the cost of sales figure. Assuming that there are no retention monies, and no cash has been received from the client, an amount of £150,000 is due.

## 16.5 Conclusions

In this chapter we have looked at three techniques associated with specific-order costing.

Job costing is used when customers specify their requirements and the job is relatively small and short in duration.

Batch costing is often used if the individual units of production are small or homogeneous. Each batch is considered as a separate, identifiable job and the costs are collected in the same way as for job costing. When the batch has been completed, the total batch cost is divided by the number of good units produced to give the cost per unit.

Contract costing is a costing technique applied to long-term contracts, such as construction and civil engineering projects. A particular problem of long-term projects is how to determine the annual profits to be taken to the profit and loss account when the contract is incomplete. This requires the valuation of work in progress at the end of the financial year. When work has been done, but has not yet been certified, it is valued at cost, without any profit element.

Having completed this chapter, you should now be able to:

- explain what is meant by specific order costing;
- calculate the profit or loss for a job;
- calculate the profit or loss for a batch;
- calculate the profit or loss for a completed contract;
- calculate the profit or loss for an incomplete contract to date and the profit or loss in suspense.

---

## Exercises

Complete the following sentences:

**1** Specific-order costing assesses ...................................................................

**2** Job costing is appropriate ......................................................................

**3** Batch costing is appropriate .....................................................................

**4** Contract costing is appropriate ..................................................................

**5** Rectification costs are ........................................................................

Are the following statements true or false?

**6** Costing a batch is very similar to costing a job.

**7** Subcontractors' wages are normally regarded as direct labour.

**8** Retention monies are a proportion of the price withheld by the client.

**9** Completed work on a contract which has not been certified is valued without a profit element.

**10** No profit can be taken at the period end unless the contract is complete.

You may wish to read more widely than this book to answer the following questions fully, but you can check the main points by referring to the appropriate sections in this chapter.

**11** What are the main stages in job costing? (Section 16.2)
**12** What is meant by batch costing? (Section 16.3)
**13** What are the main features of contract costing? (Section 16.4)
**14** Explain the different methods which can be used for charging plant and machinery to a contract. (Section 16.4)

Multiple choice questions (more than one answer may apply):

**15** A materials requisition note is sent to:

    **a** the purchasing department
    **b** the client
    **c** the stores department
    **d** the architect.

**16** A job card shows:

    **a** the instructions to be carried out for the completion of a job
    **b** all the costs which have been incurred on a job
    **c** the calculation of the overhead absorption rate
    **d** the selling price quoted to the customer.

**17** Subcontractors working on a long-term contract are considered as:

    **a** overheads
    **b** direct expenses
    **c** direct materials
    **d** direct wages.

**18** If rectification costs normally occur, they are charged:

    **a** to the most expensive job
    **b** to administration overheads
    **c** to production overheads
    **d** as a discount on the selling price.

**19** If a contract is unfinished at the year end:

    **a** no profit can be taken
    **b** the expected profit on the entire contract can be taken
    **c** a proportion of the expected profit on the entire contract can be taken
    **d** none of these.

**20** Retention monies are:

    **a** the profit on an unfinished construction contract
    **b** the charge for plant on a contract account
    **c** a proportion of the contract value withheld by the client
    **d** the value of work certified by the architect.

Practice questions:

**21** A company has established the following annual budgets:

| Factory | Total fixed overhead | £33,000 |
| | Total direct labour hours | 22,000 |
| Dept 1 | Total variable overhead | £18,000 |
| | Total direct labour hours | 9,000 |
| Dept 2 | Total variable overhead | £16,000 |
| | Total direct labour hours | 10,000 |

A job has been accepted which has the following direct costs:

Direct materials    18 kg @ £5.10 per kg
Direct wages:
   Dept 1          18 hours @ £3.50 per hour
   Dept 2          32 hours @ £3.00 per hour

Calculate the total cost of the job and the profit as a percentage of costs if the selling price is £500.

**22** Prepare a contract account for Bradford-on-Avon Building Ltd based on the following information as at 31 December 1998:

---

**Contract 267**
**Commencement date 1 January 1997**

|  | £ |
|---|---|
| Contact price | 550,000 |
| Materials delivered to site | 42,220 |
| Wages | 68,880 |
| Site expenses | 16,250 |
| Value of plant on 1 January | 250,000 |
| Materials on site at 31 December | 3,850 |
| Work certified | 210,000 |
| Cost of work completed but uncertified | 10,500 |
| Estimated costs of completion | 286,250 |

Plant is depreciated at 20% per annum

---

**23** Quickprint, a jobbing printer, recovers production overheads at £2.50 per direct labour hour and adds 20% for general overheads to the total production costs to arrive at the total cost of a job. A further 25% is added to the total cost to arrive at the selling price. Calculate the selling price of an order for printing wedding invitations from the following information:

| | |
|---|---|
| Materials | £30 |
| Labour | 4 hours |
| Wages | £5 per hour |

**24** Jill Collis has decided to start a business as a garden designer. She wishes to pay herself a salary of £25 per hour and rents an office for £300 per month. Her other estimated monthly costs are as follows:

|  | £ |
|---|---|
| Telephone | 140 |
| Lighting | 20 |
| Advertising | 80 |
| Car | 300 |

She anticipates that in a month she should be able to work for 80 hours and intends to quote for work at total cost plus 15% profit. A potential client invites her to quote for a garden design and she calculates the cost of materials in terms of photographs, drawings, etc. will be £70. What price should she quote if the job is likely to take 30 hours?

**25** Catbrook Construction Ltd is undertaking a contract where the price is £320,000 and the estimated total cost of the contract is estimated at £260,000. At the end of the financial year the cost of work certified is £140,000 and the cost of work done but not certified is £34,000. The company intends to calculate its profit at the year end using costs as the basis of the estimated degree of completion. What is the share of profit at the year end on the incomplete contract?

(Answers on pp.338–9)

# 17 Continuous-operation Costing

## 17.1 Introduction

Cost accounting methods can be divided into two main groups. We looked at the first group, specific-order costing, in Chapter 16. The second group is *continuous-operation costing*, which is a system of costing applied to industries where the method of production is in continuous operation – for example, bottling or electricity generation. This costing system is essentially a form of *average costing*, which is a method of obtaining unit costs in which the items produced have a high degree of homogeneity. The unit cost is obtained by dividing the total production cost by the number of items produced.

In this chapter we look first at *output costing*, which has some of the features of job costing or batch costing (see Chapter 16) insofar as the aim is to calculate the cost per unit. However, output costing is used where standardised goods or services are produced from a single operation over a period of time.

We then go on to look at two methods of continuous-operation costing: *service costing* and *process costing*. Service costing is used when specific functions or services such as a canteen or personnel department, are costed. It can be used to ascertain the cost of a service provided internally or a service provided for external customers. Process costing is used where production is carried out in a series of stages or processes. Costs are accumulated for the whole production process and *average unit costs* of production computed at each stage. Special rules are applied to the valuation of work in progress, normal and abnormal losses, and it is usual to distinguish between the main product of the process, by-products and joint products.

## 17.2 Output Costing

*Output costing* is used when basically only one product is being manufactured, although various types or grades of the product may be made. It is commonly used in highly mechanised industries, such as quarrying and cement manufacture. Costs are collected for the financial period, usually by nature, and the total is divided by the number of units produced to give an *average cost per unit*. Any partly completed units at the end of the financial period are usually ignored, as they are likely to be insignificant compared with the total number of whole units produced. In addition, the amount of unfinished units tends to be constant at the end of each period.

The *cost statements* used by companies vary according to the nature of the industry and the information needs of managers. To allow some control, it is normal to show the costs classified by their nature for the period and the cost per unit. It is useful if some basis of comparison is also given, such as the results for the previous period or the budgeted figures. The following example shows a unit cost statement for 1 kg of material being produced:

### Unit cost statement for January
### (Total units produced 10,000)

| | | Cost per kg | |
| Item | Cost | Actual | Budget |
| | £ | £ | £ |
|---|---|---|---|
| Wages and salaries | 25,000 | 2.50 | 2.55 |
| Materials | 40,000 | 4.00 | 4.02 |
| Packaging | 2,000 | 0.20 | 0.21 |
| Transport | 3,500 | 0.35 | 0.33 |
| Depreciation | 4,500 | 0.45 | 0.45 |
| Electricity | 8,000 | 0.80 | 0.75 |
| Rates and rent | 7,500 | 0.75 | 0.74 |
| Repairs and maintenance | 1,500 | 0.15 | 0.12 |
| Total cost | 92,000 | 9.20 | 9.18 |

## 17.3  Service Costing

*Service costing* is used when specific services or functions, such as service centres, departments or functions, are to be costed. The services may be offered to external parties, such as hotel accommodation or car hire, or the business may be a manufacturing organisation which needs to know the cost of services provided internally, such as the canteen, stores or maintenance department. The main problem is identifying a *cost unit* so that the service being provided can be measured. For example, a hotel may decide on an occupied bed night; a bus company on a passenger mile. If particular industries have agreed on common cost units, it is possible to make *inter-company comparisons*.

Many of the organisations using service costing are large, national businesses. Rigorous systems and procedures are therefore needed to collect and analyse the costs. Such organisations are often subject to fluctuating demands for their services – for example, there are peak periods of demand during the day for electricity, water, bus and rail services. This fluctuating demand means that managers will need information to distinguish between *fixed costs* and *variable costs* (see Chapter 13) and we will be examining how these costs are treated in Chapter 18. However, not all service organisations use service costing because if the services provided do not have a high degree of homogeneity, a form of *job costing* (see Chapter 16) must be used. This is the case with the services provided by accountants and architects, for example, where services are tailored to the needs of individual clients.

There are a number of features associated with service costing. Usually the cost of direct materials is relatively small compared with direct labour and overhead costs. The service may not be a revenue earner, so the purpose of service costing is not to establish a profit or a loss, but to provide information to managers for the purpose of cost control and the predicting future costs.

A simple example of service costing in operation is that of a company canteen. The organisation needs to know the cost of running the canteen and the average cost per meal. A monthly statement is drawn up showing the various costs. Typically, these would include the following:

- *Labour costs* – Hourly paid staff need to complete time sheets to provide this information; the salaries of any supervisors and managers would be regarded as fixed costs.
- *Food and beverages* –These costs are collected from the suppliers' invoices. A separate stores may be in operation for food and beverage supplies which will require the usual controls and procedures (see Chapter 14).
- *Consumables* – These are items such as crockery, cutlery and cleaning materials which all require regular renewal.
- *Ovens, equipment and furniture* – A depreciation charge is made for these fixed assets (see Chapter 6).
- *Occupancy or building costs* – Some apportionment is made so that the canteen carries a fair share of the costs incurred through the space it occupies (see Chapter 15).

All these costs are recorded for the month to give a total cost figure for running the canteen. By dividing this figure by the number of meals serviced during the period, the average cost per meal can be calculated.

## Activity

A training college in the tourism industry has annual running costs per student of £800,000. It provides a basic training course which can be taken full-time, block release or as a sandwich course. The following table gives details of the courses and the student numbers.

| Mode of study | Number of students | Number of attendance days |
|---|---|---|
| Full-time | 60 | 125 |
| Block release | 300 | 34 |
| Sandwich | 180 | 85 |

Determine a suitable cost unit for the training college and calculate the cost per unit.

Although it is possible to use a student as a cost unit, this would not provide a meaningful figure because of the different modes of study. Therefore, it would be more useful to use a student day as the cost unit by multiplying the number of students by the number of attendance days for each mode of study, as follows:

| Mode of study | Number of students | Number of attendance days | Student days |
|---|---|---|---|
| Full-time | 60 | 125 | 7,500 |
| Block release | 300 | 34 | 10,200 |
| Sandwich | 180 | 85 | 15,300 |
| | | | 33,000 |

$$\text{Cost per student day} = \frac{£800,000}{33,000}$$

$$= £24.24$$

## 17.4 Process Costing

*Process costing* is a method of costing applied to production when the process is carried out in a series of chemical or operational stages. The finished output at one stage of production becomes the input for the next stage in the process. At the end of all the stages the completed production is sold or transferred to finished goods stock. This type of production is often found in chemical works, oil refineries and paint manufacturers.

Costs are accumulated for the whole production process and *average unit costs* of production are computed at each stage in the production process. In process costing special rules are applied to the valuation of *work in progress (WIP)*, *normal losses* and *abnormal losses* and it is usual to distinguish between the main product of the process, *by-products* and *joint products*. We shall be looking at each of these later on in this chapter.

For each stage in the process, both direct costs, such as materials and labour, and production overheads are charged. By dividing the costs on one process by the number of units, the average cost per unit is calculated. Cost units which are similar in nature pass through each of the production processes. It is essential that appropriate cost units are chosen (see Chapter 13). For a liquid product the cost unit might be a litre; for a solid product a kilogram or a tonne would be more appropriate. As cost units move from one process to another, the costs incurred accumulate and are transferred with them. Although the actual method of process costing varies from one organisation to another, the main features of process costing systems are as follows:

- There are separate processes which can be defined easily and the costs collected to them.
- The output from one process forms the input of the next process.
- Both direct costs and overheads are charged to the processes.
- Costs are accumulated in respect of cost units as production goes through the various processes.
- The *average unit cost* is calculated by dividing the total cost of a process for a period of time by the number of cost units for the period.

The latter can be expressed as a formula:

$$\text{Average cost per unit} = \frac{\text{Costs incurred during period}}{\text{Number of units produced}}$$

We will use an example to show how it is used in practice to arrive at the average cost per unit for the period. Brilliant Paints produced 50,000 completed units in January. Direct materials cost £5,000 and direct labour £3,500. Production overheads were £1,500. Therefore, total costs incurred during the period were £10,000. Substituting the figures in the formula:

$$\text{Average cost per unit} = \frac{£10,000}{50,000} = £0.20$$

Of course, at the end of the period it is likely that there will be some units which are not yet complete because they have only been partly processed. This balance of unfinished work remaining in the production operation is known as *work in progress (WIP)*. The costs incurred for the period relate to all the units, whether completed or only partly completed. To find out the average cost per unit when there are partly completed units we must first convert them to *equivalent units* – in other words, equivalent of whole units. For example, if there were 2,000 partly finished units in work-in-progress which are 50% complete, they would be counted as 1,000 equivalent units

$(2,000 \times 50\%)$. We can now adjust the formula for calculating the average cost per unit for the period as follows:

Average cost per unit

$$= \frac{\text{Costs incurred during period}}{\text{Completed units produced} + \text{Equivalent units in WIP}}$$

In February Brilliant Paints produced 55,000 completed units. WIP was 2,000 units which were 50% complete. Direct materials cost £5,500 and direct labour £4,000. Production overheads were £1,500. Therefore total costs incurred during the period were £11,000. Substituting the figures in the formula:

$$\text{Average cost per unit} = \frac{£11,000}{55,000 + (2,000 \times 50\%)} = £0.20$$

The costs incurred in production comprise the usual elements of direct materials, direct labour and production overheads. When WIP is examined at the end of a period the degree of completion may vary for each cost element. For example, the units may be almost complete as far as materials are concerned, but further substantial labour and overhead costs may be incurred in order to complete the units. In such cases the cost elements must be treated separately in order to find out the number of equivalent units before the average cost per unit can be calculated.

## Activity

Moving on to the month of March, the following figures are available for Process No. 1 at Brilliant Paints:

| Cost element | £ |
| --- | --- |
| Direct materials | 8,050 |
| Direct labour | 12,375 |
| Production overheads | 8,400 |

There are 5,000 completed units and 1,000 units in WIP. The units in WIP are 75% complete for materials, 50% complete for labour and 25% for production overheads. Calculate the average cost per unit.

Using the formula, you should not have had too much difficulty with this activity. First you need to calculate the value of WIP for each of the cost elements as follows:

| Cost element | Formula | Cost per unit £ |
|---|---|---|
| Direct materials | $\dfrac{£8,050}{5,000 + (1,000 \times 75\%)}$ | 1.40 |
| Direct labour | $\dfrac{£12,375}{5,000 + (1,000 \times 50\%)}$ | 2.25 |
| Production overheads | $\dfrac{£8,400}{5,000 + (1,000 \times 25\%)}$ | 1.60 |
| Total cost per unit | | 5.25 |

| | | £ | £ |
|---|---|---|---|
| Direct materials | 750 equivalent units @ £1.40 | 1,050 | |
| Direct labour | 500 equivalent units @ £2.25 | 1,125 | |
| Production overheads | 250 equivalent units @ £1.60 | 400 | 2,575 |
| Value of completed units | 5,000 units @ £5.25 | | 26,250 |
| | | | 28,825 |

You may have noticed that the value of WIP (£2,575) plus the value of the completed units (£26,250) equals the total cost incurred for Process No 1 for March (£28,825). This is a check which should always be carried out.

So far we have only considered the first process. Let us take the above figure of 5,000 completed units at the end of March for Process No 1 and add information concerning the second stage of production. At the end of April the following information is available:

| Cost element | £ |
|---|---|
| Direct materials | 6,000 |
| Direct labour | 3,800 |
| Production overheads | 2,850 |

There were 4,500 completed units transferred to stock and 500 units in WIP which were 50% complete. With this information we can calculated the value of WIP and the completed production transferred to finished goods store at the end of April. However, there are two points to note here. First, Process No 2 starts with the 5,000 units transferred from Process No 1 at the end of March. Secondly, when calculating the number of equivalent units, there will be no further materials costs incurred, as materials were needed at the start of the process. WIP is therefore 100% complete as far as direct materials are concerned. To tackle the calculations in a logical way, the information can be drawn up in the form of a table:

## Brilliant Paints
## Process No 2 Costs for April

| Cost element | Total costs £ | No. of completed units | Equivalent units in WIP | Total effective units | Cost per unit £ | Value of WIP £ |
|---|---|---|---|---|---|---|
| Previous process costs | 26,250 | 4,500 | 500 | 5,000 | 5.25 | 2,625 |
| Direct materials | 6,000 | 4,500 | 500 | 5,000 | 1.20 | 600 |
| Direct labour | 3,800 | 4,500 | 250 | 4,750 | 0.80 | 200 |
| Production overheads | 2,850 | 4,500 | 250 | 4,750 | 0.60 | 150 |
|  | 38,900 |  |  |  | 7.85 | 3,575 |

|  | £ |
|---|---|
| Value of completed units (4,500 @ £7.85) | 35,325 |
| *Add*   Value of WIP | 3,575 |
|  | 38,900 |

This example illustrates a number of important points. The first and second columns in the table are straightforward; the third column shows the number of completed units transferred to finished goods stock. The fourth column shows the number of equivalent units in WIP. There are 500 units in WIP and for previous process costs and materials costs the units are 100% complete. By definition, previous process costs are always complete. In this example the materials were added at the beginning of the process. This means that even when there are partly finished units in WIP at the end of the period, the units must be complete as far as the material cost element is concerned. This is a favourite examination topic and the following rules should be applied:

1 If any cost elements are added at the start of the process, no further costs of this nature will be incurred.
2 If any cost elements are added at the end of the process, as the units in WIP have not reached this stage, no part of the cost element can be included in WIP.
3 Having calculated the number of equivalent units this is added to the number of completed units to give the number of total effective units. The total cost for each element in the second column is divided by the number of total effective units to give the cost per unit in the sixth column. To find the value of WIP, the number of equivalent units in WIP for each element is multiplied by the cost per unit.
4 The final stage is to calculate the value of the completed units at the bottom of the table and add the value of WIP. These total of these two figures must agree with the figure of total costs as shown in the second column.

Closing WIP for a process at the end of one period forms the opening WIP for the same process at the start of the next period. This raises the problem of how WIP should be valued. Certain assumptions can be made to decide the method of valuation. Management may assume that the units comprising WIP are completed during the current period and use the *first in, first out (FIFO)* method (see Chapter 14). Alternatively, it may be assumed that the partly finished units forming the opening WIP are mixed with the current period's production and as it is not known which units are completed at the end of the period the *average cost method* can be used. We will use an example to illustrate both methods.

Brilliant Paints has three production processes. For the month of December the opening WIP for Process No 2 was 300 units (50% complete) valued at £4,500. At the start of the period there were 900 completed units transferred from Process No 1 which were valued at £2,700. The total costs for Process No 2 for the month were £8,100. At the end of December 1,000 completed units were transferred to Process No 3 and the closing WIP was 200 units which were 25% complete.

We will now calculated the value of closing WIP using FIFO. The various calculations can be broken down into a number of steps as follows:

**1** Number of effective units produced by Process No 2 during December:

|  |  | Units |
|---|---|---|
| | Closing WIP (200 × 25%) | 50 |
| *Add* | Completed units transferred to Process No 3 | 1,000 |
| | | 1,050 |
| *Less* | Opening WIP (300 × 50%) | 150 |
| | Effective units manufactured in period | 900 |

**2** Costs incurred in period to produce 900 effective units:

|  |  | £ |
|---|---|---|
| | Transferred from Process No 1 | 2,700 |
| *Add* | Other costs incurred in period | 8,100 |
| | | 10,800 |

**3** Valuation of closing WIP:

$$\frac{\text{Costs incurred in period}}{\text{No. of effective units}} = \frac{£10,800}{900} = £12 \text{ per unit}$$

No. of equivalent units in closing WIP (200 × 25%) = 50

Value of closing WIP = 50 units @ £12 = £600

**4** Value of 1,000 completed units transferred to Process No 3:

|  |  | £ |
|---|---|---:|
|  | Value of opening WIP | 4,500 |
| *Add* | Costs transferred from Process No 1 | 2,700 |
|  | Other costs incurred in period | 8,100 |
|  |  | 15,300 |
| *Less* | Value of closing WIP | 600 |
|  | Value of completed units transferred to Process No 3 | 14,700 |

In the average cost method the opening WIP valuation plus the period costs are used to calculate the average cost per unit. The same average cost per unit is used to value both the closing WIP and the completed units. The steps are as follows:

**1** Total number of effective units:

|  |  | Units |
|---|---|---:|
|  | Completed units transferred to Process No 3 | 1,000 |
| *Add* | Closing WIP (200 25%) | 50 |
|  |  | 1,050 |

**2** Total costs incurred:

|  |  | £ |
|---|---|---:|
|  | Opening WIP valuation | 4,500 |
| *Add* | Costs transferred from Process No 1 | 2,700 |
|  | Other costs incurred in period | 8,100 |
|  |  | 15,300 |

**3** Valuation of closing WIP:

$$\text{Average cost per unit} = \frac{\text{Total costs incurred}}{\text{Total number of effective units}}$$

$$= \frac{£15,300}{1,050} = £14.5714$$

Closing WIP $= (200 \times 25\%) \times £14.5714 = £728.57$

**4** Valuation of 1,000 completed units transferred to Process No 3:

|  |  | £ |
|---|---|---:|
|  | Transferred to Process No 3 (1,000 units @ £14.5714) | 14,571.40 |
| *Add* | Value of closing WIP | 728.57 |
|  | Value of completed units transferred to Process No 3 | 15,299.97 |

The above examples demonstrate the input of the different WIP valuations on the value of completed units transferred to the next process. The consequence is that under the two different methods the final profit for the business will also differ. Therefore, once a policy has been established, it is essential to use the specified method consistently.

## 17.5 Waste

Even in a highly efficient production process there is likely to be some *waste* or spoilage. This is the amount of material lost as part of a production process. Acceptable levels of waste, known as *normal loss*, are part of the cost of production and are allowed for in the product costs. It is possible for losses to take place at any point in the process. Where waste occurs part-way through a process, some of the loss is charged to WIP. If the loss takes place at the end of a process, perhaps at the final inspection stage, only units which have been completed during the period are charged with the loss. The procedure for dealing with normal loss occurring at the end of the process is as follows:

1 Complete a table for process costs as explained in Section 17.4.
2 The third column of the table should show all the completed units, both the good units and those which have been designated as normal loss.
3 Complete the table and use the cost per unit to calculate the value of the normal loss.
4 Divide the value of the normal loss by the number of good completed units and add to the original cost per unit to obtain a revised cost per unit.

We will now illustrate this with an example. Brilliant Paints has provided the following information for the period:

| Cost element | £ |
| --- | --- |
| Materials (added at start of process) | 18,000 |
| Direct labour | 31,000 |
| Production overheads | 15,725 |

There were 2,000 units of closing WIP at the end of the period. which were 50% complete as far as labour costs were concerned and 25% complete with regard to production overheads. There were 18,000 completed units of which 1,000 units were scrapped. Using this information, we can construct a table to calculate the process costs:

**Brilliant Paints**
**Normal loss process costs for period**

| Cost element | Total costs £ | No. of completed units | Equivalent units in WIP | Total effective units | Cost per unit £ | Value of WIP £ |
|---|---|---|---|---|---|---|
| Direct materials | 18,000 | 18,000 | 2,000 | 20,000 | 0.90 | 1,800 |
| Direct labour | 31,350 | 18,000 | 1,000 | 19,000 | 1.65 | 1,650 |
| Production overheads | 15,725 | 18,000 | 500 | 18,500 | 0.85 | 425 |
| | 65,075 | | | | 3.40 | 3,875 |

| | | | |
|---|---|---|---|
| Value of normal loss (1,000 units @ £3.40 | | £3,400 | 0.20 |
| allocated to 17,000 units) | | 17,000 | |
| Revised cost per unit | | | 3.60 |

| | £ |
|---|---|
| Value of completed units (17,000 units @ £3.60) | 61,200 |
| *Add*  Value of WIP | 3,875 |
| | 65,075 |

*Abnormal loss* is the loss arising from a manufacturing or chemical process through abnormal waste, shrinkage, seepage or spoilage in excess of the normal loss. It may be expressed as a weight or volume or in other units appropriate to the process and is usually valued on the same basis as the good output. An *abnormal gain* is an unexpected surplus of output that may occur if the actual loss is less than the normal loss. The abnormal losses must carry their share of the costs of the normal losses. It is important to do this calculation before working out the value of the abnormal loss to be charged to the profit and loss account. The procedure is as follows:

1 Complete a table for process costs, as explained in Section 17.4.
2 The third column of the table should show all the completed units: the good units, those which have been designated as normal loss and the abnormal loss.
3 Complete the table and use the cost per unit to calculate the value of the *normal loss.*
4 Divide the value of the normal loss by the number of good completed units and abnormal loss units and add to the original cost per unit to obtain a revised cost per unit.
5 Multiply the revised cost per unit by the number of units of abnormal loss to obtain the value of the abnormal loss to be charged to the profit and loss account.

# Activity

Brilliant Paints has provided the following information for the period:

| Cost element | £ |
|---|---|
| Materials (added at start of process) | 50,000 |
| Direct labour | 47,500 |
| Production overheads | 18,000 |

There were 2,000 units of closing WIP at the end of the period. which were 75% complete as far as labour costs were concerned and 50% complete with regard to production overheads. There were 8,000 completed units. Normal loss is 500 units, but actual waste in the period was 750 units. Using this information, construct a table to calculate the process costs.

If you were able to follow the procedure for calculating normal loss, you should not have had too many problems with this activity. Check your answer against the following:

## Brilliant Paints
## Abnormal loss process costs for period

| Cost element | Total costs £ | No. of completed units | Equivalent units in WIP | Total effective units | Cost per unit £ | Value of WIP £ |
|---|---|---|---|---|---|---|
| Direct materials | 50,000 | 8,000 | 2,000 | 10,000 | 5.00 | 10,000 |
| Direct labour | 47,500 | 8,000 | 1,500 | 9,500 | 5.00 | 7,500 |
| Production overheads | 18,000 | 8,000 | 1,000 | 9,000 | 2.00 | 2,000 |
| | 115,500 | | | | 12.00 | 19,500 |

| | | |
|---|---|---|
| Value of normal loss (500 units @ £12.00 allocated to 7,500 remaining units) | £6,000 7,500 | 0.80 |
| Revised cost per unit | | 12.80 |
| | £ | |
| Value of completed units (7,250 units @ £12.80) | 92,800 | |
| *Add* Value of WIP | 19,500 | |
| Value of abnormal loss charged to profit and loss (250 units @ £12,80) | 3,200 | |
| | 115,500 | |

## 17.6 By-products and Joint Products

*By-products* are the output of a process that have secondary economic significance to the main product of the process and may require further processing to make them marketable. *Joint products* are the output of a process in which there is more than one product and all the products have similar or equal economic importance. They use the same commonly processed materials up to a certain point (the *split-off point*), although they may require further processing to make them marketable.

By-products and joint products are very common in the meat, oil refining, chemical and mining industries. Because the definition of the terms depends on the perceived significance of the sales value of the products, companies tend to have differing views as to whether a product can be regarded as a joint or by-product.

There are three main methods of costing by-products:

1 No attempt is made to distinguish between the main product and the by-product. Any sales value from the by-product is added to the sales of the main product and all costs are set against this to show the total profit. The view is taken that as there is a common process, it is unrealistic to attempt to attribute a proportion of the costs to the by-product.
2 If the sales value of the by-product is very small it may be shown directly in the profit and loss account as 'other income'. Any costs incurred after the split-off point to bring the by-product into a saleable condition are deducted from its income before showing in the profit and loss account.
3 The preferred method is to deduct the sales value of the by-product less any costs incurred after the split-off point from the total cost of production.

We can illustrate the third method with an example. The following information is available from Paisley Poultry Ltd:

| | |
|---|---|
| Costs of production for period | £200,000 |
| Opening stock | Nil |
| Closing stock of main product | 5% of production |
| Sales revenue of main product | £220,000 |
| Net sales value of by-product | £2,200 |
| Subsequent costs of by-product | £200 |

**Paisley Poultry Ltd**
**By-product costing statement**

| | | £ | £ |
|---|---|---|---|
| | Sales of main product | | 220,000 |
| | Cost of production (£200,000 − £2,000) | 198,000 | |
| *Less* | Closing stock (5%) | 9,900 | |
| | Cost of sales | | 188,100 |
| | Profit | | 31,900 |

With joint products the common costs incurred up to the split-off point must be *apportioned* in some way. Subsequent costs arising after that point relate to each specific product and do not require apportionment. There are two methods by which common costs can be apportioned:

1 The *physical units* basis apportions the costs according to the physical weight or volume of the products.
2 The *sales value* basis apportions the costs in proportion to the relative sales value of the products.

Both methods allow a closing value to be placed on the closing stock of each of the joint products and permit the costs and profits of each of the joint products to be determined. In addition, they both provide management information. It is important to remember that one product cannot be manufactured independently of the other: the profit of one product is affected by the way the common costs are apportioned.

The physical units basis of apportionment can be used only when the joint products separate after the split-off point into comparable states. Therefore, this method cannot be used if one product is a solid and the other a gas after the separation point, for example. In addition, if the products have very different sales values this is not reflected in the attributable profits and could lead to one product appearing to be very profitable and the other less so. The physical units basis of apportionment is easy to apply: the joint costs are simply apportioned on the basis of the output of each product to the total output measure by weight or volume, as shown in the following example. The following information is available for the period for Pampered Pet Foods Ltd:

| | |
|---|---|
| Joint processing costs | £6,000 |
| Output of joint product A | 2,000 kg |
| Output of joint product B | 10,000 kg |
| Sales value of product A | £1.10 per kg |
| Sales value of product B | £0.55 per kg |

**Pampered Pet Foods Ltd**
**Joint product costing statement**
**(Physical units basis of apportionment)**

| | Product A | Product B | Total |
|---|---|---|---|
| Output | 2,000 kg | 10,000 kg | 12,000 kg |
| | £ | £ | £ |
| Sales | 2,200 | 5,500 | 7,700 |
| Apportioned costs | 1,000 | 5,000 | 6,000 |
| Profit | 1,200 | 500 | 1,700 |
| Profit/sales percentage | 54.5% | 9.1% | 22.1% |

The apportioned costs for Product *A* are calculated as follows:

$$\frac{\text{Product } A \text{ output}}{\text{Total output}} = \frac{2,000 \, \text{kg}}{12,000 \, \text{kg}}$$

The profit/sales percentage for Product *A* is calculated as follows:

$$\frac{\text{Product } A \text{ profit}}{\text{Product } A \text{ sales}} \times 100 = \frac{£1,200}{£2,200} \times 100 = 54.5\%$$

The advantage of the sales value basis of apportionment is that it gives the same profit/sales percentage for each product. As managers often operate on an assumed relationship between costs and profits, this method is widely used. In applying this method the joint costs are apportioned in the proportion that the total sales value of each product bears to the total sales value for all out put of the joint processes. The selling price per unit is not used to apportion. The following example uses the same data as above:

---

**Joint product costing statement**
**(Sales value basis of apportionment)**

|                          | Product *A* | Product *B* | Total  |
|--------------------------|-------------|-------------|--------|
|                          | £           | £           | £      |
| Sales                    | 2,200       | 5,500       | 7,700  |
| Apportioned costs        | 1,714       | 4,286       | 6,000  |
| Profit                   | 486         | 1,214       | 1,700  |
| Profit/sales percentage  | 22.1%       | 22.1%       | 22.1%  |

---

The apportioned costs for product A are calculated as follows:

$$\frac{\text{Product } A \text{ sales}}{\text{Total sales}} \times \text{Joint processing costs} = \frac{£2,200}{£7,700} \times £6,000 = £1,714$$

Whichever method is used, the total profit remains the same, but the profit per product can be significantly different.

Some products incur further costs after the split-off point to put them into a saleable condition. This means that there is no sales value at the split-off point which can be used to apportion costs. If it is not possible to determine what the relative sales value should be at the split-off point, the subsequent processing costs should be deducted from the final sales value to give a *notional sales value* at split-off point. The notional sales value is then used to apportion costs in the way described.

## 17.7 Conclusions

In this chapter we have looked at a number of techniques associated with continuous-operation costing.

Output costing is used when essentially only one product is being manufactured and the average cost per unit is calculated.

Service costing is used when specific services or functions are costed, and once a cost unit has been identified the average cost per unit can be calculated.

Process costing is used to determine product costs when production is carried out in a series of processes. Costs for each process are accumulated and the average cost per unit calculated. Special rules are applied to the valuation of work-in-progress and waste. There are three main methods by which by-products can be costed and two methods for costing joint products.

Having completed this chapter, you should now be able to:

- explain what is meant by continuous-operation costing;
- use unit costing to calculate the average cost per unit;
- use service costing to calculate the average cost per unit;
- use process costing to calculate the average cost per unit for products, including by-products and joint products.

## Exercises

Complete the following sentences:

**1** In continuous-operation costing, the unit cost is obtained by ........................

...................................................................................................................

**2** Output costing is used when ........................................................................

**3** Service costing is used when .......................................................................

**4** Process costing is used when .......................................................................

**5** In process costing, normal losses are part of ............................................

Are the following statements true or false?

**6** Service costing is only used by very small organisations.

**7** Service costing can be used for internal and external services.

**8** Process costing is used in the quarrying industry.

**9** The advantage of process costing is that there is no work in progress (WIP).

**10** In process costing both direct costs and overheads are charged to the processes.

You may wish to read more widely than this book to answer the following questions fully, but you can check the main points by referring to the appropriate sections in this chapter.

**11** For which industries is output costing best suited to and why? (Section 17.2)

**12** What are the main features of service costing? (Section 17.3)

**13** What are the main features of process costing? (Section 17.4)

**14** How are the costs of waste dealt with in process costing? (Section 17.5)

Multiple choice questions (more than one answer may apply):

**15** If a business has fluctuating demands for its services, it will need to identify:

   **a** fixed costs only
   **b** variable costs only
   **c** fixed costs and variable costs separately
   **d** total costs only.

**16** To calculate the unit cost of production for a period using output costing:

   **a** the depreciation cost is included
   **b** the depreciation cost is excluded
   **c** the cash spent on assets is included
   **d** there is never any deprecation cost.

**17** In a service organisation the costs of materials is normally:

   **a** higher than labour costs
   **b** lower than labour costs
   **c** the same as labour costs
   **d** there are never any material costs.

**18** In process costing the costs incurred for the period apply to:

   **a** completed units only
   **b** work in progress only
   **c** both completed units and work in progress
   **d** wastage only.

**19** If there are 10,000 units which are 25% finished at the end of the period, the number of equivalent units is:

   **a** 7,500
   **b** 2,500
   **c** 25,000
   **d** 75,000.

**20** In process costing abnormal losses:

   **a** carry their share of the costs of normal losses
   **b** do not carry their share of the costs of normal losses
   **c** are never costed separately
   **d** are set against abnormal gains.

Practice questions:

**21** A pollution control company carries out 240 standard tests in its laboratory per month for traces of hydrocarbons. The annual costs of running the laboratory are as follows:

| | £ |
|---|---|
| Technician's wages | 12,000 |
| Materials | 2,500 |
| Laboratory costs | 15,500 |
| | 30,000 |

Calculate the cost per test.

**22** Distinguish between normal losses, abnormal losses and explain their costing treatments.

**23** A large company has a distribution department with its own garages and vehicles. Suggest **six** headings under which the costs of the department might be collected.

**24** In one period a processing company had the following information:

| | |
|---|---|
| Units received for previous process | 16,000 |
| Value of units received | £910,000 |
| Processing costs: | |
| Labour and overheads | £701,200 |
| Materials introduced | £49,500 |

There was no WIP at the beginning of the period, but at the end of the period there was WIP of 3,800 units which were 100% complete for materials and 50% complete for labour and overheads. Calculate the number of equivalent units produced.

**25** Using the information given in Question 24, calculate the cost per equivalent unit.

(Answers on pp. 339–40)

# 18 Marginal Costing

## 18.1 Introduction

This chapter investigates the impact of changes in the volume of activity undertaken by a business on costs and profits. To examine these changes and the financial implications, a technique known as *marginal costing* (also known as *variable costing*) is used. Marginal costing principles are also used in *cost–volume–profit (C–V–P) analysis* and *break-even analysis*.

In marginal costing variable costs are charged to cost units and the fixed costs for the period are written off in full, without attempting to charge them to individual cost units. Thus, marginal costing is differs considerably from absorption costing, the other major technique for ascertaining the cost of a unit (see Chapter 15).

Marginal costing is a very valuable decision-making technique. It helps management to set prices, compare alternative production methods, set production activity levels, close production lines and choose which of a range of potential products to manufacture. The theory behind marginal costing is simple to understand and the principles can be easily applied to straightforward problems. Although in practice there are some difficulties and limitations to marginal costing, it is nevertheless a very useful technique.

## 18.2 Cost Behaviour

In Chapter 13 we defined *direct costs* as those costs which can be identified with a specific product or saleable service, and *indirect costs* as those which cannot. We defined *fixed costs* as those costs which in total tend to remain the same regardless of changes in the level of activity, and *variable costs* as those which in total tend to change in direct proportion to changes in the level of activity. From this, we can deduce that direct costs will always be variable costs. The words 'tend to change' are used in the definition because there is not always a direct relationship and some costs are *semi-variable*. This means that they contain both a fixed and a variable element.

A *marginal cost* is regarded by accountants as the average variable cost and is assumed to be constant in the short term.

## Activity

Which of the costs in the following list are normally classified as fixed and which are normally classified as variable in a manufacturing organisation?

- Accountants' salaries
- Advertising
- Depreciation
- Direct labour
- Direct materials
- Machine operators' wages
- Rates
- Rent
- Salesmen's commission
- Warehouse wages.

Even if you do not have any experience of working in a manufacturing environment you should have been able to identify these from the definitions of fixed and variable costs. Accountants' salaries, advertising, depreciation, rates, rent and warehouse wages are all examples of fixed costs. Direct labour, direct materials, machine operators' wages and salesmen's commission are usually considered as variable costs because they change when the level of activity changes.

## Activity

In Sam Reeve's taxi business, which we used as an example in Chapter 13, the average mileage by a taxi in one quarter is 15,000 miles and the costs, analysed by nature, are as follows:

| Expense | Total for quarter £ |
|---|---|
| Driver's salary | 2,670 |
| Petrol and oil | 1,050 |
| Annual service | 450 |
| Taxation and insurance | 1,110 |
| Depreciation | 870 |
| Total | 6,150 |

Sam has been invited to submit a quotation for a special job which will involve an additional 500 miles per quarter. This mileage can be done in the driver's current time allowance, so no additional salary will be incurred. Sam needs to know the costs of the additional 500 miles per quarter, so that he can quote for the job.

Explain how the following figures have been calculated. Is one of them the correct figure of cost for the additional 500 miles?

**a** £205
**b** £116
**c** £35.

---

Answer **a**, £205, is the result of multiplying the mileage of 500 miles by the total cost per mile of 41p. The total cost per mile is calculated by dividing the total cost for the quarter by the average mileage for the quarter of 15,000 miles. However, we know that no additional wages for the driver will be incurred, so it would be incorrect to take £205 as the cost of the additional 500 miles. The driver's wages, in this example, can be considered as a *fixed cost*. In our example, activity is measured in miles.

Answer **b**, £116, has been calculated by multiplying the 500 miles by 23.2p; that is, the total cost per mile less the driver's element. But this is not the correct answer to the question, because if you look at the list of costs you will see that the driver's salary is not the only fixed cost. Certain other costs will not increase because of the additional 500 miles per quarter. Taking them in the order in which they are listed, the costs for petrol and oil will obviously rise with the increased mileage, so they are not fixed. With regard to servicing and repairs, some routine servicing will be carried out regardless of the mileage and this is therefore a fixed cost. However, other servicing and repair costs depend on the mileage. Clearly, tax and insurance are fixed costs and, like the driver's salary, should be excluded from our calculations of the cost for the additional 500 miles. Depreciation, to some extent, is influenced by the amount of mileage, but in a taxi business, depreciation depends mainly on the passage of time.

The above identification of fixed costs should help you with answer **c** suggested, £35. This has been calculated by multiplying the 500 miles by 7p, the cost of petrol and oil per mile. In view of the information we have available, this is the best answer. If we are to be more precise, we will need more details of the service and repair costs so that we can identify which are fixed.

---

## Activity

Circle the correct answer in the following statements:

**a** If activity increases the total fixed cost will increase/decrease/stay the same.
**b** If activity increases the fixed cost per unit will increase/decrease/stay the same.
**c** If activity decreases the total fixed cost will increase/decrease/stay the same.
**d** If activity decreases the fixed cost per unit will increase/decrease/stay the same.

---

You should have had little difficulty in deciding the answers to **a** and **c**. These are drawn straight from the definition and in both cases the total fixed costs stay the same regardless of changes in the level of activity. You may have found the answers to **b** and **d** a little more difficult, and some simple figures may help. We will take as our example a factory where the rent is £8,000 per annum, a fixed cost. The output of the factory each year is 1,000 units. The cost for rent per unit is therefore £8. If the factory makes 1,500 units one year, what is the rent per unit? The total rent cost will stay the same at £8,000 so the cost per unit for rent will decrease to £5.33. Therefore, the answer to **b** is that if activity increases the fixed cost per unit will decrease. The reasoning is similar with statement **d**: if activity decreases the fixed cost per unit will increase.

## Activity

Circle the correct answer in the following statements:

**a** If activity increases, the total variable cost will increase/decrease/stay the same.
**b** If activity increases, the variable cost per unit will increase/decrease/stay the same.
**c** If activity decreases, the total variable cost will increase/decrease/stay the same.
**d** If activity decreases, the variable cost per unit will increase/decrease/stay the same.

You should have found this activity fairly straightforward after the earlier example. The answer to statements **b** and **d** is that if activity increases or decreases the variable cost per unit will stay the same. The answer to statement **a** is that when activity increases the total variable cost will increase. Similarly with statement **c**, when activity decreases, the total variable cost decreases.

## 18.3 Calculating Contribution

In Chapter 15 we examined absorption costing, which is a method of charging all costs to the product or service. *Marginal costing* is a technique whereby only the *variable* or *marginal costs* of production are charged to the cost units. Marginal costing is sometimes called *direct costing* and in some text books it is described under the heading of *cost–volume–profit (C–V–P) analysis*. The advantage of marginal costing over absorption costing is that it recognises that costs behave differently as activity changes.

As we saw in Section 18.2, total *fixed costs* tend to remain the same despite changes in levels of production or sales activity. Total *variable costs* tend to increase or decrease in line with production or sales activity. *Semi-variable costs* contain both fixed and variable cost elements and must be analysed so that the fixed cost elements can be added to other fixed costs and the variable cost elements to the other variable costs. Because some costs change and others stay the same when activity changes, so the total cost for all production and the total cost per unit changes, but not directly. We therefore need a technique which will provide useful information if we are interested in an organisation where activity levels fluctuate. Marginal costing is such a technique.

Under marginal costing, only the variable costs are charged to the units. The difference between the selling price and the variable cost is not a profit, since no allowance has been made for fixed costs. The difference between the selling price and the variable costs per unit is the *contribution* (to fixed costs), and can be calculated for one unit or for any chosen level of sales. As soon as the total fixed costs have been covered by the contribution, the organisation starts making a profit. The following example illustrates these points.

Mementoes Ltd manufactures ceramic models of historic buildings for the tourist trade. The materials for each model cost 60p and the labour costs are 30p per unit. The presentation boxes cost 15p per unit. The selling price is £2.30 each. The total fixed costs or overheads for the business are £850 per week. The normal weekly output is 1,000 units. With this information we can draw up a marginal cost statement, calculating the contribution per 1,000 units and per single unit:

### Mementoes Ltd
### Marginal cost statement for one week

| Output | 1,000 units | | 1 unit | |
|---|---|---|---|---|
| | £ | £ | £ | £ |
| **Sales** | | 2,300 | | 2.30 |
| **Variable costs** | | | | |
| Materials | 600 | | 0.60 | |
| Labour | 300 | | 0.30 | |
| Packaging | 150 | 1,050 | 0.15 | 1.05 |
| **Contribution** | | 1,250 | | 1.25 |
| *Less* Total fixed costs | | 850 | | |
| **Net profit/(loss)** | | 400 | | |

Marginal costing is useful for a number of short-term decisions such as:

- setting the selling price of products, particularly in times of trade depression and when introducing new products;
- evaluating the proposed closure or temporary cessation of part of the business;
- deciding the value of accepting a special contract or order;
- comparing the cost implications of different methods of manufacture.

For example, the management of Mementoes Ltd might want to know what the lowest selling price is that could be set for its models. If you look back at the marginal cost statement you will see that the answer is £1.05 – any lower than that would mean that the company does not recoup all the variable costs it incurs in making one unit. Even at £1.05 the company is not obtaining a contribution towards its fixed costs. We will now look at some other examples.

## Activity

Iceblock Ltd makes three types of ice lolly and shares its fixed overheads equally over the three types. A summary of the financial statement for last month is shown below:

### Iceblock Ltd

|  | Fruit Ice | Choc Ice | Kool Ice | Total |
|---|---|---|---|---|
| Total number produced | 11,200 | 9,000 | 6,000 | |
| | £ | £ | £ | £ |
| Total sales | 5,500 | 4,500 | 2,400 | 12,400 |
| Variable costs | 2,400 | 1,800 | 1,300 | 5,500 |
| Contribution | 3,100 | 2,700 | 1,100 | 6,900 |
| Fixed costs | 2,000 | 2,000 | 2,000 | 6,000 |
| Net profit/(loss) | 1,100 | 700 | (900) | 900 |

The sales director has suggested that as sales of all ice lollies are expected to decrease by 10% next month, production of Kool Ice should be stopped until demand picks up. Redraft the above statement, first showing what will happen if there is a 10% decrease in demand, and second, if production of Kool Ice is halted.

Check your answer against the following figures:

### Iceblock Ltd

|  | Fruit Ice | Choc Ice | Kool Ice | Total |
|---|---|---|---|---|
| Total number produced | 10,080 | 8,100 | 5,400 | |
| | £ | £ | £ | £ |
| Total sales | 4,950 | 4,050 | 2,160 | 11,160 |
| Variable costs | 2,160 | 1,620 | 1,170 | 4,950 |
| Contribution | 2,790 | 2,430 | 990 | 6,210 |
| Fixed costs | 2,000 | 2,000 | 2,000 | 6,000 |
| Net profit/(loss) | 790 | 430 | (1,010) | 210 |

The above statement shows the impact of the 10% decrease on profit as well as the fact that Kool Ice is making a contribution to fixed costs.

If production of Kool Ice is stopped, then the net profit would turn into a net loss as the following figures show:

|  |  | £ |
|---|---|---|
| **Contribution** |  |  |
| Fruit Ice | 2,790 |
| Choc Ice | 2,430 |
|  | 5,220 |
| *Less* **Fixed costs** | 6,000 |
| **Net loss** | (780) |

The difference between the old profit of £210 and the new position, a loss of £780, is £990 and this is the lost contribution of Kool Ice. The loss of £780 results because we assume that the £6,000 of fixed costs will stay the same, at least in the short term, regardless of changes in activity or the cessation of one of the product lines. The general rule is that, if a product or service makes a contribution towards fixed costs, it is financially worthwhile continuing to provide it. There may be other business reasons for dropping it, or it may be financially preferable to direct the activities of the organisation in another direction. However, in this example it is financially advisable to continue production of Kool Ice.

Let us assume that a large hotel has approached Iceblock Ltd and offers to place an order for 600 Kool Ices per month if the price is reduced from 40p to 30p per lolly. The order would restore demand, but should the company accept it in view of the low price offered? The general rule is that, if you have idle production capacity, it is worthwhile accepting a special order as long as it makes a contribution. The key figures for Kool Ice, calculated to the nearest penny, are as follows:

| | Per unit | | Per unit |
|---|---|---|---|
| Present selling price | 40p | Suggested selling price | 30p |
| Variable costs | 22p | Variable costs | 22p |
| Contribution | 18p | Contribution | 8p |

As the special price will still give a contribution of 8p, it is worthwhile accepting, but there may be other factors which must be considered, such as the reaction of other customers who may learn of this discounted price, before making a final decision.

Now the production manager says he can change the production method so that up to 12,000 Fruit Ices can be produced per month for an additional fixed cost of £500 per month. He estimates that this will save variable costs of 4p per Fruit Ice. Do you think this plan should be implemented? There is no need to do a full calculation again, but look instead at the maximum possible savings in variable costs and compare them with the fixed costs. The maximum savings will be 4p × 12,000 = £480. Since this is lower than the £500 additional fixed costs incurred, the proposal is not worthwhile.

## 18.4 Limiting Factors

A *limiting factor* is a key factor which constrains the growth of an organisation. Examples are sales or shortages of materials or labour. The limiting factor should be identified and production arranged so that the contribution per unit of limiting factor is maximised. In the examples we have looked at so far in this chapter we have assumed that there are no factors present which would prevent the organisations from achieving the level of activity required to break even or to make the desired level of profit. However, this is rarely the case in business and there is nearly always some factor present – such as the maximum sales which can be made or the production capacity of machinery – which prevents unlimited growth. In making decisions using contribution, we have to take such factors into account. We can explain this by turning back to Mementoes Ltd.

## Activity

Mementoes Ltd makes models of historic buildings, but we said that there was only one model priced at £2.30 with variable costs of £1.05. Let us assume that this model is of Winchester Cathedral. One of their designers suggests that they make a model of Windsor Castle instead of Winchester Cathedral. The fixed costs of the business would stay the same, but the variable costs and selling price would be as follows:

| | Winchester Cathedral | | Windsor Castle | |
|---|---|---|---|---|
| | £ | £ | £ | £ |
| Selling price | | 2.30 | | 3.00 |
| Variable costs: | | | | |
| Materials | 0.60 | | 0.90 | |
| Labour | 0.30 | | 0.35 | |
| Packaging | 0.15 | 1.05 | 0.20 | 1.45 |
| Contribution | | 1.25 | | 1.55 |

Based on the above information, do you recommend that the company makes models of Winchester Cathedral or Windsor Castle?

You should have had no difficulty with this because the contribution per unit Mementoes gets from Windsor Castle is £1.55 compared with £1.25 from Winchester Cathedral. The general rule is that if there are no limiting factors present, select the activity which gives the highest contribution. This is assuming that you are certain that you can sell them!

Supposing the company finds that the supply of materials is limited and therefore it can make only a limited number of models. It uses the same materials for both models, but as can be seen from the above costs, Windsor Castle uses 50% more materials. Which model should the company makes to obtain the maximum profit? This is slightly more difficult. When there is a particular limiting factor present – in this case, materials – the general rule is to maximise the contribution per unit of limiting factor. In other words, select the model which gives the greatest contribution for the materials used. We do not know the amount of materials. If we did, we could calculate the contribution per kilo by dividing the contribution per unit by the number of kilos per unit. However, as we know the cost of materials for each model, we can calculate the contribution we get for each penny of materials, as follows:

|  | Winchester Cathedral | Windsor Castle |
|---|---|---|
|  | £ | £ |
| Contribution per unit | 1.25 | 1.55 |
| Materials per unit | 0.60 | 0.90 |
| Contribution per 1p of materials | 0.208 | 0.172 |

In this example, if materials are limited it would be best to manufacture models of Winchester Cathedral since this has the highest contribution per unit per limiting factor. As you can see, if we only had £100 of materials, we could get a contribution of £20.80 from Winchester Cathedral, but only £17.20 from Windsor Castle.

## 18.5 **Break-even Analysis**

*Break-even analysis* is an extension of marginal costing and is used to identify the *break-even point* of a business. The break-even point is where the business makes neither a profit nor a loss and can be determined by constructing a graph or by applying the following formula:

$$\text{Break-even point in units} = \frac{\text{Total fixed costs}}{\text{Contribution per unit}}$$

You will remember that contribution per unit is the selling price less the variable costs per unit. The above formula gives the same answer as would be arrived at by constructing a break-even graph, but with more complex figures it permits a greater degree of accuracy.

Continuing to use the example of Mementoes Ltd, the company sells each model for £2.30. Materials cost 60p, labour 30p and packing costs 15p per unit. The fixed costs were £850 per week. With this information we can calculate the break-even point. Substituting the figures for the formula, the calculations are:

$$\text{Break-even point} = \frac{\pounds850}{\pounds1.25} = \text{approximately 680 models}$$

The sales value at the break-even point can be found by using the following formula:

$$\text{Sales value at break-even point} = \frac{\text{Total fixed costs} \times \text{Sales value}}{\text{Total contribution}}$$

The amounts for sales value and contribution can be at the maximum level of activity, per unit or any other level. Using the formula we can now calculate the sales value at the break-even point for Mementoes Ltd:

$$\text{Sales value at break-even point} = \frac{\pounds850 \times \pounds2,300}{\pounds1,250} = \pounds1,564$$

If the organisation has a specific target profit, the level of activity that will achieve it can be found by using the following formula:

$$\text{Selected level of activity in units} = \frac{\text{Fixed costs} + \text{Target profit}}{\text{Contribution per unit}}$$

Using the formula, we can work out how many models Mementoes would have to make and sell if the company wanted to make a profit of £200 per week.

$$\text{Selected level of activity} = \frac{\pounds850 + \pounds200}{\pounds1.25} = \text{840 models}$$

The difference between the selected level of activity (840 models) and the break-even point (680 models) is known as the *margin of safety*. Mementoes could miss its target of 840 models by 160 models before it goes under the break-even point and starts making a loss. All this information can be shown on a break-even graph. The procedure for constructing a break-even graph is as follows:

1 Draw a horizontal axis to measure activity.
2 Draw a vertical axis to measure costs and revenue.
3 Plot a fixed cost line which will be parallel to the horizontal axis.
4 Plot a total cost line by adding the variable costs to the fixed costs, re-membering that at nil activity there will be no variable costs, but there will be the total fixed costs.
5 Plot the revenue line.

The point where the revenue line and the total cost line intercept is the *break-even point*.

---

## Activity

Draw a break-even graph for Mementoes Ltd. Assume that the maximum level of activity is 900 models.

---

If you have drawn your graph accurately, you should have obtained the same break-even point as you calculated using the formula. Your completed graph should look like this:

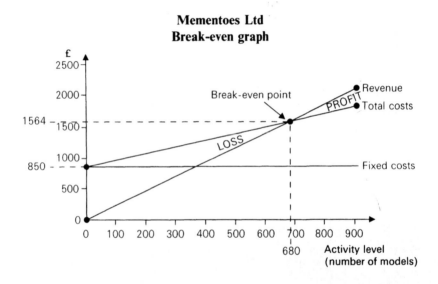

**Mementoes Ltd**
**Break-even graph**

Break-even analysis makes the same assumptions about the behaviour of fixed and variable costs as marginal costing. These rarely hold true over a complete range of activity and a period of time. Fixed costs may move in steps as additional facilities such as another machine, more factory space, etc. are brought into use as production increases. Variable costs may rise steeply in the early stages because production is not very efficient. They may also rise again at the peak of activity due to pressure of work causing inefficiencies.

The limited range of activity over which the assumptions on cost behaviour hold true is known as the *relevant range*, and decisions should be restricted to this range unless investigations are conducted.

In this section we have concentrated on calculating the break-even point. However, the same principles can be used for calculating the profit at different levels of activity. For this reason, some text books prefer to use the term *cost–volume–profit (C–V–P) analysis*, as this focuses on what will happen to the financial results if a level of activity or volume fluctuates.

## 18.6  Conclusions

In this chapter we have considered the impact on cost and profit of changes in activity levels. We have explained how a marginal cost statement is drawn up and how the contribution of various products is calculated. We have discussed the importance of limiting factors, which may constrain the growth of an organisation and therefore affect the decision-making process. We have also explained the general rules for calculating which product will be more profitable to produce when limiting factors are present. Finally, we have drawn a break-even graph and used it to find the break-even point as well as using a number of formulae.

Having completed this chapter. you should now be able to:

- differentiate between fixed and variable costs;
- draw up a marginal cost statement;
- explain the importance of calculating the contribution;
- calculate the break-even point of an activity;
- describe the effect of limiting factors.

## Exercises

Complete the following sentences:

**1** When activity increases, fixed costs per unit ............................................................
**2** Marginal costing is a technique ............................................................
**3** Contribution is calculated by ............................................................
**4** The break-even point is where ............................................................
**5** The margin of safety is ............................................................

Are the following statements true or false?

**6** When activity increases, total variable costs increase.
**7** When activity decreases, total fixed costs decrease.
**8** When activity increases, fixed costs per unit increase.
**9** When activity decreases, fixed costs per unit increase.
**10** When activity increases, variable cost per unit stay the same.

You may wish to read more widely than this book to answer the following questions fully, but you can check the main points by referring to the appropriate sections in this chapter.

**11** Distinguish between the behaviour of fixed and variable costs when activity increases. (Section 18.2)
**12** Explain the concept of contribution. (Section 18.3)
**13** What is meant by the margin of safety? (Section 18.4)
**14** Why are limiting factors important? (Section 18.5)

Multiple choice questions (more than one answer may apply):

**15** If the selling price per unit is £27.00 and the variable costs per unit are £13.00, the contribution per unit is:

  **a** £40.00
  **b** £14.00
  **c** £13.00
  **d** none of these.

**16** If the variable costs per unit are £6.00 and 500 units have been sold for £5,000, the total contribution is:

  **a** £4,000
  **b** £2,000
  **c** £3,000
  **d** £8,000.

**17** If the contribution per unit is £2.00 and the total variable costs for 100 units is £300, the total sales figure for those 100 units is:

  **a** £200
  **b** £500
  **c** £700
  **d** £100.

**18** If the total fixed costs are £12,000, the selling price per unit is £12 and the variable costs are £8 per unit, the break-even point is:

  **a** 12,000 units
  **b** 3,000 units
  **c** 1,500 units
  **d** 4,500 units.

**19** If fixed costs are £80,000 and contribution is 50p per unit, the number of units to be sold to achieve a target profit of £50,000 is:

  **a** 60,000 units
  **b** 260,000 units
  **c** 600,000 units
  **d** 200,000 units.

**20** If the contribution for 1,000 units is £650 and the variable cost is 45p per unit, the total sales figure for 350 units is:

  **a** £492.50
  **b** £157.50
  **c** £385.00
  **d** £70.00.

Practice questions:

**21** Describe the circumstances in which you would use marginal costing to make a decision.
**22** Explain the impact of limiting factors and how you would allow for them. Use a worked example to illustrate your answer.
**23** A business has fixed costs of £1,000 and sells its product for £2.50 per unit. The variable costs are £1.20 per unit. Draw a break-even graph.
**24** Describe the limitations of marginal costing.

**25** You are an assistant management accountant in a company which manufactures fairground equipment. The company uses absorption costing and like many other firms in recent years, has been suffering in the economic recession. Steve Wrench, the production manager, is worried because his total cost per unit is increasing despite the strict cost controls he exercises. Diane Flowers, the marketing manager, is complaining that in order to maintain sales volume, the selling price per unit must be reduced. They have had a meeting and calculated that the price Diane has suggested is lower than the total cost per unit as calculated by Steve. They have come to the conclusion that if they lower the price and increase their sales volume, it will lead to even larger losses.

Write a report addressed to Mr Wrench and Ms Flowers explaining:

**a** why the total cost per unit increases as production decreases;
**b** why marginal costing may be more appropriate than absorption costing for decision-making in times of recession.

(Answers on pp. 340–1)

# **19** Capital Investment Appraisal

## 19.1 **Introduction**

This chapter considers a number of techniques which can be used to make a decision when investing in a long-term capital project. When a business wishes to invest in a new factory, computer facilities, production line or any other major project that requires capital investment, there are a number of decisions to be made. Some are organisational and personnel decisions, but it is crucial that the financial implications of any decisions are considered. At the very least, management will want to know that the business will get its money back. In this chapter and Chapter 20 we will be looking at the different interpretations of this phrase and the techniques of *capital investment appraisal* most commonly used.

## 19.2 **Purpose of Capital Investment Appraisal**

When a business is considering whether to invest a large amount of *capital* in a long-term project, it needs to be sure that the amount of money received during the life of the project will be higher than the amount originally invested. The annual profit and the distinction between fixed and variable costs is therefore of less importance than the timing and amount of the cash going in and out of the business. In some cases an investment is made not to generate more cash, but to make a saving on costs. For example, a business may be deciding whether to replace a machine with a new model which is less expensive to run. The question that the business needs to answer is whether the savings in costs are sufficiently high to warrant the investment in the new machine. Once again, cash is the most important factor.

## Activity

A company has a choice between three machines, each costing £100,000 to purchase. Each machine will last for 3 years and the company estimates that over that period the positive net cash flows – that is, the difference between the cash coming in and going out each year – will be as follows:

| Year | Machine 1 £ | Machine 2 £ | Machine 3 £ |
|------|-------------|-------------|-------------|
| 1 | 60,000 | 20,000 | 10,000 |
| 2 | 40,000 | 40,000 | 20,000 |
| 3 | 20,000 | 60,000 | 95,000 |

Which machine would you recommend that the company purchases?

In order to make the comparison, you need to total the above cash flows:

| Year | Machine 1 £ | Machine 2 £ | Machine 3 £ |
|------|-------------|-------------|-------------|
| 1 | 60,000 | 20,000 | 10,000 |
| 2 | 40,000 | 40,000 | 20,000 |
| 3 | 20,000 | 60,000 | 95,000 |
| Total | 120,000 | 120,000 | 125,000 |

Machines 1 and 2 both give the same total net cash inflow of £120,000 over the 3-year period and therefore either would be a worthwhile investment. However, you may decide that machine 1 is preferable because the cash comes in more quickly. Machine 3 looks better than the other two because the total net cash inflow is £125,000. However, you have to wait until year 3 before you get most of the cash and this means that the risk is increased. With all three machines the company has estimated the cash flows and the further into the future the estimate is, the more unreliable it is likely to be. It is therefore difficult to decide which is the 'best' machine to buy and we need a specific technique to help us.

We are going to describe a number of different techniques of project appraisal in this chapter and Chapter 20. Each has advantages and disadvantages and may give different answers to the same problem. Therefore, management must decide which is the *most appropriate technique* to use in the circumstances.

## 19.3 Payback Period

Calculating the *payback period* is a simple technique for appraising the acceptability of projects and is very popular with non-accountants. The project is considered purely from the point of view of its cash flow over the life of the project. The objective is to recover the cash outlay in the shortest possible time.

For example, supposing you are considering buying an ice cream van, which will last for 5 years, and you want to employ someone to operate it. Cash spent on buying the van would be £12,000. For each year, you estimate the cash flows will be as follows:

|  | £ | £ |
|---|---|---|
| **Cash in** | | |
| Sales | | 20,000 |
| **Cash out** | | |
| Purchases (ingredients) | 5,000 | |
| Wages for operator | 9,000 | |
| Expenses (petrol, tax, insurance, repairs, etc.) | 2,000 | 16,000 |
| **Net cash flow** | | 4,000 |

With this information, we can calculate the payback period as follows:

| Year | Yearly net cash flows | Cumulative net cash flows |
|---|---|---|
|  | £ | £ |
| 0 | (12,000) | (12,000) |
| 1 | 4,000 | (8,000) |
| 2 | 4,000 | (4,000) |
| 3 | 4,000 | Nil |
| 4 | 4,000 | 4,000 |
| 5 | 4,000 | 8,000 |

As you can see, depreciation of the van is not included because depreciation is not a cash flow. The cash flow relating to the van is the cash paid for van when it was bought. But there are several other things in this table which need explaining:

- Year 0 is a conventional way of saying start of year 1. Year 1, 2, 3, etc. means end of year 1, 2, 3, etc.
- It is customary to assume that cash flows during a year will be received at the end of that year. Of course, this is not true, but it simplifies the calculation and errs on the side of conservatism by giving a slightly pessimistic rather than an optimistic view if the cash flows are positive. It is possible to produce cash flows on a quarterly or monthly basis, but this is seldom done in payback calculations, because forecasting to this degree of refinement is rarely possible.
- Negative cash flows (cash going out) are shown in brackets, whereas positive cash flows (cash coming in) are not.
- The cumulative cash flows are shown as nil at the end of year 3. This means that at the end of year 3 the cash flowing in from the project has reached the figure of £12,000, which is same as the initial cash outflow in

payment for the van at the start of year 1. Therefore, we can say that the payback period for the project is 3 years.

## Activity

The net cash flows for a project have been budgeted as follows:

| Year | Yearly net cash flows £ |
|------|-------------------------|
| 0 | (18,000) |
| 1 | 8,000 |
| 2 | 8,000 |
| 3 | 8,000 |
| 4 | 8,000 |
| 5 | 8,000 |

What is the payback period?

You need to work out the cumulative net cash flows over the period. Check your answer against the following:

| Year | Yearly net cash flows £ | Cumulative net cash flows £ |
|------|-------------------------|------------------------------|
| 0 | (18,000) | (18,000) |
| 1 | 8,000 | (10,000) |
| 2 | 8,000 | (2,000) |
| 3 | 8,000 | 6,000 |
| 4 | 8,000 | 14,000 |
| 5 | 8,000 | 22,000 |

The answer lies somewhere between 2 and 3 years. Assuming the cash flow is regular throughout the year, it should be easy to see that the answer is $2\frac{1}{4}$ years or 2 years and 3 months. If the figures are not simple, the way to calculate the part year is:

| Year | Cumulative net cash flow £ |
|------|-----------------------------|
| 2 | (2,000) |
| 3 | 6,000 |

Add the two cumulative cash flows, ignoring the fact that the first figure is negative (in brackets):

$$2,000 + 6,000 = 8,000$$

Then divide the earlier figure (2,000) by the total:

$$\frac{2,000}{8,000} = \frac{1}{4} \text{ of a year}$$

Therefore the payback period is $2 + \frac{1}{4} = 2\frac{1}{4}$ years.

The main *advantages* of the payback period technique are as follows:

- The technique is very simple to calculate and is understood by managers who are not very numerate.
- It produces results which are useful for risky projects, where the prediction of cash flows for more than the first few years is difficult, due to possible changes in the market. For example, changes in technology may make a product obsolete in a year or so, although the current market for the product seems assured.
- Some businesses may need to consider short-term cash flows more important than long-term cash flows, perhaps due to lack of capital adequate to sustain long-term objectives. It is not much use aiming for long-term profitability if the business fails in 6 months' time from lack of cash.

The main *disadvantages* of the payback period technique are:

- Net cash inflows in year 5 are given the same degree of importance as those for year 1. Cash now or soon is worth more than the same amount of cash in 5 years' time. This is known as the *time value of money.*
- The technique ignores cash flows after the payback period.

---

## Activity

Returning to the example of the three machines at the beginning of this chapter, which machine would you recommend purchasing on the basis of the payback period technique?

---

Your answer should be machine 1, because this has a payback period of only 2 years compared with longer periods for the other two machines. However, using the payback period would mean that we would not select machine 3, which gave the greatest return of cash. This is one of the disadvantages of the technique.

## 19.4 Accounting Rate of Return

Whereas the payback period method is concerned with cash flows, the *accounting rate of return (ARR)* is concerned with profit and average capital employed. We will define profit as *profit before interest and tax.* The other figure used to calculate the accounting rate of return is *average capital employed.* 'Capital employed' means the money that is tied up in the business and this can be defined as *fixed assets plus current assets less current liabilities.* 'Average capital employed' means that if the capital employed is £18,000 at the beginning of next year and £22,000 at the end of next year, then the average capital employed for next year is £20,000 (£18,000 + £22,000 ÷ 2 years). ARR is calculated as profit before interest and tax as a percentage of average capital employed. The formula is:

$$\frac{\text{Profit before interest and tax}}{\text{Average capital employed}} \times 100$$

## Activity

Richard Pillinger is contemplating developing his farm by opening a farm shop selling his organically grown produce or opening a restaurant serving food that has been prepared using the farm's organic produce. Estimates for these projects are as follows:

|  | Farm shop £ | Restaurant £ |
|---|---|---|
| Sales | 62,000 | 109,000 |
| Cost of sales including expenses | 43,400 | 82,000 |
| Average capital employed | 100,000 | 180,000 |

What are the accounting rates of return for the two projects, and which project do you consider is the better one?

You should have calculated the figures needed for the formula before working it out:

|  |  | Farm shop £ | Restaurant £ |
|---|---|---|---|
|  | Sales | 62,000 | 109,000 |
| *Less* | Cost of sales | 43,400 | 82,000 |
|  | Profit before interest and tax | 18,600 | 27,000 |
| ARR | $\dfrac{\text{Profit before interest and tax}}{\text{Average capital employed}} \times 100$ | $\dfrac{18,600}{100,000} \times 100 = 18.6\%$ | $\dfrac{27,000}{180,000} \times 100 = 15\%$ |
|  | Rank | 1 | 2 |

If we rank these projects by their ARR, then the farm shop is ranked first, as it has an ARR of 18.6% compared with 15% for the restaurant. However, Richard would be well advised not to base his decision purely on this method of project appraisal. For example, it would be interesting to know what the payback periods would be, although we do not have sufficient information to calculate them. Also, you can see that the restaurant requires more capital than the farm shop (an average of £180,000 compared with £100,000), but the restaurant makes more profit than the farm shop in absolute terms (£27,000 compared with £18,600).

Assuming that the capital required for the restaurant is available for investment, and since the farm shop requires less than half this amount, what is Richard to do with the difference? He could put it in a building society, but the return would be likely to be much less than the 15% for the restaurant. He might want to consider investing in another project similar to the farm shop, but this might not be possible. In other words, ARR is too poor a technique to be a satisfactory basis for a decision. It leaves too many questions unanswered.

The main *advantages* of the accounting rate of return technique are as follows:

- Calculations are very simple.
- The entire life of the project is taken into account.

The main *disadvantages* of the accounting rate of return technique are:

- The timing of cash movements is completely ignored.
- There are a number of different definitions of profit and capital employed and therefore the calculation of the accounting rate of return can result in different figures.
- The crucial factor in investment decisions is cash flow and the accounting rate of return uses profits.
- The technique takes no account of the time value of money; a topic we discuss in Chapter 20.
- It takes no account of the incidence of profits.
- Averages can be misleading.

## 19.5 Conclusions

In this chapter we have described two techniques of project appraisal: the payback period technique and the accounting rate of return. The payback period technique is concerned with cash flows and calculates the time it will take to recover the cash invested in the project. The accounting rate of return is concerned with profit and expresses this as a percentage of the average capital employed in the project. In addition, we have considered the main advantages and disadvantages of these two techniques.

Having completed this chapter, you should now be able to:

- explain the purpose of capital investment appraisal;
- apply the payback period technique to a project;
- apply the accounting rate of return technique to a project;
- explain the advantages and disadvantages of these two techniques.

# Exercises

Complete the following sentences:

**1** The payback technique has the disadvantage of ignoring ...............................
...........................................................................................................................

**2** The accounting rate of return (ARR) is calculated as ...................................
...........................................................................................................................

**3** When investing in a long-term project, a business wishes to ensure that .........
...........................................................................................................................

**4** The aim of the payback technique is ...........................................................

**5** The accounting rate of return (ARR) is simple and ......................................
...........................................................................................................................

Are the following statements true or false?

**6** With the accounting rate of return, the cash flows of the project are taken into account.

**7** The payback period takes account of the time value of money.

**8** The payback technique is good for high-risk projects.

**9** With capital investment projects you must separate the fixed costs from the variable costs.

**10** You must know the cash flows in order to calculate the accounting rate of return.

You may wish to read more widely than this book to answer the following questions fully, but you can check the main points by referring to the appropriate sections in this chapter.

**11** What is the main concern of a business when making a capital investment? (Section 19.2)

**12** What are the main advantages and disadvantages of the payback period technique? (Section 19.3)

**13** What is the difference between the payback period and the accounting rate of return? (Sections 19.3 and 19.4)

**14** How would you calculate the accounting rate of return? (Section 19.4)

Multiple choice questions (more than one answer may apply):

**15** The payback period is the time in years it takes for cash inflows of a project to equal:

**a** the average capital employed
**b** the cost of capital employed
**c** the cash overdraft limited agreed with the bank
**d** the cash outflows.

**16** A project has a cash outflow in year 0 of £17,100 and cash inflows for the first and subsequent years of £3,600 per annum. The payback period is:

**a** $4\frac{1}{4}$ years
**b** $4\frac{3}{4}$ years
**c** $4\frac{1}{2}$ years
**d** 4 years $7\frac{1}{2}$ months.

**17** The average profit before tax for the next 3 years of a project is budgeted at £8,500 per annum. The average capital employed over the 3 years is budgeted at £50,000. The ARR is:

**a** 17%
**b** 58%
**c** 51%
**d** 19.33%.

**18** To calculate the ARR, you need to know:

**a** the cash inflows
**b** the cash outflows
**c** both of them
**d** neither of them.

**19** The advantage of the ARR technique is that it:

**a** allows for the timing of cash movements
**b** takes account of the entire life of the project
**c** takes account of the incidence of profit
**d** takes account of the time value of money.

**20** You would use the payback period technique when:

**a** you want to know the profitability of the project
**b** you want to know the return on capital employed
**c** the full life of the project must be taken into account
**d** the cash investment must be recovered in the shortest possible time.

Practice questions:

**21** Explain why the payback period technique is preferable to the accounting rate of return.
**22** Describe the limitations of the payback period technique.
**23** Describe the limitations of the accounting rate of return.
**24** Farmer George Tractors Ltd has £500,000 to invest. The net cash flows of two possible projects are as follows:

| Year | Project 1 £ | Project 2 £ |
|------|-------------|-------------|
| 1 | 80,000 | 90,000 |
| 2 | 100,000 | 110,000 |
| 3 | 180,000 | 190,000 |
| 4 | 140,000 | 110,000 |
| 5 | 100,000 | 80,000 |

Which project should the management choose, and why?
**25** Film Animation Ltd wishes to expand and has £800,000 to invest. The details of two potential projects are as follows:

| | Project A £ | Project B £ |
|------|-------------|-------------|
| Sales | 318,500 | 358,000 |
| Cost of sales including expenses | 240,500 | 264,400 |
| Average capital employed | 650,000 | 780,000 |

Which project should the management choose, and why?

(Answers on pp. 341–2)

# 20 Discounted Cash Flow

## 20.1 Introduction

In Chapter 19 we looked at two techniques of investment appraisal, the payback period and the accounting rate of return. However, as we discussed, both these techniques suffer from severe limitations. Because capital investment appraisal is so crucial to decision-making, managers need to use a technique that provides valuable financial information. *Discounted cash flow (DCF)* does just this.

The main concept of DCF is that there is a *time value to money*. In the first part of this chapter we explain this fairly straightforward principle and, once you have mastered it, you will find the calculations in this chapter relatively simple. In the remainder of the chapter we introduce two further techniques, *net present value* and the *internal rate of return*, which can be used to make a decision when investing in a long-term capital project. Both these techniques are very important and the concept of discounting is so crucial that it is now also being used in financial accounting.

## 20.2 Main Principles

In Chapter 19, we said that the project appraisal techniques of payback and accounting rate of return take no account of the *time value of money*. The basic principle is that £1 received now is worth more than £1 received at some time in the future. One reason for this is that money received now can be invested. For example, supposing someone wanted to borrow money from you now and promised to pay you £100 in a year's time, how much would you be willing to lend them if the usual interest rate is 10%? One concern you may have is whether you are likely to be paid the £100. If you consider it is doubtful, you may decide not to lend the money or, if you do, to charge a higher rate of interest because of the higher risk. If you consider the loan is safe, then you may be willing to lend £90.90. In a year's time this would give interest of £9.10 to make the sum of £100 which you are repaid.

## Activity

How much would you be willing to lend now, if the interest rate is 15% and the borrower promises to repay £500 in 3 years' time?

You probably have had to make some complex calculations to arrive at the correct answer of £329. However, there is an easy method if you turn to the *discounted cash flow tables* in Appendix 2 (p. 346) and look at Table 1, Present Value Factors. The question we are trying to answer is what is the *present value* of £500 received in 3 years' time, if the interest rate is 15%. If you look in the left-hand column at 3 years and read across to the 15% column, you will see that the *discount factor* is 0.658. This is for £1, so we need to multiply this by £500. This gives the figure of £329 which is the amount you would be willing to lend now. You can check this by working out 15% compound interest on £329 for 3 years:

|  | £ |
|---|---|
| Principal | 329.00 |
| Interest Year 1 | 49.35 |
|  | 378.35 |
| Interest Year 2 | 56.75 |
|  | 435.10 |
| Interest Year 3 | 65.27 |
| Total at end of 3 years | 500.37 |

It is the above concept of the time value of money which underpins the two most sophisticated techniques in capital investment appraisal, *net present value* and *internal rate of return*, which we will look at next.

## 20.3 Net Present Value

*Net present value (NPV)* converts the future net cash flows into present-day values and the project with the largest net present value is the one preferred. Many problems, both in real life and in exams, are concerned with choosing between alternatives, even if one alternative is to do nothing.

## Activity

Keith Hacker is considering whether to buy a computer which will improve his cash flows by £30,000 per annum for the next 5 years, at the end of which time the computer will be out of date and of no value. The computer will cost £75,000 and will be bought for cash. The discount rate which Keith thinks is suitable is

15%. Using the following pro forma and Table 1, Present Value Factors, in Appendix 2, calculate the net present value of this project:

| Year | Detail | Cash flows £ | Discount factor at 15% | Present value £ |
|------|--------|--------------|------------------------|-----------------|
| 0 | Purchase of computer | (75,000) | 1.000 | (75,000) |
| 1 | Net cash inflow | | | |
| 2 | Net cash inflow | | | |
| 3 | Net cash inflow | | | |
| 4 | Net cash inflow | | | |
| 5 | Net cash inflow | | | |
| | **Net present value** | | | |

If you had problems with this activity, you may find the following comments helpful.

- The purchase of the computer is a negative cash flow, and is shown in brackets. The discount factor is 1.000 because the cash outflow is at year 0.
- It is assumed that the cash flow always takes place at the end of the year.

The solution is as follows:

| Year | Detail | Cash flows £ | Discount factor at 15% | Present value £ |
|------|--------|--------------|------------------------|-----------------|
| 0 | Purchase of computer | (75,000) | 1.000 | (75,000) |
| 1–5 | Net cash inflow | 30,000 | 3.352 | 100,560 |
| | **Net present value** | | | 25,560 |

You should have got the same NPV of £25,560, but you will see that we have taken a short cut. The *discount factor* of 3.352 can be found in Appendix 2, Table 2, Cumulative Present Value Factors (p. 349), and is used to save the effort of multiplying £30,000 in turn by the individual figures from Table 1 for years 1–5 inclusive. You can use this short cut only when it is the same amount of cash each year, otherwise you must use Table 1.

The NPV of the project is a positive £25,560. It is called 'net' because the initial outlay on the machine has been deducted from the total of the discounted inflows. Since the project has a positive NPV, Keith will be getting a return on his investment of more than 15%. If the NPV had been nil, his return would be 15%. If the project had shown a negative NPV, the return would be less than 15%, and it would not therefore be worth undertaking.

## 20.4 Internal Rate of Return

The *internal rate of return (IRR)* uses the same principles as NPV, but the aim is to find the discount rate which gives a net present value of 0 for the project. In other words, the aim of the technique is to show the percentage return you obtain on the investment.

## Activity

In the previous example we concluded that at a discount rate of 15%, a positive NPV of £25,560 made Keith's investment worthwhile. In other words Keith would be getting a return on the project in excess of 15%. Using the following pro forma, and Discount Table 2 in Appendix 2, recalculate the NPV, using discount rates of 20%, 25% and 30%:

| Year | Cash flows £ | At 20% Discount factor | At 20% Present value £ | At 25% Discount factor | At 25% Present value £ | At 30% Discount factor | At 30% Present value £ |
|------|------|------|------|------|------|------|------|
| 0 | (75,000) | 1.000 | (75,000) | 1.000 | (75,000) | 1.000 | (75,000) |
| 1–5 | 30,000 | | | | | | |

Check your answer against the following:

| Year | Cash flows £ | At 20% Discount factor | At 20% Present value £ | At 25% Discount factor | At 25% Present value £ | At 30% Discount factor | At 30% Present value £ |
|------|------|------|------|------|------|------|------|
| 0 | (75,000) | 1.000 | (75,000) | 1.000 | (75,000) | 1.000 | (75,000) |
| 1–5 | 30,000 | 2.991 | 89,730 | 2.689 | 80,670 | 2.436 | 73,080 |
| | | | 14,730 | | 5,670 | | (1,920) |

The information we now have can be summarised as follows:

- At a discount rate of 15%, the NPV is a positive £25,560.
- At a discount rate of 20%, the NPV is a positive £14,730.
- At a discount rate of 25%, the NPV is a positive £5,670.
- At a discount rate of 30%, the NPV is a negative £1,920.

Looking at this, you can see that the higher the discount rate, the smaller the NPV becomes, until it eventually becomes negative somewhere between 25% and 30%. The IRR lies at the point where the NPV changes from positive to negative, i.e. where it is nil.

This can be illustrated by plotting the NPVs on a graph against the appropriate discount rates. The discount rates are marked on the $x$ axis, and NPVs on the $y$ axis.

**Keith Hacker**
**Internal rate of return**

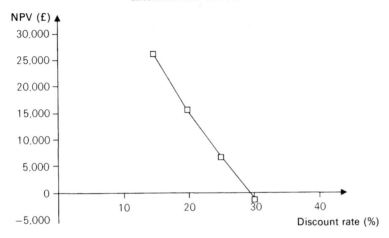

You will see that the line joining the four points is a slight curve, but for all practical purposes, we can assume that it is a straight line, provided the points are not too far apart. We shall use the data at 25% and 30% discount rates. The discount rate at which the line crosses the *x* axis, where NPV is nil, is somewhere between 25% and 30% – i.e. 25 plus a number between 0 and 5 (30–25). The calculation involves *linear interpolation* (linear, because it assumes a straight line), and is as follows:

$$5\left(\frac{5{,}670}{5{,}670 + 1{,}920}\right) + 25 = 28.7\%$$

The calculation shows that Keith will get a return of 28.7% on the project. The figures in square brackets represent the proportion of 5 that we require to be added to 25:

$$\frac{\text{NPV of 25\% rate}}{\text{NPV of 25\% rate plus NPV of 30\% rate}}$$

We ignore the fact that the NPV of the 30% rate (£1,920) is negative, i.e. that the difference (or distance) between 5,670 and (1,920) is the total of the two figures, ignoring the fact that the second figure is negative. If you find this difficult to understand, the following explanation may help. If yesterday you had £100 in the bank (positive figure), and today find you have an overdraft of £50 (negative figure), how much money have you drawn out of the bank since yesterday? The answer is £100 + £50 = £150.

The main *advantages* of the net present value and internal rate of return techniques are as follows:

- They use the concept of the time value of money.
- The entire life of the project is taken into account.
- They permit comparisons with other opportunities to be made.
- They enable the organisation to decide on its financing policy.

The main *disadvantages* of the net present value and internal rate of return techniques are:

- The calculations are complex.
- It is difficult to decide what is the most appropriate discount rate to use.
- Managers may have difficulty in understanding the technique.

## 20.5 **Information Required**

Although *net present value* and *internal rate of return* are useful techniques, they are also slightly complex and managers without any knowledge of accounting may have difficulty in understanding the results. Since the main purpose of management accounting is to help managers by providing useful information, if the information presented is hard to interpret it makes less useful. As well as managers having problems in understanding the results of the calculations, the management accountant may have problems in obtaining the figures to do the calculations. These problems are common to all investment appraisal techniques based on cash flows.

## **Activity**

What sort of problems do you think might be associated with investment appraisal techniques based on cash flows?

One major problem is concerned with predicting the amount of *cash* that is likely to come in and go out of the business over the life of the project. Some projects last for many years and it is impossible to forecast the amounts with certainty. For this reason, many companies prefer the payback period, because it is based on the earliest cash flows. One cash flow which can arise at the end of a project is the sale of the machinery and equipment which was originally purchased for the project. With a large investment in machinery, the second-hand or scrap value may be very high, even after many years of use. The expected proceeds from the sale of any such assets must be shown as a cash inflow in the calculations.

Another problem which has not yet been mentioned is the choice of *discount factor*. In this chapter we have used a number of different rates as illustrations, but in practice management, with advice from the management accountant, must decide which rate to use. You will appreciate that the choice of discount factor is critical to the results of the calculation. One basis on which to choose the discount rate is to use the current rate of return the organisation receives on capital employed. Another method is to use the current cost of capital. Alternatively, the return on other projects available could be used or the rate which could be received if the organisation invested the capital externally.

When answering questions on capital appraisal, it is easy for students to concentrate on the calculations and forget these other aspects. The calculations are relatively easy, but the above issues make capital investment appraisal techniques complex. However, it is vital that the management accountant makes use of them, as they assist management in determining the likely return they will get from a long-term project and deciding whether it is acceptable in view of the risks involved.

## 20.6 Conclusions

In this chapter we have described two further techniques of project appraisal, net present value and internal rate of return, and considered their advantages and disadvantages. These techniques are concerned with discounted cash flow and take account of the time value of money. The specific information required for discounted cash flow techniques presents some problems, but if available these methods of capital investment appraisal greatly assist management decision-making.

Having completed this chapter, you should now be able to:

- appraise a capital investment project using a number of techniques;
- explain the advantages and disadvantages of the techniques;
- explain the importance of the concept of the time value of money;
- use discounted cash flow tables.

## Exercises

Complete the following sentences:

1 The time value of money concept ...........................................................................
2 Net present value (NPV) converts ........................................................................
3 The aim of the internal rate of return (IRR) is to ...............................................
4 Positive net cash flow is ..........................................................................................
5 Two major problems associated with discounting are .......................................

Are the following statements true or false?

6 If a project has a positive NPV, it is not worth undertaking.
7 In capital investment appraisal, cash is more important than profit.
8 For NPV you need to know the cash inflows and the cash outflows.
9 Discount rates should always be 1% higher than the bank rate.
10 The NPV for projects will always be positive.

You may wish to read more widely than this book to answer the following questions fully, but you can check the main points by referring to the appropriate sections in this chapter.

**11** What is meant by the time value of money? (Section 20.2)
**12** Explain the principle of the calculations for NPV. (Section 20.3)
**13** Explain the calculation for linear interpolation. (Section 20.4)
**14** What are the main advantages and disadvantages of the discounted cash flow (DCF) techniques? (Section 20.4)

Multiple choice questions (more than one answer may apply):

**15** Any scrap value at the end of a project is:

    **a** treated as a negative cash flow
    **b** treated as positive cash flow
    **c** ignored completely
    **d** not discounted.

**16** The aim of IRR is to

    **a** identify the highest NPV
    **b** identify the lowest NPV
    **c** find the correct discount rate
    **d** find the percentage return on the investment.

**17** If a project gives a negative NPV with a discount rate of 12% this means that:

    **a** a mistake has been made
    **b** a different discount rate should be selected
    **c** the project is worth undertaking
    **d** the project is not worth undertaking.

**18** One advantage of NPV is that:

    **a** the discount rate is always known
    **b** it gives the percentage return on the investment
    **c** it gives the return on capital employed
    **d** the entire life of the project is taken into account.

**19** Using a 18% rate of discount, the present value of £753 to be received in 10 years' time is:

    **a** £380.00
    **b** £243.00
    **c** £143.00
    **d** £83.00.

**20** A project has the following cash flows:

| Year | Cash flows |
|------|-----------|
| 0 | (£20,000) |
| 1 | £10,000 |
| 2 | £10,000 |
| 3 | £10,000 |

Using a 15% discount rate, the NPV is:

    **a** £22,830
    **b** £2,830
    **c** £283
    **d** (£2,830).

Practice questions:

**21** What are the advantages and disadvantages of using DCF?
**22** Describe the procedures for calculating the NPV of a project.
**23** What issues should be considered when deciding the discount factor?
**24** Compare NPV with the technique of IRR.
**25** Kerry Melrose has a conference organising business and is thinking of buying some computer-controlled audio visual equipment. She has done her calculations on a cash basis and has discovered that the equipment will cost £10,000. At the end of the first year she will have to spend £5,000 on training and advertising, and this should generate an additional £1,000 worth of business. In the second year, she estimates that the advertising costs will reduce to £3,000, but an additional £2,000 worth of business will be generated. In the third and fourth years no advertising will be required and the additional business generated will be £3,000 in year 3 and £8,000 in year 4. Kerry believes that by the end of year 5 the equipment will be out of date, but she should be able to generate a further £6,000 worth of business in that year and be able to sell the equipment at the end of the year for £4,000.

Write a report for Kerry Melrose which shows:

**a** the payback period of the project
**b** the net present value of the project using a discount rate of 12%
**c** an explanation of the two techniques, and an interpretation of their results
**d** your recommendation as to whether Kerry should go ahead with the project, and any financial considerations she should bear in mind.

(Answers on pp. 342–3)

# 21 Budgetary Control

## 21.1 Introduction

This chapter introduces the technique of *budgetary control*, the process by which financial control can be exercised within a business using *budgets* for income and expenditure for each function of the organisation. A budget is a financial or quantitative statement prepared in advance of a specified accounting period. These budgets are compared with actual performance to establish any *variances*.

In all but the smallest of organisations, budgetary control is a major technique for planning and control. Individual function managers are made responsible for the controllable activities within their budgets and are expected to take action to remedy unacceptable adverse variances. There are very few managers who do not encounter a budgetary control system during their career. Budgetary control is used in service and manufacturing businesses, as well as not-for profit organisations. Apart from the government's budgets, some of the most publicly announced budgets are those of major films, where even the credits at the end of the film give the name of the accountant!

In this chapter we explain the importance of budgetary control and describe the procedures for setting up the system. We also explain how it is used to generate valuable information for managers in their task of planning and controlling the activities of the organisation and making decisions.

## 21.2 Business Planning

The importance of *business planning* can be shown by looking at an example. Cascade plc manufactures bathroom fittings. Based on past production records, the production manager believes that 15,000 shower units will be needed and buys all the materials and stores them in a warehouse. The marketing manager has heard that the water companies are considering adopting a metered water system, based on usage, rather than a system of water rates based on property value, and has therefore launched a massive sales campaign. He believes that 30,000 shower units will be sold. The financial accountant has received a letter from the bank stating that overdraft facilities will be withdrawn. He has therefore decided to stop any expenditure which is not absolutely necessary. The designer has come up with a new design using recycled water. The personnel manager believes that the recession will get worse and has started issuing redundancy notices to the workforce.

This example illustrates how a lack of coordination of the various activities, and managers following their own ideas, can lead to resources not being matched to the demands made on them and result in waste and inefficiency. This is remedied by business planning. The first stage of business planning is for the owners or directors of the business to set out their assumptions of what is going to happen to the organisation's markets and business environment. Non-trading organisations also operate in a business environment and planning is just as crucial to them.

## Activity

Make a list of the factors the owners or directors of an organisation should examine when arriving at their assumptions of what is going to happen to their markets and the business environment.

Depending on the type of organisation you were thinking of, the sort of factors you may have included are:

- changes in the size of the organisation's market and its anticipated share of the market;
- possible strategies of the organisation's competitors;
- likely changes in interest rates or sources of funding;
- likely cost increases and availability of energy, materials and labour;
- possibility of legislation or social pressures which will affect the organisation;
- effect of the activities of other related organisations;
- trends in climatic, demographic, environmental and other factors likely to affect the organisation's activities.

Having set out their assumptions, the owners or directors can then make *forecasts* about what is likely to happen in the year ahead. If they were to leave it at that, they would not be discharging their managerial responsibilities. For example, they might forecast that the organisation will become bankrupt. Although this may be accurate, it would clearly be unacceptable. They must find ways of minimising any threats to the organisation and taking advantage of any opportunities. By setting out the actions which must be taken in view of their predictions, they are making business plans.

The plans and policies established by the owners and directors must be converted into detailed plans covering all aspects of the organisation's activities. These are normally broken down on a monthly basis for a year or a longer period. Initially the plans may be in *quantitative terms* – for example the number of products to be made, the quantity of materials to be ordered. However, they will be converted into *financial terms* to form the budgetary control system. We will be looking at a formal definition of a budget in Section 21.3, but at this stage we can consider a budget to be a plan expressed in financial terms covering a specified length of time. Next, the detailed plans must be translated into actions for each manager to pursue.

---

## Activity

Using the example of Cascade plc again, both the production manager and the marketing manager need to know how many shower units they plan to sell in the coming year so that they can ensure that the number of shower units to be made will meet the anticipated demand. What suggestions would you make if either of the following circumstances arose:

**a**  Many more shower units are made than can be sold?
**b**  Many more orders are received than the number of shower units made?

---

In situation **a**, you may have decided that it is necessary to cut back severely on production. This could lead to redundancies with machines and other resources not being used to their full capacity. Alternatively, you may have suggested that production continues at the same level and the excess production is stored, which could be very expensive. Finally, you may consider that the organisation should boost sales through price reductions or increased marketing. Both these options could also be very expensive.

In situation **b**, although you may think that this is a good position for the business to be in, it can lead to considerable problems. If the company attempts to boost production, it may need overtime working at a higher wage rate. More machines and larger premises may be required, which may require taking out a loan to pay for them. If the company fails to meet the orders, customers will become dissatisfied and the firm's reputation will be harmed; customers may go to competitors where the service is better.

Whichever of the above alternatives the company chooses, the policy will have to be communicated to all managers. This will ensure that detailed plans can be drawn up which minimise the potential damage to the company's financial performance. However, even if detailed plans are made available to all managers so that activities are coordinated, it does not mean that there is *control*. Because the plans are based on predictions, events will occur which mean that the plans cannot be achieved. Prices may rise unexpectedly; new competitors may enter the market and offer cheaper products; machines may break down; suppliers may not be able to deliver materials on time. If an organisation is going to achieve control, regular *monitoring* must take place so that what actually happens can be compared with the original plan. In this way, action can be taken whenever circumstances dictate.

The following diagram shows the process of business planning and monitoring which leads to budgetary control:

**Business planning and control**

```
                    ┌─────────────┐
                    │ Assumptions │
                    └──────┬──────┘
                           ▼
                    ┌─────────────┐
                    │ Predictions │
                    └──────┬──────┘
                           ▼
                    ┌───────────────┐
                    │ Detailed plans│
                    └──────┬────────┘
           ┌───────────────┴───────────────┐
  ┌────────────────┐              ┌────────────────────┐
  │ Revise plans/  │              │ Actual performance │
  │ Corrective action│            │    by managers     │
  └────────────────┘              └─────────┬──────────┘
           ▲                                ▼
  ┌────────────────┐              ┌────────────────────┐
  │ Comparison of  │◄─────────────│ Measurement of     │
  │ actual with plan│             │ actual performance │
  └────────────────┘              └────────────────────┘
```

If there is no formal system of planning and control in an organisation, there will be an informal system. In small organisations, managers may be responsible for all the stages. In larger organisations, there is probably a formal system with a greater division of responsibility at each stage. Assumptions and predictions are normally made at board level following consultation throughout the organisation.

Collecting information to measure actual performance is part of the accounting function and accountants are also responsible for issuing financial statements which compare the actual performance with the plan. At this stage most managers find that they have a role in explaining any differences which have taken place between the plan and actual, and suggesting the appropriate course to pursue.

## 21.3 Purpose of Budgetary Control

As explained, budgetary control is the setting of plans or budgets which lay down policies for which managers are responsible. A regular comparison is made of what is actually achieved with the plan, so that individual managers can remedy any divergence from the plan or revise the plan if necessary. The overall *purpose* of budgetary control is to help managers to plan and control the use of resources. However, there are a number of other, more specific, purposes:

- A formal system of budgetary control enables an organisation to carry out its *planning* in a systematic and logical manner.
- *Control* can be achieved only by setting a plan of what is to be accomplished in a specified time period and managers regularly monitoring progress against the plan, taking corrective action where necessary.
- By setting plans, the activities of the various functions and departments can be *coordinated*. For example, the production manager can ensure that the correct quantity is manufactured to meet the requirements of the sales team, or the accountant can obtain sufficient funding to make adequate resources available to carry out the task, whether this is looking after children in care or running a railway network.
- A budgetary control system is a *communication system* which informs managers of the objectives of the organisation and the constraints under which it is operating. The regular monitoring of performance helps keep management informed of the progress of the organisation towards its objectives.
- By communicating detailed targets to individual managers, *motivation* is improved. Without a clear sense of direction, managers will become demotivated.
- By setting separate plans for individual departments and functions, managers are clear about their responsibilities. This allows them to *make decisions*, as long as they are within their budget responsibilities, and avoids the need for every decision to be made at the top level.
- By comparing actual activity for a particular period of time with the original plan any *variance* (difference), expressed in financial terms, is identified. This enables managers to assess their performance and decide what *corrective action*, if any, needs to be taken.
- By predicting future events, managers are encouraged to collect all the relevant information, analyse it and *make decisions in good time*.
- An organisation is made up of a number of individuals with their own ambitions and goals. The budgetary control process allows these individual goals to be modified and integrated with the overall objectives of the organisation: it thus encourages *consensus*. Managers can see how their personal aims fit into the overall context and how they might be achieved.

---

## Activity

Give an example of a budget.

---

A *cash flow forecast* is a good example of a budget. You will have met this if you have done financial accounting. A cash flow forecast is a statement which shows the amount of cash which is expected to come in and go out during some period in the future. It is usually drawn up for each month over a 12-month period, and shows the monthly cash inflows and outflows, as well as the net cash flows and the cumulative cash position. A cash flow forecast is not a tool for control because it is only a plan. In order to achieve control, comparison must be made with the actual figures.

## 21.4 **The Budgetary Control Process**

We explained at the beginning of this chapter that a budget is expressed in monetary terms and shows the income and/or expenditure needed during a financial period to achieve the given objective. However, in the first instance, the calculation may be carried out with quantities such as labour hours or kilograms of materials. Budgets are drawn up for individual departments and functions (for example, the sales budget and the production budget), as well as for capital expenditure, stock holding and cash flow. All the budgets are interrelated and incorporated into the *master budget*, which includes a budgeted profit and loss account and balance sheet. The following diagram shows the interrelationship of budgets in a simple organisation:

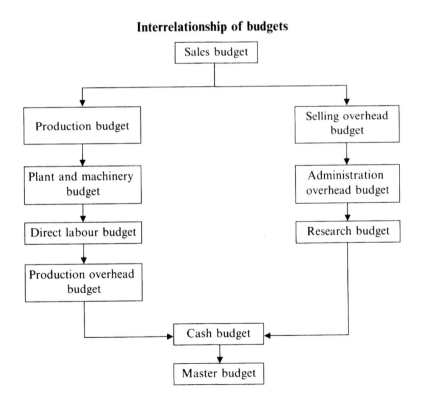

**Interrelationship of budgets**

The following example shows how the budgets are linked. Portalight Ltd manufactures torches. The sales director has estimated that the following quantities will be sold over the next 6 months:

|        | Jan   | Feb   | Mar   | Apr   | May   | Jun   |
|--------|-------|-------|-------|-------|-------|-------|
| Sales  | 1,000 | 1,200 | 1,500 | 1,600 | 1,600 | 1,750 |

The production department will manufacture the torches in the month before the sales take place and it has been agreed that a buffer stock of 200 torches will be maintained. On December 1 there is a stock of 100 torches.

## Activity

How many torches must the production department manufacture each month?

The best way to tackle this problem is to draw up a table giving all the information:

|               | Dec   | Jan   | Feb   | Mar   | Apr   | May   | Jun   |
|---------------|-------|-------|-------|-------|-------|-------|-------|
| Opening stock | 100   | 1,200 | 1,400 | 1,700 | 1,800 | 1,800 | 1,950 |
| Production    | 1,100 | 1,200 | 1,500 | 1,600 | 1,600 | 1,750 |       |
| Sales         |       | 1,000 | 1,200 | 1,500 | 1,600 | 1,600 | 1,750 |
| Closing stock | 1,200 | 1,400 | 1,700 | 1,800 | 1,800 | 1,950 |       |

Having calculated the number of torches which must be produced, we need to consider the decisions that the production manager now take and which budgets will be affected. The most immediate decisions concern whether there is sufficient machine capacity to make the torches, and whether there is sufficient labour. It may be that more machines and labour are required in the busy months and more space will be required in the factory; therefore all these budgets will be affected. The accountant will be concerned with the cash requirements for any changes and will want to ensure that the implications of these decisions are shown in the cash budget. It is because of the interrelated nature of budgets that a change in any one can affect all the other budgets.

The process of preparing budgets for each of the functions and other activities in an organisation and drawing up a master budget can take a number of months. The budgets must be communicated to managers before the start of the appropriate financial period, called the *budget period*, so that they know what the plans are for their own departments and can implement them. Some organisations adopt a 'top-down' approach to budget-setting: the owners or directors decide the individual plans for each department and function, and these plans are given to the individual managers to implement. Other organisations use a 'bottom-up' approach to budget-setting: individual managers construct their own budgets which are given to the owners or directors who coordinate the individual budgets into a master budget. These are the two extremes, and most organisations fall somewhere between the two.

A *budget committee* may be formed, made up of the functional or departmental managers and chaired by the chief executive. The management accountant usually occupies the role of committee secretary, and he or she coordinates and assists in the preparation of the budget data provided by each manager. The budget committee reviews the budgets submitted by individual managers and ensures that each has the following characteristics:

● conforms to the policies formulated by the owners or directors;
● shows how the objectives are going to be achieved, and recognises any constraints under which the organisation will be operating;
● is realistic;
● integrates with the other budgets;
● reflects the responsibilities of the manager concerned.

If a budget does not display all these characteristics, it will need to be revised. This may affect other budgets and there may need to be negotiations between the managers concerned to introduce the necessary budget changes. When the budgets have been approved by the budget committee, they are submitted to the directors for approval prior to the commencement of the budget period. If the directors accept the budget, it is then adopted by the organisation as a whole and becomes the working plans.

There are a number of different types of budgets. A *fixed budget* is not changed even when actual activity levels differ from those set. A *flexible budget* is one which is changed to allow for the behaviour of variable costs at different levels of budgeted and actual activity. We shall be looking at flexible budgets in more detail later in this chapter.

## 21.5 Variance Analysis

*Variance analysis* is the investigation of the factors which have caused the differences between the actual and the budgeted figures (the differences are known as *variances*). Actual progress is measured from the beginning of the budget period, which is usually a year. Each month, the actual figures are compared with the plan and reported to the managers responsible.

If the actual costs are lower than the budgeted costs, there will be a *favourable variance* and this will result in a higher final profit. But if the actual costs are higher than the budgeted costs, the variance is known as an *adverse variance* which will result in a lower profit. There may also be income variances. If actual income is higher than budgeted income, there will be a favourable variance and this will result in a higher final profit. On the other hand, if actual income is lower than budgeted income, there will be an adverse variance which will result in a lower final profit. Adverse variance figures are usually shown in brackets.

## Activity

Richard Pillinger, who we met in Chapter 19, has now made up his mind and has decided to invest in a farm shop selling organic produce from his farm. The farm produces early tomatoes, new potatoes and cauliflowers. Complete the following budget report by filling in the variances:

**Farm Shop**
**Budget report for May**

|  | Budget £ | Actual £ | Variance £ |
|---|---|---|---|
| **Income** | | | |
| Tomatoes | 25,000 | 24,500 | |
| Potatoes | 18,000 | 17,200 | |
| Cauliflowers | 19,000 | 19,600 | ——— |
| Subtotal | 62,000 | 61,300 | ——— |
| **Costs** | | | |
| Salaries | 28,400 | 29,000 | |
| Expenses | 12,500 | 12,000 | |
| Administration | 1,800 | 1,700 | |
| Miscellaneous | 700 | 300 | ——— |
| Subtotal | 43,400 | 43,000 | ——— |
| **Profit** | 18,600 | 18,300 | ——— |

You should not have had too much difficulty in calculating the variances as it is simply a matter of subtracting the actual figures from the budgeted figures. Check your answer against the completed budget report below, making sure that you have remembered to show the adverse variances in brackets:

**Farm Shop**
**Budget report for May**

|  | Budget £ | Actual £ | Variance £ |
|---|---|---|---|
| **Income** |  |  |  |
| Tomatoes | 25,000 | 24,500 | (500) |
| Potatoes | 18,000 | 17,200 | (800) |
| Cauliflowers | 19,000 | 19,600 | 600 |
| Subtotal | 62,000 | 61,300 | (700) |
| **Costs** |  |  |  |
| Salaries | 28,400 | 29,000 | (600) |
| Expenses | 12,500 | 12,000 | 500 |
| Administration | 1,800 | 1,700 | 100 |
| Miscellaneous | 700 | 300 | 400 |
| Subtotal | 43,400 | 43,000 | 400 |
| **Profit** | 18,600 | 18,300 | (300) |

The budget report shows that in May, Richard made a profit which was £300 lower than planned. This was due to lower income from sales of early tomatoes and new potatoes than planned, combined with higher salaries paid. Now he must decide whether these adverse variances require any action on his part. The salary increase may not have been planned but is nevertheless necessary. The lower sales income may be due to factors beyond his control, such as unexpected bad weather affecting yield. Most businesses experience peaks and troughs during the year, especially where there are seasonal factors which affect production and demand, and these need to be reflected in the monthly budget figures. On the other hand, Richard may discover it is due to poor marketing or distribution problems. Before he can decide what action, if any, to take to remedy the adverse variances, Richard must first investigate the cause.

## 21.6 Fixed and Flexible Budgets

A *fixed budget* is a budget which is not changed once it has been established, regardless of changes in activity level. It may be revised if the situation so demands, but a fixed budget is not changed solely because the actual activity level differs from the budgeted activity level. This can be a considerable disadvantage because a fixed budget may show an adverse variance on costs which is simply due to an increase or decrease in variable costs. As you will remember from Chapter 18, total variable costs increase or decrease in proportion with changes in activity level.

A *flexible budget* changes in accordance with activity levels and reflects the different behaviours of fixed and variable costs. Therefore, in a flexible budget, any cost variance can be assumed to be due to an increase or decrease in fixed costs. A flexible budget may be used at the planning stage to illustrate the impact of achieving different activity levels. It can also be used at the control stage at the end of a month to compare the actual results with what they should have been.

The following example shows the importance of flexible budgeting. Portalight Ltd's budget for January is based on an output of 1,000 torches. The following budget report shows the budgeted and actual figures for the month when 1,100 torches were sold:

**Portalight Ltd**
**Budget report for January**

|  | Budget £ | Budget £ | Actual £ | Actual £ |
|---|---|---|---|---|
| Sales |  | 1,500 |  | 1,650 |
| Variable costs | 750 |  | 880 |  |
| Variable overheads | 250 |  | 260 |  |
| Fixed overheads | 200 |  | 200 |  |
| Total costs |  | 1,200 |  | 1,340 |
| Profit |  | 300 |  | 310 |

The managing director has been sent the above budget statement and is delighted that the actual profit is £10 above the budget.

## Activity

Write a brief report to the managing director explaining why he should not be so pleased with the results. Support your report with calculations.

After all the work you have done on marginal costing in Chapter 18, the words *variable costs* should immediately have alerted you to the problem of comparing the actual results with the original budget when there has been a change in activity level. In this case the number of torches sold was 1,100 compared with the planned amount of 1,000. Although the sales department must be congratulated on achieving increased sales, the company needs to construct a flexible budget to see if they have controlled their variable costs. This is done by multiplying the planned variable costs per unit by the actual level of production.

The variable costs were originally set at £750 for 1,000 torches, which is 75p per torch. The variable overheads were originally set at £250 for 1,000 torches, which is 25p per torch. If we assume that as the number of torches manufactured increases, the total variable costs increase, the flexible budget compared with the actual results is as follows:

**Portalight Ltd**
**Budget report for January**

|  | Flexible budget | | Actual | |
|---|---|---|---|---|
|  | £ | £ | £ | £ |
| Sales (at £1.50 per unit) |  | 1,650 |  | 1,650 |
| Variable costs (1,100 × 75p) | 825 |  | 880 |  |
| Variable overheads (1,100 × 75p) | 275 |  | 260 |  |
| Fixed overheads | 200 |  | 200 |  |
| Total costs |  | 1,300 |  | 1,340 |
| Profit |  | 350 |  | 310 |

The flexible budget shows that at an output of 1,100 torches, a profit of £350 should have been made. A comparison of the figures shows that although variable overheads have been reduced, there is an overspend on variable costs which should be investigated.

## 21.7 Advantages and Disadvantages

Sometimes management implements a system of budgetary control, but becomes disillusioned with it; the disadvantages seem to outweigh the advantages. In this chapter we have described the way in which budgetary control systems are operated and the use of flexible budgets. However, there is no single model of a perfect budgetary control system and each organisation needs a system that meets its own particular needs. The following list shows the main requirements for an effective system of budgetary control:

- A sound and clearly defined organisation with the managers' responsibilities clearly indicated.
- Effective accounting records and procedures which are understood and applied.
- Strong support and the commitment of top managers to the system of budgetary control.
- The education and training of managers in the development, interpretation and use of budgets.
- The revision of the original budgets where circumstances show that amendments are required to make them appropriate and useful.
- The recognition throughout the organisation that budgetary control is a management activity and not an accounting exercise.
- An information system which provides data for managers so that they can make realistic predictions.
- The correct integration of budgets and their effective communication to managers.

- The setting of budgets which are reasonable and achievable.
- The participation of managers in the budgetary control system.

## Activity

When an organisation has a budgetary control system, internal planning and control should be improved, which must be a considerable advantage. What other advantages might there be, and what are the disadvantages of a budgetary control system?

The main *advantages* are as follows:

- Decisions are based on the examination of future problems in sufficient time for the organisation to take corrective action.
- With clearly defined objectives and the monitoring of achievement, motivation of the entire management team is improved.
- Plans can be reviewed regularly in the light of changing circumstances and can be amended where appropriate.
- The resources of the organisation are given the fullest and most economical use.
- The activities of all the various functions in the organisation are properly coordinated.
- Capital and effort are put to the most profitable use.
- The advantages are of a flexible budgetary control system over fixed budgeting are that flexible budgeting provides clearer information to management for decision-making and control purposes. By comparing the actual results with what should have been achieved at that level of activity, a more accurate measure is given.

There are quite a number of potential drawbacks with a budgetary control system. How damaging they are depends on the way the system is operated. The main *disadvantages* are as follows:

- The process of drawing up budgets is time-consuming, and managers may be deflected from their prime responsibilities of running the organisation.
- The future is always uncertain and budgets may be unrealistic. This can lead to poor control and the disillusionment of managers.
- Budgets may be imposed by top management with no consultation; consequently managers may feel demotivated.
- If a fixed budget is set and actual activity fluctuates from the planned level, the budget may become irrelevant.
- Managers may consider the budgets as 'being set in stone' and instead of taking effective and sensible decisions when the circumstances warrant it, may be constrained by the original budget.

## 21.8 Conclusions

In this chapter we have looked at the need for business planning and the entire cycle of planning and control in an organisation. We have examined the way in which budgets are established for separate functions and integrated into a master budget and considered what organisational factors are required to operate an effective system of budgetary control. Finally, we have looked at the advantages and disadvantages of budgetary control, and of using fixed and flexible budgets.

Having completed this chapter, you should now be able to:

- identify the main features of a budgetary control system;
- describe the requirements for an effective system of budgetary control;
- list the advantages and disadvantages of a budgetary control system.

---

## Exercises

Complete the following sentences:

**1** A budget is .................................................................................................................
**2** A flexible budget is ..........................................................................................................
**3** A good example of a budget is ..........................................................................................
**4** All individual budgets are incorporated into a .................................................................
**5** An adverse cost variance is ..............................................................................................

Are the following statements true or false?

**6** For control to be achieved, regular monitoring of actual performance must take place.
**7** A fixed budget changes as activity levels change.
**8** A budget committee comprises all the accountants in an organisation.
**9** A variance is the difference between a predetermined and an actual figure.
**10** Once budgets have been set for a financial period, they should never be changed.

You may wish to read more widely than this book to answer the following questions fully, but you can check the main points by referring to the appropriate sections in this chapter.

**11** Why is business planning important? (Section 21.2)
**12** What are the purposes of budgetary control? (Section 21.3)
**13** Describe what is meant by variance analysis. (Section 21.5)
**14** What are the requirements for an effective system of budgetary control? (Section 21.7)

Multiple choice questions (more than one answer may apply):

**15** Budgetary control is used in the following types of organisation:

    **a** limited companies
    **b** charities
    **c** sole traders
    **d** any organisation.

**16** Budget periods may be for:

  **a** 1 year
  **b** 1 month
  **c** 1 week
  **d** any period.

**17** Budgets are used for:

  **a** motivation
  **b** planning
  **c** control
  **d** all of these.

**18** The major drawback of fixed budgets is that:

  **a** they are drawn up for a single level of activity only
  **b** they cannot show the differences between budgeted and actual cost
  **c** they can never be used for cost control purposes
  **d** they are drawn up for short-term use only.

**19** Flexible budgets should only be used where:

  **a** the actual level of activity is likely to fluctuate
  **b** production and sales are equal
  **c** costs are classified according to cost behaviour
  **d** all variances are normally adverse.

**20** Variance analysis is concerned with investigating:

  **a** differences between variable costs and fixed costs
  **b** differences between variable direct costs and variable indirect costs
  **c** differences between fixed and flexible budgets
  **d** differences between budgeted and actual results.

Practice questions:

**21** Describe the main features of a budgetary control system.
**22** What are the advantages and disadvantages of a budgetary control system?
**23** Distinguish between a fixed budget and a flexible budget.
**24** What behavioural aspects would you expect to be associated with a system of budgetary control?
**25** The director of Leisure Magazines Ltd recently introduced a budgetary control system. An accountant was appointed who drew up budgets for the advertising and editorial departments based on the actual results for the last 3 years. At the end of the first month of the new financial period, the actual total revenue was higher than planned, but the total advertising department costs were higher than budgeted. The editorial department actual costs were the same as those budgeted and the actual profit for the period was higher. On receiving the first month's results, the director threatened to dismiss the advertising manager for exceeding the budgeted costs. The advertising manager retaliated by saying that he would resign unless the budgetary control system was scrapped. The accountant left to join another company.

You work for the firm of consultants which has been asked to advise the company. Prepare a preliminary report covering the following:

**a** an analysis of the problems, and how you think they have arisen;

**b** guidelines for the operation of a successful and effective budgetary control system;

**c** recommendations as to what action the director of the client company should take.

(Answers on p. 343)

# 22 Standard Costing

## 22.1 Introduction

This chapter introduces the technique of *standard costing*, which is a method of financial control that compares predetermined costs, known as *standard costs*, and actual costs. Standard costing is a system of financial control which is closely associated with *budgetary control*. Many organisations use both systems, although one can be used without the other. However, it is less common to find a standard costing system in operation without a budgetary control system being present.

Budgetary control is applied to departments, budget centres and the organisation as a whole, and is a technique which can be used in any organisation, whether it is a business, charity, university, hospital, etc. Standard costing is mainly applied to products and processes. Therefore it is a technique that is more commonly used in manufacturing organisations, although it may also be useful in service industries. As in a budgetary control system, it allows the comparison of predetermined costs and income with the actual costs and income achieved. Any *variances*, or differences, can then be investigated. Managers within the organisation can be held responsible for these variances and, by analysing the reasons for the variances, control can be achieved.

## 22.2 Setting Standards

The predetermined costs are known as *standard costs*. These are the costs which are incurred under defined working conditions. The standard cost is calculated from technical specifications, which give the quantity of materials, labour and other elements of cost required, and relate them to the prices and wages it is anticipated will be in place for the period in which the standard cost is to be used. It is usual to measure the time in which it is planned to complete a certain volume of work in *standard hours* or *standard minutes.* This means that a standard hour is a measure of production output, rather than a measure of time.

---

## Activity

A company has set 1 standard hour's production at 500 units. In a 7-hour day, 4,000 units are produced. What is this output in standard hours?

---

You will have needed to make the following calculation to answer this question:

$$\frac{4,000 \text{ units}}{500 \text{ units per standard hour}} = 8 \text{ standard hours' production}$$

The type of standard used depends on the philosophy of the organisation. We can define a 'standard' as a measurable quantity established in defined conditions. Organisations can set *ideal standards* or *attainable standards*. Ideal standards are based on the best possible working conditions, but attainable standards are more widely used. The main reason why attainable standards are more popular than ideal standards is because attainable standards are based on realistic efficient performance and allow for problems such as machine breakdown, material wastage, etc. Although ideal standards are useful for management decision-making, there is the risk that employees will be demotivated by the impossibility of achieving them.

## 22.3 Variance Analysis

*Variance analysis* is the investigation of the factors causing the differences between the standard and actual results. As in budgetary control, these differences are known as *variances.* Any variances are analysed to reveal their constituent parts, so that sufficient information is available to permit investigation by management. *Favourable variances* are those which improve the predetermined profit and *adverse variances* are those which reduce the predetermined profit.

---

## Activity

In the Stitching Department of Jarvis Jackets Ltd 100 pockets can be made in 1 standard hour. In an 8-hour day, 950 pockets are produced. Will this give rise to a favourable or adverse variance? Why is this?

---

The first step is to calculate how many pockets should be made in an 8-hour day:

$$100 \text{ units per standard hour} \times 8 \text{ actual hours}$$

$$= 800 \text{ standard hours production}$$

Next you should have calculated the variance by subtracting the standard hours production (800) from the actual production (950) to arrive at a figure of 150. This is a favourable variance because 150 more pockets are produced than the 800 planned. Now we are ready to make this part of the standard costing system, by expressing the variance in financial terms.

## 22.4 Direct Materials Variance

In a manufacturing organisation the direct product costs are normally *direct materials* and *direct labour*. The reasons for overspending or underspending on either of these costs is based on the following simple concept:

$$\text{Total cost} = \text{Quantity used} \times \text{Unit price}$$

The difference between standard and actual total cost must be due to variations in the quantity used, the unit price or a combination of both. Predetermined standards are set both for the *usage level* of direct materials for a given volume of production and the *price* allowed per unit of direct materials. The price standards are based on the price per unit expected to be paid or budgeted for the level of purchases projected over the period for which the standard is to be applied.

In general, any price variance is regarded as the responsibility of the purchasing manager or buyer and variation in the volume or quantity of materials consumed is regarded as the responsibility of the production manager. However, due to the interdependence of price and usage, responsibilities may be difficult to assign.

The *direct materials variance* is based on the following formula:

$$\text{Total direct materials cost} = \text{Quantity used} \times \text{Price per unit}$$

Standards are set for the *quantity* of materials to be used for a specific volume of production and the *price* to be paid per unit of direct materials. The total direct materials variance is calculated by using the following formula:

(Standard quantity used × Standard price per unit) − (Actual quantity used × Actual price per unit)

## Activity

Jarvis Jackets Ltd has decided to extend its range to include denim jackets. One jacket requires a standard usage of 3 metres of direct materials which has been set at a standard price of £2.20 per metre. In the period, 80 jackets were made and 260 metres of materials consumed at a cost of £1.95 per metre. Calculate the total direct materials variance.

To answer this question you should have put the figures into the above formula. However, the first stage is to calculate the standard quantity of materials for the actual level of production. As 80 jackets were made, and the company planned to use 3 metres of denim per jacket, the standard quantity for that level of production is 240 metres. Substituting the figures in the formula:

$$(240 \text{ metres} \times £2.20) - (260 \text{ metres} \times £1.95)$$

$$= £528 - £507$$

$$= £21 \text{ favourable variance}$$

The difference of £21 between the planned cost and the actual cost is a favourable variance because we have spent less on our materials than we planned for that level of production. Although this information is useful, it needs to be more precise to enable the management to take any action required. The reason why actual materials costs can differ from the planned materials costs for a given level of production is due to two factors. Either we have used more or less materials than planned and/or we have paid more or less per unit of materials than we planned.

The total direct materials variance can be divided into a *usage variance* and a *price variance*, as shown in the following diagram:

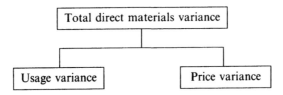

The *usage variance* is the difference between the standard quantity specified for the actual production and the actual quantity used at standard price per unit. The formula is:

(Standard quantity × Standard price per unit) − (Actual quantity × Standard price per unit)

Depending on the data you are given, you may find it more convenient to shorten this formula to the following:

(Standard quantity – Actual quantity) × Standard price per unit

## Activity

Calculate the usage variance from the data for Jarvis Jackets Ltd.

Once again, to answer this question you needed to insert the figures into the formula. The answer is:

$$(240 \text{ metres} - 260 \text{ metres}) \times £2.20$$

$$= (£44.00) \text{ adverse variance}$$

In this instance, there is an adverse variance because the company has used more materials than planned for that level of production.

The final stage is to find out the *price variance*. This is the difference between the standard and actual purchase price per unit for the actual quantity of materials purchased or used in production. The formula is:

(Standard price per unit × Actual quantity) – (Actual price per unit × Actual quantity)

As with the usage variance, if the data is readily available, it may be more convenient to use the following shortened formula:

(Standard price per unit – Actual price per unit) × Actual quantity

## Activity

Calculate the price variance from the data for Jarvis Jackets Ltd.

The answer is:

$$(£2.20 - £1.95) \times 260 \text{ metres} = £65.00 \text{ favourable variance}$$

The variance is favourable because the company has paid less for the materials than planned for that level of production. If you deduct the adverse usage variance of £44 from the favourable price variance of £65 you obtain the total direct materials variance of £21 favourable. The first two variances therefore explain the last.

Of course, working out the figures is not the end of the task. Managers need to investigate the reasons for the variances and to determine whether any corrective action is required. There are a number of reasons for the adverse usage variance. Perhaps inferior materials were used and this led to higher wastage than planned, or the labour force was inexperienced and this led to high levels of wastage. Alternatively, some materials may have been lost or stolen.

One strong possibility for the price variance is that the company has used poorer quality, and therefore less expensive, materials. This would tie in with the possible reason for the adverse usage variance. Other reasons may be that the business is using a different supplier than originally intended or has negotiated a bulk discount.

## 22.5 Direct Labour Variances

The same principles apply to the calculation of the *direct labour variances* as for the direct materials variances. Standards are established for the rate of pay to be paid for the production of particular products and the labour time taken for their production. The standard time taken is expressed in *standard hours* or *standard minutes* and becomes the measure of output. By comparing the standard hours allowed and the actual time taken, labour efficiency can be assessed. In practice, standard times are established by *work, time and method study* techniques.

The direct labour variance is based on the following formula:

$$\text{Total labour cost} = \text{Hours worked} \times \text{Rate per hour}$$

The *total direct labour variance* is calculated by using the following formula:

(Standard direct labour hours × Standard rate per hour) – (Actual direct labour hours × Actual rate per hour)

## Activity

The management of Jarvis Jackets Ltd decides that it takes 6 standard hours to make 1 denim jacket and the standard rate paid to labour is £8 per hour. The actual production is 900 units and this took 5,100 hours at a rate of £8.30 per hour. Calculate the total direct labour hour variance.

With your knowledge of the calculation of materials variances, this activity should have caused you few problems. The first stage is to calculate the standard direct labour hours for this level of production which is

900 jackets × 6 standard hours = 5,400 standard hours. The variance can then be calculated as follows:

(5,400 standard hours × £8.00) − (5,100 actual hours × £8.30)

= £43,200 − £42,330

= £870 favourable variance

The variance is favourable because the total labour cost is less than planned for that level of production. The total direct labour variance can be broken down into a *direct labour rate variance* and a *direct labour efficiency variance*, as shown in the following diagram.

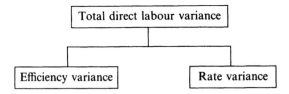

The direct labour efficiency variance, sometimes referred to as the *labour productivity variance*, is the difference between the actual production achieved, measured in standard hours, and the actual hours worked, valued at the standard labour rate. The formula is:

(Standard hours × Standard rate per hour) − (Actual hours × Standard rate per hour)

Depending on the data you have available, it may be more convenient to shorten the formula to:

(Standard hours − Actual hours) × Standard rate per hour

---

## Activity

Calculate the direct labour efficiency variance from the data for Jarvis Jackets Ltd.

---

The answer is:

(5,400 standard hours − 5,100 actual hours) × £8.00

= £2,400 favourable variance

The *direct labour rate variance* is the difference between the standard and actual direct labour rate per hour for the actual hours worked. The formula is:

(Standard rate per hour × Actual hours) – (Actual rate per hour × Actual hours)

Depending on the data you are given, you may find the following shortened formula more convenient:

(Standard rate per hour – Actual rate per hour) × Actual hours

---

## Activity

Calculate the direct labour rate variance from the data for Jarvis Jackets Ltd.

---

The answer is:

$$(£8.00 – £8.30) × 5,100 \text{ actual hours}$$

$$= (£1,530) \text{ adverse variance}$$

The variance is adverse because we have paid the workforce more than we planned for that level of production.

If you deduct the adverse direct labour rate variance of £1,530 from the favourable efficiency variance of £2,400, you get the favourable total direct labour variance of £870.

The most likely reason for the labour rate and efficiency variances is that the company has used more highly skilled labour than originally planned. Therefore, the rate paid was higher, but the output was greater than planned. There are other possible reasons – for example, the business may have given a pay rise, or overtime may have been worked. Further investigation would be required to identify the actual reasons and to determine whether any corrective action is required.

## 22.6 **Advantages and Disadvantages**

As with budgetary control, many of the benefits of standard costing are associated with the processes of planning. Control is improved and it compels managers to make decisions, coordinate activities and communicate with one another.

## Activity

What other advantages might there be and what are the disadvantages of standard costing?

With your knowledge of budgetary control, you should not have had many problems with this activity. The main *advantages* of standard costing are as follows:

- Standard-setting establishes a benchmark against which actual costs can be compared.
- The technique permits a thorough examination of the organisation's production and operations activities.
- As the standards are based on future plans and expectations, the information provided to management is much more accurate than that based merely on past performance.
- By examining the reasons for any variances between standard and actual costs and income, management needs to concentrate only on the exceptions to the planned performance. This leads to greater managerial efficiency.
- Variance analysis may result in cost reductions, and control of costs is improved.

The main *disadvantages* are:

- It may be difficult to set standards, particularly in a new or dynamic organisation.
- The standard costing system may be expensive to maintain and the additional record-keeping may become a burden to busy managers.
- Standards will naturally become out of date and require revision. In a very dynamic organisation this may happen so quickly that managers lose confidence in the system.
- Information provided by the system is of value only if it is used by managers for control purposes. If the information has no credibility or is not understood, it has no value.

## 22.7 Conclusions

In this chapter we have looked at standard costing and the calculation of variances. We have described how to calculate variances for both total materials costs and total labour costs. We have also examined the calculation of the subvariances and considered the reasons why they have occurred. Finally, we have examined the advantages and disadvantages of a standard costing system.

Having completed this chapter, you should now be able to:

- describe the technique of standard costing;
- calculate the direct materials variances;
- calculate the direct labour variances;
- discuss the advantages and disadvantages of standard costing.

# Exercises

Complete the following sentences:

**1** Ideal standards are based on ...........................................................................
**2** Variance analysis is the ...............................................................................
**3** Differences between standard and actual costs must be due to .......................
................................................................................................................
**4** A materials price variance is the responsibility of ........................................
**5** The subvariances of the total direct material variance are ............................
................................................................................................................

Are the following statements true or false?

**6** If actual income is higher than planned the variance will be adverse.
**7** If actual cost is higher than planned the variance will be adverse.
**8** If more hours are worked than planned there will be a usage variance.
**9** The price variance is the difference between the standard price and the actual price per unit multiplied by the standard quantity.
**10** The rate variance is the difference between the standard and the actual direct labour rate per hour for the actual hours worked.

You may wish to read more widely than this book to answer the following questions fully, but you can check the main points by referring to the appropriate sections in this chapter.

**11** Compare ideal and attainable standards. (Section 22.2)
**12** What is variance analysis? (Section 22.3)
**13** What are the possible reasons for materials usage variances? (Section 22.4)
**14** What is meant by a standard hour? (Section 22.5)

Multiple choice questions (more than one answer may apply):

**15** The formula for the materials price variance is:

    **a** (Standard price per unit−Actual price per unit) × Standard quantity
    **b** (Standard quantity − Actual quantity) × Standard price per unit
    **c** (Standard price per unit − Actual price per unit) × Actual quantity
    **d** (Standard quantity − Actual quantity) × Actual price per unit.

**16** The formula for the materials usage variance is:

    **a** (Standard price per unit − Actual price) × Standard quantity
    **b** (Standard quantity − Actual quantity) × Standard price per unit
    **c** (Standard price per unit − Actual price per unit) × Actual quantity
    **d** (Standard quantity − Actual quantity) × Actual price per unit.

**17** The formula for the labour efficiency variance is:

    **a** (Standard rate per hour – Actual rate per hour) × Actual hours
    **b** (Standard hours – Actual hours) × Actual rate per hour
    **c** (Standard hours – Actual hours) × Standard rate per hour
    **d** (Standard rate per hour – Actual rate per hour) × Standard hours.

**18** The formula for the labour rate variance is:

    **a** (Standard rate per hour – Actual rate per hour) × Actual hours
    **b** (Standard hours – Actual hours) × Actual rate per hour
    **c** (Standard hours – Actual hours) × Standard rate per hour
    **d** (Standard rate per hour – Actual rate per hour) × Standard hours.

**19** A favourable materials price variance arises when:

    **a** more materials are used than planned
    **b** more is paid per unit of materials than planned
    **c** less is paid per unit of materials than planned
    **d** the quantity of materials used is less than planned.

**20** Standard costing is used for:

    **a** motivation
    **b** planning
    **c** control
    **d** all of these.

Practice questions:

**21** Calculate and suggest possible reasons for the materials price variance from the following data:

Standard price per kilo is £4
Standard usage per unit is 5 metres
Actual price per kilo is £3
Actual usage per unit is 5 metres

**22** Calculate and suggest possible reasons for the materials usage variance from the following data:

Standard price per tonne is £50
Standard usage is 1,000 tonnes
Actual price per tonne is £50
Actual usage is 995 tonnes

**23** A manufacturing company has set a standard price for materials of £100 per kilo and anticipates that it will make 4 units from 1 kilo of materials. The actual production is 200 units and 52 kilos of materials are used at a price of £98 per kilo. Calculate all the material variances and discuss the possible reasons for them.

**24** A company plans to make 1 unit every 10 hours and the standard rate per hour is set at £9. In a financial period 50 units are made and this takes 460 hours. The total labour cost for the period is £5,060. Calculate all the labour variances and discuss the possible reasons for them.

**25** Four years ago, your Uncle Mike set up a small manufacturing company, Aphrodite Showers, in Cyprus which manufactures shower screens. There are two models: the Paphos, which is the standard model, and the Nicosia, the deluxe model. Both models are made from frosted glass and have an aluminium frame and fittings. The standard model has plain glass and silver satin finish to the frame and fittings. The deluxe model has an attractive design on the glass and a polished gold finish to the frame and fittings.

Once a year your Uncle Mike comes back to spend Christmas with you and your family. This year, knowing that you are studying management accounting on your course, he asks for your advice. He explains that despite a buoyant market and excellent sales figures, his profits have been very disappointing and he wants to embark on a cost-cutting exercise. After discussions, you find that he does not operate a standard costing system and does not seem to know what it is. However, he is very keen to learn and as he is only staying a few days, asks you to write to him in Cyprus with full details. He also invites you to visit him for a holiday during the summer.

Write your Uncle Mike a letter explaining the advantages of a standard costing system, how it can be implemented and the information he can expect to obtain.

(Answers on pp. 343–4)

# 23 Developments in Management Accounting

## 23.1 Introduction

Over the last 10 years or so there have been a number of developments in management accounting. In part, these changes have been brought about by dissatisfaction with the more traditional approaches to management accounting and the information which has been generated. Other influences have been related to changes in the nature of organisations and the activities they undertake, and the increasingly complex and competitive business environment.

As with all new systems and procedures, in the early days it is difficult to assess how successful they are and how long it will be before they are replaced by other novel approaches. In this chapter we concentrate on three developments that have become firmly established and are widely accepted in principle, if not in practice. We consider them in alphabetical order to avoid implying any ranking of importance.

The first topic we consider is *activity-based costing (ABC)*, which is a method of costing that recognises that costs are incurred by each activity that takes place within an organisation and that products or customers should bear costs according to the activities they use. The second topic is *strategic management accounting*, which is a management accounting system that attempts to provide management with the information needed to help make long-term strategic decisions, rather than being limited to the more traditional provision of short-term cost information. The final topic we examine is known as *throughput accounting (TA)*. This is an approach to short-term decision-making in manufacturing, in which all conversion costs are treated as if they were fixed costs and products are ranked if a particular constraint or scarce resource exists.

## 23.2 Activity-based Costing

*Activity-based costing (ABC)* first became prominent in the UK in the late 1980s and has been adopted in various forms by a number of organisations.

It seeks to obtain a more realistic approach to ascertaining the total cost of a cost unit than is generated by traditional *absorption costing* (see Chapter 15). ABC is most closely associated with organisations which have some form of advanced manufacturing technology (AMT), including such features as computer-aided design (CAD), computer-aided manufacturing (CAM), flexible management systems (FMS), and total quality management (TQM). The main reasons for the popularity of ABC are as follows:

- Organisations are operating in an increasingly complex and competitive environment, and managers need more sophisticated information systems.
- The diversity of product ranges have increased, requiring better data collection and recording procedures.
- The proportion of overheads have been increasing, making a rational and realistic basis for allocating and apportioning them even more critical.

A fundamental aspect of ABC is the assumption that most overhead costs can be analysed into two main groups:

- *short-term variable costs* that vary with the volume of production (such overheads can be charged to the cost unit by using recovery rates based on direct labour hours or machine hours, as we demonstrated with absorption costing in Chapter 15); and
- *long-term variable costs* that do not vary with volume of production, but with some other form of activity – for example, the costs of handling stock may be more dependent on the range of items manufactured and their technical complexity rather than the actual volume of production.

ABC is a costing method that seeks to recognise these differences by focusing on the activities in the organisation which incur costs. Any activity or series of activities that takes place within an organisation and causes costs to be incurred is known as a *cost driver*. Examples of cost drivers are the volume of raw materials handled in the organisation, the number of orders placed by customers or the number of machine hours. The cost drivers for short-term variable overheads are based on volume of activity as measured by direct labour hours or machine hours. The cost driver for long-term variable overheads could be the number of job runs for an activity, such as machine set-up costs.

A collection of costs charged to products by the use of a common cost driver is known as a *cost pool*. You should not confuse cost pools with departments. In one department there can be a range of activities which cause costs to be incurred. For example, in the production department the power used is related to the machine hours, but the costs incurred in the handling of raw materials may be related to the number of purchase orders made, and the costs incurred in setting up the various machines related to the number of different jobs undertaken.

We will now use an example to illustrate how ABC is used. Teddies Galore Ltd makes three products, the details of which for a financial period are as follows:

| Product | Output (units) | Number of production runs | Material cost per unit | Direct labour hours per unit |
|---|---|---|---|---|
| Standard teddy | 50 | 10 | £10 | 2 |
| Deluxe teddy | 50 | 10 | £30 | 6 |
| Mini teddy | 500 | 20 | £5 | 1 |

The direct labour costs are £10 per hour and for the financial period the overhead costs are as follows:

| | £ |
|---|---|
| Short-term variable overheads | 18,000 |
| Machine set-up costs | 10,000 |
| Material handling cost | 26,000 |
| Total | 54,000 |

First we need to calculate the *cost per unit* using absorption costing:

**Teddies Galore Ltd**
**Cost per unit using absorption costing**

| | Standard teddy | Deluxe teddy | Mini teddy | Total |
|---|---|---|---|---|
| Number of units | 50 | 50 | 500 | 600 |
| | £ | £ | £ | £ |
| Direct materials | 500 | 1,500 | 2,500 | 4,500 |
| Direct labour | 1,000 | 3,000 | 10,000 | 14,000 |
| Direct costs | 1,500 | 4,500 | 12,500 | 18,500 |
| Overheads[1] | 6,000 | 18,000 | 30,000 | 54,000 |
| Total cost | 7,500 | 22,500 | 42,500 | 72,500 |
| Cost per unit | £150 | £450 | £85 | |

*Notes*:
1 Overhead absorption rate, based on a total of 900 direct labour hours:

$$\frac{£54,000}{900 \text{ hours}} = £60 \text{ per hour}$$

Now we need to repeat the procedure for ABC. The details are as before, but the cost drivers are as follows:

| Short-term variable overheads: | Direct labour hours |
|---|---|
| Machine set-up costs: | Number of production runs |
| Material handling costs: | Number of production runs |

**Teddies Galore Ltd**
**Cost per unit using ABC**

| | Standard teddy | Deluxe teddy | Mini teddy | Total |
|---|---|---|---|---|
| Number of units | 50 | 50 | 500 | 600 |
| | £ | £ | £ | £ |
| Direct materials | 500 | 1,500 | 2,500 | 4,500 |
| Direct labour | 1,000 | 3,000 | 10,000 | 14,000 |
| Direct costs | 1,500 | 4,500 | 12,500 | 18,500 |
| Short-term overheads[1] | 2,000 | 6,000 | 10,000 | 18,000 |
| Machine set-up[2] | 2,500 | 2,500 | 5,000 | 10,000 |
| Material handling[3] | 6,500 | 6,500 | 13,000 | 26,000 |
| Total costs | 12,500 | 19,500 | 40,500 | 72,500 |
| Cost per unit | £250 | £390 | £81 | |

*Notes:*

1 Short-term variable overheads: $\dfrac{£18,000}{900\text{ hours}} = £20$ per direct labour hour

2 Machine set-up costs: $\dfrac{£10,000}{40} = £250$ per production run

3 Material handling costs: $\dfrac{£26,000}{40} = £650$ per production run

At the beginning of this section we explained the reasons for the introduction of ABC and those organisations which have implemented the method successfully would claim that this method of costing offers the following advantages:

- Costs are attributed to the activity that caused them to be incurred. In absorption costing the costs are allocated and apportioned on an arbitrary basis to various parts of the organisation, and in marginal costing the fixed costs are ignored. ABC avoids these problems by associating costs with the actual activity, and if the level of that activity changes one would expect to see a change in the level of costs incurred in the longer term.
- As costs are related to the activity that causes them to be incurred, the information produced is more useful for managers in planning and controlling the activities of the business. The products and services that caused the costs to be incurred are charged with these costs on a realistic basis.
- The increasing complexity of diverse product ranges and the potential impact on costs is recognised under this method of costing. For example, an order that requires a high level of technical input, or is for a low volume and therefore only needs a small production run, is charged with the costs that it incurs.

Although ABC appears to offer a number of advantages, there are critics of the method who argue that these are illusory or rarely enjoyed in practice. Some critics contend that ABC is no more than a more sophisticated version of absorption costing and that organisations have been using this sort of approach for a number of years; it is only consultants and academics inventing a new terminology that has given the method prominence. Other disadvantages of ABC are:

- The system is costly to implement and operate. Numerous cost drivers and cost pools have to be identified for the system to be fully effective. For many organisations this is neither practical nor possible.
- Although the information generated by the system may be more sophisticated, managers do not have the time or the knowledge to analyse it fully. ABC generates more information than is needed by the practising manager.
- ABC is only a method of collecting and recording costs and claims too much for itself. An organisation is a complex, dynamic combination of many disciplines, including behavioural ones; ABC does not take account of the context in which businesses operate.

## 23.3 Strategic Management Accounting

Much of what has been written about management accounting, including ABC, takes a strictly internal perspective of the organisation. It considers what goes on inside the organisation, concentrating on the visible products and services, and the information managers need about activities inside the business. *Strategic management accounting* attempts to introduce a new dimension to the subject by emphasising the external environment and the importance of reporting information on such matters as markets and competitors.

Strategic management accounting is therefore not a method, technique, procedure or a system, but a philosophy which underpins the entire approach to management accounting. A number of writers have described their own versions of strategic management accounting and some of the main strands are summarised below:

- Data should be collected on such matters as the costs, prices and market share of competitors, so that managers have some comparisons to determine the strategies they should be pursuing.
- More emphasis should be placed on generating data that is of direct help in setting pricing policy. In particular, assessing competitors' costs structures and relating this to their pricing policy when changes in levels of activity take place.
- Businesses can adopt a strategy of *cost leadership* where they are the lowest cost-producers within the industry. This requires an analysis of all the

organisation's activities, from procuring raw materials to delivering the goods to the customers, and the costs associated with each. Comparison must be conducted with other companies to identify opportunities for cost reduction.

- It should be recognised that a consumer buys a product, not only for its basic function, but also for a number of other attributes such as guarantees, after sales service and appearance. Therefore, an analysis should be conducted to link the costs to the attributes that are considered to be of strategic importance in the eyes of the (final) consumer.

A major criticism of many of the different approaches to strategic management accounting is that it is impossible to obtain detailed information on competitors. A further criticism is that strategic management accounting strays into areas that traditionally are the preserve of other disciplines, such as strategic management. Whatever the merits of these criticisms, strategic management accounting offers a fresh perspective and acknowledges the importance of managerial action being placed in a context that is not formed solely by cost information generated about internal activities.

## 23.4 **Throughput Accounting**

*Throughput accounting (TA)* is an approach to management accounting that focuses on the fact that a number of organisations are constrained in the level of activity they can achieve by the presence of bottlenecks in the operations process. A *bottleneck* is a point at which the flow is constricted. For example, there may be a particular machine at the centre of the production activity which acts as a bottleneck to the entire process, or at peak times there may be such a queue of customers that service cannot be given fast enough to keep them moving through. It is the responsibility of managers to identify such bottlenecks and either attempt to remove them or ensure that they are always operating at full capacity.

If a bottleneck cannot be removed, the remainder of the operations process must be scheduled to ensure that it does not generate more than the bottleneck can absorb, as this leads to inefficiencies. In manufacturing, this will lead to stocks of *work in progress (WIP)* being held before they can be cleared through the bottleneck. The process of identifying the bottlenecks and taking action to remove them is known by the somewhat elaborate title of the *theory of constraints*. The theory can be applied in organisations by using TA.

Under TA it is argued that managers can increase profitability by increasing throughput and, at the same time, reducing the costs of holding inventories and operational expenditure. However, in the short term, little action can be taken on operational expenditure, which is mostly fixed in nature, so managers should concentrate on throughput followed by inventories. This implies that all operating expenses, including direct labour, is regarded as fixed. Only direct materials are regarded as a variable cost.

For decision-making, TA uses a similar approach to *marginal costing* (see Chapter 18), but the definition of 'variable costs' is far stricter. To apply throughput accounting the following formula is used:

$$\text{Throughput accounting (TA) ratio} = \frac{\text{Return per factory hour}}{\text{Costs per factory hour}}$$

where:

$$\text{Return per factory hour} = \frac{\text{Sales price} - \text{Material cost}}{\text{Time on key resource}}$$

$$\text{Cost per factory hour} = \frac{\text{Total factory cost}}{\text{Total time available on key resource}}$$

We will now use an example to show how the formula is used. Blue Glass Ltd produces two types of drinking glasses for the export market. Both are finely engraved on two separate machines and the details are as follows:

|  | Goblets | Schooners |
|---|---|---|
| Estimated sales demand | 1,500 glasses | 1,500 glasses |
| Selling price per glass | £8.00 | £7.50 |
| Direct material costs | £2.00 | £2.50 |
| **Engraving machine hours required per glass** | | |
| Machine 1 | 1 hour | 1 hour |
| Machine 2 | 4 hours | 2 hours |

The machine capacity in the financial period is limited to 4,000 hours for each machine and the total operating expenses are £12,000

The first step is to find out where the bottleneck is, and we do this by calculating the machine hours required to meet the sales demand:

|  | Goblets | Schooners | Total |
|---|---|---|---|
| Machine 1 | 1,500 hours | 1,500 hours | 3,000 hours |
| Machine 2 | 6,000 hours | 3,000 hours | 9,000 hours |

It is evident that the bottleneck is Machine 2 which will have capacity in the financial period for only 4,000 hours, but the estimated sales demand is for 9,000 hours. Our calculation of the TA ratio will be based on Machine 2:

|  | **Goblets** | **Schooners** |
|---|---|---|
| Return per factory hour | $\dfrac{£6}{4 \text{ hours}} = £1.50$ | $\dfrac{£5}{2 \text{ hours}} = £2.50$ |
| Cost per factory hour | $\dfrac{£12,000}{4,000 \text{ hours}} = £3.00$ | $\dfrac{£12,000}{4,000 \text{ hours}} = £3.00$ |
| TA ratio | $\dfrac{£1.50}{£3} = 0.50$ | $\dfrac{£2.50}{£3} = 0.83$ |

On a ranking basis it is therefore more profitable to meet the demand for schooners fully before starting to manufacture goblets. This will mean that the production of 1,500 schooners will use 3,000 of the machine hours on Machine 2 and the remaining 1,000 hours of machine capacity may be used for manufacturing 250 goblets. Of course, having identified the bottleneck, management should ascertain what scope it has to alleviate its impact.

For those who are familiar with marginal costing, throughput accounting offers no novel technical development and as such suffers the drawbacks of any technique which uses variable costs. Under marginal costing we could treat direct materials as the only variable cost and proceed to compute the contribution per unit of limiting factor – in this case, machine hours – to give the ranking to arrive at the same result as above. The value of throughput accounting is the emphasis on concentrating on bottlenecks and eradicating them. It may also help management to review what are the true variable costs in the short run.

## 23.5 Conclusions

In this chapter we have looked at three developments in management accounting. We have explained why ABC has assumed a position of importance, how it differs from absorption costing and how to calculate the cost per unit using ABC. We have also considered strategic management accounting and explained how it is attempting to achieve a more outward-looking approach. Finally, we have examined throughput accounting and demonstrated how it might be applied if there are bottlenecks in an organisation.

Having completed this chapter, you should now be able to:

- explain what is meant by activity-based costing (ABC);
- calculate the cost per unit using activity-based costing;
- discuss strategic management accounting;
- explain what is meant by the theory of constraints;
- determine machine utilisation by applying throughput accounting (TA).

# Exercises

Complete the following sentences:

**1** Activity-based costing (ABC) is a method of costing that .................................................
.............................................................................................................................................

**2** Strategic management accounting is a management accounting system that attempts to ...........................................................................................................................

**3** The theory of constraints is .........................................................................................

**4** A cost driver is .............................................................................................................

**5** A cost pool is ...............................................................................................................

Are the following statements true or false?

**6** Activity-based costing (ABC) is not appropriate in an advanced manufacturing technology environment.

**7** The theory of constraints is concerned with identifying bottlenecks in an organisation.

**8** Short-term variable overheads could be charged to the cost unit by using direct labour hours.

**9** Throughput accounting (TA) treats direct materials as a fixed cost.

**10** Throughput accounting (TA) uses some of the same concepts as marginal costing

You may wish to read more widely than this book to answer the following questions fully, but you can check the main points by referring to the appropriate sections of this chapter.

**11** What are the main reasons for activity-based costing (ABC) increasing in popularity? (Section 23.2)

**12** What are the criticisms of activity-based costing (ABC)? (Section 23.2)

**13** What are the main themes of strategic management accounting? (Section 23.3)

**14** Explain the formulae used in throughput accounting (TA). (Section 23.4)

Multiple choice questions (more than one answer may apply):

**15** . Strategic management accounting is:

    **a**  a method for controlling production costs

    **b**  a philosophy of management accounting

    **c**  a sophisticated technique for forecasting future costs and profits

    **d**  an industry wide procedure for management accounting.

**16** In throughput accounting (TA) the return per factory hour is calculated by:

    **a**  deducting all direct costs from the selling price and dividing by the time of the key resource

    **b**  deducting all direct material costs from the selling price and dividing by the time of the key resource

    **c**  dividing direct material costs by the selling price

    **d**  dividing the selling price by the direct material costs.

**17** In activity-based costing (ABC), activities that cause costs to be incurred are:

    **a**  cost units

    **b**  cost centres

    **c**  cost pools

    **d**  cost drivers.

**18** A business has three products with the following TA ratios: Product $X = 0.63$; Product $Y = 0.82$; Product $Z = 0.75$. The product(s) you would concentrate on if there is a bottleneck is/are:

   **a** $X$ and $Z$
   **b** $Y$ and $Z$
   **c** $X$
   **d** $Y$.

**19** Activity-based costing (ABC) assumes that costs are incurred by and can be associated with:

   **a** departments
   **b** products
   **c** activities
   **d** direct labour hours.

**20** In throughput accounting (TA):

   **a** all costs are regarded as fixed
   **b** all costs are regarded as variable
   **c** direct labour costs are regarded as variable
   **d** direct material costs are regarded as variable.

Practice questions:

**21** When using ABC, what types of cost drivers are appropriate for short-term variable overhead costs?

**22** What are the main problems associated with strategic management accounting?

**23** How is the throughput ratio calculated?

**24** Compare and contrast marginal costing and throughput accounting.

**25** What influences have encouraged new developments in management accounting?

(Answers on pp. 344–5)

# Appendix 1

# Answers to Exercises

## Part I Introduction to Accounting

### Chapter 1

1 Accounting is concerned with identifying, measuring, recording and communicating the economic transactions of organisations.
2 Financial accounting is concerned with the classification, measurement and recording of business transactions and the preparation of annual financial statements.
3 Management accounting is concerned with the use of financial and statistical techniques and methods to provide information to managers.
4 A qualified accountant must be a member of a recognised professional accounting body.
5 The prudence concept requires a cautious view of an organisation's transactions and no profits or revenues should be anticipated.
6 True.
7 False.
8 True.
9 False (other currencies may be used).
10 True.
11–14 Check the main points of your answer by referring to the appropriate sections in the chapter.
15 a and d.
16 b.
17 b.
18 b.
19 d.
20 d.
21 You should identify the key responsibilities of the financial accountant compared to the management accountant. Answers should identify that management accounting is for internal purposes and financial accounting is mainly for external purposes and is subject to a regulatory framework.
22 Reference should be made to the value to the preparers, users and auditors of financial statements. Descriptions of the four assumptions should be comprehensive.
23 You need to identify the fact that money is not a stable unit of measurement and reference should be made to the effect on the balance sheet. Higher marks are likely to be awarded if you give specific examples, such as the impact on stock valuations and the effect on profit.
24 You should identify such aspects as the skill and loyalty of the workforce, the reputation of the organisation, relationship with suppliers, customer lists, proven production methods, efficient administrative procedures.

**25** A typical answer will select matching and prudence with the costs having been incurred and some doubt on revenue/profits. You should identify that the prudence concept should prevail.

## Chapter 2

**1** A sole trader and a partnership have unlimited liability, which means that the owners are liable for any debts incurred by the business.

**2** The main source of financial information on a limited liability company is the annual report and accounts.

**3** Financial information can assist managers in their responsibilities of controlling, planning and decision-making.

**4** Shareholders require information about a company for the purpose of share-trading decisions and for generally evaluating the performance of the organisation.

**5** Lenders require financial information on a company to ascertain whether the interest will be paid and the loan repaid.

**6** True.

**7** True.

**8** False.

**9** False.

**10** False.

**11–14** Check the main points of your answer by referring to the appropriate sections in the chapter.

**15 c.**

**16 a.**

**17 b.**

**18 d.**

**19 b.**

**20 b** and **d**.

**21** You must discuss the concept of limited liability. Mention should also be made of the different legislative requirements and the issues of control and finance.

**22** Annual reports and accounts, directories, electronic databases and the press should be included in all answers. Higher marks are likely to be awarded if you give the names of specific sources (e.g. Datastream, Fame, etc.) and the type of information you can obtain (e.g. share prices, annual results, etc.).

**23** You should discuss the points raised in the chapter.

**24** Marks are likely to be equally weighted between the identification of user needs and how well these are met by the annual report and accounts. A sound and early contribution to the debate was the *Corporate Report* published by the Accounting Standards Steering Committee in 1975, which you should read if you need to study this topic in depth.

**25** The information is given in the chapter, but you need to discuss the absence of limited liability and the legal matters concerning partnerships as contained in the Partnership Act 1890.

# Part II  Financial Accounting

## Chapter 3

**1** The term 'cash' refers to all money, whether in the form of coins, notes, cheques or any other way of making payment which does not involve credit.

**2** Profit is the excess of revenue less the costs incurred for a financial period, irrespective of whether cash has been paid or received.

**3** Positive cash flow is cash coming into an organisation.
**4** Negative cash flow is cash going out of an organisation.
**5** Net cash flow is the difference between the cash going out and the cash coming into an organisation.
**6** False.
**7** False.
**8** True.
**9** False.
**10** False.
**11–14** Check the main points of your answer by referring to the appropriate sections in the chapter.
**15** b.
**16** c.
**17** a.
**18** d.
**19** c.
**20** a.
**21**

---

### Cash flow statement

|  | January £ | February £ |
|---|---|---|
| **Cash in** | | |
| Cash sales | 200 | 200 |
| Credit sales | 500 | 600 |
| Subtotal | 700 | 800 |
| **Cash out** | | |
| Purchases | 600 | 650 |
| Other expenses | 200 | 220 |
| Subtotal | 800 | 870 |
| **Cash surplus/(deficit)** | (100) | (70) |
| **Cumulative cash position** | (100) | (170) |

---

**22** You need to explain the terms positive cash flow, negative cash flow and net cash flow. A distinction should be made between the monthly movements and the cumulative position. Sensible comments should be made when there is either a cumulative surplus or deficit.

**23**

---

### Philip Trigg
### Cash flow forecast January to June 1998

|  | Jan £ | Feb £ | Mar £ | Apr £ | May £ | Jun £ |
|---|---|---|---|---|---|---|
| **Cash in** | | | | | | |
| Sales *A* | | | 792 | 858 | 858 | 990 |
| Sales *B* | | 1,300 | 1,300 | 1,560 | 1,560 | 1,560 |
| Subtotal | | 1,300 | 2,092 | 2,418 | 2,418 | 2,550 |
| **Cash out** | | | | | | |
| Rent | 1,500 | | | 1,500 | | |
| Light and heat | | 120 | 120 | 120 | 120 | 120 |
| Telephone | | | 50 | | | 50 |
| Packaging | | | 130 | 209 | 242 | 242 |
| Expense | 25 | 25 | 25 | 25 | 25 | 25 |

| | | | | | | |
|---|---|---|---|---|---|---|
| Equipment | 2,500 | 1,000 | 500 | – | – | – |
| Subtotal | 4,025 | 1,145 | 825 | 1,854 | 387 | 437 |
| **Cash surplus/(deficit)** | (4,025) | 155 | 1,267 | 564 | 2,031 | 2,113 |
| **Cumulative cash position** | (4,025) | (3,870) | (2,603) | (2,039) | (8) | 2,105 |

A capital investment of £4,025 is required to prevent the business from going into overdraft.

**24** With a loan of £5,000 and drawings of £500 per month, the figures for Philip Trigg are:

| | Jan | Feb | Mar | Apr | May | Jun |
|---|---|---|---|---|---|---|
| | £ | £ | £ | £ | £ | £ |
| Cumulative balance | 475 | 130 | 747 | 811 | 2,342 | 3,805 |

**25** You should draw up a logical list of expenses, but it is likely that the main marks will be given for identifying sources of information (e.g. if labour has to be hired the local press or job centre will give a guide to prevailing wage rates).

# Chapter 4

**1** A goods received note is raised by the ordering organisation when the goods are delivered.

**2** Clock cards are used to record the time spent at work by employees.

**3** Double-entry bookkeeping is an effective method for recording financial transaction in a way which allow financial statements to be prepared.

**4** Capital is the amount invested in a business by the owner(s).

**5** The accounting equation is: Assets = Capital + Other liabilities or Capital = Assets – Other liabilities.

**6** False.

**7** True.

**8** False.

**9** False.

**10** False.

**11–14** Check the main points of your answer by referring to the appropriate sections in the chapter.

**15** b.

**16** b.

**17** d.

**18** c.

**19** d.

**20** c.

**21**

## Castle Tours

### Capital account

| 1998 | | £ | 1998 | | £ |
|---|---|---|---|---|---|
| | | | 1 March | Bank | 5,000 |
| | | | | | |

### Loan account

| 1998 | | £ | 1998 | | £ |
|------|--|---|------|--|---|
| | | | 1 March | Bank | 4,700 |
| | | | 1 March | Cash | 300 |
| | | | | | |

### Bank account

| 1998 | | £ | 1998 | | £ |
|------|--|---|------|--|---|
| 1 March | Loan | 4,700 | | | |
| | Capital | 5,000 | | | |
| | | | | | |

### Cash account

| 1998 | | £ | 1998 | | £ |
|------|--|---|------|--|---|
| 1 March | Loan | 300 | | | |
| | | | | | |

**22**                     **Ashley Kennels**

### Purchases account

| 1998 | | £ | 1998 | | £ |
|------|--|---|------|--|---|
| 1 August | Bowin Ltd | 1,500 | | | |
| | | | | | |

### Bowin Ltd

| 1998 | | £ | 1998 | | £ |
|------|--|---|------|--|---|
| 2 August | Returns outward | 50 | 1 August | Purchases | 1,500 |
| | | | | | |

### Returns outward account

| 1998 | | £ | 1998 | | £ |
|------|--|---|------|--|---|
| | | | 2 August | Bowin Ltd | 50 |
| | | | | | |

**23**

## Mary's Cake Shop

### Bank account

| 1998 | | £ | 1998 | | £ |
|---|---|---|---|---|---|
| 1 March | Opening balance | 2,500 | 12 June | Goodwin Wholesale Ltd | 1,000 |
| | | | | | |
| | | | | | |

### Goodwin Wholesale Ltd

| 1998 | | £ | 1998 | | £ |
|---|---|---|---|---|---|
| 12 June | Bank | 1,000 | 1 March | Purchases | 3,000 |
| | | | | | |

### Purchases account

| 1998 | | £ | 1998 | | £ |
|---|---|---|---|---|---|
| 1 March | Goodwin Wholesale Ltd | 3,000 | | | |
| | | | | | |

**24**

## Wellworth Fencing

### Capital account

| 1998 | | £ | 1998 | | £ |
|---|---|---|---|---|---|
| | | | 1 June | Bank | 50,000 |
| | | | | | |

### Bank account

| 1998 | | £ | 1998 | | £ |
|---|---|---|---|---|---|
| 1 June | Capital | 50,000 | 1 June | Lorry | 16,000 |
| | | | 1 June | Lorry insurance | 1,400 |
| | | | 1 June | Premises rent | 4,500 |
| | | | 2 June | Equipment | 5,400 |
| | | | 2 June | Purchases | 850 |
| | | | 2 June | Advertising | 420 |
| | | | | | |

### Lorry account

| 1998 | | £ | 1998 | | £ |
|---|---|---|---|---|---|
| 1 June | Bank | 16,000 | | | |
| | | | | | |

### Lorry insurance account

| 1998 | | £ | 1998 | | £ |
|---|---|---|---|---|---|
| 1 June | Bank | 1,400 | | | |
| | | | | | |

### Premises rent account

| 1998 | | £ | 1998 | | £ |
|---|---|---|---|---|---|
| 1 June | Bank | 4,500 | | | |
| | | | | | |

### Equipment account

| 1998 | | £ | 1998 | | £ |
|---|---|---|---|---|---|
| 1 June | Bank | 5,400 | | | |
| | | | | | |

### Purchases account

| 1998 | | £ | 1998 | | £ |
|---|---|---|---|---|---|
| 2 June | Bank | 850 | | | |
| 4 June | Timber Supplies | 120 | | | |

### Advertising account

| 1998 | | £ | 1998 | | £ |
|---|---|---|---|---|---|
| 2 June | Bank | 420 | | | |
| | | | | | |

### Timber Supplies

| 1998 | | £ | 1998 | | £ |
|---|---|---|---|---|---|
| | | | 4 June | Purchases | 120 |
| | | | | | |

**25**                                               **Lavender & Lace**

### Sales account

| 1998 | | £ | 1998 | | £ |
|------|--|---|------|--|---|
| | | | 2 July | Cash | 138 |
| | | | 3 July | Cash | 192 |
| | | | | | |

### Postage account

| 1998 | | £ | 1998 | | £ |
|------|--|---|------|--|---|
| 1 July | Cash | 25 | | | |
| 2 July | Cash | 31 | | | |
| | | | | | |

### Window cleaning account

| 1998 | | £ | 1998 | | £ |
|------|--|---|------|--|---|
| 1 July | Cash | 10 | | | |
| | | | | | |

### Stationery account

| 1998 | | £ | 1998 | | £ |
|------|--|---|------|--|---|
| 1 July | Cash | 15 | | | |
| 1 July | Cash | 36 | | | |
| | | | | | |

### Miscellaneous account

| 1998 | | £ | 1998 | | £ |
|------|--|---|------|--|---|
| 1 July | Cash (parking) | 2 | | | |
| 2 July | Cash (parking) | 2 | | | |
| 3 July | Cash (parking) | 2 | | | |
| | | | | | |

**Petrol account**

| 1998 | | £ | 1998 | | £ |
|---|---|---|---|---|---|
| 1 July | Cash | 18 | | | |
| 2 July | Cash | 18 | | | |
| | | | | | |

**Purchases account**

| 1998 | | £ | 1998 | | £ |
|---|---|---|---|---|---|
| 2 July | Cash | 104 | | | |
| 3 July | Cash | 89 | | | |
| | | | | | |

## Chapter 5

**1** The purpose of a trial balance is to prove the mathematical accuracy of the bookkeeping entries.
**2** The credit column of a trial balance is a list of all the revenues, provisions and liabilities.
**3** To find out if you have transposed figures in the accounts you calculate the difference and check if the result is dividable by 9.
**4** In double-entry bookkeeping, for every debit entry there is a credit entry.
**5** The final accounts prepared from a trial balance are the profit and loss account and the balance sheet.
**6** True.
**7** True.
**8** False.
**9** True.
**10** True.
**11–14** Check the main points of your answer by referring to the appropriate sections in the chapter.
**15 c.**
**16 b.**
**17 d.**
**18 d.**
**19 b.**
**20 c.**
**21**

**Bank account**

| 1998 | | £ | 1998 | | £ |
|---|---|---|---|---|---|
| 1 October | Opening balance | 6,400 | 2 October | Purchases | 750 |
| 12 October | Sales | 1,800 | 3 October | Advertising | 1,120 |

| 15 October | Paul Plummer | 950 | 16 October | Purchases | 2,300 |
|---|---|---|---|---|---|
| 18 October | Paul Plummer | 950 | 18 October | Janet Mayo | 780 |
| 20 October | Sales | 1,450 | 20 October | Purchases | 3,400 |
| | | | 20 October | Balance c/d | 3,200 |
| | | 11,550 | | | 11,550 |
| 21 October | Balance b/d | 3,200 | | | |
| | | | | | |

**22**

### Jean's Farm Eggs
### Trial balance as at (date)

| | Debit £ | Credit £ |
|---|---|---|
| Capital | | 61,200 |
| Sales | | 16,800 |
| Purchases | 17,500 | |
| Cash at bank | 13,500 | |
| Equipment | 24,000 | |
| Motor vehicles | 21,000 | |
| Office expenses | 2,000 | |
| | 78,000 | 78,000 |

**23**

### Turner Tyres

| 1998 | | £ | 1998 | | £ |
|---|---|---|---|---|---|
| 2 May | Sales | 850 | 31 May | Cash | 1,900 |
| 12 May | Sales | 1,650 | 31 May | Balance c/d | 1,900 |
| 18 May | Sales | 260 | | | |
| 21 May | Sales | 400 | | | |
| 25 May | Sales | 640 | | | |
| | | 3,800 | | | 3,800 |
| 1 June | Balance b/d | 1,900 | | | |
| | | | | | |

**24**

### Harlech Health Foods
### Trial balance as at (date)

|                        | Debit £ | Credit £ |
|------------------------|--------:|---------:|
| Capital                |         | 18,000   |
| Sales                  |         | 26,200   |
| Purchases              | 36,770  |          |
| Returns inward         | 900     |          |
| Returns outward        |         | 460      |
| Discounts allowed      | 720     |          |
| Discounts received     |         | 620      |
| Wages                  | 1,600   |          |
| Cash at bank           | 1,500   |          |
| Equipment              | 2,000   |          |
| Rent                   | 1,400   |          |
| Miscellaneous expenses | 390     |          |
|                        | 45,280  | 45,280   |

**25**

### Country Furniture
### Trial balance as at 31 December 1998

|                   | Debit £ | Credit £ |
|-------------------|--------:|---------:|
| Capital           |         | 14,000   |
| Bank loan         |         | 25,000   |
| Sales             |         | 96,000   |
| Bank              | 4,000   |          |
| Trading expenses  | 8,000   |          |
| Premises          | 75,000  |          |
| Purchases         | 32,000  |          |
| Stock             | 16,000  |          |
|                   | 135,000 | 135,000  |

## Chapter 6

**1** Gross profit is the difference between the sales and the cost of sales for the financial period.

**2** Net profit is the gross profit less all other operating expenses which have been incurred during the financial period.

**3** An accrual is an expense which has been incurred but has not gone through the books of account.

**4** Depreciation is the allocation of the cost of an asset less its residual value over the financial periods which will benefit from its use.

**5** A provision for doubtful debts is intended to show a prudent approach to the figure recorded as sales in the profit and loss account and as debtors on the balance sheet.

**6** False.

**7** True.

**8** False.

**9** False.

**10** True.

**11–14** Check the main points of your answer by referring to the appropriate sections in the chapter.

**15** b.

**16** d.

**17** c.

**18** b.

**19** d.

**20** c.

**21**

|  | a<br>£ | b<br>£ | c<br>£ | d<br>£ | e<br>£ |
|---|---|---|---|---|---|
| Opening stock | 100 | 50 | 1,020 | 232 | 14,960 |
| Purchases | 400 | 680 | 10,210 | 1,924 | 163,570 |
|  | 500 | 730 | 11,230 | 2,156 | 178,530 |
| Closing stock | 50 | 210 | 1,550 | 150 | 18,815 |
| Cost of sales | 450 | 520 | 9,680 | 2,006 | 159,715 |

**22**

|  | a<br>£ | b<br>£ | c<br>£ | d<br>£ | e<br>£ |
|---|---|---|---|---|---|
| Sales | 10,000 | 600 | 17,000 | 18,150 | 27,750 |
| Cost of sales | 6,000 | 450 | 13,500 | 680 | 24,590 |
| Gross profit | 4,000 | 150 | 3,500 | 17,470 | 3,160 |
| Total expenses | 3,500 | 100 | 3,250 | 15,370 | 2,420 |
| Net profit | 500 | 50 | 250 | 2,100 | 740 |

**23**

|  | a | b | c | d | e |
|---|---|---|---|---|---|
| Cost of asset | £10,000 | £9,500 | £16,400 | £1,500 | £24,750 |
| Scrap value | £2,000 | £500 | £1,400 | £200 | £1,850 |
| Useful life | 4 years | 3 years | 30 years | 5 years | 10 years |
| Annual depreciation charge | £2,000 | £3,000 | £500 | £260 | £2,290 |

**24** The annual depreciation charge is £120,000 – £24,000 = £96,000 ÷ 8 = £12,000. The full cost of the machine will appear in the cash flow in July and the depreciation charge for the 6 months of £6,000 will appear in the profit and loss account. If you explain all these aspects correctly you are likely to be awarded high marks.

**25** You need to explain the calculation of opening stock plus purchases less closing stock equals cost of goods sold. This matching process against the sales figure allows the gross profit to be calculated. You are likely to receive high marks if you discuss the impact of stock valuations, wastage and theft, and the use of mark ups and margins.

## Chapter 7

**1** The accounting question demonstrates that at any one point in time the assets equals the capital plus the liabilities.

**2** In the UK, the most common presentation of the balance sheet is the vertical format.

**3** Debtors represent money owed to the organisation.

**4** Creditors represent money owed by the organisation.

**5** Drawings are money or goods taken by the owner of a business for their own use and appear on the balance sheet as a reduction of capital.

**6** True.

**7** True.

**8** False.

**9** False.

**10** False.

**11–14** Check the main points of your answer by referring to the appropriate sections in the chapter.

**15** d.

**16** c.

**17** b.

**18** b.

**19** b.

**20** c.

**21**

|  | a<br>£ | b<br>£ | c<br>£ | d<br>£ | e<br>£ |
|---|---|---|---|---|---|
| Capital | 8,400 | 14,000 | 6,050 | 3,200 | 12,000 |
| Liabilities | 3,600 | 1,400 | 7,120 | 14,800 | 25,160 |
| Assets | 12,000 | 15,400 | 13,170 | 18,000 | 37,160 |

**22**

### Nick Lucas
### Horizontal balance sheet as at 31 December 1998

|  | £ | £ |  | £ |
|---|---|---|---|---|
| **Fixed assets** |  |  | **Capital** | 256,000 |
| Land and buildings | 100,000 |  | *Less* **Creditors: amounts due within one year** |  |
| Machinery | 94,000 |  | Trade creditors | 30,000 |
| Fixtures and fittings | 42,000 | 236,000 |  |  |
| **Current assets** |  |  |  |  |
| Stock | 32,000 |  |  |  |
| Debtors | 12,000 |  |  |  |
| Cash | 6,000 | 50,000 |  |  |
|  |  | 286,000 |  | 286,000 |

### Nick Lucas
### Vertical balance sheet as at 31 December 1998

|  | £ | £ | £ |
|---|---|---|---|
| **Fixed assets** |  |  |  |
| Land & buildings |  | 100,000 |  |
| Machinery |  | 94,000 |  |
| Fixtures and fittings |  | 42,000 | 236,000 |

|  | **Current assets** | | | |
|---|---|---|---|---|
|  | Stock | 32,000 | | |
|  | Debtors | 12,000 | | |
|  | Cash | 6,000 | 50,000 | |
| *Less* | **Creditors: amounts due within one year** | | | |
|  | Trade creditors | | 30,000 | |
|  | **Working capital/Net current assets** | | | 20,000 |
|  | | | | 256,000 |
|  | Capital | | | 256,000 |

**23**

|  | **Asset** | **Liability** | **Capital** |
|---|---|---|---|
| Stock purchased on credit | +Stock | +Creditors | |
| Cash paid for stock | +Stock | | |
|  | −Cash | | |
| Loan repaid | −Cash | −Loan | |
| Cash received from debtor | +Cash | | |
|  | −Debtors | | |
| Cash withdrawn by owner | −Cash | | −Capital |

**24** You need to explain how the statements are related. For example, you should mention that the total cash figure from sales on the cash flow statement when deducted from sales in the profit and loss account gives the figure of debtors in the balance sheet. You are likely to receive higher marks if you introduce the more complex terms (such as depreciation) into your answer.

**25** You should comment on the underpinning of the accounting equation and note with limitations the items not included on the balance sheet, the problems over asset valuations and the possible unrepresentativeness of the particular balance sheet date.

# Chapter 8

**1** An accrual is an estimate in the accounts of a business of a liability that is not supported by an invoice or a request for payment.

**2** A prepayment is a payment made by the business for goods or services before they are received.

**3** Net current assets are calculated by deducting current liabilities from current assets.

**4** Drawings are the amounts withdrawn from the business by the owners in anticipation of profit.

**5** Net book value is the original cost of an asset less the cumulative depreciation.

**6** False.

**7** False.

**8** False.

**9** True.

**10** False.

**11–14** Check the main points of your answer by referring to the appropriate sections in the chapter.

**15** b and d.

**16** d.

**17** c.
**18** d.
**19** b.
**20** c.
**21**

---

### Top-to-Toe
### Trading and profit and loss account for the
### year ending 31 December 1998

|  |  | £ | £ |
|---|---|---:|---:|
|  | **Sales** |  | 72,100 |
| *Less* | **Cost of sales** |  |  |
| *Add* | Purchases | 11,160 |  |
| *Less* | Closing stock | 790 | 10,370 |
|  | **Gross profit** |  | 61,730 |
| *Add* | Rent received |  | 1,500 |
|  |  |  | 63,230 |
| *Less* | **Expenses** |  |  |
|  | Wages | 12,000 |  |
|  | Insurance | 7,400 |  |
|  | Rent | 18,000 |  |
|  | Electricity | 2,380 |  |
|  | Advertising | 3,600 |  |
|  | Telephone | 1,740 |  |
|  | Provision for doubtful debts | 240 |  |
|  | Administration expenses | 1,410 |  |
|  | Depreciation | 3,750 | 50,520 |
|  | **Net profit** |  | 12,710 |

---

### Top-to-Toe
### Balance sheet as at 31 December 1998

|  |  | £<br>Cost | £<br>Depreciation | £<br>Net book<br>value |
|---|---|---:|---:|---:|
|  | **Fixed assets** |  |  |  |
|  | Equipment | 15,000 | 3,750 | 11,250 |
|  | **Current assets** |  |  |  |
|  | Stock |  | 790 |  |
|  | Debtors |  |  |  |
|  |  | 1,200 |  |  |
| *Less* | Provision for doubtful debts |  | 960 |  |
|  |  | 240 |  |  |
|  | Prepayments |  | 260 |  |
|  | Bank |  | 1,060 |  |
|  |  |  | 3,070 |  |
| *Less* | **Creditors: amounts due within one year** |  |  |  |
|  | Creditors | 1,620 |  |  |
|  | Accruals | 990 | 2,610 |  |
|  | **Net current assets** |  |  | 460 |
|  | **Total assets less current liabilities** |  |  | 11,710 |
|  | Capital at beginning of year |  | 15,000 |  |
| *Add* | Profit for year |  | 12,710 |  |
|  |  |  | 27,710 |  |
| *Less* | Drawings |  | 16,500 | 11,710 |

**23**

---

### Walters Watches
### Balance sheet as at 7 April 1998

| | £ | £ |
|---|---:|---:|
| **Fixed assets** | | |
| Fixtures and fittings | | 50,000 |
| **Current assets** | | |
| Stock | 31,000 | |
| Debtors | 10,000 | |
| Bank | 3,000 | |
| | 44,000 | |
| *Less* **Creditors: amounts due within one year** | | |
| Creditors | 9,000 | |
| **Net current assets** | | 35,000 |
| **Total assets less current liabilities** | | 85,000 |
| | | |
| Capital at beginning of year | | 85,000 |

---

**24** The main points you should make in your letter to Rob Walters are as follows: The balance sheet is a financial statement, the purpose of which is to provide a snapshot of the business at one particular point in time (the date on which it is drawn up). There are two formats: vertical and horizontal. The vertical format is the one most frequently used in the UK. The information shown is identical in both formats; it is only the presentation that differs. The balance sheet shows the assets held by the business and the liabilities and capital which have helped fund the assets. The balance sheet is based on the accounting equation that assets equal capital plus liabilities. It must be remembered that the balance sheet is normally drawn up on an historical cost basis which means that the amounts shown do not necessarily represent the current values. Not everything that is of value to the business – for example, loyalty of employees, skilled workforce, good customer contacts, network of suppliers, good credit rating, etc. – is necessarily shown in the balance sheet.

**25**

---

### Back Up Business Services
### Trading and profit and loss account for the
### year ending 31 December 1998

| | £ | £ |
|---|---:|---:|
| **Sales** | | 42,800 |
| *Less* **Cost of sales** | | |
| Opening stock | 500 | |
| *Add* Purchases | 2,600 | |
| | 3,100 | |
| *Less* Closing stock | 560 | 2,540 |
| **Gross profit** | | 40,260 |
| *Add* Rent received | | 500 |
| | | 40,760 |
| *Less* **Expenses** | | |
| Wages | 15,600 | |
| Lighting and heating | 2,750 | |
| Postage and stationery | 550 | |
| Insurance | 1,250 | |
| Telephone | 950 | |

| | | | |
|---|---|---|---|
| Provision for doubtful debts | | 450 | |
| Depreciation – Equipment | | 3,000 | |
| – Car | | 3,000 | 27,550 |
| **Net profit** | | | 13,210 |

---

### Back Up Business Services
### Balance sheet as at 31 December 1998

| | | £ | £ | £ |
|---|---|---|---|---|
| | | Cost | Depreciation | Net book value |
| **Fixed assets** | | | | |
| | Premises | 55,000 | – | 55,000 |
| | Equipment | 20,000 | 6,000 | 14,000 |
| | Car | 9,000 | 6,000 | 3,000 |
| | | | | 72,000 |
| **Current assets** | | | | |
| | Stock | | 560 | |
| | Debtors | 7,150 | | |
| *Less* | Provision for doubtful debts | 450 | 6,700 | |
| | Bank | | 1,950 | |
| | | | 9,210 | |
| *Less* | **Creditors: amounts due within one year** | | | |
| | Creditors | 11,750 | | |
| | Accruals | 750 | 12,500 | |
| | **Net current assets** | | | (3,290) |
| | **Total assets less current liabilities** | | | 68,710 |
| | Capital at beginning of year | | | 55,500 |
| *Add* | Profit for year | | | 13,210 |
| | | | | 68,710 |

---

## Chapter 9

**1** Partners are entitled to a salary if they have made an agreement to that effect.

**2** In the absence of a specific agreement between the partners the provisions of the Partnership Act 1890 apply.

**3** The value of any goodwill is considered to be an asset of the partnership and a new partner will have to recompense the existing partners for a share of it.

**4** Profits on the realisation of a partnership are shared among the partners in their profit-sharing ratios.

**5** The main disadvantage of a partnership compared to a limited company is that the partners have unlimited liability.

**6** False.

**7** False.

**8** False.

**9** False.

**10** True.

**11–14** Check the main points of your answer by referring to the appropriate sections in the chapter.

**15** c.

**16** b and c.

**17** c.
**18** c.
**19** c.
**20** c.

---

### H&G Tool Hire
### Appropriation account for the year ending 31 December 1998

| | | | £ | £ | £ |
|---|---|---|---|---|---|
| **Net profit available for appropriation** | | | | | 95,000 |
| *Add* | Interest on drawings | Harold | | 1,500 | |
| | | George | | 1,000 | 2,500 |
| | | | | | 97,500 |
| *Less* | Salaries | Harold | 15,000 | | |
| | | George | 10,000 | 25,000 | |
| | Interest on capital | Harold | 1,000 | | |
| | | George | 3,000 | 4,000 | 29,000 |
| | | | | | 68,500 |
| **Balance of profits to be shared** | | | | | |
| | | Harold 60% | | 41,100 | |
| | | George 40% | | 27,400 | 68,500 |

**22**

---

### H&G Tool Hire
### Current accounts

| | | Harold Cobb | George Cobb |
|---|---|---|---|
| | | £ | £ |
| | Salary | 15,000 | 10,000 |
| *Add* | Interest on capital | 1,000 | 3,000 |
| *Add* | Share of profits | 41,100 | 27,400 |
| | | 57,100 | 40,000 |
| *Less* | | | |
| | Interest on drawings | 1,500 | 1,000 |
| | Drawing | 35,000 | 32,000 |
| | **Closing balance** | 20,600 | 7,000 |

**23**

---

### J&B Services

| | £ |
|---|---|
| Total net assets of the new partnership (£2000,000 × 3) | 600,000 |
| Identifiable net assets of the old partnership (£120,000 × 2) plus the investment by the new partner (£200,000) | 440,000 |
| Difference (goodwill) | 160,000 |

### Goodwill account

| | | £ | | | £ |
|---|---|---|---|---|---|
| Jarvis | | 80,000 | | | |
| Berry | | 80,000 | | | |

### Capital account: Jarvis

|  | £ |  | £ |
|---|---|---|---|
|  |  | Opening balance | 120,000 |
|  |  | Goodwill | 80,000 |

### Capital account: Berry

|  | £ |  | £ |
|---|---|---|---|
|  |  | Opening balance | 120,000 |
|  |  | Goodwill | 80,000 |
|  |  |  |  |

### Capital account: Lindsay

|  | £ |  | £ |
|---|---|---|---|
|  |  | Bank | 200,000 |
|  |  |  |  |

**24.**

### Page & Partners
### Appropriation account for the year ending 31 December 1998

|  |  |  | £ | £ | £ |
|---|---|---|---|---|---|
| **Net profit available for appropriation** |  |  |  |  | 131,950 |
| *Add* | Interest on drawings | Page |  | 2,750 |  |
|  |  | Jones |  | 1,000 |  |
|  |  | Beattie |  | 1,400 | 5,150 |
|  |  |  |  |  | 137,100 |
| *Less* | Salaries | Page | 15,000 |  |  |
|  |  | Jones | 10,000 |  |  |
|  |  | Beattie | 10,000 | 45,000 |  |
|  | Interest on capital | Page | 5,000 |  |  |
|  |  | Jones | 7,500 |  |  |
|  |  | Beattie | 8,500 | 21,000 | 66,000 |
| **Balance of profits to be shared** |  |  |  |  | 71,100 |
|  |  | Page |  | 23,700 |  |
|  |  | Jones |  | 23,700 |  |
|  |  | Beattie |  | 23,700 | 71,100 |

## Current accounts

|  |  | Page £ | Jones £ | Beattie £ |
|---|---|---|---|---|
|  | Opening balance | 4,500 | 2,000 | 5,000 |
| *Add* |  |  |  |  |
|  | Salary | 15,000 | 10,000 | 10,000 |
|  | Interest on capital | 5,000 | 7,500 | 8,500 |
|  | Share of profits | 23,700 | 23,700 | 23,700 |
|  |  | 48,200 | 43,200 | 47,200 |
| *Less* |  |  |  |  |
|  | Interest on drawings | 2,750 | 1,000 | 1,400 |
|  | Drawings | 55,000 | 20,000 | 28,000 |
|  | **Closing balance** | (9,550) | 22,200 | 17,800 |

**25**

## Mourne, Noonan & Knight

### Realisation account

|  | £ |  | £ |
|---|---|---|---|
| Premises | 50,000 | Bank: Sale of premises | 47,500 |
| Stock | 48,600 | Bank: Sale of stock | 41,100 |
| Debtors | 28,200 | Bank: Debtors realised | 26,800 |
|  |  | Loss on realisation: Mourne | 3,800 |
|  |  | Noonan | 3,800 |
|  |  | Knight | 3,800 |
|  | 126,800 |  | 126,800 |

### Bank account

|  | £ |  | £ |
|---|---|---|---|
| Realisation: Premises | 47,500 | Opening balance | 28,700 |
| Realisation: Stock | 41,100 | Creditors | 78,300 |
| Realisation: Debtors | 26,800 | Payment to Mourne | 5,400 |
|  |  | Payment to Noonan | 3,000 |
|  | 115,400 |  | 115,400 |

## Capital accounts

|  | Mourne | Noonan | Knight |  | Mourne | Noonan | Knight |
|---|---|---|---|---|---|---|---|
|  | £ | £ | £ |  | £ | £ | £ |
| Loss on realisation | 3,800 | 3,800 | 3,800 | Opening balance | 8,000 | 6,000 | 2,000 |
| Knight* | 800 | 600 |  | Current accounts | 2,000 | 1,400 | 400 |
| Bank | 5,400 | 3,000 |  | Mourne* |  |  | 800 |
|  |  |  |  | Noonan* |  |  | 600 |
|  | 10,000 | 7,400 | 3,800 |  | 10,000 | 7,400 | 3,800 |

*\* Garner* v. *Murray* (1904)

## Chapter 10

**1** With limited companies, the shareholders' liability is limited to the money they have agreed to invest.

**2** The three elements of the regulatory framework are the Companies Act 1985, as amended by the Companies Act 1989, accounting standards and Stock Exchange regulations.

**3** The Accounting Standards Committee (ASC) was replaced in 1990 by the Accounting Standards Board (ASB).

**4** A summary financial statement is an abbreviated version of the full report and accounts.

**5** The two bodies working together to achieve international harmonisation of accounting standards are the IASC and IOSCO.

**6** True.

**7** False.

**8** True.

**9** True.

**10** False.

**11–14** Check the main points of your answer by referring to the appropriate sections in the chapter.

**15** c.

**16** d.

**17** d.

**18** b.

**19** b.

**20** c.

**21** The contents of the annual report and accounts of a listed company are the chairman's statement, the directors' report, the accounting policies, the profit and loss account, the statement of total recognised gains and losses, the balance sheet, the cash flow statement, the notes to the accounts and the auditors' report.

**22** You need to describe the annual reports and accounts which show the annual results; interim statements which show the half-yearly results; and preliminary announcements which show any profit or loss and are published as soon as the annual results have been agreed with the auditors.

**23** The main point you should cover in your answer is that the ASB issues financial reporting standards (FRSs) which apply to all accounts intended to give a true and fair view. An offshoot of the ASB, the Urgent Issues Task Force (UITF) is responsible for issuing guidance on urgent matters.

**24** In your answer you need to explain that the Companies Act 1985 provides the legal framework and applies to all limited companies. The ASB issues financial reporting standards (FRSs) which add further requirements to the legislation. In addition, the London Stock Exchange (LSE) has its own rules, but these apply only to listed companies.

**25** You should make reference in your answer to the objectives of the ASC, the problems it confronted and the reasons for its replacement by the ASB. Higher marks are likely to be awarded for a discussion on the Dearing Report and reference to specific standards to illustrate the arguments.

## Chapter 11

**1** Minority interests represent the interests of individual shareholders in a subsidiary company.

**2** Debentures are long-term loans to the company.

**3** Share capital is calculated by multiplying the number of shares issued by their face value.

**4** FRS 1 requires companies to produce a cash flow statement.

**5** The statement of total recognised gains and losses is intended to show all recognised gains and losses which have occurred during the period.

**6** False.

**7** False.

**8** False.

**9** False.

**10** False.

**11–14** Check the main points of your answer by referring to the appropriate sections in the chapter.

**15** c.

**16** a.

**17** d.

**18** c.

**19** b.

**20** b.

**21** The main items you would expect to see are corporation tax, dividends and, in some cases, minority interests.

**22** The main items are share capital, debentures, minority interests and reserves. A description of what these terms mean is given in the chapter.

**23** Under FRS 3 a breakdown of turnover and operating profit by continuing operations, acquisitions and discontinued operations must be disclosed. A description of what these terms mean is given in the chapter.

**24** Earnings per share is the profit attributable to the ordinary shareholders divided by the number of ordinary shares issued. Investors regard it as a key measure of financial performance.

**25** The main items in a consolidated cash flow statement are described in the chapter.

## Chapter 12

**1** Return can be defined as profit before interest and tax.

**2** The prime ratio is calculated by expressing profit before interest and tax as a percentage of capital employed.

**3** Ratios may be misleading if there is high inflation.
**4** The definition of capital employed is fixed assets plus current assets less current liabilities.
**5** Capital turnover measures the level of activity in the business as reflected by sales in relation to the capital employed.
**6** False.
**7** False.
**8** True.
**9** True.
**10** False.
**11–14** Check the main points of your answer by referring to the appropriate sections in the chapter.
**15 c.**
**16 c.**
**17 d.**
**18 c.**
**19 c.**
**20 c.**
**21** Gross profit margin = 26.9%
Gross profit mark up = 36.8%
**22** ROCE = 8.76%
Profit margin = 15.2%
Capital turnover = 0.57 times
**23** Current test = 1.69 : 1
Acid test = 0.51 : 1
**24**

|  | Adams Ltd | Evelyn Ltd |
| --- | --- | --- |
| Prime ratio | 10.5% | 6.9% |
| Profit margin | 8.3% | 5.8% |
| Gross profit margin | 20.2% | 22.1% |
| Capital turnover | 1.26 times | 1.18 times |

**25** The main ratios you could have calculated are:

| | |
| --- | --- |
| Prime ratio/ROCE | 19.8% |
| Gross profit margin | 71.18% |
| Net profit margin | 28.58% |
| Capital turnover | 0.67 times |
| Current test | 3.66 : 1 |
| Acid test | 2.12 : 1 |
| Debt collection period | 134 days |
| Credit period | 204 days |

# Part III Management Accounting

## Chapter 13

**1** A cost unit can be defined as a quantitative unit of the product or service to which costs are allocated.
**2** Direct costs can be identified with a specific product or saleable service.
**3** In the short term, fixed costs tend to remain the same irrespective of changes in the level of activity.

**4** A cost centre is an identifiable part of an organisation for which costs can be collected.

**5** Production overheads are the indirect costs of production that cannot be traced directly to the product or cost unit.

**6** False.

**7** True.

**8** False.

**9** True.

**10** True.

**11–14** Check the main points of your answer by referring to the appropriate sections in the chapter.

**15** a.

**16** d.

**17** c.

**18** a.

**19** c.

**20** a.

**21** The essence of this question is that the purpose of management accounting is to supply information that is useful. The more detailed the information and the more relevant to the problem, the more useful it will be. By classifying costs in different ways, detailed information can be provided which is relevant to the problem.

**22** This is taken from the chapter. A cost unit is the quantitative unit of the product or service to which costs are allocated; in other words, the output. A cost centre is an identifiable part of the organisation for which costs can be collected. Cost units pass through cost centres.

**23** The main point is to explain that product costs are related to the products themselves, whereas period costs relate to a period of time.

**24** Motor vehicles' licences – selling and distribution cost
Depreciation of factory machinery – production cost
Commission paid to sales team – selling and distribution cost
Salary of finance director's secretary – administration cost
Salary of factory security guard – production cost
Fees to advertising agency – selling and distribution cost
Buildings' insurance – administration cost
Lubricants for factory machinery – production cost
Depreciation of fork lift truck – production cost
Accounting software – administration cost
Bonuses for factory staff – production cost
Training course for clerical staff – administration cost

**25** Julie's Jardinières
    **a** Prime cost £16,200
    **b** Production cost £27,600
    **c** Total cost £36,000
    **d** Administration overhead £3,800
    **e** Selling overhead £3,300
    **f** Distribution overheads £1,300

## Chapter 14

**1** A purchase requisition note is sent to the purchasing department by the production department or stores department.

**2** The average price method of pricing issues of materials uses a simple average or a weighted average price.

**3** Piecework tickets are used for costing labour at each stage of manufacture.
**4** Job cards record how long each activity takes to pass through the production process.
**5** Labour costing is closely related to the method of remuneration operated by the organisation.
**6** False.
**7** False.
**8** False.
**9** True.
**10** False.
**11–14** Check the main points of your answer by referring to the appropriate sections in the chapter.
**15** b.
**16** d.
**17** c.
**18** c.
**19** b.
**20** a.
**21** This is taken direct from the chapter, but it is valuable to specify the information that should be given on the documents and even draw up specimen documents.
**22** This is taken direct from the chapter, but you should be able to give a numerical example and explain some of the management issues concerning stock control.
**23** It is likely that you will be given higher marks for an original and relatively complex worked example.
**24** As well as identifying issues of absenteeism, lateness, inaccuracies, fraud etc. you should also discuss the procedures you envisage and the costs and practicalities of operating such procedures.
**25**

| Product | | Hours |
|---|---|---|
| A | 12 units @ 0.8 hours | 9.6 |
| B | 30 units @ 0.6 hours | 18.0 |
| C | 24 units @ 0.5 hours | 12.0 |
| | | 39.6 |

Therefore, total pay $= 39.6$ hours @ £5 per hour $=$ £198.

## Chapter 15

**1** Cost apportionment is the sharing of overheads over a number of cost centres.
**2** An overhead analysis allows the apportionment and allocation of overheads to cost centres.
**3** The overhead absorption rate is the method for charging overheads to cost units.
**4** The overheads for service cost centres must be apportioned to production cost centres.
**5** The direct labour hour absorption rate is calculated by dividing the overheads for the cost centre by the total direct labour hours for that cost centre.
**6** False.
**7** True.

**8** False.
**9** False.
**10** False.
**11–14** Check the main points of your answer by referring to the appropriate sections in the chapter.
**15** b.
**16** d.
**17** c.
**18** d.
**19** c.
**20** a.
**21** Where the overhead has been incurred in making available machine time, and this will be evidenced by the number of machine hours available. You should also mention that the products should also be dissimilar and require uneven resources. If the products were the same the cost unit absorption rate could be used, and this would be easier to administer.
**22** Administration is best apportioned to the other overheads where possible. The most common treatment for selling and distribution overheads is still a percentage addition to the factory cost, and you can usefully discuss how relevant this approach now is.
**23** You will probably find it easier to think of the disadvantages and the misleading figures produced by 'averages' of any type. You should also consider the advantages, as the factory-wide rate is cheap to administer, easy to calculate and rapid in execution, and it could be appropriate and acceptable in certain conditions (e.g. similar production processes and products).
**24** You should start by explaining what is meant by under of overabsorption and why it arises. You need to note that it must be brought into the calculation of the final profit figure. You will probably receive higher marks if you mention that a suspense account can be used for periodic adjustment.
**25**

## West Wales Windsurfers Ltd

| | Shaping dept | Finishing dept | Canteen | Total |
|---|---|---|---|---|
| | £ | £ | £ | £ |
| Allocated overhead | 680,000 | 390,000 | 160,000 | 1,230,000 |
| Canteen (number of employees) | 100,000 | 60,000 | | |
| Total | 780,000 | 450,000 | | |
| | | | | |
| Machine hours | 260,000 | | | |
| Labour hours | | 180,000 | | |
| Budgeted overhead absorption rate | £3.00 | £2.50 | | |

| | Fun Wave | Hot Racer |
|---|---|---|
| | £ | £ |
| Materials | 80 | 50 |
| Labour | | |
| Shaping department | 150 | 180 |
| Finishing department | 80 | 80 |
| Overheads | | |
| Shaping department | 90 | 240 |
| Finishing department | 100 | 100 |
| Total | 500 | 650 |

## Chapter 16

**1** Specific-order costing assesses the individual costs of performing each particular job.

**2** Job costing is appropriate when customers specify their requirements and the job is small and of short duration.

**3** Batch costing is appropriate when the individual units of production are small or homogeneous.

**4** Contract costing is appropriate for large, long-term projects.

**5** Rectification costs are the costs incurred in remedying any defects in the output.

**6** True.

**7** False.

**8** True.

**9** True.

**10** False.

**11–14** Check the main points of your answer by referring to the appropriate sections in the chapter.

**15** c.

**16** a.

**17** b.

**18** c.

**19** c.

**20** c.

**21**

| | |
|---|---|
| Cost of job | £413 |
| Selling price | £500 |
| Profit | £87　(21%) |

**22**

| | |
|---|---|
| Cost of work | £163,000 |
| Profit on contract to date | £34,058 |
| Profit in suspense | £12,942 |

**23**

---

### Quick Print
### Job No. 123: Wedding invitations

| | | £ |
|---|---|---|
| Materials | | 30 |
| Wages | (4 hours @ £5 per hour) | 20 |
| Production overheads | (4 hours @ £2.50 per hour) | 10 |
| Production costs | | 60 |
| General overheads | (20%) | 12 |
| | | 72 |
| Profit | (25%) | 18 |
| | | 90 |

---

**24**

---

### Jill Collis
### Job No. 4: Garden design

| | | £ |
|---|---|---|
| Materials | | 70 |
| Salary | (30 hours @ £25 per hour) | 750 |
| Overheads | (30 hours @ £10.50 per hour) | 315 |

| | | |
|---|---|---|
| Total cost | | 1,135 |
| Profit | (15%) | 170 |
| Quoted price | | 1,305 |

Overhead absorption rate $\dfrac{£840}{80 \text{ hours}} = £10.50$

**25**

### Catbrook Construction

| | | £ |
|---|---|---|
| Cost of work done: | Work certified | 140,000 |
| | Work not certified | 34,000 |
| | | 174,000 |
| Estimated contract profit: | Contract price | 320,000 |
| | Estimated total costs | 260,000 |
| | | 60,000 |
| Profit at year end: | $\dfrac{£174,000}{£260,000} \times £60,000 =$ | £40,150 |

## Chapter 17

**1** In continuous-operation costing the unit cost is obtained by dividing the total production cost by the number of items produced.
**2** Output costing is used when basically only one product is produced.
**3** Service costing is used when specific services or functions are to be costed.
**4** Process costing is used when the output of one stage of the production operation forms the input for the next.
**5** In process costing, normal losses are part of the cost of production.
**6** False.
**7** True.
**8** False.
**9** False.
**10** True.
**11–14** Check the main points of your answer by referring to the appropriate sections in the chapter.
**15** c.
**16** a.
**17** b.
**18** c.
**19** b.
**20** a.
**21**

Total annual costs = £30,000
Monthly costs   = £2,500

Cost per test     = $\dfrac{£2,500}{240} = £10.42$

**22** Normal losses are acceptable levels of waste which are regarded as part of the costs of production and are allowed in the product costs. Abnormal losses are due to abnormal waste and are normally valued on the same basis as the good output. Abnormal losses must carry their share of the cost of normal losses.

**23** The costs should be classified under the headings of direct and indirect costs. Examples include the following:

Direct costs:
Drivers' wages
Running costs
Repairs and servicing
Annual costs (such as road tax, insurance, depreciation, etc.)

Indirect costs:
Salary of transport manager
Cost of running garages

**24**

| No. of units | Materials | | Labour/Overheads | |
| | Completed | Equivalent units | Completed | Equivalent units |
|---|---|---|---|---|
| 12,200 | 100% | 12,200 | 100% | 12,200 |
| 3,800 | 100% | 3,800 | 50% | 1,600 |
| Equivalent units produced | | 16,000 | | 13,800 |

**25**

Unit costs: Materials $\dfrac{£960,000^*}{16,000} = £60,000$

Labour/Overheads $\dfrac{£701,200}{13,800} = £50.81$

*Note*: * Materials costs: From previous process £910,500
Materials introduced     £49,500
£960,000

# Chapter 18

**1** When activity increases, fixed costs per unit decrease.

**2** Marginal costing is a technique whereby only the variable or marginal costs of production are charged to cost units.

**3** Contribution is calculated by deducting variable costs from sales.

**4** The break-even point is where the business makes neither a profit nor a loss.

**5** The margin of safety is the difference between the selected level of activity and the break-even point.

**6** True.

**7** False.

**8** False.

**9** True.

**10** True.

**11–14** Check the main points of your answer by referring to the appropriate sections in the chapter.

**15** b.

**16** b.

**17** b.

**18** b.

**19** b.

**20** c.

**21** You need to emphasise the short-term nature of marginal costing and the assumptions it uses in their answers. If you cite specific uses, you should demonstrate why the concept of contribution is valuable in those uses. You need to refer to uses such as fixing the selling price, ascertaining the break-even point and deciding on the cessation of a product.

**22** Your answer will probably be based on materials or labour as the limiting factors. You should indicate how you have calculated the contribution per unit of limiting factor and how the selection will maximise the overall profit of the organisation.

**23** Your graph should enable you to read off the break-even point of 769 units. You are likely to be given higher marks if you include a suitable scale for the graph and it is correctly headed and labelled.

**24** This is direct from the text, but you will be able to get higher marks if from your wider reading you suggest how the limitations can be overcome and discuss the importance of the relevant range and the treatment of semi-variable costs.

**25 a.** The total cost per unit increases because some costs are fixed in nature and therefore the same total amount of cost has to be shared over fewer units. **b.** Marginal costing focuses on the contribution to fixed costs. In periods of recession most decision-making is concerned with achieving the best contribution. Although in the long term it is essential that fixed costs are recovered, marginal costing can give a new perspective on the problems confronted by the organisation.

## Chapter 19

**1** The payback technique has the disadvantage of ignoring the time value of money and cash flows after the payback period.

**2** The accounting rate of return (ARR) is calculated as the return expressed as a percentage of the average capital employed.

**3** When investing in a long-term project, a business wishes to ensure that it will get its money back

**4** The aim of the payback technique is to recover the cash in the shortest possible time.

**5** The accounting rate of return (ARR) is simple and takes the entire life of the project into account.

**6** False.

**7** False.

**8** True.

**9** False.

**10** False.

**11–14** Check the main points of your answer by referring to the appropriate sections in the chapter.

**15** d.

**16** b.

**17** a.

**18** d.

**19** b.

**20** d.

**21** You need to draw a distinction between the importance of cash in the payback period and profit in the accounting rate of return. You should also comment on the inconsistencies of definitions of the accounting rate of return.

**22** Cash flows are ignored after the payback period, so a potentially highly favourable project with late, high cash flows may be excluded. Also the technique does not make any allowance for the time value of money.

**23** The importance of the timing and amount of cash flow is ignored and no allowance is made for the time value of money. In addition, the definition and calculation of profit and capital employed may not be sufficiently rigorous.

**24** With the information you have been given, you can use only the payback period technique. Both projects have a payback period of 4 years, so either could be chosen. Some businesses may choose Project 1 as this gives the largest cash return over the entire life of the project. Others may choose Project 2 as the largest cash flows are in the early years. Neither of these decisions are part of the payback period technique.

**25** With the information you have been given, you can use only the accounting rate of return technique.

| **Project A** | **Project B** |
|---|---|

$$\text{ARR} = \frac{£78,000}{£650,000} = 12\% \qquad \frac{£93,000}{£78,000} = 12\%$$

Both projects have an accounting rate of return of 12% and therefore on the basis of this technique are identical. Some businesses may choose Project **A** if they can invest the £150,000 not required in another project which provides a return in excess of 12%.

## Chapter 20

**1** The time value of money concept is concerned with calculating the present value of future cash flows.

**2** Net present value (NPV) converts future cash flows into present-day net values.

**3** The aim of the internal rate of return (IRR) is to find the discount rate which gives a net present value (NPV) of 0 for the project.

**4** Positive net cash flow is where the sum of the cash coming in is greater than the sum of the cash going out.

**5** Two major problems associated with discounting are predicting the cash flows over the life of the project and the choice of discount factor.

**6** False.

**7** True.

**8** True.

**9** False.

**10** False.

**11–14** Check the main points of your answer by referring to the appropriate sections in the chapter.

**15** b.

**16** d.

**17** d.

**18** d.

**19** c.

**20** b.

**21** The advantages and disadvantages are listed in the text, but it is crucial that you discuss the concept of the time value of money.

**22** Essentially, you need to comment on the identification of the timing and amount of cash flows over the entire life of the project. You should explain the use of the discount factor and how to look it up in the tables. You also need to comment on the interpretation of the NPV figure.

**23** This is a large and complex area and you need show reading of more advanced texts, such as *Management and Cost Accounting* by Colin Drury.

For high marks, you should identify the practical as well as the theoretical difficulties.

**24** You should be able to provide a basic answer from the chapter, but for higher marks you need to give evidence of further reading.

**25** The payback period is 4½ years and the NPV is (£1,475). You need to point out the contradiction of the answers: the project appears to be viable using the payback technique, but the NPV, which takes the time value of money into account, shows that this is not the case.

## Chapter 21

**1** A budget is a plan expressed in financial terms covering a specified period of time.

**2** A flexible budget is one which is changed to allow for the behaviour of variable costs at different levels of activity.

**3** A good example of a budget is a cash flow forecast.

**4** All individual budgets are incorporated into a master budget.

**5** An adverse cost variance is where the actual costs are higher than the budgeted costs.

**6** True.

**7** False.

**8** False.

**9** True.

**10** False.

**11–14** Check the main points of your answer by referring to the appropriate sections in the chapter.

**15 d.**

**16 d.**

**17 d.**

**18 a.**

**19 a.**

**20 d.**

**21** These issues have been covered in the chapter and you should be able to give a comprehensive answer.

**22** Although you may wish to concentrate on the advantages of budgetary control, for higher marks you should also exhibit a sound knowledge of the disadvantages.

**23** This is covered briefly in the chapter. For higher marks, you will need to expand on this from information gained in lectures or further reading and give a simple worked example.

**24** This is an extensive area and you need to cover aspects related to the implementation of the system, budget-setting, actual performance, analysis of variances and revision of plans and/or corrective action.

**25** Your answers must be in report form. A variety of approaches can be taken, but a useful method of analysis is to use the list of features which should be present for an effective system of budgetary control given in the chapter. Your recommendations will depend on the assumptions you make, but they need to be credible and set within a business context.

## Chapter 22

**1** Ideal standards are based on the best possible working conditions.

**2** Variance analysis is the investigation of the factors which have caused the differences between the standard and actual results.

**3** Differences between standard and actual costs must be due to variations either in quantity used or unit price, or both.

**4** A materials price variance is the responsibility of the purchasing manager.

**5** The subvariances of the total direct materials variance are the usage variance and the price variance.

**6** False.

**7** True.

**8** False.

**9** False.

**10** True.

**11–14** Check the main points of your answer by referring to the appropriate sections in the chapter.

**15** c.

**16** b.

**17** c.

**18** a.

**19** c.

**20** d.

**21** £5 favourable (could be due to inferior quality materials, cheaper supplier, bulk discounts).

**22** £250 favourable (could be due to more expensive materials with less wastage, efficient production processes, experienced workforce with less wastage).

**23** Total materials cost variance (£96) adverse
Usage variance (£200) adverse
Price variance £104 favourable.
Possible reasons are that an inferior type of material has been used and wastage is higher than planned. Another supplier may have been used and the materials had a slightly different specification, leading to higher usage. You are likely to achieve higher marks if you suggest where the responsibility possibly lies and give recommendations for further action.

**24** Total labour variance (£560) adverse
Rate variance (£920) adverse
Efficiency variance £360 favourable.
A possible reason may be that more highly skilled labour were employed than originally planned and their output has been greater. It may be that unplanned bonus payments were made to encourage higher output. The effect of the actions has led to an overall £560 adverse variance and higher-grade students should suggest what possible actions can be taken to remedy the situation.

**25** You need to identify the advantages and discuss in general terms the process for setting-standards and the information in terms of the variances that the system should produce. For higher marks, you should relate your answer to the particular context (e.g. by discussing the setting of separate standards for glass and aluminium). You should also take into account that there are two products, with the deluxe product using more expensive materials.

## Chapter 23

**1** ABC is a method of costing that recognises that costs are incurred by each activity and that products or customers should bear costs according to the activities they use.

**2** Strategic management accounting is a management accounting system that attempts to provide information needed to help make long-term strategic decision, rather than short-term cost information.

**3** The theory of constraints is the process of identifying bottlenecks and taking action to remove them.

**4** A cost driver is an activity or series of activities that takes place within an organisation and causes costs to be incurred.

**5** A cost pool is a collection of costs charged to products by the use of a common cost driver.

**6** False.

**7** True.

**8** True.

**9** False.

**10** True.

**11–14** Check the main points of your answer by referring to the appropriate sections in the chapter.

**15** b.

**16** b.

**17** d.

**18** d.

**19** c.

**20** d.

**21** With short-term variable overheads the cost drivers are normally the direct labour hours or direct machine hours. It is essential that you emphasise in your answer that the activities or series of activities that cause costs to be incurred are the cost drivers.

**22** Although strategic management accounting provides a fresh perspective, it is difficult to determine how some of the data relating to external organisations might be obtained.

**23** The throughput ratio is calculated by dividing the return per factory hour by the costs per factory hour. The former is the sales price less materials costs divided by the time on the key resource. The cost per factory hour is calculated by dividing the total factory cost by the total time available on the key resource.

**24** There is considerable similarity between the technique of marginal costing and throughput accounting, as both are based on variable costs. In marginal costing, however, direct labour is normally assumed to be variable, whereas in throughput accounting it is regarded as fixed. Throughput accounting offers the advantage that it concentrates on bottlenecks with the intention of eradicating them

**25** The main influences are dissatisfaction with the more traditional approach; the need for more useful information; changes in the nature of organisations and the greater overhead burden; the increasingly complex and competitive business environment.

# Appendix 2

# Present Value Tables

**Table 1** *Present Value Factors*

| Future years | | | | | | | | Rate of discount | | | | | | | | |
|---|---|---|---|---|---|---|---|---|---|---|---|---|---|---|---|---|
| | 1% | 2% | 3% | 4% | 5% | 6% | 7% | 8% | 9% | 10% | 11% | 12% | 13% | 14% | 15% | 16% |
| 1 | 0.990 | 0.980 | 0.971 | 0.962 | 0.952 | 0.943 | 0.935 | 0.926 | 0.917 | 0.909 | 0.901 | 0.893 | 0.885 | 0.877 | 0.870 | 0.862 |
| 2 | 0.980 | 0.961 | 0.943 | 0.925 | 0.907 | 0.890 | 0.873 | 0.857 | 0.842 | 0.826 | 0.812 | 0.797 | 0.783 | 0.770 | 0.756 | 0.743 |
| 3 | 0.971 | 0.942 | 0.915 | 0.889 | 0.864 | 0.840 | 0.816 | 0.794 | 0.772 | 0.751 | 0.731 | 0.712 | 0.693 | 0.675 | 0.658 | 0.641 |
| 4 | 0.961 | 0924 | 0.889 | 0.855 | 0.823 | 0.792 | 0.763 | 0.735 | 0.708 | 0.683 | 0.659 | 0.636 | 0.613 | 0.592 | 0.572 | 0.552 |
| 5 | 0.952 | 0.906 | 0.863 | 0.822 | 0.784 | 0.747 | 0.713 | 0.681 | 0.650 | 0.621 | 0.594 | 0.567 | 0.543 | 0.519 | 0.497 | 0.476 |
| 6 | 0.942 | 0.888 | 0.838 | 0.790 | 0.746 | 0.705 | 0.666 | 0.630 | 0.596 | 0.565 | 0.535 | 0.507 | 0.480 | 0.456 | 0.432 | 0.410 |
| 7 | 0.933 | 0.871 | 0.813 | 0.760 | 0.711 | 0.665 | 0.623 | 0.584 | 0.547 | 0.513 | 0.482 | 0.452 | 0.425 | 0.400 | 0.376 | 0.354 |
| 8 | 0.924 | 0.854 | 0.789 | 0.731 | 0.677 | 0.627 | 0.582 | 0.540 | 0.502 | 0.467 | 0.434 | 0.404 | 0.376 | 0.351 | 0.327 | 0.305 |
| 9 | 0.914 | 0.837 | 0.766 | 0.703 | 0.645 | 0.592 | 0.544 | 0.500 | 0.460 | 0.424 | 0.391 | 0.361 | 0.333 | 0.308 | 0.284 | 0.263 |
| 10 | 0.905 | 0.820 | 0.744 | 0.676 | 0.614 | 0.558 | 0.508 | 0.463 | 0.422 | 0.386 | 0.352 | 0.322 | 0.295 | 0.270 | 0.247 | 0.227 |
| 11 | 0.896 | 0.804 | 0.722 | 0.650 | 0.585 | 0.527 | 0.475 | 0.429 | 0.388 | 0.350 | 0.317 | 0.287 | 0.261 | 0.237 | 0.215 | 0.195 |
| 12 | 0.887 | 0.789 | 0.701 | 0.625 | 0.557 | 0.497 | 0.444 | 0.397 | 0.356 | 0.319 | 0.286 | 0.257 | 0.231 | 0.208 | 0.187 | 0.168 |
| 13 | 0.879 | 0.773 | 0.681 | 0.601 | 0.530 | 0.469 | 0.415 | 0.368 | 0.326 | 0.286 | 0.258 | 0.229 | 0.204 | 0.182 | 0.163 | 0.145 |
| 14 | 0.870 | 0.758 | 0.661 | 0.578 | 0.505 | 0.442 | 0.388 | 0.341 | 0.299 | 0.263 | 0.232 | 0.205 | 0.181 | 0.160 | 0.141 | 0.125 |
| 15 | 0.861 | 0.743 | 0.642 | 0.555 | 0.481 | 0.417 | 0.362 | 0.315 | 0.275 | 0.239 | 0.209 | 0.183 | 0.160 | 0.140 | 0.123 | 0.108 |
| 16 | 0.853 | 0.728 | 0.623 | 0.534 | 0.458 | 0.394 | 0.339 | 0.292 | 0.252 | 0.218 | 0.188 | 0.163 | 0.142 | 0.123 | 0.107 | 0.093 |
| 17 | 0.844 | 0.714 | 0.605 | 0.513 | 0.436 | 0.371 | 0.317 | 0.270 | 0.231 | 0.198 | 0.170 | 0.146 | 0.125 | 0.108 | 0.093 | 0.080 |
| 18 | 0.836 | 0.700 | 0.587 | 0.494 | 0.416 | 0.350 | 0.296 | 0.250 | 0.212 | 0.180 | 0.153 | 0.130 | 0.111 | 0.095 | 0.081 | 0.069 |
| 19 | 0.828 | 0.686 | 0.570 | 0.475 | 0.396 | 0.331 | 0.277 | 0.232 | 0.195 | 0.164 | 0.138 | 0.116 | 0.098 | 0.083 | 0.070 | 0.060 |
| 20 | 0.820 | 0.673 | 0.554 | 0.456 | 0.377 | 0.312 | 0.258 | 0.215 | 0.178 | 0.149 | 0.124 | 0.104 | 0.087 | 0.073 | 0.061 | 0.051 |

**Table 1** (continued)

| Future years | Rate of discount | | | | | | | | | | | | | | | |
| | 17% | 18% | 19% | 20% | 21% | 22% | 23% | 24% | 25% | 26% | 28% | 30% | 35% | 40% | 45% | 50% |
|---|---|---|---|---|---|---|---|---|---|---|---|---|---|---|---|---|
| 1 | 0.855 | 0.847 | 0.840 | 0.833 | 0.826 | 0.820 | 0.813 | 0.807 | 0.800 | 0.794 | 0.781 | 0.769 | 0.741 | 0.714 | 0.690 | 0.667 |
| 2 | 0.731 | 0.718 | 0.706 | 0.694 | 0.683 | 0.672 | 0.661 | 0.650 | 0.640 | 0.630 | 0.610 | 0.592 | 0.549 | 0.510 | 0.476 | 0.444 |
| 3 | 0.624 | 0.609 | 0.593 | 0.579 | 0.565 | 0.551 | 0.537 | 0.525 | 0.512 | 0.500 | 0.477 | 0.455 | 0.406 | 0.364 | 0.328 | 0.296 |
| 4 | 0.534 | 0.516 | 0.499 | 0.482 | 0.467 | 0.451 | 0.437 | 0.423 | 0.410 | 0.397 | 0.373 | 0.350 | 0.301 | 0.260 | 0.226 | 0.198 |
| 5 | 0.456 | 0.437 | 0.419 | 0.402 | 0.386 | 0.370 | 0.355 | 0.341 | 0.328 | 0.315 | 0.291 | 0.269 | 0.223 | 0.186 | 0.156 | 0.132 |
| 6 | 0.390 | 0.370 | 0.352 | 0.335 | 0.319 | 0.303 | 0.289 | 0.275 | 0.262 | 0.250 | 0.227 | 0.207 | 0.165 | 0.133 | 0.108 | 0.088 |
| 7 | 0.333 | 0.314 | 0.296 | 0.279 | 0.263 | 0.249 | 0.235 | 0.222 | 0.210 | 0.198 | 0.178 | 0.159 | 0.122 | 0.095 | 0.074 | 0.059 |
| 8 | 0.285 | 0.266 | 0.249 | 0.233 | 0.218 | 0.204 | 0.191 | 0.179 | 0.168 | 0.157 | 0.139 | 0.123 | 0.091 | 0.068 | 0.051 | 0.039 |
| 9 | 0.243 | 0.226 | 0.209 | 0.194 | 0.180 | 0.167 | 0.155 | 0.144 | 0.134 | 0.125 | 0.108 | 0.094 | 0.067 | 0.048 | 0.035 | 0.026 |
| 10 | 0.208 | 0.191 | 0.176 | 0.162 | 0.149 | 0.137 | 0.126 | 0.116 | 0.107 | 0.099 | 0.085 | 0.073 | 0.050 | 0.035 | 0.024 | 0.017 |
| 11 | 0.178 | 0.162 | 0.148 | 0.135 | 0.123 | 0.112 | 0.103 | 0.094 | 0.086 | 0.079 | 0.066 | 0.056 | 0.037 | 0.025 | 0.017 | 0.012 |
| 12 | 0.152 | 0.137 | 0.124 | 0.112 | 0.102 | 0.092 | 0.083 | 0.076 | 0.069 | 0.063 | 0.052 | 0.043 | 0.027 | 0.018 | 0.012 | 0.008 |
| 13 | 0.130 | 0.116 | 0.104 | 0.094 | 0.084 | 0.075 | 0.068 | 0.061 | 0.055 | 0.050 | 0.040 | 0.033 | 0.020 | 0.013 | 0.008 | 0.005 |
| 14 | 0.111 | 0.099 | 0.088 | 0.078 | 0.069 | 0.062 | 0.055 | 0.049 | 0.044 | 0.039 | 0.032 | 0.025 | 0.015 | 0.009 | 0.006 | 0.003 |
| 15 | 0.095 | 0.084 | 0.074 | 0.065 | 0.057 | 0.051 | 0.045 | 0.040 | 0.035 | 0.031 | 0.025 | 0.020 | 0.011 | 0.006 | 0.004 | 0.002 |
| 16 | 0.081 | 0.071 | 0.062 | 0.054 | 0.047 | 0.042 | 0.036 | 0.032 | 0.028 | 0.025 | 0.019 | 0.015 | 0.008 | 0.005 | 0.003 | 0.002 |
| 17 | 0.069 | 0.060 | 0.052 | 0.045 | 0.039 | 0.034 | 0.030 | 0.026 | 0.023 | 0.020 | 0.015 | 0.012 | 0.006 | 0.003 | 0.002 | 0.001 |
| 18 | 0.059 | 0.051 | 0.044 | 0.038 | 0.032 | 0.028 | 0.024 | 0.021 | 0.018 | 0.016 | 0.012 | 0.009 | 0.005 | 0.002 | 0.001 | 0.001 |
| 19 | 0.051 | 0.043 | 0.037 | 0.031 | 0.027 | 0.023 | 0.020 | 0.017 | 0.014 | 0.012 | 0.009 | 0.007 | 0.003 | 0.002 | 0.001 | 0.000 |
| 20 | 0.043 | 0.037 | 0.031 | 0.026 | 0.022 | 0.019 | 0.016 | 0.014 | 0.012 | 0.010 | 0.007 | 0.005 | 0.002 | 0.001 | 0.001 | 0.000 |

**Table 2** *Cumulative Present Value Factors*

Rate of discount

| Future years | 1% | 2% | 3% | 4% | 5% | 6% | 7% | 8% | 9% | 10% | 11% | 12% | 13% | 14% | 15% | 16% |
|---|---|---|---|---|---|---|---|---|---|---|---|---|---|---|---|---|
| 1 | 0.990 | 0.980 | 0.971 | 0.962 | 0.952 | 0.943 | 0.935 | 0.926 | 0.917 | 0.909 | 0.901 | 0.893 | 0.885 | 0.877 | 0.870 | 0.862 |
| 2 | 1.970 | 1.942 | 1.913 | 1.886 | 1.859 | 1.833 | 1.808 | 1.783 | 1.759 | 1.736 | 1.713 | 1.690 | 1.668 | 1.647 | 1.626 | 1.605 |
| 3 | 2.941 | 2.884 | 2.829 | 2.775 | 2.723 | 2.673 | 2.624 | 2.577 | 2.531 | 2.487 | 2.444 | 2.402 | 2.361 | 2.322 | 2.283 | 2.246 |
| 4 | 3.902 | 3.808 | 3.717 | 3.630 | 3.546 | 3.465 | 3.387 | 3.312 | 3.240 | 3.170 | 3.102 | 3.037 | 2.974 | 2.914 | 2.855 | 2.798 |
| 5 | 4.853 | 4.713 | 4.580 | 4.452 | 4.329 | 4.212 | 4.100 | 3.993 | 3.890 | 3.791 | 3.696 | 3.605 | 3.517 | 3.433 | 3.352 | 3.274 |
| 6 | 5.795 | 5.601 | 5.417 | 5.242 | 5.076 | 4.917 | 4.767 | 4.623 | 4.486 | 4.355 | 4.231 | 4.111 | 3.998 | 3.889 | 3.784 | 3.685 |
| 7 | 6.728 | 6.472 | 6.230 | 6.002 | 5.786 | 5.582 | 5.389 | 5.206 | 5.033 | 4.868 | 4.712 | 4.564 | 4.423 | 4.288 | 4.160 | 4.039 |
| 8 | 7.652 | 7.325 | 7.020 | 6.733 | 6.463 | 6.210 | 5.971 | 5.747 | 5.535 | 5.335 | 5.146 | 4.968 | 4.799 | 4.639 | 4.487 | 4.344 |
| 9 | 8.566 | 8.162 | 7.786 | 7.435 | 7.108 | 6.802 | 6.515 | 6.247 | 5.995 | 5.759 | 5.537 | 5.328 | 5.132 | 4.946 | 4.772 | 4.607 |
| 10 | 9.471 | 8.983 | 8.530 | 8.111 | 7.722 | 7.360 | 7.024 | 6.710 | 6.418 | 6.145 | 5.889 | 5.650 | 5.426 | 5.216 | 5.019 | 4.833 |
| 11 | 10.368 | 9.787 | 9.253 | 8.760 | 8.306 | 7.887 | 7.499 | 7.139 | 6.805 | 6.495 | 6.207 | 5.938 | 5.687 | 5.453 | 5.234 | 5.029 |
| 12 | 11.255 | 10.575 | 9.954 | 9.385 | 8.863 | 8.384 | 7.943 | 7.536 | 7.161 | 6.814 | 6.492 | 6.194 | 5.918 | 5.660 | 5.421 | 5.197 |
| 13 | 12.134 | 11.348 | 10.635 | 9.986 | 9.394 | 8.853 | 8.358 | 7.904 | 7.487 | 7.103 | 6.750 | 6.424 | 6.122 | 5.842 | 5.583 | 5.342 |
| 14 | 13.004 | 12.106 | 11.296 | 10.563 | 9.899 | 9.295 | 8.745 | 8.244 | 7.786 | 7.367 | 6.982 | 6.628 | 6.302 | 6.002 | 5.724 | 5.468 |
| 15 | 13.865 | 12.849 | 11.938 | 11.118 | 10.380 | 9.712 | 9.108 | 8.559 | 8.061 | 7.606 | 7.191 | 6.811 | 6.462 | 6.142 | 5.847 | 5.575 |
| 16 | 14.718 | 13.578 | 12.561 | 11.652 | 10.838 | 10.106 | 9.447 | 8.851 | 8.313 | 7.824 | 7.379 | 6.974 | 6.604 | 6.265 | 5.954 | 5.668 |
| 17 | 15.562 | 14.292 | 13.166 | 12.166 | 11.274 | 10.477 | 9.763 | 9.122 | 8.544 | 8.022 | 7.549 | 7.120 | 6.729 | 6.373 | 6.047 | 5.749 |
| 18 | 16.398 | 14.992 | 13.754 | 12.659 | 11.690 | 10.828 | 10.059 | 9.372 | 8.756 | 8.201 | 7.702 | 7.250 | 6.840 | 6.467 | 6.128 | 5.818 |
| 19 | 17.226 | 15.678 | 14.324 | 13.134 | 12.085 | 11.158 | 10.336 | 9.604 | 8.950 | 8.365 | 7.839 | 7.366 | 6.938 | 6.550 | 6.198 | 5.877 |
| 20 | 18.046 | 16.351 | 14.877 | 13.590 | 12.462 | 11.470 | 10.594 | 9.818 | 9.129 | 8.514 | 7.963 | 7.469 | 7.025 | 6.623 | 6.259 | 5.929 |

**Table 2** (continued)

|  |  |  |  |  |  |  |  | Rate of discount |  |  |  |  |  |  |  |  |
|---|---|---|---|---|---|---|---|---|---|---|---|---|---|---|---|---|
| Future years | 17% | 18% | 19% | 20% | 21% | 22% | 23% | 24% | 25% | 26% | 28% | 30% | 35% | 40% | 45% | 50% |
| 1 | 0.855 | 0.847 | 0.840 | 0.833 | 0.826 | 0.820 | 0.813 | 0.806 | 0.800 | 0.794 | 0.781 | 0.769 | 0.741 | 0.714 | 0.690 | 0.667 |
| 2 | 1.585 | 1.566 | 1.547 | 1.528 | 1.509 | 1.492 | 1.474 | 1.457 | 1.440 | 1.424 | 1.392 | 1.361 | 1.289 | 1.224 | 1.165 | 1.111 |
| 3 | 2.210 | 2.174 | 2.140 | 2.106 | 2.074 | 2.042 | 2.011 | 1.981 | 1.952 | 1.923 | 1.868 | 1.816 | 1.696 | 1.589 | 1.493 | 1.407 |
| 4 | 2.743 | 2.690 | 2.639 | 2.589 | 2.540 | 2.494 | 2.448 | 2.404 | 2.362 | 2.320 | 2.241 | 2.166 | 1.997 | 1.849 | 1.720 | 1.605 |
| 5 | 3.199 | 3.127 | 3.058 | 2.991 | 2.926 | 2.864 | 2.803 | 2.745 | 2.689 | 2.635 | 2.532 | 2.436 | 2.220 | 2.035 | 1.876 | 1.737 |
| 6 | 3.589 | 3.498 | 3.410 | 3.326 | 3.245 | 3.167 | 3.092 | 3.020 | 2.951 | 2.885 | 2.759 | 2.643 | 2.385 | 2.168 | 1.983 | 1.824 |
| 7 | 3.922 | 3.812 | 3.706 | 3.605 | 3.508 | 3.416 | 3.327 | 3.242 | 3.161 | 3.083 | 2.937 | 2.802 | 2.508 | 2.263 | 2.057 | 1.883 |
| 8 | 4.207 | 4.078 | 3.954 | 3.837 | 3.726 | 3.619 | 3.518 | 3.421 | 3.329 | 3.241 | 3.076 | 2.925 | 2.598 | 2.331 | 2.109 | 1.922 |
| 9 | 4.451 | 4.303 | 4.163 | 4.031 | 3.905 | 3.786 | 3.673 | 3.566 | 3.463 | 3.366 | 3.184 | 3.019 | 2.665 | 2.379 | 2.144 | 1.948 |
| 10 | 4.659 | 4.494 | 4.339 | 4.192 | 4.054 | 3.923 | 3.799 | 3.682 | 3.571 | 3.465 | 3.269 | 3.092 | 2.715 | 2.414 | 2.168 | 1.965 |
| 11 | 4.836 | 4.656 | 4.486 | 4.327 | 4.177 | 4.035 | 3.902 | 3.776 | 3.656 | 3.543 | 3.335 | 3.147 | 2.752 | 2.438 | 2.185 | 1.977 |
| 12 | 4.988 | 4.793 | 4.611 | 4.439 | 4.278 | 4.127 | 3.985 | 3.851 | 3.725 | 3.606 | 3.387 | 3.190 | 2.779 | 2.456 | 2.196 | 1.985 |
| 13 | 5.118 | 4.910 | 4.715 | 4.533 | 4.362 | 4.203 | 4.053 | 3.912 | 3.780 | 3.656 | 3.427 | 3.223 | 2.799 | 2.469 | 2.204 | 1.990 |
| 14 | 5.229 | 5.008 | 4.802 | 4.611 | 4.432 | 4.265 | 4.108 | 3.962 | 3.824 | 3.695 | 3.459 | 3.249 | 2.814 | 2.478 | 2.210 | 1.993 |
| 15 | 5.324 | 5.092 | 4.876 | 4.675 | 4.489 | 4.315 | 4.153 | 4.001 | 3.859 | 3.726 | 3.483 | 3.268 | 2.825 | 2.484 | 2.214 | 1.995 |
| 16 | 5.405 | 5.162 | 4.938 | 4.730 | 4.536 | 4.357 | 4.189 | 4.033 | 3.887 | 3.751 | 3.503 | 3.283 | 2.834 | 2.489 | 2.216 | 1.997 |
| 17 | 5.475 | 5.222 | 4.990 | 4.775 | 4.576 | 4.391 | 4.219 | 4.059 | 3.910 | 3.771 | 3.518 | 3.295 | 2.840 | 2.492 | 2.218 | 1.998 |
| 18 | 5.534 | 5.273 | 5.033 | 4.812 | 4.608 | 4.419 | 4.243 | 4.080 | 3.928 | 3.786 | 3.529 | 3.304 | 2.844 | 2.494 | 2.219 | 1.999 |
| 19 | 5.584 | 5.316 | 5.070 | 4.843 | 4.635 | 4.442 | 4.263 | 4.097 | 3.942 | 3.799 | 3.539 | 3.311 | 2.848 | 2.496 | 2.220 | 1.999 |
| 20 | 5.628 | 5.353 | 5.101 | 4.870 | 4.657 | 4.460 | 4.279 | 4.110 | 3.954 | 3.808 | 3.546 | 3.316 | 2.850 | 2.497 | 2.221 | 1.999 |

# Index